£ 22,50

## MODULES 1-7

# Pass ECDL5

**European Computer Driving Licence Version 5**

F.R. Heathcote

P.M. Heathcote

O.H.U. Heathcote

R.P. Richards

## Using Microsoft Office 2007

D1342105

**www.payne-gallway.co.uk**

✓ Free online support
✓ Useful weblinks
✓ 24 hour online ordering

01865 888070

PAYNE-GALLWAY
Part of Pearson

Payne-Gallway is an imprint of Pearson Education Limited, a company incorporated in England and Wales, having its registered office at Edinburgh Gate, Harlow, Essex, CM20 2JE. Registered company number: 872828

www.payne-gallway.co.uk

Text © F.R. Heathcote, P.M. Heathcote, O.H.U. Heathcote, R.P. Richards 2007

This edition first published 2009

13 12 11
10 9 8 7 6 5 4 3

British Library Cataloguing in Publication Data
A catalogue record for this book is available from the British Library.

ISBN 978 1 905292 38 7

Edited by Alex Sharpe
Additional text in Module 8 © Alex Sharpe
Typeset by Standard Eight Limited www.std8.com
Illustrated by Direction Marketing & Communications Ltd
Picture research by Liz Alexander
Cover photo © Richard Chasemore
Printed in Spain by Graficas

Acknowledgements
The authors and publisher would like to thank the following individuals and organisations for permission to reproduce photographs:

Dreamstime.com/Dinoablakovic pp. 3, 5; istockphoto.com/Eimantas Buzas p. 4; istockphoto.com/Rafa Gabowski p. 5; istockphoto.com/Ranplett p. 6; Pearson Education Ltd/Gareth Boden p. 6; Intel p. 9; Dreamstime.com/Curtpick p. 10; istockphoto.com/Wojtek Wojtowicz p. 10; istockphoto.com/Craig Barhorst p. 10; Dreamstime.com/Krzysiek Poczty p. 11; Dreamstime.com/Albo p. 11; Shutterstock/Dino O p. 11; istockphoto.com/Michal Rozanski p. 12; istockphoto.com/Ugur Evirgen p. 12; istockphoto.com/Greg Nicholas p. 13; istockphoto.com/Jaroslaw Wojcik p. 13; istockphoto.com/Jami Garrison p. 13; Dreamstime.com/Motionero p. 14; istockphoto.com/Craig DeBourbon p. 14; istockphoto.com/Marcus Jones p. 15; istockphoto.com/Tyler Boyes p. 15; istockphoto.com/Bluestocking p. 15; istockphoto.com/Matjaz Boncina p. 15; istockphoto.com/Craig Jewell p. 16; istockphoto.com/Tom Gufler, p. 16; istockphoto.com/Lee Dot p. 17; Digital Vision p. 30; istockphoto.com/Norman Chan p. 47; Punchstock/stockbyte p. 95; WWF-Canon/Martin Harvey pp. 417, 419–20, 423–4, 432, 434, 438, 443; Pearson Education Ltd – www.payne-gallway.co.uk pp. 448–9; Google Search page – www.google.co.uk pp. 455–7, 463, 466, 471; Home page of www.Number10.gov.uk reproduced under the terms of the Click-Use Licence p. 456; Home Office Identity & Passport Service reproduced under the terms of the Click-Use Licence pp. 477–8.

The authors and publisher would like to thank the following individuals and organisations for permission to reproduce material used in this book:

Microsoft screenshots throughout the publication: Microsoft product screenshots reprinted with permission from Microsoft Corporation.

Every effort has been made to contact copyright holders of material reproduced in this book. Any omissions will be rectified in subsequent printings if notice is given to the publishers.

Websites
The websites used in this book were correct and up-to-date at the time of publication. It is essential for tutors to preview each website before using it in class so as to ensure that the URL is still accurate, relevant and appropriate. We suggest that tutors bookmark useful websites and consider enabling students to access them through the school/college intranet.

Ordering information
Payne-Gallway, FREEPOST (OF1771),
PO Box 381, Oxford OX2 8BR
Tel: 01865 888070
Fax: 01865 314029
Email: orders@payne-gallway.co.uk

Extra resources
www.payne-gallway.co.uk

## ECDL Foundation Disclaimer Text

European Computer Driving Licence, ECDL, International Computer Driving Licence, ICDL, e-Citizen and related logos are all registered Trade Marks of the European Computer Driving Licence Foundation Limited ("ECDL Foundation").

PEARSON EDUCATION LIMITED is an entity independent of ECDL Foundation and is not associated with ECDL Foundation in any manner. This courseware may be used to assist candidates to prepare for the ECDL Foundation Certification Programme as titled on the courseware. Neither ECDL Foundation nor PEARSON EDUCATION LIMITED warrants that the use of this courseware publication will ensure passing of the tests for that ECDL Foundation Certification Programme. This courseware publication has been independently reviewed and approved by ECDL Foundation as covering the learning objectives for the ECDL Foundation Certification Programme.

Confirmation of this approval can be obtained by reviewing the Partners Page in the About Us Section of the website www.ecdl.org

The material contained in this courseware publication has not been reviewed for technical accuracy and does not guarantee that candidates will pass the test for the ECDL Foundation Certification Programme. Any and all assessment items and/or performance-based exercises contained in this courseware relate solely to this publication and do not constitute or imply certification by ECDL Foundation in respect to the ECDL Foundation Certification Programme or any other ECDL Foundation test. Irrespective of how the material contained in this courseware is deployed, for example in a learning management system (LMS) or a customised interface, nothing should suggest to the candidate that this material constitutes certification or can lead to certification through any other process than official ECDL Foundation certification testing.

For details on sitting a test for an ECDL Foundation certification programme, please contact your country's designated National Licensee or visit the ECDL Foundation's website at www.ecdl.org.

Candidates using this courseware must be registered with the National Operator before undertaking a test for an ECDL Foundation Certification Programme. Without a valid registration, the test(s) cannot be undertaken and no certificate, nor any other form of recognition, can be given to a candidate. Registration should be undertaken with your country's National Licensee at an Approved Test Centre.


## BCS Disclaimer Text

The European Computer Driving Licence is operated in Britain by BCS (British Computer Society). Established in 1957, BCS is an international awarding body for a wide range of qualifications suited to both everyday IT users and to IT specialists. The leading professional body for those working in the IT industry, BCS now enjoys a world-wide membership of more than 68,000 members in over 100 countries.

# Preface

## Who is this book for?

This book is suitable for anyone studying for ECDL Version 5.0, either at school, adult class or at home. It is suitable for complete beginners or those with some prior experience, and takes the learner step-by-step from the very basics to the point where they will feel confident using a number of different software packages, using the Internet and organising their work efficiently. This book is also suitable for anyone studying for the BCS 2009 course.

## The approach

The approach is very much one of 'learning by doing'. Each module is divided into a number of chapters which correspond to one lesson. Where relevant, the student is guided step-by-step through a practical task at the computer, with numerous screenshots to show exactly what should be on their screen at each stage. Each individual in a class can proceed at their own pace, with little or no help from a teacher. At the end of most chapters there are exercises that provide invaluable practice. By the time the student has completed a module, every aspect of the ECDL syllabus will have been covered.

Each module has its own Table of Contents so that any particular topic can easily be looked up for revision.

## Software used

The instructions and screenshots are based on a PC running Microsoft Windows XP and Microsoft Office 2007 with Internet Explorer 7 and Outlook Express. However, it will be relatively easy to adapt the instructions for use with earlier versions.

## Extra resources

Answers to practice exercises and other useful supporting material can be found on the publisher's website www.payne-gallway.co.uk.

## About ECDL

The European Computer Driving Licence (ECDL) Syllabus Version 5 is the European-wide qualification enabling people to demonstrate their competence in computer skills. Candidates must study and pass the test for each of the first seven modules listed below before they are awarded an ECDL cetificate. The ECDL tests must be undertaken at an accredited test centre. For more details of ECDL tests and test centres, visit the ECDL website www.ecdl.org.

Module 1 – Concepts of Information and Communication Technology (ICT)
Module 2 – Using the computer and managing files
Module 3 – Word processing
Module 4 – Spreadsheets
Module 5 – Using databases
Module 6 – Presentation
Module 7 – Web browsing and communication

The BCS Module 1 revised syllabus on IT Security for Users and Module 2 revised syllabus on IT User Fundamentals are covered in Module 8. A table is included in Module 8 to show how the BCS syllabus maps to ECDL syllabus 5.0.

# Table of Contents

# Module 1
## Concepts of Information Technology

This module will give you an understanding of some of the main concepts of IT at a general level. You will learn about:

- types of computer and the component parts of a computer
- software used by and on a computer
- networks, including the Internet
- health and safety issues relevant to the use of computers
- security issues arising from the use of computers
- legislation such as the Data Protection Act and legal issues regarding copyright.

This training, which has been approved by the ECDL Foundation, includes exercise items intended to assist Candidates in their training for an ECDL Certification Programme. These exercises are not ECDL Foundation certification tests. For information about authorised ECDL Test Centres in different national territories, please refer to the ECDL Foundation website at www.ecdl.org

# Module **1**

# Contents

# General Concepts

**In this chapter you will find out:**

- ❗ what a computer is
- ❗ about different types of computer
- ❗ about different parts of a computer.

## A world of computers

In this module you'll learn about what a computer is and about some of the thousands of ways in which computers are used today. Amazingly, the history of commercial computing goes back only to around 1960, when the first computers were used by a very few large organisations to perform repetitive tasks such as processing the company payroll. These computers were massive, occupying whole floors in office blocks, and yet had only a fraction of the computing power of a modern pocket calculator. The computer that controlled the first manned spaceship to the moon in 1969 had less calculating capability than a modern mobile phone!

The term Information Technology (IT) refers to the use of computers to process and transfer information. Computers are now commonly used to communicate information, as well as performing tasks like word processing or calculations. Other machines, such as fax machines and telephones, contain tiny computers, and you may often hear the term Information and Communication Technology (ICT) used instead of IT to refer to these.

## Hardware and software                    Syllabus 1.1.1.1/1.2.1.1–2/1.2.1.4

In order to work, a computer needs two things – hardware and software.

Hardware is the physical part of a computer – the bits you can see and touch. The casings for computers and their associated pieces of hardware, such as monitors and printers, are usually made of tough plastic. The electronic components, such as switches and integrated circuits (commonly known as 'chips'), are mounted on boards (printed circuit boards or PCBs) inside the case.

Software is the list of instructions that are coded in a special way so the computer can understand them. These are the computer programs that tell the computer exactly what to do. There are many different types of program, for example:

- ❶ applications, such as a word processor, spreadsheet and e-mail packages

- ❶ operating systems, such as Microsoft Windows, which work in the background and let you decide which applications to run.

Many common household devices such as washing machines, microwave ovens, video recorders and digital alarm clocks contain computer hardware and specialised software to make them perform the tasks they are designed to do.

## Types of computer                                      Syllabus 1.1.1.2

Different types of computer are used for different applications.

Mainframe computers are large, fast and expensive. They are used by very big organisations such as electricity companies, banks or multinational companies. Hundreds or thousands of users may connect to and use a mainframe at the same time.

Each user has a computer terminal that is connected to the mainframe. Some types of terminal cannot be used for anything unless they are connected to the mainframe. These are known as dumb terminals. All the computer's calculations take place in the mainframe. Alternatively, an ordinary personal computer (PC) may be connected to a mainframe and this can do useful work even if it is not connected at any particular time. A PC used in this way is sometimes known as an intelligent terminal.

The terminals connected to a mainframe computer may be in different parts of the same country or they may even be overseas.

A network computer (normally referred to as a network server) has a number of PCs connected to it to create a computer network. The server is typically used to store information for use by all the users on the network.

## Personal computers                                      Syllabus 1.1.1.2–3

The personal computer (PC) has become an almost indispensable piece of equipment for office workers, from managing directors down to clerical staff.

A popular type of PC is the desktop. The main system unit is designed to sit on top of the user's desk or as a tower underneath it. The latter is becoming increasingly popular as it takes up less desk space.

The picture below shows the main parts of a desktop PC.

**Speakers:**
These let you listen to music and other sounds from your computer.

**Screen:**
This displays information from the computer.

**System unit:**
This contains the **central processing unit** (CPU), hard disk drive, removable disk drives and memory.

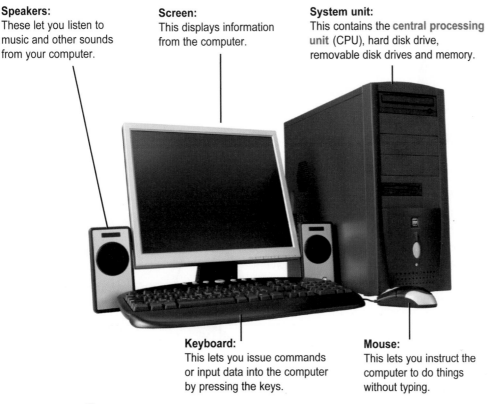

**Keyboard:**
This lets you issue commands or input data into the computer by pressing the keys.

**Mouse:**
This lets you instruct the computer to do things without typing.

**Tip:**

Hardware devices such as the screen, keyboard, mouse etc. connected to the main system unit are referred to as **peripherals**.

Portable computers were introduced so that users could easily transport their computer to different locations and even do some work en route, perhaps on a train journey. There are three main types:

- Laptops (sometimes called notebooks) are computers that have all the peripherals noted above housed in one portable case together with a rechargeable battery.

- Hand-held devices such as palmtops and Personal Digital Assistants (PDAs). They are becoming more powerful as the technology advances. Some hand-held devices let the user draw on the screen with a special pen. The drawings are then converted into text and diagrams.

The first PDAs were simple electronic organisers and looked similar to calculators. Recent models can be used as web browsers, portable media players, mobile phones and provide GPS satellite navigation.

PDAs generally have a touch screen and a detachable pen or stylus. The user taps the screen with the stylus to click buttons or to make menu choices.

ⓘ More recently, laptop-type computers called tablet PCs have been developed. The user uses a stylus in a similar way as with a PDA, but the stylus can also be used as a 'pen' to write or draw directly on the screen, thereby providing a very quick way of taking notes.

|  | Capacity | Speed | Cost | Typical users |
|---|---|---|---|---|
| Mainframe | Very large disk storage. Very large main memory. | Very fast in order to process vast amounts of data | Extremely expensive. | Large companies (often multinational), Health Authorities etc. |
| Network server | Large disk storage – gigabytes or even terabytes. Large main memory (RAM). | Fast – measured in gigahertz. | Expensive due to components and software for networking functions, backup etc. | Smaller companies, schools, hospitals etc. |
| PC | Probably smaller disk storage and main memory (RAM) than a server (especially if networked). | Fast – measured in gigahertz. | Becoming cheaper all the time. | Employees within all sizes of organisation, home users etc. |
| Laptop / Tablet PC | Similar to a PC. | Similar to a PC. | Often more expensive than for a comparably powered PC due to miniaturisation of components. | Mostly business users, commuters etc. |
| PDA | Much smaller disk storage capacity and main memory than a PC. | Slower than a PC. | Relatively expensive compared to a PC. | Mostly business users, commuters etc. |

## The digital age                                          Syllabus 1.1.1.3

The advent of the digital age has meant that computing power has been brought to many different and new devices, with many being able to perform similar functions. It is now possible to listen to music or radio broadcasts, or watch TV, on multimedia players that might be dedicated to a particular function, or on mobile phones (smartphones) that also let you use the Internet for e-mails and web browsing, and which are also digital cameras and PDAs!

# Hardware

In this chapter you will find out:

- ❗ what computer hardware is
- ❗ what computer memory is and how it is measured
- ❗ about computer performance
- ❗ what input and output devices are
- ❗ about computer storage
- ❗ what input and output ports are used for.

## Central Processing Unit                                Syllabus 1.1.1.4

Within the system unit is the central processing unit (CPU): the 'brain' of the computer. This is where all processing and calculations take place. It consists of two different parts:

- ❶ The processor.
- ❶ Memory.

## The processor                                          Syllabus 1.1.1.4

The processor consists of two main components: the control unit and the arithmetic/logic unit (ALU). The control unit fetches instructions from the computer's memory, decodes them and synchronises all the computer's operations.

The arithmetic/logic unit (ALU) is where all of the work is carried out. The ALU can perform two sorts of operations on data. Arithmetic operations include addition, subtraction, multiplication and division. Logical operations consist of comparing one data item with another to determine whether the first data item is smaller than, equal to or greater than the second data item.

Physically the processor is a silicon chip, which consists of complex electronic circuits. This chip, together with other chips that do different jobs, are mounted on printed circuit boards (PCBs).

## Computer memory                              Syllabus 1.1.1.4/1.1.3.1–2

A computer has a 'memory' which stores information. There are two kinds of memory: random access memory (RAM) and read-only memory (ROM).

RAM (sometimes known as immediate access memory) is divided into millions of addressable storage units called bytes.

Each byte consists of 8 bits (binary digits). A bit can be set either OFF or ON, depending on whether an electric current is switched off or on, representing a 0 or a 1. All numbers, text, sounds, graphics etc. are held as different patterns of 0s and 1s in the computer.

One byte can hold one character, or it can be used to hold a code representing, for example, a tiny part of a picture, a sound or part of a computer program instruction. The total number of bytes in main memory is referred to as the computer's memory size. Computer memory sizes are measured using the following units:

| Measurement | Power of 2 | Size (bytes) | Symbol |
|-------------|-----------|--------------|--------|
| 1 kilobyte | $2^{10}$ | 1,024 (just over 1 thousand) | kB |
| 1 megabyte | $2^{20}$ | 1,048,576 (just over 1 million) | MB |
| 1 gigabyte | $2^{30}$ | 1,073,741,824 (just over 1 billion) | GB |
| 1 terabyte | $2^{40}$ | 1,099,511,627,776 (just over 1 trillion) | TB |

So for example this paragraph contains approximately 250 characters or bytes. The text in this module is stored as a file on the computer's hard disk. The file contains approximately 60,000 characters (approximately 59 kB).

The amount of memory that comes with a standard PC has increased exponentially over the last 20 years. In about 1980, BBC microcomputers with 32 kB of memory were bought in their thousands for home and school use. In 1981, Bill Gates of Microsoft made his famous remark "640 kB ought to be enough for anybody". By 2003, a PC with 256 MB or 512 MB of memory was standard, costing less than £1000 including bundled software.

Program instructions and the data being processed are held in RAM. For example, if you are writing a letter using Microsoft Word, both Word and your letter will be held in RAM while you are working on it. If you accidentally switch off the machine, or there is a power cut while you are working, you will lose the letter if you have not saved it and when you restart the computer, you will have to load Word again (i.e. the Word software will be copied from your hard disk into RAM again). When you finish your letter, save it and close Word so that RAM is freed up for the next task.

RAM has these two major characteristics:

- Each location in RAM has its own unique address. It can be randomly accessed – the computer can be instructed to fetch the data it needs from any given address in memory.

- RAM is volatile – its contents are lost when the power is switched off.

A PC will also only have a very small amount of ROM. Unlike RAM, its contents can never be changed, and all the instructions held in ROM have to be 'burned' into the memory chip before it leaves the factory. The contents of ROM are not lost when the computer is switched off. The small program which starts running as soon as you switch the computer on is held in ROM. This program tells the computer to start loading the operating system (e.g. Microsoft Windows) from disk.

ROM has these two major characteristics:

1. ROM cannot be written to or used to hold ordinary user application programs such as word-processing software.

2. ROM is non-volatile – its contents are NOT lost when the power is switched off.

**Tip:**

> Many household machines contain ROM chips – for example your washing machine, dishwasher or DVD recorder. You can, for example, select which washing program to use, but you cannot change how many minutes the cycle takes or use the washing machine to cook your dinner instead!

## Computer performance

Syllabus 1.1.2.1–2

Two main factors impact on a computer's performance: processor speed and amount of RAM.

Processor speed is measured in megahertz (MHz) or gigahertz (GHz). (1 GHz is equal to one thousand megahertz.)

Each year, as technology advances, processor speed increases. Twenty years ago a computer with a processor speed of a few hundred kilohertz (kHz) would have been considered very powerful. Now a processor speed of more than 3 GHz is not unusual – that is about 10,000 times faster!

The other factor in determining the performance of a computer is the amount of memory (RAM) it has. Modern software takes up a huge amount of memory.

When you install software such as Microsoft Word on your computer, it is stored on the hard disk inside the system unit. When you open Word to write a letter, for example, the software program (Word) has to be copied into RAM before the computer can execute the program instructions which enable you to type your letter. If a computer does not have enough memory to hold all of Microsoft Word in RAM at once, it will swap bits of the program in and out of memory from disk as they are required. This takes time.

The same happens when you have several programs running at once. They all take up memory space, and your computer may run more slowly because instructions and data are being copied from disk to memory as needed.

Thus, the number of applications running at any one time also affects the performance of a computer.

Graphics (images and video) utilise considerable processing power that can adversely affect performance. A graphics processor dedicated to controlling the display of graphics will speed up your computer.

## Input devices

All the data that is fed *into* a computer is called input. The items of hardware used to input data are called input devices. These are some of the most common input devices:

### Keyboard

The most common way to enter data into a PC is by keyboard. Computer keyboards have their keys arranged in a similar way to those on a typewriter. This way of arranging keys is called QWERTY because of the order in which the keys appear in the first row of letters. Extra keys carry out specific jobs depending on the software being used.

### Mouse

A mouse is a small hand-held input device which has a ball fitted underneath. When the mouse is moved, a signal created by the movement of the ball is transmitted to the computer. This controls a pointer on the screen which moves in a direction corresponding to the direction of the mouse movement. Once the user has pointed the arrow on their screen at something, it can be selected by clicking a button on top of the mouse. There are usually two or three buttons on a mouse. The left-hand button is normally used to make selections.

Other pointing devices used instead of the mouse are tracker balls and touch pads.

- ⓘ Tracker balls are sometimes used on portable computers. The user rotates a ball directly with the fingers to move the cursor on the screen.

- ⓘ Touch pads are often found on laptops. The user moves their finger over the surface of the pad to move the cursor.

**Tip:**

> A popular way of connecting devices to a computer is by using a wireless connection. These transfer data using infrared signals. This means that fewer cables are needed; however, the wireless input devices need batteries as they do not get their power from the computer through a connecting cable.

## Microphone

If a computer has a sound card, it should have the ability to receive sound input from a microphone through the sound card microphone port. This is useful for recording voice or sounds on your computer. With suitable software, it can even be used to dictate into a word processor, or to control the computer with voice commands.

## Light pen

A light pen is a small pen-shaped wand which contains light sensors. The light pen is used to choose objects or commands on the screen either by pressing it against the screen or by pressing a small switch on its side. This sends a signal to the computer, which then works out the exact location of the light pen on the screen.

## Scanner

Scanners are used to input text, diagrams and pictures to the computer. They can be hand-held but usually they are 'flat bed' devices which sit on the desk. Printed text can be scanned using optical character recognition (OCR) software so that it can be word-processed. Images can be scanned and loaded into graphics software where they can be altered or enhanced.

## Joystick

A joystick is often used to play games on a PC. It controls the way things move on the screen and can control movement from side-to-side, up and down and diagonally. A joystick normally has at least one button that can be used in a game, for example to make a character jump or fire a missile.

## Webcam

A webcam is a small camera that is used to capture images for display on a web page. They are often low-resolution cameras providing continuous video or a series of 'stills' at regular intervals.

Webcams are also used for tele-conferencing.

### Digital camera

A major benefit of using a digital camera is that you can transfer photos directly to your PC without sending a film off to be developed. A cable supplied with the camera can connect it to a port on your PC.

Using a digital camera is very similar to using a traditional camera. They both use the basic components such as a lens, flash, shutter and viewfinder. Most digital models now incorporate an LCD screen so that you can view your subject as you take the photo, and you can then review the picture afterwards.

The quality and number of digital pictures that can be taken will depend on the amount of memory in the camera.

## Output devices                                             Syllabus 1.1.4.2

The information that a computer produces is called output. The items of hardware that receive this output are called output devices. The most common output devices are shown below:

### Screen

A screen (or monitor) displays the output information from a computer. The size of a monitor is measured in inches diagonally across the screen; 15, 17, 19 and 21 inch monitors are the most common sizes. The picture on a monitor is made up of thousands of tiny coloured dots called pixels.

The quality and detail of the picture on a monitor depends on the resolution, which is measured in pixels going across and down the screen. The more pixels the screen has, the higher the resolution and the better the picture. Resolutions typically range from 800 × 600 to 1600 × 1200.

Another factor which affects the quality of the image is its refresh rate. This is measured in hertz (Hz) and indicates how many times per second the image on the screen is updated. To avoid flickering images, which can lead to eye strain and headaches, the refresh rate of a monitor should be at least 72 Hz.

Older-type monitors work in the same way as televisions where electrical signals are converted into an image on the screen by a cathode ray tube (CRT).

Flat-screen monitors are more popular now and they take up much less desk space than CRTs. These liquid crystal display (LCD) screens are similar to those provided on portable computers.

## Printer

A good printer can help you produce professional-looking printed output from your PC. There are three main categories of printer, each of them suitable for different types of job.

Many PCs are supplied with an inkjet printer. These print pictures or characters by forcing small dots of ink through tiny holes. The ink is stored in replaceable cartridges, normally separate for colour and black ink.

These printers can also print on envelopes, labels, acetates and other specialist paper.

Laser printers produce very high quality printed output very quickly. They are suitable for large volume printouts. Colour laser printers are expensive but black and white laser printers cost only a few hundred pounds and are standard in many large and small businesses. The main running expense is the cost of replacement toner (powdered ink) cartridges every few thousand pages.

Dot matrix printers have steel pins which strike an inked ribbon to create a pattern of tiny dots which form a character. How good the print is depends on how many pins the machine has: 24 pins will produce better quality print than 9 pins.

This type of printer is not normally supplied with a PC for home use, as the quality is not as good as an inkjet or laser printer. As they work by striking the paper, they are called impact printers and are often used by businesses to print on multi-part stationery for producing documents such as invoices – a top copy goes to the customer, a second 'carbon copy' may be used as a delivery note and a third copy may be kept in the office. Laser printers and inkjet printers cannot print two or more copies of a document simultaneously in this way.

## Plotter

A plotter is another device for producing hard-copy from a computer. It uses several coloured pens to draw the computer output on paper. Plotters can produce very accurate drawings and are often used in Computer-Aided Design (CAD) applications to produce engineering or architectural drawings.

### Speakers

External speakers are supplied with multimedia PCs. These are computers that incorporate a sound card, CD-ROM and speakers. The system can then combine text, sound and graphics to run programs such as games. The quality and volume of the sound produced can be adjusted either within software or on the speakers themselves.

Computers can produce output in the form of sound by using a speech synthesiser. This converts electrical signals into sound waves. Sound software can be used to mix musical sounds and create new sounds. Some of the sounds can replicate human speech – this is called speech synthesis and is used by some telephone enquiry systems.

Headphones can be used so that other users are not disturbed.

## Input/output devices

Syllabus 1.1.4.3

Some devices can be classed as input or output devices.

### Touchscreen

A touchscreen allows the user to touch an area of the screen rather than having to type the data on a keyboard. They are widely used in tourist centres, where tourists can look up various local facilities and entertainments, in fast-food stores for entering customer orders, in manufacturing and many other environments.

## Storage devices

### Disk storage

To save your work when the computer is turned off, you need to save it onto a disk. There are three main types of disk: floppy disk, hard disk and CD-ROM.

A floppy disk comprises a flexible plastic disc with a magnetic coating (similar to cassette tape) housed inside a hard protective casing. (The name derives from the very early floppy disks which were housed in thin cardboard sleeves.) A modern floppy disk has a storage capacity of 1.44 MB. A floppy disk is portable, so you can insert it into your computer's floppy disk drive, store your work on it and then remove it. You could take the disk and insert it into another PC and carry on with your work. Before a floppy disk (or any disk) can be used it must be formatted. This means that the disk is checked for errors and set up to accept data. Nowadays the vast majority of new floppy disks are pre-formatted.

The main storage disk on a computer is the hard disk. An internal hard disks is housed permanently inside your computer. External hard disks are portable and are also useful for backing up data. These disks have a much larger storage capacity than a floppy disk, and transfer data to and from computer memory much more quickly.

The capacity of hard disks is measured in megabytes (MB) or gigabytes (GB). Most modern PCs have a hard disk with a capacity of at least 100 GB.

Users of networks are often allocated a limited amount of user space on hard disks on network servers. This provides the user with additional disk storage to that on their own computer, and has the added advantage that the contents of the user space will be regularly backed-up by the network administrator.

PCs are often fitted with a CD-ROM (Compact Disc Read Only Memory) drive. CD-ROMs are removable and can hold large amounts of programs or data. Data is often in the form of text, pictures, music and animations.

Software is often supplied on CD-ROM and it is an ideal medium for games packages. These disks are read-only, which means that you cannot save any information on them. You can only read what is already there. Up to 650 MB of data can be stored on these disks.

CD-RW (read-write) disks let you save data which can then be erased and overwritten with new data.

DVD drives are also now being supplied as removable storage, allowing you to watch films on your PC. A DVD-ROM can hold up to 135 minutes of high-quality video and CD-quality sound.

## Other storage media

Flash and memory stick storage uses memory chips to store data rather than a magnetic disc. Flash drives are as portable as floppy disks but have a capacity of 1 MB or greater so they are rapidly superseding them. Memory cards, such as those found in digital cameras, are also electronic storage devices. Flash memory is non-volatile (its contents are not lost when the power is switched off).

Magnetic tape or DAT (Digital Audio Tape) is used almost exclusively for backups and for archiving old data that needs to be kept but which will probably never be used. Large amounts of data can be stored very cheaply and compactly using this medium, which is also known as a data cartridge. Tapes are much slower to access than floppy disks or CD-ROMs.

The table below gives a comparison between the different types of removable PC storage.

| Device | Capacity | Price of drive (approx) | Price of media (approx) |
|---|---|---|---|
| Floppy disk | 1.44 MB | £25 | £0.50 |
| CD | 650 MB | £150 | £1 |
| DVD | 17 GB | £450 | £25 |
| DAT | 60 GB | £300 | £10 |
| Flash | 1–8 GB | £20 | N/A |

Tip:

These prices are changing all the time – only use this table for the sake of comparison.

## Online storage

It is possible to upload files to companies that specifically provide online storage for a fee. This is particularly useful for backup purposes because the files are stored away from the file owner's premises.

## Input/output ports Syllabus 1.1.1.5

Input and output devices are connected to the computer via ports. Common ports are:

ⓘ    serial ports – data is transferred into and out of a computer one bit at a time.

ⓘ    parallel ports – data is transferred along several wires, so it is transferred more quickly than through a serial port.

ⓘ    universal serial bus (USB) connectors – an inexpensive means of connecting peripherals to a computer, and gradually superseding serial and parallel ports. A USB port is a general purpose port that can be used for connecting a range of peripheral devices. Most desktop PCs now have at least two USB ports into which any USB-compatible device can be plugged. These include plug and play devices such as mice, keyboards, scanners, printers, joysticks, digital cameras and audio speakers. 'Plug and play' means  that the devices will automatically be recognised by Windows as soon as they are plugged in. USB devices can be swapped without restarting the PC. This is called hot-swapping. USB ports can also be used for networking.

ⓘ    network ports – rectangular sockets, often on the back of a computer, that are used to connect cables to a local area network. They are sometimes referred to as RJ-45 connectors.

ⓘ    a FireWire connector – a high-speed serial connection.

# Module 1 Concepts of Information Technology

## Exercises

1. A friend tells you that his son's new PC has 100GB of RAM. Is this plausible? Look up some advertisements for PCs to find a typical figure for RAM and hard disk capacity.

2. Describe two differences between RAM and ROM. Give a typical use for each.

3. All computers from mainframes to palmtops have certain elements in common, such as a central processing unit (CPU), input, output and storage devices.

    (a) Describe briefly a typical user of a mainframe computer and of a palmtop.

    (b) What unit is the speed of the CPU measured in?

    (c) Name the two main parts of the CPU and describe the function of each.

4. Explain the terms Information Technology, hardware and software.

5. Describe the functions of each of the following devices and state whether they are input or output devices:

    (a) Touchpad

    (b) Plotter

    (c) Joystick

    (d) Scanner

6. Suppose you have typed a page of text using a word processor. The text contains about 2000 characters including spaces. Approximately how much RAM will this text occupy?

7. What type of printer would you recommend for each of the following users? Justify your answers.

    (a) An author working at home on her latest novel.

    (b) A small garage printing purchase orders for spare parts. Three copies of each purchase order is required.

    (c) A student who needs to print out his geography project in colour at home.

8. A graphic artist needs to send artwork that he has created on his computer to his client. The graphics files are 50MB. Name and justify a suitable medium for storing and posting the files.

9. Describe two typical uses of each of the following devices attached to a PC:

    (a) Touchscreen

    (b) Speakers

    (c) DVD drive

10. Give three examples of 'plug and play' devices.

11. Give two advantages of using a wireless mouse on your PC.

# Software

In this chapter you will find out:

- what software is
- about different types of software: operating system, BIOS, applications and utilities
- about software to help the disabled.

## The operating system                                    Syllabus 1.2.1.1–2/4

Software is the list of instructions (the program) that tells a computer what to do.

An operating system is a series of programs that organise and control a computer. The computer will not work without it. Early operating systems (DOS – disk operating systems) were text-based which meant that you had to type instructions on the keyboard. Windows was developed as a graphical user interface (GUI). This meant that instead having to type complicated text commands, you can use the mouse to point at icons and commands on the screen. Recent versions of Microsoft Windows are both the operating system and the GUI. The main functions of an operating system are:

- to provide a user interface so that the user can communicate with the computer
- to communicate with all the hardware devices, such as the keyboard, screen and printer. For example, when the user gives an instruction to print, the operating system checks that the printer is switched on and ready
- to organise the storage and retrieval of data from disk. The operating system has to keep track of where every file is stored on disk so that it can be retrieved quickly
- to manage the smooth running of all the programs currently in RAM. The operating system will allocate processing time to each program in turn. For example, while you are thinking what to type into Word, the computer may be busy receiving an e-mail message or saving a spreadsheet you have just been working on.

Tip:

Examples of other operating systems include **MS-DOS, OS/2, Unix, Linux** and **Mac OS X**.

### The BIOS (Basic Input/Output System)

The BIOS is stored in ROM or in flash memory and starts up every time the PC is switched on. It is the most basic software within the PC and is responsible for the low-level functions required to make the hardware operate properly. It records basic information about the PC, such as the type and characteristics of the hard drive(s) installed, the amount of memory, date, time etc. As such, it must be correctly configured or the PC simply will not operate as intended. Initially the BIOS will be configured by the PC manufacturer. When any subsequent hardware change is made to modern PCs, the BIOS is updated automatically. So, generally, no user intervention is required.

## Application software                                    Syllabus 1.2.1.3–4

Applications are the programs that let you use your computer to do work. Common applications include word processors, spreadsheets, databases, presentation software, desktop publishing software, project management software, web page editors, graphics software, e-mail software and web browsers, and games etc. Microsoft Office includes several of these applications:

- Word – a word processor. Word processor applications are used for producing text-based documents such as letters and reports.

- Excel – a spreadsheet. Spreadsheet applications are a large array of cells that are used for calculations.

- Access – a database. Database software is used to input, store and retrieve related data.

- Publisher – a desktop publishing package. DTP software is similar to a word processor but provides additional features that let you produce professional documents such as books.

- PowerPoint – presentation software. Presentation software is used to produce slides to accompany talks or for stand-alone viewing at an exhibition for example.

Other Office applications include FrontPage (for producing web pages), Outlook (an organiser that includes an e-mail facility) and Internet Explorer (a web browser).

## Utility software

Utilities are programs that help you use your computer efficiently and securely. The operating system and applications do not need them to work, although some utilities are provided as part of the Windows operating system. There are numerous utilities available. They include:

- disk defragmenter – to organise files on a disk so the computer works more efficiently

- backup software – to let you choose and schedule files for automatic or manual backup

- ⓘ file compression software – to let you reduce file sizes to save disk space and speed up data transfer

- ⓘ anti-virus software – to prevent, detect and remove viruses

- ⓘ text editors – basic editors that do not provide all the features of professional word processors

- ⓘ compilers – that turn a text-written program into code the computer can run.

## Accessibility
Syllabus 1.2.1.5

Microsoft Windows and Office applications have special features to help those with disabilities. These include:

- ⓘ StickyKeys to help people who have difficulty typing by reducing the number of keystrokes required. An on-screen keyboard removes the need for a normal keyboard altogether by letting the user use a pointing device to select keyboard characters.

- ⓘ A screen magnifier that magnifies parts of the screen as the mouse cursor passes over them and a high contrast display option that helps people with visual disabilities.

- ⓘ Voice recognition software that lets a user say instructions or dictate directly into a word processor.

- ⓘ An on-screen reader that outputs selected text as a spoken voice through loudspeakers.

Other functions, such as predictive text, can also help those with disabilities.

## Exercises

1. Describe the purpose of:

   (a)   two applications

   (b)   two utilities.

2. Describe briefly the main functions of the operating system.

3. What is the function of the BIOS?

4. Describe two utilities that improve accessibility for the disabled.

# Networks

In this chapter you will find out:

- ❗ what networks are
- ❗ about different network configurations
- ❗ what the Internet is and how to connect to it
- ❗ about downloading, uploading and transfer rates.

## Stand-alone and networking                      Syllabus 1.3.1.1

When two or more computers are connected together so they can communicate with one another and transfer data, they are said to be networked. A network can be as small as two computers connected on the same desk, or it can connect computers in different parts of the same country or in different parts of the world. A small network within an office or within a building is called a local area network (LAN). A network that connects computers and LANs in different buildings countrywide is called a wide area network (WAN). The Internet is a WAN that connects millions of computers across the world.

Computers on a LAN are usually connected by wires or they may be wireless (i.e. using radio technology to transfer data between computers). WAN connections may be wire, fibre optic, radio (microwave) and via satellite.

A stand-alone computer is one that is not connected to any other computer. This is rare, as most computers today are connected to the Internet.

As well as letting users share data that might be on different computers, a network also makes available for sharing other resources, such as peripherals like printers and scanners etc.

## Network configurations                          Syllabus 1.3.1.2

The two common network configurations are peer-to-peer and client–server networks.

- All the computers connected in a peer-to-peer network have equal status, that is they all have the same role. There are different ways of connecting the computers in a peer-to-peer network, but essentially all the computers have access to data on the other computers and resources in the network, although it is possible to control access rights to hide sensitive data from prying eyes! A peer-to-peer network is suitable for home use where computer users, perhaps in different rooms, might want to share a single colour printer or Internet access.

- In a client–server network, all the users' computers (the clients) connect to another computer called a server. The server provides all the resources to the clients. For example, the server might provide a single point for Internet access, check for viruses on the clients, or host a database that multiple clients can access.

## The Internet    Syllabus 1.3.1.3/1.4.2.1–4

The Internet is a global network that connects individual computers and networks of computers so users can communicate and share data. The development of the Internet has made possible the following, which use it:

- The World Wide Web – a data retrieval system comprising interlinked pages. A user looks for web pages containing specific topics using a search engine and the relevant pages are displayed using a browser.

- E-mail – electronic mail that lets users communicate and transfer files as attachments.

- File transfer – direct transfer of files from a user's computer to a recipient's computer (with given access rights).

- E-commerce – all the activities associated with commercial trading, but using the Internet to communicate and share data such as electronic transfer of funds. The World Wide Web also lets traders display and sell their products online.

- Instant messaging – a communication method where a message typed at one computer appears 'immediately' on the recipient's screen.

- VoIP – Voice over Internet Protocol is a voice telephony system that uses the Internet to let users speak to each other.

- E-media – radio and television, in real time or time-shifted.

- RSS feeds – RSS variously means Rich or RDF Site Summary, but is often referred to as 'Really Simple Syndication'. RSS displays updated content (perhaps for a news or a financial website) without the user having to visit or refresh the source page.

## Intranets and extranets                                  Syllabus 1.3.1.4

An intranet is similar to the Internet, but it is usually associated with a company or organisation with access to its web pages being restricted to its employees. Intranet uses are many, but typical web pages might include topics related to a company's policies, frequently asked questions, social events, internal phone directories, company news items etc.

A company may allow the public or authorised users (such as suppliers) limited access to its intranet through the Internet. This network is called an extranet.

## Connecting to the Internet                               Syllabus 1.3.2.3–5

Most users' access to the Internet is by means of an Internet Service Provider (ISP). There are several ways of connecting a computer to the ISP's computers.

- 🛈 Dial-up – This used to be the most used connection. It utilises standard analogue telephone lines, so a computer's digital data needs to be converted using a modem (modulator-demodulator) before it can be sent. The modem also converts data returned to the computer back to digital form so the computer can work with it.
Because standard telephone lines are used, a connection needs to be established each time a user wants to connect to the ISP and then to the Internet – hence dial-up. The user will pay for the connection in the same way as a telephone call, which can become expensive if large files are being transferred or large amounts of time are spent on the Web.

- 🛈 Broadband – This is an 'always connected' digital connection so it is not necessary to contact the ISP every time Internet access is required. A broadband connection is usually provided by an ISP at a fixed monthly rate for a set data transfer limit.
Access to broadband can be limited by area availability of suitable infrastructure (high bandwidth cables and telephony equipment); however, wireless links to Internet 'points of access' and satellite links can be used instead of cables.

The 'always connected' nature of broadband means that the connected computer is more susceptible to intruder attacks. The risk is mitigated by installing a firewall to limit access to the computer from the Internet or other network connection.

## Downloading and uploading                                Syllabus 1.3.2.1–2

The process of transferring over a network a file from one computer to a second computer that is asking for the transfer is called downloading. For example, you might download an upgrade file or driver file from a manufacturer's server to your own computer.

The opposite process, that is transferring a file from your computer to another computer on a network, is called uploading. You might upload files to a server as backup copies, or you might upload files to a customer's server so they can access them easily.

Transferring data between any computers on a network is not instantaneous. How quickly data is transferred is called the transfer rate. It is measured in bits per second. A typical dial-up modem connected to the Internet has a data transfer rate of 56 kbps (kilobits per second, where kilo = thousand), which means that large files take a considerable time to transfer. A broadband connection will give transfer rates measured in megabits per second (Mbps, where mega = million). Broadband upload transfer rates (to the Internet) tend to be slower than download (from the Internet) rates.

Unless two computers are connected together directly, any data transferred between them will have to pass through other equipment on the way, each affecting the data transfer rate. The bandwidth of cables and radio links also limit transfer rate.

Today, it is possible to access the Internet to browse the Web and send e-mails etc. using a mobile phone. Internet hotspots set up in public areas such as cafés, hotels etc. allow users to wireless connect to the Internet through their mobile devices, such as laptops and PDAs.

## Exercises

1.  Describe peer-to-peer and client–server networks and list the advantages/ disadvantages of each.

2.  Describe the benefits and limitations of e-commerce:

    (a)   to a business

    (b)   to somebody wanting to purchase a product.

3.  Explain the meaning of:

    (a)   downloading

    (b)   uploading.

4.  Explain data transfer rate.

5.  What hardware is needed to connect to the Internet?

6.  Describe the differences between the Internet, an intranet and an extranet.

# CHAPTER 5

# ICT in Everyday Life

**In this chapter you will find out:**

- ❗ how ICT is used in business, government, healthcare and education
- ❗ about teleworking
- ❗ about the ergonomic, health and environmental issues related to using ICT
- ❗ about virtual communities and precautions that should be taken when online.

## IT or ICT?                                   Syllabus 1.4.1.1

Information technology (IT) describes all things related to computers and the data they process to provide information. As digital technology has spread beyond computers alone, what constitutes IT has broadened to take in electronic communications. The term Information and Communications Technology (ICT) more fully describes this wider use of digital electronics.

### Computers or people?

Computers are an indispensable part of our daily lives. There are many reasons why this is so. Computers can:

- ❶ calculate millions of times faster than humans
- ❶ never get tired or need a rest
- ❶ do jobs that it would be dangerous for a human to do
- ❶ store large amounts of data in a very small space
- ❶ find data and provide information quickly
- ❶ never lose or misplace data.

However, no computer has come up with a play or book worth reading, conjured up a new recipe for something worth eating, or given comfort, sympathy or understanding to someone in distress. Computers can aid people in these tasks, but they can never replace them.

In this chapter you'll look at some of the ways in which computers are used in organisations such as businesses, industry, hospitals, schools and in the home office.

# ICT in business
Syllabus 1.4.1.2

### Business administration systems

Computers are used in businesses for keeping customer records, recording orders, printing invoices, keeping accounts, calculating payroll and managing stock, to name just a few applications.

### Booking systems

Using a network of computers, companies are able to record a booking instantly, for example at a theatre, on a flight etc. Using a computerised booking system it is impossible to sell the same seat twice, even though many people may be making a booking at any one time.

### Online banking

Most banks now offer some form of online banking. Advantages to the customer include access to their account details at any time without the need to travel to a high-street branch. Many people are still concerned about the level of security of these systems and the lack of personal contact if problems arise. The main advantage to the banks is a reduction in the cost of running and staffing branches which can lead to job losses.

### Online trading

Websites let shops extend their presence out of the high street. Shoppers can compare prices from companies across the world. Some retailers only trade online, for example Amazon. An advantage of this is that the company does not have to pay for premises other than for warehousing, and for sales staff.

### High-street trading

The purchaser is able to purchase goods more easily using credit and debit cards, and a shop receives the money more quickly as it is electronically transferred into its account. Managers can more easily compare sales across different branches and sales trends can be analysed more simply.

Many retailers, especially large supermarkets, use automatic stock control systems that monitor sales at the tills. The store then knows when stocks of certain items are running low, and the system will automatically reorder new stock on a 'just in time' basis. This means that the store does not hold too much of any perishable goods, only receiving new stock when a predefined lower limit is reached. These systems also let a price change, such as a special offer, be reliably updated in all the retailer's branches.

# ICT in government
Syllabus 1.4.1.2

Many government-run organisations rely heavily on computers to process millions of records every month. Some of these are listed on the next page.

### Census

Every few years the government takes a census to determine how many people live in the UK, as well as various statistics on age, ethnic origin and income. These census records are held on computer and can be analysed to ensure that the right number of schools, hospitals and other facilities are made available in different areas of the country.

### Electronic voting

A voting register of all adults eligible to vote is regularly updated and held on computer. Electronic voting, either at a polling booth or from home via a computer or telephone, has been trialled in local elections and is likely to become widespread.

### Electronic petitions

You can register your name for a cause you feel strongly about by signing an electronic petition that is accessed by your MP or Downing Street. The petition website gives details of the cause and displays recent signatories.

### Vehicle registration

The DVLA computers at Swansea keep a record of every licensed vehicle in the UK, including the make of car, registration number and registered owner. It is possible to renew a vehicle's registration online.

### Revenue collection

The Inland Revenue keeps records of every tax payer (private or business), and processes their tax returns. It is possible to fill in a tax return online rather than using a paper form.

## ICT in healthcare

### Patient administration systems

Doctors' surgeries and hospitals are computerised with more patient records being introduced. Appointment booking systems are computerised and doctors automatically print out prescriptions from their PCs.

### Ambulance control systems

Many ambulance services are computerised. The objectives of such a system include:

- call-taking, accepting and verifying incident details
- determining which ambulance to send
- communicating details of an incident to the chosen ambulance
- positioning suitably equipped and staffed vehicles in locations where they are most likely to be needed, so minimising response times to calls.

### Diagnostic tools and instruments

Computerised diagnostic tools include equipment to take scans or analyse blood, urine and tissue samples. Specialised equipment is also used to monitor vital signs such as heart rate and temperature. Computerised devices such as pacemakers and prostheses (artificial limbs) have enabled tens of thousands of people to live longer and fuller lives.

### Specialist surgical equipment

Computers are now used to assist surgeons carrying out surgical operations. Special equipment can provide three-dimensional vision and eliminate hand tremor by scaling down the range of motion.

Virtual reality systems let surgeons practise complicated procedures before they undertake an operation for real.

# ICT in education
Syllabus 1.4.1.3

ICT is spreading rapidly in education from primary schools right through to universities. With ICT firmly on the National Curriculum, pupils now gain invaluable experience of ICT in the classroom before they embark on a career.

### Registration and timetable systems

Computers are widely used in schools and colleges to keep records. In some schools, pupils register their presence each day by swiping a magnetic card through a machine.

School timetable systems are commonly used to work out the timetable for each individual class or pupil.

### Computer-based training (CBT) and multimedia resources

Software packages that enable users to learn any subject at their computer screens are widely available. They are used not only in schools but also in organisations to teach anything from a foreign language to how to advise a customer on the correct mortgage. CBT gives the learner more flexibility over when and where to study.

Many school textbooks now come with a CD-ROM or web links that provide extra resources, sometimes interactive, that build upon the text, often giving more context.

### Distance learning and homework using the Internet

The Internet is a cost-effective resource to help pupils and students receive learning materials and assignments, especially for those in remote parts of the world or who are participating on a distance learning course away from a college.

Websites, used carefully, are an excellent research resource for homework. Some schools and colleges use e-mail to set and collect homework.

# Module 1 Concepts of Information Technology

## Teleworking

Syllabus 1.4.1.4

The increased availability of ICT has meant that many of the things that at one time could only be done at a company's premises can now be done from a home office. Many companies now allow their employees to telework – instead of commuting, the employees use ICT to process and transfer data to and from the company's computers.

Of course, not all jobs are suited to teleworking, but where they are, the benefits include:

- reduced cost of travelling
- long commuting journeys avoided
- opportunity to work in the comfort of their own home environment
- increased productivity and greater ability to focus on one task
- flexible schedules, for example easier childcare arrangements
- reduced company space requirements.

The drawbacks include:

- lack of personal contact with fellow workers
- lack of teamwork and participation with shared projects
- home distractions may interfere with work.

In addition, ICT availability has meant that you do not have to be an employee of a company to work from home. Many individuals have successful businesses providing services and selling products from their home which could be anywhere in the country.

## Ergonomics

Syllabus 1.4.4.1–3

As people spend more and more time using computers it is essential to consider the ergonomic efficiency of their use. Ergonomics is the study of how well people do their jobs in different working environments. This efficiency is affected by a range of factors, which include among others:

- Lighting. The room should be well lit with indirect lighting. Computers should neither face windows nor back onto a window so that the users have to sit with the sun in their eyes. The screen should be positioned so that it does not reflect the glare from a window. Adjustable blinds should be provided.

- Ventilation. The room should have opening windows to allow free circulation of air and to prevent overheating.

- Furniture. Chairs should be of adjustable height, with a backrest which tilts to support the user at work and at rest, and should swivel on a five-point base. It should be at the correct height relative to a keyboard on the desk.

- ⓘ Accessories. Document holders, mouse mats, paper trays, foot rests etc. should be provided where appropriate.

- ⓘ Hardware. The screen should tilt and swivel and be flicker-free. Ideally it should be situated so that it avoids reflecting light. An anti-glare filter placed on the screen can prevent eye strain. The keyboard should be separately attached.

All computer users should be encouraged to take frequent breaks.

## Health issues                                                        Syllabus 1.4.4.4

Computers are responsible for many health problems, from eye strain to wrist injuries and back problems.

- ⓘ Repetitive Strain Injury (RSI). This is the collective name for a variety of disorders affecting the neck, shoulders and upper limbs. It can result in numbness or tingling in the arms and hands, aching and stiffness in the arms, neck and shoulders, and an inability to lift or grip objects. The risk of getting RSI problems can be minimised by sitting correctly at the keyboard and wrist-rest, and by ensuring that other objects that you need are in easy reach on the desk. Document holders and foot rests should be used as appropriate.

- ⓘ Eye strain. Computer users are prone to eye strain from spending long hours in front of a screen. Many computer users prefer a dim light to achieve better screen contrast, but this makes it difficult to read documents on the desk. A small spotlight focused on the desktop can be helpful. There is no evidence that computer use causes permanent damage to the eyes but glare, improper lighting, improperly corrected vision (through not wearing the correct prescription glasses), poor work practices and poorly designed workstations all contribute to temporary eye strain. Users should take regular breaks away from the screen.

- ⓘ Back problems. Poor seating and bad posture whilst sitting at a computer screen can cause back problems. The likelihood of back problems can be minimised by making sure you do not sit in one position for an extended period of time.

Frequent breaks and change of routine will help prevent the onset of all the above.

Note:

The UK Health and Safety at Work Act (1974) legislates on health and safety in the workplace. It is supported by numerous regulations, such as:

- ⓘ the Control of Substances Hazardous to Health (COSHH) Regulations (2002)
- ⓘ the Manual Handling Operations Regulations (1992)
- ⓘ the Workplace (Health, Safety and Welfare) Regulations (1992)
- ⓘ the Health and Safety (Display Screen Equipment) Regulations (1992).

## Safety precautions

Computers are electrical devices and so present a safety hazard. There are a number of health and safety issues associated with setting up and using a computer, such as:

- All cables should be safely secured to prevent a trip hazard.
- Power points must not be overloaded.
- Working surfaces should be clean and tidy, with adequate space around the workstation.
- Food and drink should not be consumed at the desk or placed nearby.

Desktop computers are also heavy, so move them using the correct lifting techniques.

## The environment
Syllabus 1.4.5.1–2

There are a number of measures that computer users can take to help the environment:

- Recycle printer toner cartridges and printer paper.
- Use CD-ROM materials, electronic documents and on-screen help to reduce the need for printed materials.
- Use energy-saving features such as screen power management, hibernation and sleep modes and power-save modes that use less power when a system is inactive. These can all be set using the Windows control panel. Always switch off the monitor and computer at the end of a computing session (remembering to log off correctly first).
- Computer equipment disposal is subject to the EU Waste Electrical and Electronic Equipment (WEEE) Directive. This means that it must be disposed of in an environmentally-friendly way.

## Sharing with others
Syllabus 1.4.2.5–6/1.4.3.1–3

Online or virtual communities are groups of people who 'interact' using the Internet to communicate with one another without meeting. Social networking websites, Internet forums and chat rooms bring together people with a common interest and provide a means for them to discuss issues, ask questions and learn from their peers.

The Internet allows people to share information with unprecedented ease. It is no longer necessary to follow the more traditional publishing routes. Text, audio and video files can be uploaded to websites for access through browsers or future downloading to a user's computer. Audio and video files can be transferred to portable media players (such as Apple's iPod) or mobile phones. These are termed podcasts.

Sharing is an important part of the Internet and it is possible to place an online 'diary' on the Internet. This is called a blog (short for web log). A blog can take many formats: a diary, a commentary on a particular topic or event (say, political) etc. Sometimes readers can add comments to the blog.

The wiki is a way of editing websites. This allows collaborative websites to be built that take input from any user who wishes (or is permitted) to participate. Probably the most well-known collaborative website is Wikipedia which is an encyclopaedia entirely constructed of pages of information posted on it from users worldwide. Other users can add to topics already on the site or they can comment on the accuracy of an entry.

Collaborative websites are also used on company intranets. A typical use might be to provide IT help. An IT department can post help pages on frequently asked IT questions to help users with the use of their computers, and the users can add further comments or new topics that they feel might be useful to their colleagues.

Games are no longer limited to one computer, and players can compete with each other around the world using the Internet.

### Keeping safe

The very nature of the Internet, its open access to everyone, means that it is vulnerable to criminal activities. For this reason, it is vital that you take the following precautions when you use community-type websites and when you are online in general:

- Do not divulge too much personal information about yourself.

- Keep your personal profile private.

- Do not give any information that could locate you.

- Be aware that photos and information about you might be seen by others.

- Remember that you do not really **know** the people you are communicating with.

## Exercises

1. Describe briefly five situations when you may use or encounter computers other than your own PC in everyday life.

2. Describe briefly three large-scale uses of computers by government, describing in each case what data is held and how it may be used.

3. Give three advantages and three disadvantages of computer-based training in a school or company.

4. Describe briefly three health hazards associated with working long hours at a computer. In each case, describe one method of minimising the hazard.

5. (a) Describe briefly three ways in which users can minimise the detrimental effects of computers on the environment.

   (b) Describe three ways in which computers could be said to be contributing positively towards preserving the environment.

6. What is meant by teleworking? Name two advantages to:
   (a) the employer  (b) the employee.

7. Describe two business that could be run successfully from a home-based environment, explaining how ICT benefits them.

8. Describe a use for a collaborative website. What might be its limitations?

9. What precautions should you take when using online communities or similar?

# CHAPTER 6

# Legal Issues and Security

In this chapter you will find out:

- about the laws that affect ICT in the UK
- about access controls
- about viruses
- about backup procedures
- about staying safe and good practice.

## Laws

ICT, like many other things in everyday life, is subject to rules and regulations that are there to protect individuals from inappropriate activities and make them safe. Many of these regulations are enshrined in law. The main examples are:

- The Data Protection Act (1998) – This sets out rules for storing data about people and is intended to protect the privacy of individuals. More information can be found at www.ico.gov.uk.

- The Copyright, Designs and Patents Act (1988) – This covers a wide range of intellectual property including software. It is illegal to copy software, download copyright soundtracks or DVDs or to use someone else's work without their permission. More information can be found at www.patent.gov.uk/copy.htm.

- The Computer Misuse Act (1990) – This protects against hackers and viruses. It is illegal to obtain unauthorised access to any computer or to modify its contents.

- The Health and Safety at Work Act (1974) – This incorporates legislation to protect the health of employees working at computer workstations for long periods of time. More information can be found at www.hse.gov.uk. The Health and Safety Executive publish a useful document entitled Working with VDUs which can be downloaded from www.hse.gov.uk/pubns/indg36.pdf.

## Personal privacy
**Syllabus 1.6.2.1–3**

The right to privacy is a fundamental human right and one that we take for granted. Most of us, for instance, would not want our medical records freely circulated, and many people are sensitive about revealing their age, religious beliefs, family circumstances or academic qualifications. In the UK even the use of name and address files for mail shots is often felt to be an invasion of privacy.

With the advent of large computerised databases it became quite feasible for sensitive personal data to be stored and accessed by, say, a prospective employer, credit card company or insurance company to assess somebody's suitability for employment, credit or insurance, respectively, without an individual's knowledge.

In the UK, the Data Protection Act (1998) (DPA) sets out rules for processing data about people and applies to paper records as well as those held on computers. It is intended to protect the privacy of individuals. Not all countries have data protection laws, and those that do might differ in the detail.

## The data protection principles

Under the DPA, anyone holding personal data must comply with the eight enforceable principles of good practice. They say that data must be:

- fairly and lawfully processed

- obtained only for specific purposes

- adequate, relevant and not excessive

- accurate and up-to-date

- not kept longer than necessary

- processed in accordance with the data subject's rights

- not transferred to other countries without adequate protection

- secure and safe from others who don't have rights to it, for example other employees and hackers.

Any organisation holding personal data about people (for example employees or customers) must register with the Data Protection Registrar. They have to state what data is being held, the sources and purposes of the data and the types of organisation to whom the data may be disclosed.

As an individual you are entitled, on making a written request to a data user, to be supplied with a copy of any personal data held about yourself. The data user may charge a fee of up to £10 for each register entry for supplying this data but in some cases it is supplied free.

Usually the request must be responded to within 40 days. If not, you are entitled to complain to the Registrar or apply to the courts for correction or deletion of the data.

With some exceptions, data cannot be held about you without your consent.

For more information on data protection visit the following website: www.ico.gov.uk.

## Data security

One of the legal requirements of the DPA is that data about individuals must be kept secure. This means that it must be properly protected from unauthorised view or loss. Moreover, the data held on a computer system can be one of the most valuable assets to a company. Security controls must be put in place to protect it from damage and unauthorised access.

To deal with security risks, most organisations have an information security policy. A typical security policy will cover:

- ● administrative controls such as careful screening of prospective employees and disciplinary procedures in the event of security breaches

- ● backup procedures

- ● control of access to data by means of smart cards, ID badges, sign-in/sign-out registers

- ● protection against fire and flood

- ● access controls to computer systems and data by means of user IDs, passwords and access rights

- ● procedures for reporting security incidents

- ● training to make staff members aware of their responsibilities.

## Copyright and licences                                    Syllabus 1.6.1.1–4

Anything that is an original creation (anything that has been written and designed) is subject to copyright restrictions. This includes text, music and images. In the UK, copyright is protected by the Copyright, Designs and Patents Act (1988). Copyright material belongs to the copyright holder (usually the person who produced the material in the first place), and their permission must be obtained before the material can be used. Sometimes the user might charge a fee before permission is granted. Copyright protects the originator from unauthorised use of their material.

Files downloaded from the Internet containing text, graphics, audio or video clips are also copyright. They will say if they are free from copyright restrictions. It is illegal to use such material in your own publications without the consent of the author or creator.

Computer software is copyright material, but it is also subject to licence rules. When you buy software you are buying a licence to use it. Ownership of the source code, that is the software itself, remains with the producer, so it is illegal to make unauthorised copies. The terms and conditions of the licence are either provided in printed form or they are displayed on-screen when you install the software for the first time.

At the start of installation you will be asked to indicate your agreement to the licence conditions. This is referred to as the End User Licence Agreement (EULA). The CD or package will have a unique Product ID number which you may need to type in when installing the software. Once installed, you can see the Product ID number by clicking on the Help menu and selecting an option such as, for example, About Microsoft Word.

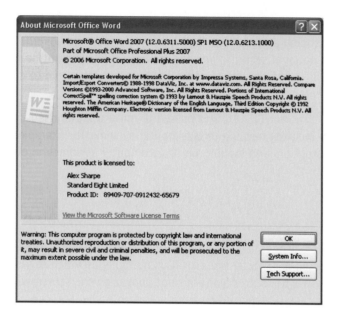

Before you can use the software, you might need to activate it. This means that the validity of the software is checked on the manufacturer's database. Software licences usually permit the user to use one copy on a single computer. It is considered to be in use if it is loaded into either the computer's temporary memory (RAM) or onto the hard disk drive. With network licences the software is often loaded onto the file server and the licence specifies how many users on the network can access it at any one time.

It is illegal to make copies of the software, except for backup purposes, so you are breaking the law if you copy software onto removable media such as floppy disks or CDs to use on another computer.

Sometimes you might be asked to register the software. This usually is a way for manufacturers to track sales and get your contact details so they can send you marketing material and information on updates. You will be told if registration is part of the authentication procedure.

Some software is classed as shareware. This can be downloaded from the Internet for evaluation. If you like the program you pay a fee and register with the manufacturer. Most programs of this type allow you to use them a limited number of times and then cease to load correctly when the evaluation period expires. Freeware programs can be downloaded from the Internet and used for no cost.

Open source software is software where the source code is available to users to modify, improve and extend.

## IT security

The data held on computers is valuable. For a company, the data might represent years of investment in developing a product or future strategies; for the government, the data might be a matter of national security; and for the individual, it might be personal data such as banking details. All of the above and other data are attractive to criminals, so it is vital that it is protected from their activities.

The UK Computer Misuse Act (1990) was passed to make unauthorised use of a computer illegal. This includes hacking into computer systems, for example to steal data or simply to cause disruption, and logging on to a computer as someone else without their permission.

## Access controls                                    Syllabus 1.5.1.1–2

Most networks require a user to log on with a user ID and password before they can gain access to the computer system. The user ID is normally assigned to you, and is open to view. The password is secret and does not appear on the screen when you type it in – the letters may be replaced by asterisks as you type. You can change your password whenever you like.

If you are authorised to access particularly sensitive data that only certain people are allowed to view, you may need to enter a second password. For example, on a company database the accounts clerks may be able to view customer records but they may not be allowed access to personal data about colleagues. These access rights are used to protect the privacy of individuals and the security of confidential data.

In order to be completely secure there are some basic rules you should follow when using a password:

- ℹ️ Never write down the password – memorise it.
- ℹ️ Never tell your password to another person.
- ℹ️ Do not use an obvious word or name as a password – a combination of at least six letters and numbers is best.
- ℹ️ Change your password regularly.

Some websites, for instance those that hold personal account information (e.g. online banks), will require you to log in securely with a user ID and password.

### Biometric security

Some computer systems might hold data that is so sensitive that password protection is not enough. It these cases sensors that check a physical feature of an individual are used. This is biometric security and it may be used for access control to computer rooms or to individual computers. Biometric security relies on the fact that some physical features, such as fingerprint, iris, face and voice patterns are unique to an individual.

## Theft Syllabus 1.5.2.3

The theft of a computer (laptops, PDAs and mobile phones are particularly vulnerable) can have disastrous consequences for the owner if they have not backed up their data. Confidential files, lists of phone numbers which could be misused, contact details or months of work can be lost if they are not properly protected and backed up. Theft can also seriously affect a company.

Hardware can be secured using cables to prevent them being stolen, and the use of passwords on screen savers and drives can prevent unauthorised access of data.

It is also important that controls are placed on the movement of data on disks, and that old disks are securely disposed of so the data does not fall into the wrong hands.

## Unauthorised access Syllabus 1.5.2.2/1.5.3.1–3

Other theft might not involve physically taking the hardware to get the data. Unauthorised access via the Internet, hacking, can cause immense damage through the loss of data or by placing malicious code (malware) on the systems.

Malware includes viruses and spyware. The latter secretly monitors what a user is doing on their computer and can even take control of it or record keystrokes to find out passwords etc.

### Viruses

Viruses are malware that can replicate and infect computers, often without the user's knowledge. Viruses have been developed with the definite intention to cause damage to computer files or, at the very least, cause inconvenience and annoyance to computer users. Precautions to avoid your PC being infected with a virus include the following:

ⓘ Virus checkers need to be installed on all computer systems so that they automatically check for any infected data when the computer is started up. Manual checkers can also be used to check for viruses on floppy disks.

ⓘ You should not share or lend removable storage media that could introduce viruses into your system.

ⓘ Care should be taken when downloading files from the Internet. The proliferation of viruses over recent years is due in part to e-mail communication. Never open an unrecognised e-mail message or an e-mail attachment from someone that you don't recognise – it could well introduce a virus to your system.

Approximately 300 new viruses are unleashed each month so it is a good idea to install a virus checker that provides an online automatic update service. The virus checking software should be capable of not only detecting the virus, but also of removing it from the infected file (this is called disinfecting the file).

**ORIGINATION**
A programmer writes a program, the virus, to cause mischief or destruction. The virus is capable of reproducing itself.

**TRANSMISSION**
Often, the virus is attached to a normal program. It then copies itself to other software on the hard disk.

**REPRODUCTION**
When another floppy disk or similar is inserted into the computer's disk drive, the virus copies itself onto the floppy disk.

**INFECTION**
Depending on what the original programmer wrote in the virus program, a virus may display messages, use up all the computer's memory, destroy data files or cause serious damage.

## Firewall

A firewall refers to software that detects and provides limited defence from unauthorised access from the Internet to a computer or network. Microsoft Windows XP and Vista include firewall software. It is important that this is configured correctly and is switched on.

## Backup procedures                                    Syllabus 1.5.2.1

Important data can be lost through accidents as well as through theft or virus infection. Copying files for backup purposes in case your hard disk crashes is an essential skill for everyone using a computer, and you will be glad you have a recent copy of your work safely tucked away.

Backing up data involves copying it to another storage device. Often users on a company network are allocated user space on a server where they can copy important data. Routine backups of the servers are taken frequently by the IT department. The backup media must be clearly labelled and should be stored in a fire-proof safe, or better still on a different site, so that, should a disaster or emergency occur, the backup media will be safe.

The most convenient form of backup storage for home users is likely to be a USB flash drive, CD, DVD or external hard drive.

For larger amounts of information, perhaps on a company network, a tape drive is normally used. This is a unit that copies the contents of the hard drive onto a magnetic cassette tape or DAT (Digital Audio Tape). If a problem occurs with the hard drive the data can all be copied back from the tape. One limitation of this procedure is that it can take some time to find a particular piece of data stored sequentially on the tape.

As broadband Internet access becomes more widely available, remote backup services are becoming more popular. This means backing up via the Internet to a remote location. This can protect against some disaster scenarios, such as a whole building being destroyed, taking PCs and backup tapes with it. One limitation can be the speed of the Internet connection which is usually a lot slower than the speed of local data storage devices, so backing up large amounts of data can be a problem. There are also potential security risks for company-sensitive information stored effectively by a third party.

## Staying safe and good practice

When using ICT-based communications, bear in mind the following principles:

- ● Protect personal information to minimise the risk of identity theft or fraud.

- ● Avoid the misuse of images which will offend others or break the law.

- ● Use language appropriate to the topic and recipient of any messages, and do not offend others. Check all recipients on a copy list should receive a particular message before you send it.

- ● Respect confidentiality.

See module 1, page 33, and module 7, page 479 for more on staying safe.

## Exercises

1. What is meant by the terms shareware and freeware? Can you use such software without paying, on your computer?

2. Before using a photograph that you have downloaded from the Internet in a publication of your own, what should you do?

3. (a) What is the name of the Act that protects the privacy of personal data held on a computer?

   (b) List four provisions of this Act.

4. What rights do you have as an individual, regarding the holding of personal data about yourself on a computer?

5. (a) What is a computer virus?

   (b) Name three measures you can take to minimise the possibility of your computer being infected with a virus.

6. Describe a suitable backup medium for:

   (a) a student using a laptop at home

   (b) a large company network.

## Ask yourself

- ❓ Can you name different types of computer and what they might be used for?
- ❓ Can you name the different parts of a desktop PC and their functions?
- ❓ Can you describe the different software types found on a desktop PC and give examples?
- ❓ Can you describe different network types and where you might find them used?
- ❓ Do you know what the Internet is and what services use it?
- ❓ Can you describe the health and safety issues surrounding computer use?
- ❓ Can you describe security issues arising from the use of computers?
- ❓ Do you know the legal aspects of using ICT?
- ❓ Can you describe how ICT has affected everyday life in the home and in business?

# Module 2
## Using the Computer and Managing Files

In this module you will learn to become competent in using the common functions of a personal computer and its operating system. You will learn how to:

- adjust main settings
- use the built-in help features
- operate effectively within the desktop environment and work with desktop icons and windows
- manage and organise files and directories/folders
- duplicate, move and delete files and directories/folders, and compress and extract files
- use virus-scanning software
- use simple editing tools and print management facilities available within the operating system
- resolve simple errors.

This training, which has been approved by the ECDL Foundation, includes exercise items intended to assist Candidates in their training for an ECDL Certification Programme. These exercises are not ECDL Foundation certification tests. For information about authorised ECDL Test Centres in different national territories, please refer to the ECDL Foundation website at www.ecdl.org

# Module **2**

# Contents

# The Desktop

In this chapter you will find out:

- about switching on and off, and restarting your computer
- about the computer desktop and parts of a window
- about using a mouse.

## First steps

This module will give you invaluable skills in using your computer's operating system – in this case Microsoft Windows XP, but other versions of Windows work in much the same way. The things you will learn in this module will help you to organise all the work you do using applications such as word processors and spreadsheets.

It will also help you to troubleshoot and know what to do when something unexpected happens. Hopefully it will take a lot of the bafflement and frustration out of using your computer!

But first, check that you will be working in a safe environment as discussed in Module 1.

## Switching on                                                    Syllabus 2.1.1.1

- If your computer has a floppy disk drive, check that there is not a disk in it.
- Press the power switch on the front of the system unit. Also remember to switch on the screen and the printer.
- If you are working on a network you will probably be asked to enter a user ID and password. Do that now. For security reasons, the password will not be displayed on the screen.

Wait for the screen to stop changing. It should end up with some small symbols (called icons), a coloured background or picture (the desktop) and a strip called the taskbar. Your computer will have been set up differently to the one shown in the image but the basic layout should be very similar.

Taskbar       Icons       Desktop

## Icons

Desktop icons can signify many different things. Here are some you might see:

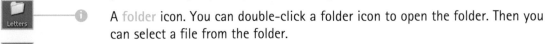 A folder icon. You can double-click a folder icon to open the folder. Then you can select a file from the folder.

A file icon. Double-click a file icon to open the file in the appropriate application – in this case, Microsoft Word.

An application icon. You can double-click an application icon to open the application.

The Recycle Bin (wastebasket). When you delete a file from your hard drive, it goes into the Recycle Bin. You can retrieve it from there if you change your mind about deleting it, so long as you haven't emptied the bin!

A printer icon. You can double-click a printer icon to control how and when documents are printed.

You will have a completely different selection of icons on your desktop, and maybe a different background as well.

## The taskbar

The taskbar at the bottom of the desktop shows application programs that are currently open. Your taskbar might show other items if it has been customised. It is possible to configure it to display shortcuts to applications you frequently use or display an icon that will display the desktop if is hidden by a running application.

Start button                            Taskbar                        Notification area

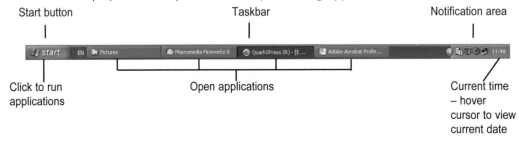

Click to run                    Open applications             Current time
applications                                                  – hover
                                                    cursor to view
                                                  current date

Hover the mouse pointer over any icon on the taskbar. A tool tip appears telling you its function. ('Hover' means move the mouse so the pointer rests over an icon, and do not click a mouse button.)

Click the open application buttons on the taskbar to switch between open windows.

### Tip:

You can switch between open windows without using the mouse by holding down the Alt key on the keyboard and pressing the tab key at the same time. The open windows are displayed as you tab through them. Release the Alt key when you reach the window you require.

## Using the mouse

The mouse is one of the main ways you can give instructions to your computer. A pointer moves across the screen as you move the mouse on the desk. The left and right buttons are used to select and activate items on the screen. Most mice have a central wheel between the buttons that can be used to scroll and zoom the image on the screen.

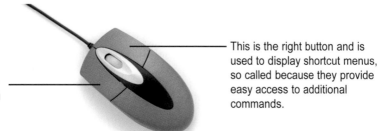

This is the left button and is the one most often used. When you are asked to click the mouse button, press this button once.

This is the right button and is used to display shortcut menus, so called because they provide easy access to additional commands.

The mouse pointer can appear as different icons depending on where it is on the screen or what the computer is doing. Here are some examples:

This is the general pointer and means the computer is ready for you to do something.

The hourglass shows the computer is busy, maybe loading a program, and you should wait until the normal pointer appears before you do anything.

When the pointer changes to a two-headed arrow you can resize a window.

## Mouse clicks

There are three ways of clicking the mouse buttons to select screen items that tell the computer what you want it to do. You will also need to drag and drop text or objects.

- Single-click. When you are told to 'click' an item, this means move the mouse so the pointer is over the required item and then press the mouse's left button once. This selects the item. Try clicking one of the desktop icons. It changes colour but nothing else happens.

- Double-click. Generally speaking, single-clicking selects an item and double-clicking activates it, but there are exceptions to this rule. Try double-clicking the My Computer icon, for example, to open the My Computer window. (If My Computer is not visible on your desktop, click Start and then click My Computer on the list displayed.) Leave this window open.

- Right-click. When you are told to right-click an item, this means move the mouse so the pointer is over the required item and then press the right-hand button once. This opens a shortcut menu showing various things that can be done. Try this by right-clicking the desktop. Click away from the menu to close it again.

    ⓘ   Drag and drop. Click an item and hold down the left mouse button while you move the mouse. The selected item will be dragged across the screen. Release the mouse button to drop the item when you have reached the desired position. Try moving a desktop icon by dragging and dropping it.

Tip:

> If you cannot move the desktop icon, right-click the Desktop and select Arrange Icons By. If Auto Arrange is ticked, click it to deselect it.

## The Start button

The Start button at the bottom left of the screen is used to select an application to run or a task that you want to do.

You'll now open a games application.

▶   Click the Start button.

▶   On the menu that appears, point to All Programs.

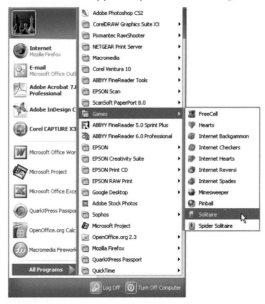

Tip:

> If your start menu looks different, right-click the Start button and click Properties. Click the Start Menu tab and select the Start menu option.

▶   On the submenu that appears, point to Games. On the next menu, click Solitaire. The Solitaire window opens.

## The parts of a window                 Syllabus 2.1.4.1–2

If you can tear yourself away from the game, or cannot figure out how to play, you'll look now at the parts of a window.

Title bar ——

Menu bar ——

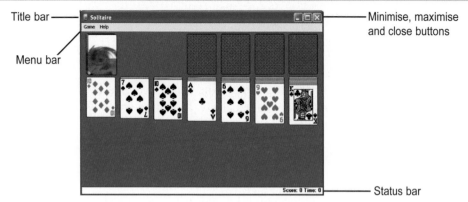

—— Minimise, maximise and close buttons

—— Status bar

All application windows have the following parts in common:

- A title bar showing the name of the program. If you can see other application windows open on your desktop, you can click the title bar to bring that application to the front so you can use it. (Alternatively, you can click the running application icon on the taskbar.)

- A menu bar of menu items that when clicked produce drop-down lists with further options to choose from.

- A status bar, which provides information about the current state of what you are viewing in the window.

- A minimise button. Click this button once in the Solitaire window. The window disappears, but the application is still open. Look in the taskbar and you will see an icon labelled Solitaire. Click it to restore the window to the desktop.

- A maximise button. Click this once in the Solitaire window. The window now occupies the full screen.
  Notice that the maximise button has now changed to a restore button. Click this once now to restore the window to its original size.

Tip:

You can double-click the title bar to maximise the window. Double-click it again to restore it to its previous size.

- A close button. Click this once to close the window. Don't do this now. If you close one of the two windows, open it up again.

- Many applications also have toolbars. These are groups of buttons that let you do related tasks. They are often placed near the menu bar, but they can be moved. The toolbars and menu bar are replaced by a ribbon in Office 2007 applications. The ribbon is context-sensitive which means the buttons shown on it change according to the task being undertaken. This is an example from Excel 2007.

## Displaying, moving and resizing a window Syllabus 2.1.4.2

Either click the icons on the taskbar or click the title bar of a window to switch between open windows. You can move a window around on the screen by dragging its title bar.

To change the size of a window, move the cursor over one of the window borders so that it changes to a double-headed arrow. Then drag one way or the other to make the window bigger or smaller.

▶ Try making the My Computer window smaller so that scroll bars appear.

If any part of the window is not shown, you can drag a scroll bar to see parts of the window that are hidden from view.

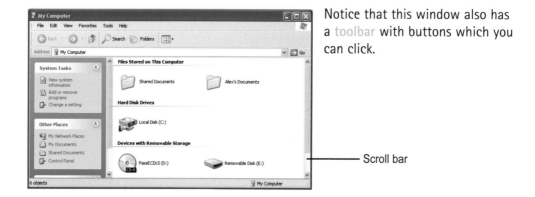 Notice that this window also has a toolbar with buttons which you can click.

—— Scroll bar

▶ Try arranging the windows on the desktop so that they don't overlap. A quick way to do this is to right-click in the taskbar and select Tile Windows Horizontally or Tile Windows Vertically from the shortcut menu.

▶ Close both the open windows when you have finished practising.

## Switching off your computer Syllabus 2.1.1.4

Before you switch off your computer you must close any programs that are open. You should then close your computer down in the recommended way. This is because the operating system performs some internal housekeeping tasks before shutting down the system. If you don't let the computer do this and you switch off the power yourself, your computer may not restart normally next time.

◯ When you have closed all your programs you should see only the Windows desktop on the screen.

◯ In the bottom left-hand corner of your screen, click Start.

◯ Click Turn Off Computer.

◯ In the box that appears click Turn Off.

◯ Your computer should power off automatically, so wait until it has before unplugging it.

## Restarting your computer                                    Syllabus 2.1.1.2

Instead of closing down your computer you can choose to restart it.

◯ When you see the Turn Off Computer box (shown above), click Restart.

## Exercises

1. Answers the following questions about your Windows desktop.

    (a) Do you have to enter a Windows username and password?

    (b) What are desktop icons?

    (c) What are the names of all the desktop icons you can see?

    (d) What is the Recycle Bin used for?

    (e) Where can you find the current date and time on your Windows desktop?

    (f) What does it mean when you see an hourglass on the screen?

    (g) How do you open an application? If you can think of more than one way, describe all of them.

2. (a) Describe the purpose of the window minimise and maximise buttons.

    (b) Describe how you would resize a window.

    (c) Draw a rough sketch of a screen with two windows tiled vertically.

3. Why must you switch off your computer correctly? Describe the procedure.

4. How might you restart your computer?

# CHAPTER 8

# Creating and Printing Files

In this chapter you will find out:

- how to open a text-editing application
- how to open an existing file
- about different file types
- how to create a document in Microsoft Word
- how to create a spreadsheet file
- about the Windows print manager and how to print a file.

In this chapter you'll open applications, some of which you will learn about in other modules, and create some sample files.

## A text-editing application                                    Syllabus 2.2.3.2

First you will create a short document in Microsoft WordPad and save it.

▶   Click Start and select All Programs, Accessories. Click WordPad.

Tip:

This is a short way of saying 'Click Start. From the submenu select All Programs. From the next submenu select Accessories. Then select WordPad.'

WordPad is a simple text editor that is included with Microsoft Windows.

In the large blank white area, you will see a small vertical blinking line. This is the text insertion point. When you type, the letters will appear on the screen at this point.

▶   Type this short sentence: This is a test document created in WordPad.

○ From the File menu, select Save.

A window will open, probably showing the default My Documents folder in the Save in: box. If it shows something different, you can either ask for help from your tutor or you can save it in the folder shown. Later, you will learn how to move it.

○ Type the name WordPad-Test in the File name: box.

Notice that by default it will be saved as a type of file called Rich Text Format. A full stop followed by the three letters rtf will be added to the end of your file name. These letters are known as the file extension.

○ Click the Save button. The window will close automatically.

 ○ Close WordPad by clicking the Close icon or by selecting File, Exit.

## Opening an existing file

Now practise re-opening WordPad and opening the new file you created.

○ Open Microsoft WordPad.

○ Select File, Open.

The Open dialogue box will be displayed, probably showing the contents of the My Documents folder. The test file you created, WordPad-Test, will be visible.

If you cannot see your test file, you will need to navigate to the correct folder. Navigation is covered in the next chapter, so you might want to ask your tutor to help you.

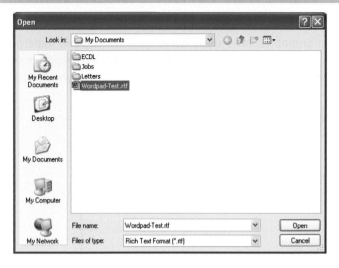

▷ Click the name of the test file to highlight it, and click the Open button.

Tip:

You can open a file by double-clicking the file name.

File types                                                    Syllabus 2.2.3.1

Windows recognises many different file types. The file type depends on which application the file was created in. Here are some examples of common file types, each identified by the three-character extension which forms part of the file name.

.avi, .mpg, .mov          Different types of video file

.bmp                      A bitmapped graphic created in a graphics package

.docx, .doc               A word-processed file created in Microsoft Word

.exe                      An executable file (that is a program that can be run)

.htm                      A web page file

.jpg, .gif, .tif          Different types of graphics file

.accdb, .mdb              A database created in Microsoft Access

.mp3, .mid, .wav          Different types of audio file

.pdf                      A file format that can be viewed in Adobe Reader

.pptx, .ppt               A presentation file created in Microsoft PowerPoint

.tmp                      A temporary file

.txt                      A plain text file

.xlsx, .xls               A spreadsheet created in Microsoft Excel

.zip                      A compressed file

## Creating Word documents

Next you will create three very short documents using Word. You need some files of different types so that you can practise moving them, copying them, renaming them and so on in the next chapter.

▷ Open Word by clicking the Start button and selecting All Programs, Microsoft Office, Microsoft Office Word 2007.

▷ Type a short invitation to your friend Sharon.

> Dear Sharon
>
> We're having a party on Friday 13th. Hope you can come!

▷ From the File menu, select Save. Save the document in the same folder as before, with the file name Sharon.

▷ Now edit the letter by changing the name Sharon to Robert.

▷ This time, you don't want to select Save from the File menu because that will overwrite the contents of the original file, leaving you with a letter to Robert with the file name Sharon. Instead, select File, Save As.

▷ Type the new file name Robert.

▷ Edit the letter once more to send an invitation to Kim.

▷ Save this file as Kim.

## Creating some spreadsheet files

Now you'll create some spreadsheet files.

- Open Microsoft Excel. This program is used to hold numerical information and you'll learn all about it in Module 4. For now, just enter a single number in cell A1.

- Type the number 1 in cell A1. Press the carriage return key on your keyboard to enter the data.

Tip:

> The carriage return key is so called because it is used on typewriters to move the platen back to the start of a new line. It is often marked with a ↵ symbol.

- Save the spreadsheet as SS1.

- Create three more spreadsheets, saving them as SS2, SS3 and SS4. You can do this in the same way as you created the three Word documents.

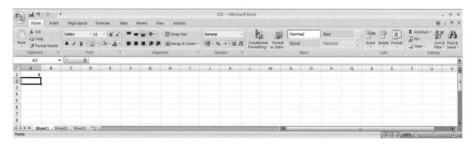

- Close Excel by clicking the Close icon or by selecting File, Exit.

## Printing a file                                        Syllabus 2.4.2.1

If you have not closed down Microsoft Word, you should see in the taskbar the name of the last document that you saved.

▶   Click the file name in the taskbar and the document will display.

▶   From the File menu select Print, to display the Print dialogue box.

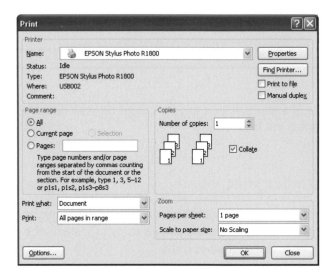

The print dialogue box allows you to set many options including which printer you want to use, which page(s) you want to print (for longer documents) and how many copies you would like.

▶   Select a printer from the Name: drop-down list by clicking the small arrow to the right of the list box and selecting the printer you want.

▶   Check that there is some paper in the printer.

▶   Make sure that only one copy is selected and click OK to print the document.

## The desktop print manager                              Syllabus 2.4.2.2

When you send a document to a printer to be printed it is added to a printer queue. This is effectively a waiting list showing all the print jobs that have been sent to a printer. When your computer sends a print job to the printer, a small printer icon appears in the notification area to the right of the taskbar. You can right-click this icon to view a print job's progress in the queue, but for small documents the appearance of this icon is often too quick to let you click it.

A more effective way to view a printer queue is as follows:

▶   Click Start, Printers and Faxes to open the Printers and Faxes window.

▶   Double-click the printer icon for your printer.

The print queue for the printer is displayed. Here you can view and control the progress of your print job.

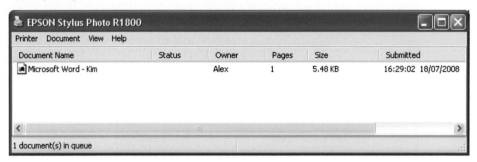

Tip:

Alternatively, if there is a shortcut icon to your printer on your desktop, you can double-click it to display the print queue.

## Pausing, restarting or deleting a print job          Syllabus 2.4.2.3

You can pause, restart or cancel a print job. You might want to do this, for example, if you accidentally start printing the whole of a long document instead of a single page from it or if the print queue status displays Error.

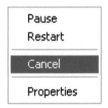 Click the file name to highlight it. A shortcut menu appears.

| Pause |
| Restart |
| Cancel |
| Properties |

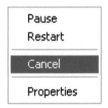    Select what you want to do from the list of options displayed.

## Exercises

1. Open a new WordPad document.

2. Enter the following text:

   Different file types include the following:

3. Move to a blank line by pressing Enter and type in the names of as many common file types as possible. Leave a couple of spaces between each one.

4. Save this document as File types.rtf in your My Documents folder.

5. Open a new Microsoft Word document.

6. In the document describe how you would access the print manager and explain what it does.

7. Save this document as Print Manager.docx in your My Documents folder.

8. Click your document File types.rtf in the taskbar and print it out.

9. Return to Print Manager.docx and print that too.

10. Add some more text to the document Print Manager.docx to explain how to cancel a job in a print queue.

11. Save the document with the name Useful tips.docx and print out a copy.

12. Close the file File types.rtf and close WordPad.

13. Close Print Manager.docx and Useful tips.docx and close Word.

# CHAPTER 9

# Working with Folders and Files

In this chapter you will find out:

- about the different disk drives on your computer
- about managing files and folders and about backing up your work
- about the Windows Recycle Bin
- about file compression
- about searching for files
- more about viruses.

## Disk drives on your computer
Syllabus 2.2.1.1–2

You might have several disk drives on your computer. Windows assigns a letter to each of them. The floppy drives (if you have any) are usually A: and B:. The hard drive is C:. Any more drives are assigned letters in order, so a second hard drive might be D:, the CD drive E: and so on. On a network the hard drive might be divided or 'partitioned' into several 'logical drives' called, for example, F:, G:, H: etc.

You can see what drives your computer has, and how much free space there is on each.

○ Go to the Desktop. You can do this by clicking the Desktop icon next to the Start button at the bottom left of the taskbar (if it is displayed), or by right-clicking in the taskbar and selecting Show the Desktop.

○ Double-click the My Computer icon. You should see a window similar to this one.

Views

**Tip:**

Alternatively, you can click Start and select My Computer from the displayed menu.

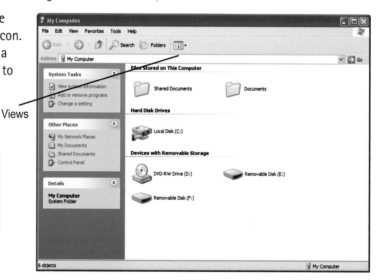

The screenshot shows a hard disk drive, C: and removeable storage drives D:, E; and F:. Your computer might be networked and have different drives. What drives are shown for your computer?

| Thumbnails |
| Tiles |
| Icons |
| List |
| ● Details |

Storage devices are covered in more detail in Module 1.

You can change the appearance of the window by clicking the Views button on the toolbar, and selecting one of the other options.

## Directories/folders                    Syllabus 2.2.1.1/2.2.1.3/2.2.2.1/2.2.3.5

All the documents you create on your PC are referred to as files. These files have to be given names (you can use up to 255 characters) and it is a good idea to use meaningful file names so that you can easily find a particular file later on.

As you use your computer more and more you will have lots of files stored on your hard drive (C:). You will need to keep your work organised so that you can go to it quickly.

Files are organised by saving them into folders that are also given names. These folders can contain subfolders. One very important folder that is set up automatically for you on the C: drive is My Documents. This is where Windows expects you to create your own subfolders to store your work.

Here is an example of a folder structure within My Documents:

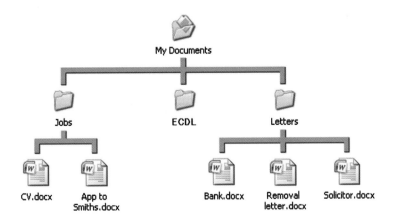

The location of files is specified by their pathname. For example in the diagram above, the pathname to the word-processed file Removal letter is:

C:\My Documents\Letters\Removal letter.docx

▶    Double-click the C: drive icon on the My Computer window.

You will now see a window displaying the folders and files in the C: drive. (Your window will have different folders.)

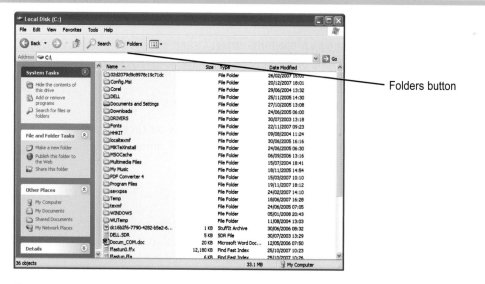

Folders button

○ Click the Folders button if it is not already selected. This shows you a more detailed view.

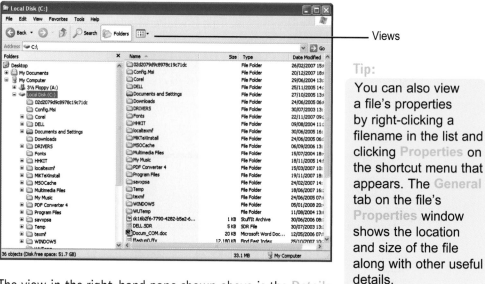

Views

**Tip:**

You can also view a file's properties by right-clicking a filename in the list and clicking Properties on the shortcut menu that appears. The General tab on the file's Properties window shows the location and size of the file along with other useful details.

The view in the right-hand pane shown above is the Details view. It shows the file size and other file properties. Click the Views button to change to this view if your screen looks different.

You can find out more about how file size is measured in Module 1.

A pathname to a file is displayed in the Address box.

## Creating a new folder                                  Syllabus 2.2.2.4

You now need to set up the folders and subfolders shown on the previous page.

○ Open the My Documents window from the desktop or Start menu.

- From the File menu, select New, Folder. A folder called New Folder is created.

- Type the name Jobs as the new folder name.

- Create the other two folders ECDL and Letters in the same way.

- Click the ECDL folder and create two subfolders Module1 and Module2 within it. (Note: these are not shown on the hierarchy tree on the previous page.)

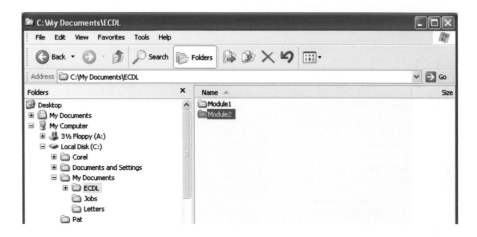

Tip:

Right-clicking on a folder and selecting Properties will tell you the total size of the folder and the number of subfolders and files it contains.

## Navigating to a file or folder                     Syllabus 2.2.2.2–3

- In the left-hand pane, click My Documents to see all the subfolders you created and all the files you saved in My Documents.

The window clearly shows the hierarchy of folders and files. The + signs in the left-hand pane indicates that there are subfolders within a folder. You can view the subfolders by clicking the + sign to expand the structure. The + sign changes to a − sign. Click the − sign to collapse the structure.

This needs practice. For example, if you click the + sign beside the ECDL folder, you will see it expanded in the left-hand window, but it is not the selected folder so the right-hand pane will still show the contents of My Documents, the selected folder.

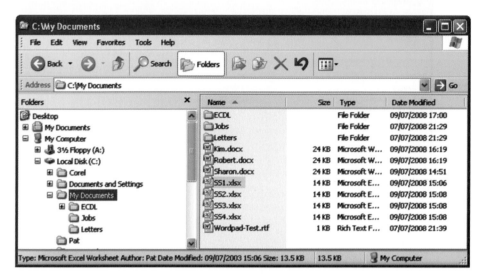

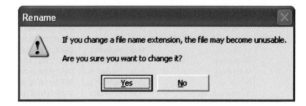 Practise clicking the + and − signs beside various folders, and selecting folders and subfolders, until you are clear about how the system works. Leave your screen looking like the one above for the next task.

Renaming a file                                        Syllabus 2.2.3.5–6

You can rename any file or folder.

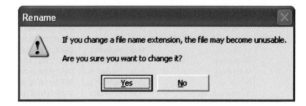 Right-click Kim.docx. Then select Rename.

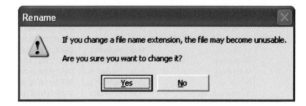 Change the file name to Tom.docx by typing the new name over the old one and pressing Enter. If you do not enter .docx correctly, you will be warned that changing the extension may make the file unusable. Be sure to get it right!

| Rename | ✕ |
|---|---|
| ⚠ | If you change a file name extension, the file may become unusable. Are you sure you want to change it? |
| | [ Yes ]    [ No ] |

## Changing file status                                    Syllabus 2.2.3.3

> Right-click the filename Robert.docx. Then select Properties.

The Properties window appears. Here you can change the file status to Read-only if you don't want to change the file accidentally. You set a file to be read-only by ticking the relevant Attributes: box. Sometimes you may find that a file has accidentally been set to read-only. You can reset it in this window by clicking the Attributes: box to remove the tick.

When a file is set to be read-only, you won't be able to save any changes you make to it unless you change the filename. This way the original file remains unchanged.

## Sorting files                                           Syllabus 2.2.3.4

You can change the order in which files are displayed in the right-hand window by clicking in the bar at the top of the Name, Size, Type or Date Modified columns. For example:

> Click once on Name. The files will be sorted in alphabetical order of name, from A to Z.

> Click again on Name. The files will be sorted in reverse alphabetical order from Z to A.

Try sorting the files in different categories, for example by file type. Leave the files sorted in ascending order of name.

## Selecting files and folders                             Syllabus 2.2.4.1

Sometimes you need to reorganise your files, perhaps moving them into different folders. Other times you may want to copy one or more files into a different folder or onto a floppy disk for backup.

You can select them one at a time or you can select all the files you want to move and then move them in one operation.

- To select an individual file or folder, click it to highlight it.

- To select several adjacent files or folders, click the first filename. Then hold down the Shift key while you click the last filename you want to select.

- To select non-adjacent files, hold down the Ctrl key while you select each one.

## Copying and moving files and folders                     Syllabus 2.2.4.2–3

You can copy a file to another folder or disk drive by first copying it to the Clipboard, and then pasting it to the desired location.

The Clipboard is a temporary storage area which will hold the latest file or folder that you cut or copy. The next time you cut or copy something, the previous contents will be overwritten. Until it is replaced, however, you can paste it elsewhere as many times as you like.

You will copy all the Word documents to the Letters folder.

- With the .docx files selected, click Edit, Copy. This copies all these files to the Clipboard.

- In the left-hand window, click the folder name Letters.

- Select Edit, Paste. The files will be copied to the Letters folder.

Now there are two copies of each of these files: in My Documents and in Letters.

Note that folders can be copied in the same way. When you copy a folder, all its contents are copied too. You can copy to another drive such as the A: drive in exactly the same way.

You can move files and folders by clicking Edit, Cut, and then pasting the item(s) where you want them. Moving an item does not leave a copy of it in the original location. However, you might find it safer to copy them first before deleting the originals.

## Making backup copies and storing online Syllabus 2.2.1.4–5

Copying files for backup purposes is an essential skill for everyone using a computer! Sooner or later some disaster will occur such as your hard disk crashing, your laptop being stolen, or your file being infected with a virus. That's when you will be glad you have a recent copy of your work on a floppy disk safely tucked away in your desk drawer at home. See Module 1 page 40 for more on backups.

Online storage is not only useful for backup purposes. It also has the benefit of convenient access, and like a LAN, you can share files easily with others if you give them access to your allocated storage space.

## Deleting files and folders Syllabus 2.2.5.1

You can delete folders and documents from their original location.

○ Click My Documents and select the .docx files again.

○ Press the Delete key on the keyboard. Alternatively, you can right-click the filenames and select Delete from the shortcut menu. You will see a message:

○ If you are sure you have selected the correct items, click Yes.

## The Recycle Bin Syllabus 2.2.5.1–2

When you delete a file or folder, it is not completely deleted. It is moved to a storage area called the Recycle Bin. This is very useful because it means that if you deleted the wrong file by mistake, you can retrieve it from the bin.

If you realise your mistake immediately, the easiest way to get your files back is to click the Undo button.

Suppose you just want to restore the file Tom.docx.

○ Display the Desktop and double-click the Recycle Bin icon.

A window opens showing the contents of the Recycle Bin.

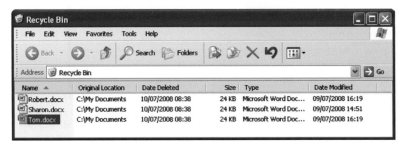

> Right-click Tom.docx and from the shortcut menu, select Restore.

Your file will be restored to the My Documents folder. You can restore deleted folders in the same way.

## Emptying the Recycle Bin                                    Syllabus 2.2.5.3

The contents of the Recycle Bin take up space on your hard disk and it is a good idea to empty it now and then. Once emptied the files cannot be restored!

> On the Desktop, right-click the Recycle Bin and select Empty Recycle Bin. You will be asked to confirm your request.

## Drag and drop

Another way of copying or moving a file or folder is to select it and then drag it into the new location.

Be aware of the following rules:

ⓘ  Dragging an item to a new location on the same drive moves the item.

ⓘ  Dragging an item to a different drive copies the item.

If you want to use drag and drop to copy a file to a new location on the same drive, hold down the Ctrl key while you drag.

You'll use drag and drop to move the spreadsheet files to the folder Module2, which is a subfolder of ECDL.

> Display the C: window (it may be minimised in the taskbar).

> Click the + sign next to the ECDL folder name so that its two subfolders are visible.

> Click SS1, then hold down Shift and click SS4 to select the four spreadsheets.

> Hold down the left mouse button while you drag the files and drop them into Module2.

Tip:

Another way of looking at and working with files and folders is by using Windows Explorer. You will see a screen similar to the one you opened from My Computer.

## Compressing files

If you want to send a file as an attachment to an e-mail, compressing it will make it smaller so it will be faster to send and receive. Some ISPs cannot receive large files. As a general rule if the size of the file you are sending is more than half a megabyte (500 kB) then you should compress it.

- ◗ Use My Computer to find a large file.
- ◗ Right-click the file and choose Send to. Then select Compressed (zipped) folder.

In the screenshot below cat.jpg has been compressed, and a new folder cat.zip appears.

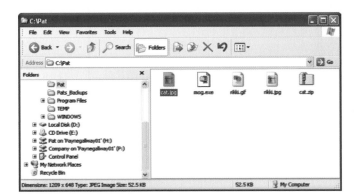

At the bottom of the screen it will tell you how big the current file is. Compare the zipped file with the unzipped file – is it a lot smaller?

## Extracting a compressed file

To unzip the file, right-click it and select Extract All. An Extraction Wizard will appear, and you can follow the steps to extract the file.

## Searching for files

If you lose a file you can use the Search facility in My Computer or in My Documents to find it again. You will look for Sharon.docx.

▶ Open My Computer if it is not already open. Navigate to C: and click the Search button. You will see the following window:

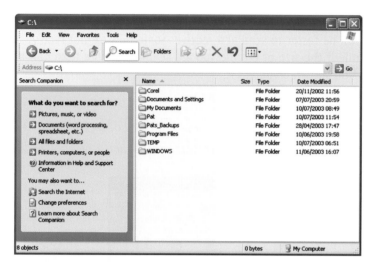

▶ In the box on the left-click Documents.

If you know that you created or modified the document within the last week, say, you can click the appropriate box.

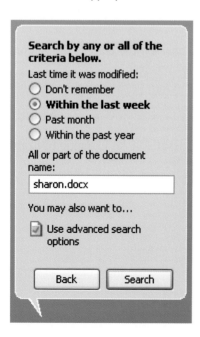

You can click Use advanced search options to search by a range of other criteria such as size.

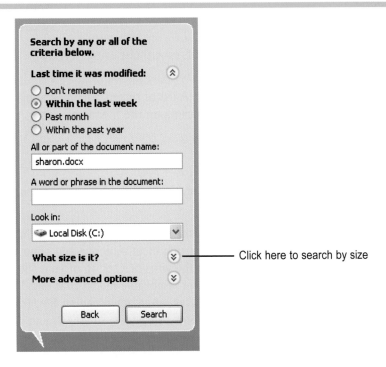

Click here to search by size

If you can't remember the whole filename, you can use a wildcard in place of any unknown characters. Use ? to stand for a single character, or * to stand for any number of characters together. So, for example, instead of the filename you could enter *.* to find all files, *.docx to find all files with a .docx extension, or sh*.docx to find all documents starting with the letters sh.

You can also search for a word or phrase contained in the document, or for files of a particular size.

⊙    Click Search.

The computer will find the file you are looking for.

You can open the file by double-clicking it.

It is possible to list and open recently used files without using Search.

▷    From the Start menu, select My Recent Documents or just Documents, depending on your computer's setup. A list of recent documents will be displayed and you can open any of them by clicking on the filename.

## Viruses                      Syllabus 2.3.2.1–3

This chapter ends with an important warning about viruses, and advice on how to avoid them.

Viruses are small programs developed with the specific intention of causing damage to computer files or, at the very least, of causing inconvenience and annoyance to computer users. An example might be that the virus deletes all of your files. You should not share or lend floppy disks or other removable media that could introduce viruses into a system, and care should be taken when downloading files from the Internet. Viruses are often sent as attachments to e-mails, so you should never open an attachment that you don't recognise. You will generally see a message similar to the one below when you attempt to open an e-mail attachment.

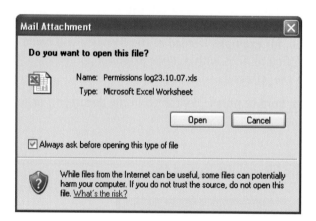

You should take precautions to avoid the potentially disastrous effects of viruses. You should ensure that a virus checker is installed on all computer systems so that they automatically check for any infected data when the computer is started up. Manual checkers can also be used to check for viruses on floppy disks, hard drives etc.

Typical anti-virus software enables you to specify which drives, folders or files you wish to scan and disinfects the file (i.e. removes the virus) if a virus is found. In this example drive A: (the floppy disk) is scanned with McAfee VirusScan. A different virus checker might be installed on your computer.

▷    From the Start menu select the VirusScan software.

▷    Click Browse to show your files and folders and select which drive, folder or file you wish to scan.

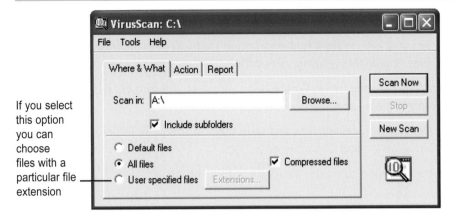

If you select
this option
you can
choose
files with a
particular file
extension

○ Click Scan Now.

The software will check all the files on drive A: and report any problems in the bottom
section of the window.

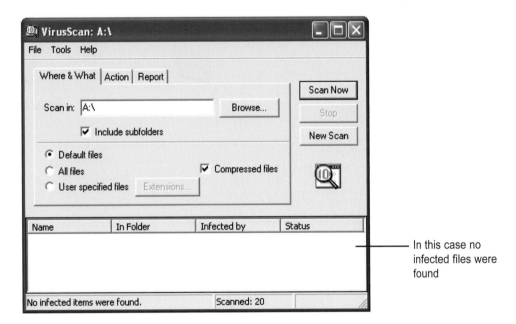

In this case no
infected files were
found

New viruses are being discovered all the time, so the anti-virus software companies
issue frequent updates to ensure that all the viruses are detected. It is a good idea to
install a package that provides an online update service. The virus checking software
will send you a message to remind you to update, which you can then do online.

## Exercises

In these exercises you will create a folder structure that will help organise the computerised files of a double-glazing sales office.

1. Create a folder named Sales. Create two subfolders within the Sales folder. Name these folders Quotes and Appointments.

2. Create two word-processed files and save them in the Sales folder. Name these files Windows.docx and Conservatories.docx.

3. Create the following subfolder structure within the Appointments subfolder.

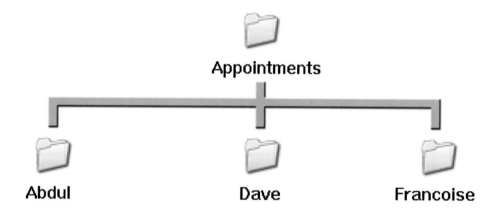

4. Copy the files Windows.docx and Conservatories .docx to the Quotes folder.

5. Rename the folder Francoise as Francis.

---

6. Use My Computer to search for a large file on your disk drive.

7. Send this to a compressed folder and see how much smaller it becomes.

8. Use the Search facility within My Computer to find the file Useful tips.docx you created in the practice exercise at the end of Chapter 8.

9. Make a note of how large this file is.

10. Enter some text giving three tips to help prevent your computer being infected by a virus.

11. Next enter some text explaining how you can view recently used files.

12. Edit the document so that each section of text has an appropriate heading.

13. Save and print this file.

14. Use My Computer to check the size of this file after the extra text was added.

# Basic Desktop and System Maintenance

In this chapter you will find out:

- about customising your computer's desktop
- about getting basic information about your computer
- how to install and uninstall a software application
- how to install a new printer and set a default printer
- how to shut down a non-responding application
- where to get help.

## Understanding your computer setup

It is useful to know where to find some of the most relevant areas of a computer setup. The Start menu can lead you to many useful features that let you configure your desktop and set up your computer in a way that suits how you use it.

## Creating and removing a desktop icon                    Syllabus 2.1.3.3–4

You can create a shortcut on the desktop to any item (program, folder, file etc.) so that you can open it instead of using the Start menu.

- ▷  From the Start menu select All Programs and find the Solitaire program.
- ▷  This time right-click the word Solitaire and move the mouse pointer over Send to.
- ▷  Click Desktop (create shortcut) from the menu.

A shortcut icon will appear on the desktop.

- ▷  Drag and drop the icon to the position you want.
- ▷  Open the Solitaire program using your new shortcut icon, then close it again.
- ▷  Remove the shortcut by right-clicking it and selecting Delete. This removes the shortcut icon, not the program.

### Creating a printer desktop icon

It can be useful to have the default printer icon on your desktop so that you can check the print status of any job.

- ○ From the Start menu select Settings, Printers and Faxes.
- ○ Drag and drop the default printer icon (the one with the tick mark against its name) to the desktop.

## Creating and using a file icon

If, for example, you are in the middle of working on a book or a project which is likely to take a few weeks, it is useful to have the file icon on the desktop. You can then open the document in the correct software (e.g. Word or Excel) simply by clicking on the icon.

Try this with a document you created in Word.

- ○ Use My Computer to navigate to a document, e.g. Sharon.docx. Drag and drop the filename on the desktop.

- ○ Now double-click the icon to open the file.

## Basic system information                                            Syllabus 2.1.2.1

It is useful to be able to view basic information about a computer system.

- ○ From the Start menu, click Control Panel, Performance and Maintenance, System. Click the General tab.

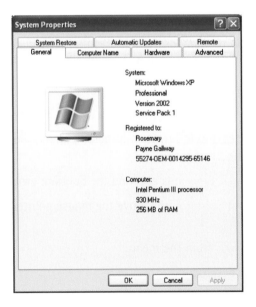

This tells you which operating system and version number you are using (in this example, Windows XP Professional version 2002, Service Pack 1). It also tells you which processor type is installed and its speed (Intel Pentium III (930 MHz)). Finally it tells you how much Random Access Memory is installed in the system (256 MB).

This kind of information can be useful if you are reporting a fault on your computer, or want to check whether your computer has the recommended minimum amount of RAM to run a new software package.

## Changing the background

If you don't like the desktop background you can easily change it.

◉ Right-click the mouse on the desktop picture.

◉ In the menu that appears left-click the Properties option to display the Display Properties dialogue box.

◉ Click the Desktop tab and scroll down the Background: list and click a background to highlight it. You will see a preview of what it looks like.

◉ When you find one you like, click Apply (and OK if you want to close the box).

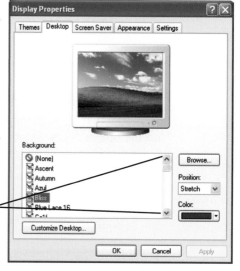

Click one of these arrows to scroll through the list.

## Setting up a screen saver

A screen saver is a moving picture or still pattern that appears on your screen when you have not used the mouse or keyboard for a specified period of time. As well as being fun, screen savers can help protect the screen from burn-out in particular spots. A password can be used to hide a screen from prying eyes if you are not at your desk.

◉ If you closed the Display Properties dialogue box, then open it again and click the Screen Saver tab.

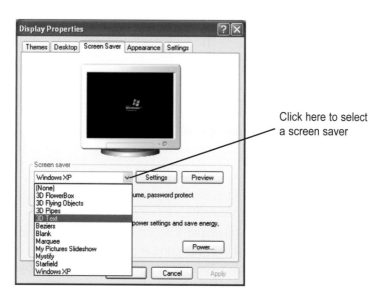

Click here to select a screen saver

○ Click the down-arrow on the right of the Screen Saver list box to view screen savers installed on your computer.

○ Click a screen saver name to highlight it and then click the Preview button to see what the option you chose will look like.

○ When you have decided on one, click Apply (and OK if you want to close the box).

## Changing the screen resolution
Syllabus 2.1.2.2

Screen resolution is the setting that determines the amount of data that appears on your screen. It is measured in pixels. Low resolution, such as 640 × 480, makes items on the screen appear large and 'blocky'. High resolution, such as 1280 × 1024, makes individual items such as text and graphics appear small but clearly defined.

○ If you closed the Display Properties dialogue box, then open it again and click the Settings tab.

○ Drag the slider in the Screen resolution panel to change the resolution.

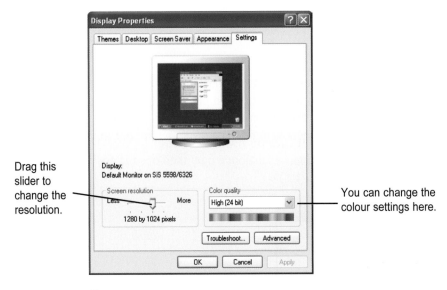

Drag this slider to change the resolution.

You can change the colour settings here.

○ When you find the resolution you want, click Apply. The screen will momentarily go black and then the dialogue box will be redisplayed.

○ Click OK if you want to close the box.

## Other display settings

You can use the Display Properties dialogue box Themes tab to set up themes which comprise a background plus a set of sounds, icons and other elements to help you personalise your computer. If you click the Appearance tab you can change the appearance of fonts, windows and dialogue boxes.

## Changing keyboard language

Your computer will have a language set as default, probably English (United Kingdom).

If you need to enter text in a different language you can add different keyboard layouts.

> From the Start menu click Control Panel, Date, Time, Language, and Regional Options, Regional and Language Options.

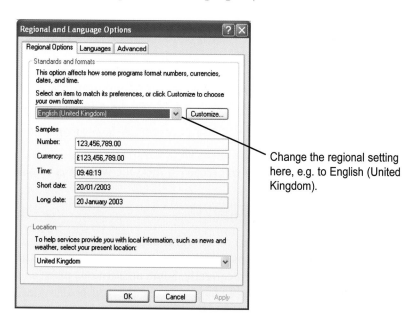

Change the regional setting here, e.g. to English (United Kingdom).

> Click the Languages tab, then click the Details button.

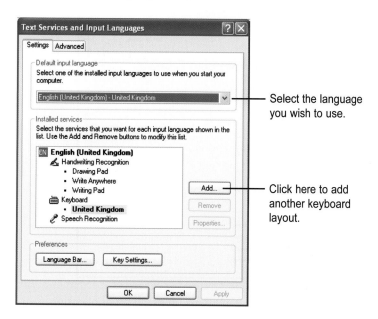

Select the language you wish to use.

Click here to add another keyboard layout.

## Formatting a floppy disk

Most floppy disks are pre-formatted when you buy them. However, if you need to format one this is the procedure:

- Insert the disk into the floppy drive.
- From the Start menu select My Computer.
- Click the disk you want to format (usually 3½ Floppy (A:) for a floppy disk) to highlight it.
- From the File menu, select Format... .
- Click the Quick Format option and then click Start.

You will receive a message warning you that all the data on the disk will be erased and asking you if you want to continue. This is in case you are reformatting an old disk that already has data on it.

- Click OK.

The formatting will begin and you will receive a message when it is complete.

## Installing/uninstalling a software application                    Syllabus 2.1.2.4

Most application programs supplied on CD-ROM auto-run when the CD is inserted into the drive and on-screen instructions explain how to proceed. To remove an application program file, it must be uninstalled correctly. Some applications place an uninstall routine in the Start menu. Otherwise you should use the Add or Remove Programs tool in the Control Panel.

- From the Start menu, select Control Panel, Add or Remove Programs.

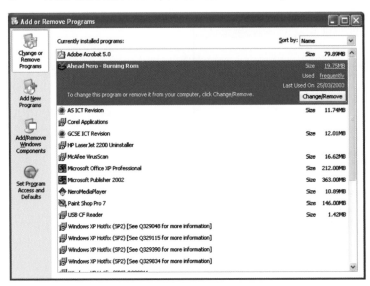

- Click Change or Remove Programs to uninstall an application.
- Click Add New Programs to install a new application.

## Print screen facility

Sometimes it is useful to be able to take a screenshot of what is on your screen and paste it into a document. You can either capture the whole screen or just the current window.

◉ Press the Print Screen key (sometimes labelled Prt Scr) on the keyboard.

This copies a picture of the whole screen to the Clipboard. If you now open a new or existing Word document, you can paste it in by selecting Paste from the Edit menu.

To capture the current window, press the Alt key at the same time as pressing Prt Scr.

**Tip:**

You can see what has been copied to the Clipboard by selecting Edit, Office Clipboard in an Office application. This opens the Clipboard on the right-hand side of the screen. Click any item to paste.

## Viewing printers and changing the default

The default printer is the printer option displayed when you click Print on the File menu of Microsoft Office applications. (It is also the printer used if you use the print icon on an Office toolbar.) To change the default printer:

◉ From the Start menu, select Printers and Faxes.

◉ Right-click the printer you want to use as the default printer, and then click Set as Default Printer.

The default printer is identified by a tick.

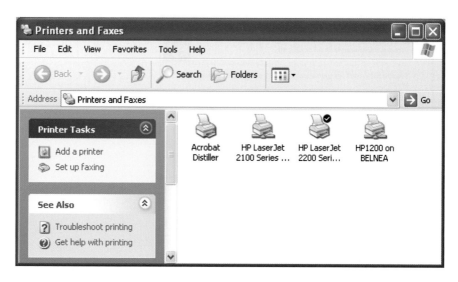

## Installing a new printer                                    Syllabus 2.4.1.2

Most printers are now 'plug and play' devices. This means that you can attach a new device to your computer and begin using it right away, without having to configure it or install additional software. If you are using an older printer it may not be 'plug and play'. In this case you should use the Add Printer Wizard supplied with Windows XP.

○ From the Start menu, select Printers and Faxes to display the Printers and Faxes window.

○ Click Add a printer under Printer Tasks to display the Add Printer Wizard.

○ Click the Next > button to display the Local or Network Printer window.

○ Select whether you are installing a network printer or a local printer (i.e. one directly connected to your PC) and click Next >.

○ Follow through the remaining stages of the wizard: you will be asked which printer port you want to use.

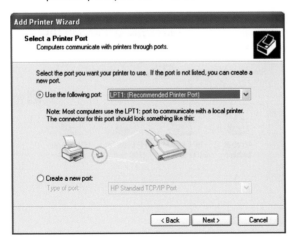

○ Select a port and click Next >.

You will then be asked for manufacturer and model of the printer.

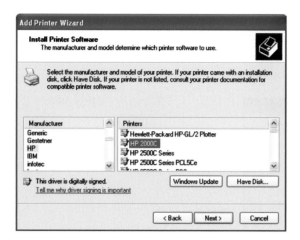

◉ Make your selection and click Next >.

◉ On the next wizard screens you can assign a name to the printer and select whether or not you want to share the printer with other network users. You will also be given the option to print a test page.

◉ Click Finish on the final wizard screen to complete the installation.

## Basic settings                                                Syllabus 2.1.2.2

### Changing the computer's date and time

The correct time zone should have been set by the supplier/manufacturer. The computer will take account of seasonal clock changes. However there might be occasions when you want to change it (e.g. when you take a laptop abroad).

◉ From the Start menu, select Control Panel, Date, Time, Language, and Regional Options, Change the date and time. Make any changes in the Date and Time Properties dialogue box and click OK.

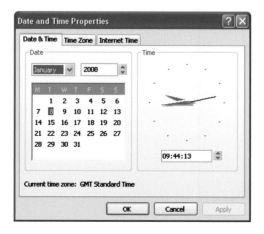

## Changing the volume settings

◯ From the Start menu, select Control Panel, Sounds, Speech, and Audio Devices, Adjust the system volume.

◯ In the Sounds and Audio Devices Properties dialogue box, Volume tab, drag the slider to adjust the sound level.

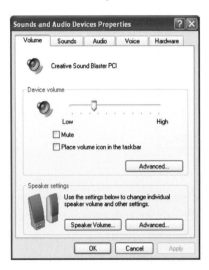

## Shutting down a non-responding application                    Syllabus 2.1.1.3

From time to time, just when you think things are going really well and that you are getting to grips with using a PC, everything suddenly grinds to a halt and it refuses to respond. Your application has crashed! If this happens:

◯ Press the Ctrl, Alt and Del(ete) keys (all at the same time) to open the Windows Task Manager.

All the applications currently running in your computer are listed under the Applications tab. One of them will probably show a status of Not Responding. This will be the offending program that has crashed your computer.

◉ Click the name of the program to highlight it and click the End Task button.

This should close down the faulty program and allow you to carry on working.

Unfortunately, you will lose anything you have been working on in the application, for example all the changes to a document since you last saved it. The only lesson to be learned is to save your work every few minutes. Everything that you have saved to a floppy disk, pen drive or hard disk is safe.

Tip:

A quick way to save a document you are currently working on is to press Ctrl-S (Ctrl and S together) on the keyboard. Alternatively, click the Save icon.

## Identifying disk drives

Syllabus 2.2.1.2

The Windows operating system automatically names each of the drives on your computer. You can use My Computer to see which disk drives your computer has, together with some basic information about them (e.g. size and free space available).

◉ Open the My Computer window. It will look similar to this example, but will show the disk drives for your system.

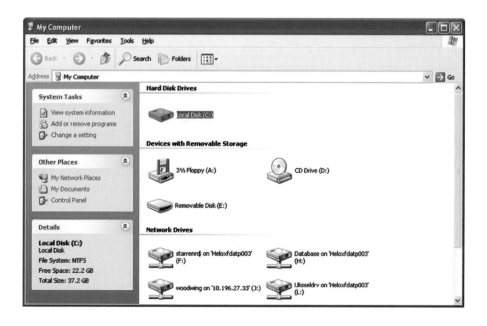

Here are some drive icons you might see:

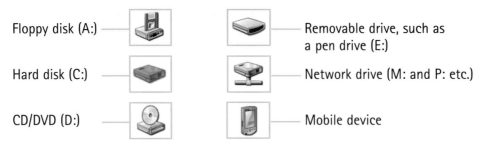

Floppy disk (A:)

Hard disk (C:)

CD/DVD (D:)

Removable drive, such as a pen drive (E:)

Network drive (M: and P: etc.)

Mobile device

Access to network drives is controlled by a network administrator who will set up the permissions. These are the rules that dictate who can access each drive. A network administrator will also set up the drive mapping on each user's computer which will allow them to connect to the appropriate drives. When a user logs on to the network with their username and password they will only be able to access the drives (and folders) agreed during this process. If the drive mapping has failed, or there is a problem connecting to the network drives, you will see a red cross through the drive icon. This means that you cannot access it because there is a fault.

Some drives cannot be accessed by normal network users, such as the one which holds the network's operating software and other important system information. These are usually only available to the network administrator.

## Getting help                                                   Syllabus 2.1.1.5

If you have problems with any of the Windows tasks or with your hardware you can get help on your computer, by phone from manufacturers' help lines or from manuals.

### Basic steps

Whether you are using a PC at work or in the home it is surprising how quickly you start to depend on the system and how frustrating it can be when things go wrong. There are several levels of support you can call upon, but, before wasting precious time, carry out some of the most basic checks:

- **Power supplies** – Is everything connected to the power supply? Has there been any break in supply? Is there any dodgy wiring?

- **External connections** – Have you checked all the connections between the peripherals and the system unit? Is the connection to the telephone outlet secure? Has the telephone line been down?

- **Supplies of consumables** – Is there paper in the printer? Does the print cartridge need replacing?

If you are experiencing an intermittent problem you should log information about the fault, for example when it occurred, how it manifested itself, any error messages that were displayed etc.

## Manufacturer support

A new PC should be covered by a standard one-year warranty. This may mean that you are expected to return the PC to the manufacturer at your own expense (a 'return to base' warranty). It is often a good idea to opt for an enhanced warranty such as a 'collect and return' or, better still, an 'on-site' warranty, which means an engineer visits you to fix it. You should also look out for extended warranties, but check the small print to see what is actually covered. The supplier or manufacturer may also offer telephone or online support, but watch out for premium charged phone lines.

When you request support be ready to provide information about your system setup and details of the problems you have experienced.

## Manuals

Even if you do not need the manufacturer's manual to set up your computer initially, keep it in a safe place as it may help if problems arise at a later date. Many have specific 'troubleshooting' chapters which save you having to wade through the whole book.

Many companies now supply very brief paper manuals and supplement these with online documents which are often in Adobe Acrobat .pdf format. These can only be opened using the Acrobat Reader program which can be downloaded free from www.adobe.co.uk.

## Windows Help and Support Centre

Windows has a comprehensive built-in help system which you can visit for help with a wide range of problems.

⊙ On the Start menu, click Help and Support to open the Help and Support Centre. The screen will look similar to this, but it may have been customised by the manufacturer to include specific help for their computers.

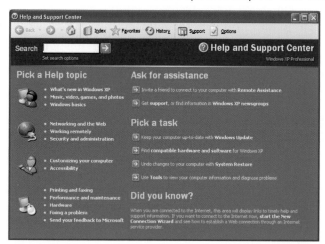

⊙ Either click a topic or type a keyword into the Search box.

⊙ If you click Fixing a problem in the bottom left of the window you can access 'troubleshooters' which help sort out problems by asking you a series of questions.

Each individual application that you run on your computer (e.g. a game, word processor, spreadsheet etc.) will have its own Help system too.

## Error reporting

When an error occurs in Windows and all operations stop, an error code might be displayed. It is generally necessary to restart the computer. When an error occurs in a program (such as Microsoft Word) an error message will be displayed and the program will stop working.

If you are using Microsoft software you can report system and program errors to Microsoft. This reporting system allows Microsoft to monitor and deal with common problems.

When an error occurs, a dialogue box will be displayed asking whether or not you want to report the problem. If you agree, technical information is collected from your computer and then sent to Microsoft over the Internet. The chances are that a similar problem will already have been reported by other people and Microsoft will supply a link to any further information that might be of help.

## Software updates

Updates to improve the reliability and security of software are often supplied free of charge by the manufacturer. For example, you can download Windows Service Pack updates and Office Service Pack (or Release) updates from the Microsoft website (www.microsoft.com) to keep your PC up-to-date with the latest versions. Alternatively, you can set up a facility called Automatic Updates to automatically download and install any important Windows updates for you at a time that you choose or to notify you whenever any high-priority updates become available.

▶ From the Start menu, click Control Panel, Performance and Maintenance, System to display the System Properties dialogue box.

▶ Click the Automatic Updates tab.

▶ Select the option you require.

Tip:

You will need an active Internet connection to receive notification of any available updates.

### Device drivers

Most parts of PC hardware require software programs called drivers to make them work properly with the operating system. New peripherals will often be supplied with a CD-ROM containing an installation program which loads the device driver onto the hard disk. Installation instructions should be supplied. If not, the manufacturer's website should have the information.

Many minor problems with new PCs are caused by incorrect or out-of-date driver software. Windows Automatic Updates will sometimes find and install more up-to-date drivers. Alternatively it is often possible to search the Internet to locate an updated driver that will sort out your problems. You can try the following sites:

- www.microsoft.com/downloads
- www.windrivers.com

Tip:

If you install an updated driver, make sure you follow the instructions for the correct version of Windows.

## Exercises

1. (a) How can you determine which printers are installed on your system?

   (b) How can you identify the default printer?

2. Describe two ways of switching between open applications.

3. How would you close a non-responsive application?

4. Why is it important to save your work regularly?

5. How can you find out how much free space is left on the hard drive?

7. Describe two functions of the Windows Control Panel.

---

8. Open My Computer and navigate to the file Useful tips.docx.

9. Create a shortcut to this document on the desktop.

10. Open the document using the shortcut icon.

11. In the Useful tips.docx document make a note of the type of processor and amount of RAM your computer has.

12. Now enter some text to describe how you would change the desktop background.

13. Open the Printer and Faxes dialogue box from the Start menu to view the printers that your computer has access to.

14. Take a screenshot of this and paste it into the Useful tips.docx document together with some notes on how to change the default printer.

15. Save and print the word-processed document.

16. Close the file and close Word.

## Ask yourself

- Do I know how to use and customise the Windows desktop?
- Can I perform basic system maintenance tasks and resolve simple errors?
- Do I know where to get help?
- Do I know how to manage folders and files?
- Do I know how to use simple editing tools to create a document, and then save and print it?

In this module you should have created and saved the following files:

Conservatories.docx
Kim.docx
Print Manager.docx
Robert.docx
Sharon.docx
Tom.docx
Useful tips.docx
Windows.docx

File types.rtf
WordPad–Test.rtf

SS1.xlsx
SS2.xlsx
SS3.xlsx
SS4.xlsx

# Module 3
## Word Processing

This module covers the basics of word processing. You will learn how to accomplish everyday tasks associated with creating, formatting and finishing small documents. You will learn how to:

- copy and move text within or between documents
- create standard tables
- use pictures and images within a document
- use mail merge tools
- print documents
- recognise and apply good practice in aligning text
- recognise and apply good practice in paragraph spacing
- recognise and apply good practice in adding new pages.

# Module **3** — Contents

# First Steps

In this chapter you will find out:

- ❶ how to run and close Microsoft Word
- ❶ about special keys on the keyboard, and the Word screen
- ❶ how to create a new document in Word
- ❶ about some text editing techniques
- ❶ how to open, save and close your documents
- ❶ how to change some of the Word defaults and preferences
- ❶ how to preview and print a document.

For this module you will be using Microsoft Word 2007, one of many word-processing packages. You should be able to follow the instructions if you are using a different version of Word.

For some of the exercises you will need to download files from our website.

- ▶ Log on to the Payne-Gallway website www.payne-gallway.co.uk.
- ▶ Navigate to the ECDL5 Student pages for Pass ECDL5 Modules 1-7.
- ▶ Click Resource file Module 3.exe.
- ▶ Click Run. If a security warning appears click Run again.
- ▶ Click Browse. Choose a convenient folder to save the files in. Click OK.
- ▶ Click Unzip. A window will appear telling you that the files have been unzipped.
- ▶ Close the window. You're ready to start!

## Loading Microsoft Word                    Syllabus 3.1.1.1

- ▶ Load Microsoft Word. You can do this in one of two ways:
- ▶ *Either* double-click the Word icon (if it is on your desktop)
- ▶ *Or* click Start, All Programs, then click Microsoft Office Word 2007. (Note: depending on how your computer is set up, you might need to click Start, All Programs, Microsoft Office, Microsoft Office Word 2007.)

# Module 3 Word Processing

## The opening screen

Word's opening screen will look something like this:

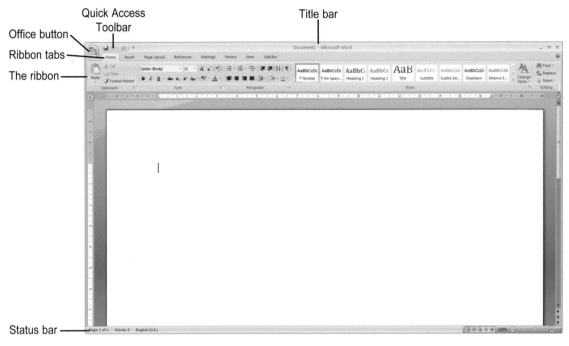

Quick Access Toolbar

Title bar

Office button

Ribbon tabs

The ribbon

Status bar

ℹ️ The Title bar shows the name of your document, which might be, for example, a story or letter. If you have only just opened Word or have not yet given your document a name, it will say Document1. It will say Document2 if this is your second document since you started Microsoft Word in this chapter.

ℹ️ The Office button has options for you to choose from. You'll be using it when you need to open, close, print or save your document.

ℹ️ The Ribbon is where you can find all the functions you will need to create and edit your document. The functions are shown as buttons with pictures called icons. They are grouped by related commands. The functions available on the ribbons can also change according to what you are currently working on. In this way they can be thought of as being context-sensitive toolbars. A ribbon is displayed by selecting its Ribbon tab.

ℹ️ The white area represents the page in which you type your document.

ℹ️ The Status bar shows what page you are on and how many pages there are in the document.

ℹ️ The Quick Access Toolbar provides some more useful commands.

ℹ️ Some functions open a context-sensitive task pane at the side of the screen (not shown in the figure above). This lets you choose further options related to the task in hand.

## The keyboard

Your keyboard will look similar to this:

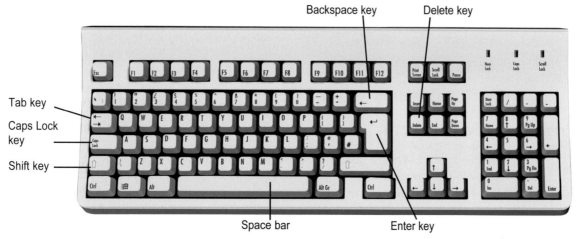

Backspace key    Delete key

Tab key

Caps Lock key

Shift key

Space bar    Enter key

The position of the following keys is labelled on the diagram above:

    ❶    The Shift key. As long as you hold this down, all the letters you type will be in capitals.

    ❶    The Caps Lock key. If you want a whole sentence to be in capitals, you can use this rather than holding down the shift key. Just press it once and release it. All the letters you type after that will be capitals. Press Caps Lock again when you want to stop typing capitals.

    ❶    The Backspace key. This deletes the letter to the left of where the cursor is flashing. If you are typing something and press a wrong letter, pressing Backspace will delete it and you can then type the right letter. Very useful!

    ❶    The Delete key. This deletes the letter to the right of where the cursor is flashing.

    ❶    The Tab key – Use this to advance the cursor to the next tab stop. Tabs are used to indent text by set amounts.

    ❶    The Enter key – Use this when you want to go to a new line.

Tip:

There are two **Enter** keys on the keyboard - one marked with a bent arrow and the other marked '**Enter**'. They both do exactly the same thing. People who are typing lists of numbers find it easier to use the key near the numbers, while those using the main part of the keyboard to type text probably prefer the one near the letters.

## Ribbon group used in this chapter

In this chapter you will use the following button in the **Paragraph** group on the Home ribbon:

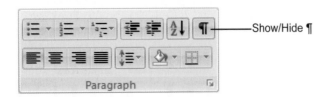
Show/Hide ¶

## Creating a new document

**Syllabus 3.1.1.2**

When you start Word, a new blank document automatically appears on the screen. It is possible to create a new document in Word based on provided designs (these are called **templates**), but for now you will start writing your new document directly on the blank page displayed (the **normal** template). You can see in the title bar that it is called Document1.

You can start to type straight away. The letters will appear at the flashing | cursor.

- ▶ Type the beginnings of a letter:    Dear Mrs Coates,

**Tip:**

Use the **shift** key, not the **caps lock** key, to type the upper case letters **D**, **M** and **C**.

## The pointer, cursor and insertion point

**Syllabus 3.2.1.2**

As you move the mouse around, the pointer moves around the screen. The pointer looks different depending on where it is on the screen.

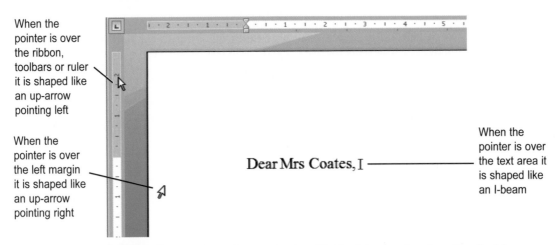

When the pointer is over the ribbon, toolbars or ruler it is shaped like an up-arrow pointing left

When the pointer is over the left margin it is shaped like an up-arrow pointing right

When the pointer is over the text area it is shaped like an I-beam

Dear Mrs Coates, I

If you click in different places in your text, with the I-beam showing, the flashing vertical line (called the **cursor**) appears in different places. It marks the insertion point – that is, the point at which text will be inserted when you start to type.

- ▶ Position the I-beam pointer at the end of the line.

- ● Press Enter twice. (Pressing Enter inserts a new blank line, so pressing it twice will leave one blank line between the line you have typed and the new insertion point.)

- ● Type the following sentences. Do not press Enter at the end of each line, the text will automatically wrap to a new line – only press Enter when you want to start a new paragraph.
  You must leave one space after a comma (but not before it). You must leave one or two spaces after a full stop – decide which you prefer and then stick to it!

> I am writing to invite you on a trip to Tanzania to see some of the current conservation work being sponsored by the Global Environment Association. You will be able to see at first-hand the areas your money is reaching and the difference it can make.

## Editing text
Syllabus 3.2.2.3

Now you can practise inserting and deleting text.

There are two 'editing modes' known as insert and overtype. By default, Word does not display which mode is currently active. It is useful to show it.

- ● Right-click anywhere on the status bar to display the Customize Status Bar menu.

- ● Click Overtype. A tick appears to show it is selected, and the word Insert appears on the status bar.

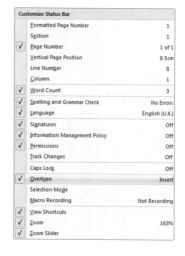

- ● Click the word Insert to change it to Overtype.

The status bar button acts as a toggle switch.

In overtype mode, when you click in your text to edit it, the letters you type replace those already there. In insert mode, the letters you type are inserted into the existing text.

- ● Make sure that you are in insert mode. If you are not, press Insert once.

- ● Place the cursor just after the a of on a trip. Click to create an insertion point and type n interesting. The text should now read

I am writing to invite you on an interesting trip …

You can alter text by highlighting it and then typing the new text. For more guidance on selecting text see page 120, but for now you are going to select a single word.

- ● Double-click the word interesting to select it. It should now appear on a coloured background.

interesting

○ Type the word exciting. This will replace the selected word.

**Tip:**

When text is selected you don't have to delete it before typing over it.

○ Place the cursor just after the t of current and click to create an insertion point. Press the Backspace key several times to delete the word current. Insert the word currently after work.

○ Now click at the end of the paragraph you have typed, and press enter twice.

○ Finish off the letter by typing

> Yours sincerely,
>
>
> Brian Harding
>
> Fundraising Executive

Don't forget to leave room for a signature!

Your letter should now look like this:

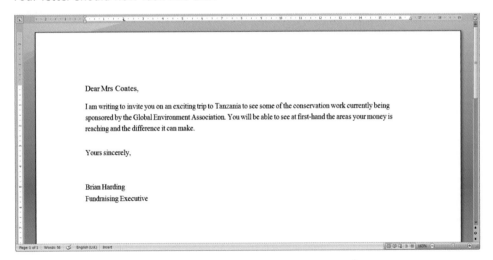

(Note: your copy of Word might have the left and right margin widths set differently to those shown above – this will mean that the text layout might be slightly different.)

## Saving your work
Syllabus 3.1.1.3

If you want to keep your work, so that you are able to add to it or change it at any time, you must keep it safe in a file on a disk. (This is called saving a file.)

You can save files on the hard disk inside the computer, or on a floppy disk or other removable storage medium that you can take out when you have finished saving.

○ Click the Office button, and then click Save on the menu that appears.

You'll see a screen rather like that below, but you will have different folders and subfolders from the ones shown.

Folder name                                    Create New Folder

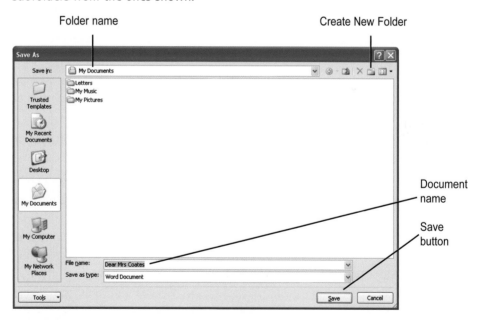

Document name

Save button

Word provides a name for your file, which will be the first word or first few words you typed. The name appears in the File name: box. The file name will be highlighted to show that it is selected ready for you to change it if you want to.

◉    Type a the file name TanzaniaLetter. You can choose any name but it should remind you of what the file contains.

Microsoft Word will add a full stop and the letters docx to the name you choose. This shows that it is a document created using Microsoft Word 2007.

You can choose in which folder you wish to save your document.

In the figure shown, Letters is a subfolder of My Documents. If you want to create a subfolder in your own My Documents folder, click the Create New Folder button and then give your folder a suitable name.

To save in the Letters folder shown in the figure:

▶ Double-click Letters to put it in the Save in: box.

▶ Leave the Save as type: box as Word Document. Before you click the Save button, read the next section. Clicking Save saves your document and automatically closes the dialogue box.

## Saving as another file type                                    Syllabus 3.1.1.4

By default your letter will be saved as a Word 2007 document, shown by the file extension .docx at the end of the file name. If you click the down-arrow on the right of the Save as type: box, you will see that you have the options of saving the file as other types.

ⓘ Saving a document as a Web Page (i.e. with the extension .htm.) saves it in a format suitable for viewing in a web browser.

ⓘ Saving a document in Rich Text Format (extension .rtf) is a useful format if you wish to transfer text between different word-processing packages or versions without losing formatting information.

ⓘ Saving a document as Plain Text (extension .txt) saves it without any formatting so it can be imported into another type of package.

ⓘ Saving a document as a Document Template (extension .dotx) creates a template on which you can base other documents such as a customised fax. Templates are discussed in Chapter 14.

Scroll down to see other options. For example, you can save a document so that it can be read in an earlier version of Word (e.g. choose Word 97–2003 for .doc files) or with a software specific file extension (e.g. .wps for Works 2000).

▶ Leave the file types as Word Document and click Save.

Tip:

Click the **Office button** and move the mouse pointer over **Save As** to display a list of options that allow you to save a file as a different type.

## Closing a document

 ◗ Click the Office button, and then click Close on the menu that appears.

## Opening an existing document

You can open your document again any time to edit or print it.

 ◗ Click the Office button. You will see a list of the most recently used documents.

◗ Click the file name TanzaniaLetter. Your document opens ready for you to work on.

◗ Now close the file again so that you can practise opening it a different way.

◗ Click the Office button, and then click Open [ Open ] on the menu that appears. You will see a window similar to the one on the next page.

◗ Navigate to the Letters folder in My Documents if it is not already showing in the Look in: list box.

○ Double-click TanzaniaLetter to open the file. Alternatively, you can single-click it and then click the Open button.

## Changing defaults and preferences                    Syllabus 3.1.2.1

By default (i.e. unless you tell it otherwise) Word saves your documents in a folder called My Documents on the C: drive. You can change this default as well as many other preferences.

○ Click the Office button, and then click Word Options on the window that appears.

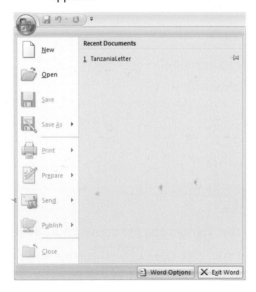

○ Click the Save option.

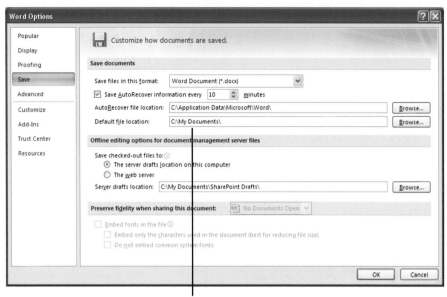

Here you can change the default folder for opening and saving files.

You can also change various other default settings such as how frequently your document is automatically saved.

Clicking Popular on the menu will open a window in which you can change the name of the author of documents you write. This name appears in a 'tip' as you hover over a file name in Windows Explorer or when opening a file.

## Inserting a paragraph                                    Syllabus 3.3.2.1

You will now insert the recipient's address and a date at the head of the letter. You can assume that the letter will be printed on headed stationery, so you need to leave some space at the top of the page for this.

> ○ Make sure the insertion point is at the top of the letter.
>
> ○ Press Enter several times to give yourself some blank lines, and then press the up-arrow key to put the cursor on the new blank line.
>
> ○ Type a name and address, followed by today's date, pressing Enter at the end of each line.
>
> ○ Check your letter carefully and if all is correct, save it again by selecting Save on the Office button menu. This time you won't be asked to name the file. The new version will overwrite your original letter.

**Tip:**

Click the **Save** button 🖫 on the **Quick Access Toolbar** to save a document.

### Merging two paragraphs

If you want to join two paragraphs together, simply place the text insertion point at the end of the first paragraph, and then press Delete until the second paragraph follows directly on from the first.

## Previewing and printing a document

Before you print a document it is always a good idea to look at it in Print Preview mode. This displays the printed appearance of the document on-screen. It lets you check you haven't missed something that needs correcting before sending it to the printer.

### Tip:

You can show paragraph breaks (and other layout features) by clicking the **Show/Hide ¶** non-printing characters icon in the **Paragraph** group on the **Home** ribbon. A paragraph mark is shown by a ¶ (pilcrow) symbol.

> Click the Office button, move the mouse pointer over Print on the menu and then click Print Preview in the right-hand pane.

Your letter will appear on the screen exactly as it will be printed, as shown below:

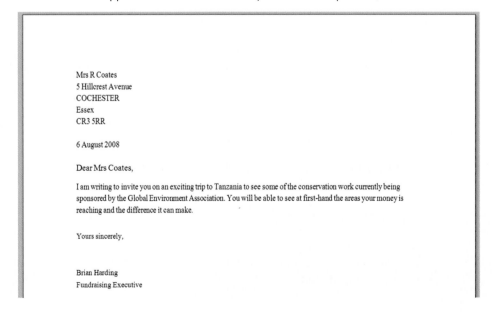

If you need to make any further corrections, press Esc or click the Close Print Preview button in the Preview group on the Print Preview ribbon.

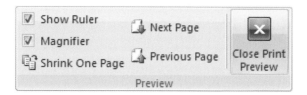

 When you have made any corrections and saved them, look at the document again in Print Preview, and then click Print 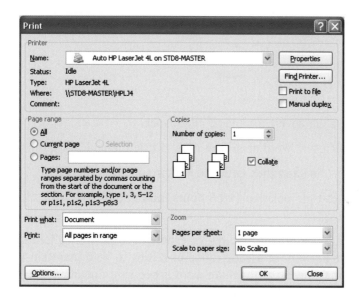 from the Office button menu to display the following window:

This window lets you select print options such as: print entire document, print specified pages, print specified number of copies, as well as other options.

You can also select which printer to send the document to. If you have no printer available, you can click the Print to file tick box to send a print file to, say, a floppy disk from where it can be printed later by another computer that is attached to a printer.

▶ Make sure that your computer is connected to a printer, that the printer is turned on and that paper is loaded.

▶ Select the printer you are going to use and select the print options to print one copy of All the pages of your document.

▶ Click OK to print the document TanzaniaLetter.

 ▶ If all is well, click Close on the Office button menu to close the document.

## Closing Microsoft Word                                        Syllabus 3.1.1.1

 ◑   Click the Office button, and then click Exit Word on the window that appears.

## Exercise

You are preparing a job advert for a local newspaper.

1.  In a new Microsoft Word document enter a title Clerical Assistant.

2.  Leave a blank line and then enter the following information:

    This is a part-time position (18.5 hours) and is temporary for six months in the first instance.

    A small insurance broker requires an experienced person to join the team and assist in the delivery of a wide range of duties to help maintain this busy office. Regular duties will include word processing documents, dealing with queries from the public and from staff, and maintaining records. Experience of working in a team is important, as is a good working knowledge of Microsoft Office.

3.  Make the sentence beginning Experience of... a new paragraph.

4.  Insert blank lines between paragraphs.

5.  Change the word important to essential.

6.  Add the following sentence to the end of the third paragraph:

    Experience of working in a personnel environment is preferable, although training will be provided.

7.  Leave two blank lines at the end and enter the following text:

    Closing date: 18th July

    Contact: Jane Hall on 01578 23455

8.  Delete the words in the first instance in the first paragraph.

9.  Save the document as Job advert.

Clerical Assistant

This is a part-time position (18.5 hours) and is temporary for six months.

A small insurance broker requires an experienced person to join the team and assist in the delivery of a wide range of duties to help maintain this busy office. Regular duties will include word processing documents, dealing with queries from the public and from staff, and maintaining records.

Experience of working in a team is essential, as is a good working knowledge of Microsoft Office. Experience of working in a personnel environment is preferable, although training will be provided.

Closing date: 18th July

Contact: Jane Hall on 01578 23455

## Ask yourself

❓   Can I run and close Microsoft Word?

❓   Do I know the different pointers/cursors used in Word and what they signify?

❓   Can I identify the Paragraph group on the Home ribbon?

❓   Can I create a document and do some simple editing?

❓   Can I save a document and do I understand why I might save a document as different file types and with different names?

❓   Can I open an existing document

❓   Do I know how to set Word's defaults and preferences?

In this chapter you should have created and saved the following files:
Job advert.docx
TanzaniaLetter.docx

In this chapter you have been introduced to the following buttons:

Close Print Preview in the Preview group on the Print Preview ribbon
Show/Hide ¶ in the Paragraph group on the Home ribbon

# CHAPTER 12

# Formatting

**In this chapter you will find out:**

- ❶ about the use of formatting to improve the appearance of a document
- ❶ about fonts and styles
- ❶ about simple formatting such as alignment, bold and colour
- ❶ about line spacing and paragraph indents.

You will use the document Itinerary.docx that you downloaded at the beginning of this module. Alternatively, you can type it yourself. The text is given below. You are to imagine that you work for an environmental organisation called the Global Environment Association (GEA). You are preparing an itinerary for a visit to Tanzania of a group of Association members.

---

Itinerary
Day 1
Depart London Heathrow on British Airways flight
Day 2
Arrive at Dar es Salaam Airport. Our representative will meet and transfer the group to the hotel. The morning will be at leisure to rest after the overnight flight. After lunch our representative will meet and escort you to the GEA offices. The Country Representative, Dr David Moshi, will give a presentation and brief you on the GEA projects in Tanzania.
Day 3
After breakfast your guide will meet you for the transfer to Mikumi Kiboga Camp.
Dinner and Overnight – Mikumi Kiboga Camp
Day 4
You will be met and escorted for an early morning game drive through the Mikumi Park. Return to your accommodation for breakfast.
Following breakfast your guide will escort you on the transfer to Udzungwa Mountain National Park. Followed by an accompanied late afternoon walk in the forest
Day 5
The day includes trekking and sightseeing in the area.
After breakfast your guide will escort the group on a leisurely walk to Sanje Falls, with a chance to take a refreshing swim in the falls. A picnic lunch will be provided.

---

## Ribbon groups used in this chapter

In this chapter you will use the following buttons and features in the Clipboard, Font, Paragraph and Styles groups on the Home ribbon:

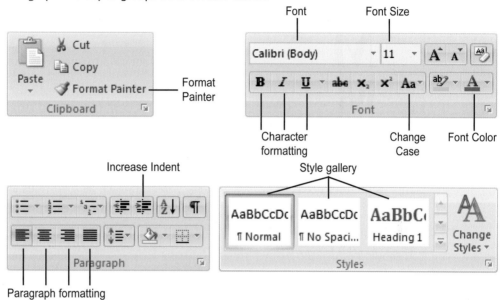

## Saving with another name                                        Syllabus 3.1.1.3

 ● Open Word if it is not already open. If you have saved the downloaded document Itinerary.docx in your own folder, click the Office button and select Open to open the document now.

 ● If you have not downloaded and saved the document, you can either do so now, or type it in as shown on the previous page.

When you click the Save icon on the Quick Access Toolbar or use the Office button Save command, your document will automatically be saved using the same file name as the one that you have previously used when saving it. If you want to keep the original copy safe and save a second version of the file, you should use the Save As... option on the Office button menu, which allows you to save the document using a different name to the same or a new folder.

 ● Click the Office button, rest the mouse pointer over Save As and click Word Document to save the document as NewItinerary.docx.

## Fonts

Nowadays the word font is used as an alternative word for typeface. Both words describe the actual shape of the letters that appear on the screen when you are typing. Fonts have different names like Times New Roman, Arial, and Comic Sans MS.

## Types of font

There are two basic types of font, called serif and sans serif. A serif is the little tail at the top and bottom of each letter.

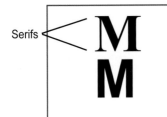

Serifs

This is written in a serif font called Times New Roman.

This is written in a sans serif font called Arial.

Taken from the French for 'without serif', sans serif fonts are very clear and are used in places where text needs to be clear and easy to read, such as road signs and textbooks.

Serif fonts are more often used for large amounts of text that will be read quickly, such as in newspapers or books. The serifs 'lead your eye' from one word to the next.

You should not use too many different fonts on a page – it can end up looking a mess.

## Font sizes

Font sizes are measured in points. 6 point is about the smallest font you can read without the aid of a magnifying glass.

This is 6 point Times New Roman.

This is 12 point Times New Roman.

# This is 24 point Times New Roman.

## Applying an existing style to a word, line or paragraph   Syllabus 3.3.3.1–2

Look at the Font group on the Home ribbon. The name of the current font is shown in the Font list box and its size is shown in the Font Size list box. When you open a new document the displayed font will be the default font – this is the font that Microsoft Word will choose for you automatically, before you change it to whatever you wish.

Font          Font Size

Times New Roman          11

You can use the Styles gallery in the Styles group on the Home ribbon to apply different built-in styles to different parts of a document.

| AaBbCcDc | AaBbCcDc | AaBbCc | AaBbCc | AaB | AaBbCc. | AaBbCcDc | AaBbCcDc |
|---|---|---|---|---|---|---|---|
| ¶ Normal | ¶ No Spaci... | Heading 1 | Heading 2 | Title | Subtitle | Subtle Em... | Emphasis |
| AaBbCcDc | AaBbCcDc | AaBbCcDc | AaBbCcDc | AABBCCDC | AABBCCDC | AABBCCDC | AaBbCcDc |
| Intense E... | Strong | Quote | Intense Q... | Subtle Ref... | Intense R... | Book Title | ¶ List Para... |

- ◉ Click the word Itinerary and click the Heading 1 style in the Styles group on the Home ribbon. The style of the word will change.

- ◉ Now click in the second line, Day 1 and select the Heading 2 style.

- ◉ Select the next paragraph and change the style to Normal if it is not already selected.

Tip:

> You can apply a built-in style to a character, word, sentence, paragraph or whole document by selecting it first. Move the mouse pointer over the **Styles** group to see the effect of applying a built-in style before you click it. Simply click in a paragraph to apply a style to all the paragraph text.

- ❶ You can display the styles in the Styles task pane by clicking the Dialogue Launcher (see the Note on page 113) on the Styles group. A character style, indicated by ə , is the applied font, font size, font colour and emphasis (such as bold, italic and underlining). A paragraph style, indicated by ¶, is the format applied to the paragraph as a whole, and includes line spacing, indents, alignment etc.

Elements of both these types of formatting are covered in the sections that follow.

Note:

> When you select text, a mini-toolbar will appear – faded at first. Move the mouse cursor over the mini-toolbar to see command buttons similar to those on the ribbon.

## Changing font and font size                                     Syllabus 3.3.1.1

Character formatting changes the look of a single word or character. First select what you want to format.

- ◉ Double-click the title word Itinerary to select it.

- ◉ Click the down-arrow beside the Font box in the Fonts group on the Home ribbon, and click the Arial font if it is not already selected.

- ◉ Click the down-arrow beside the Font Size box and select Font Size 24.

Tip:

> Move the mouse pointer over the **Font** or **Font Size** to see the effect of applying the character formatting before you select it.

## Text alignment and emboldening            Syllabus 3.3.1.2/3.3.2.3–4

You can position text horizontally on the page using the Paragraph formatting buttons in the Paragraph group on the Home ribbon, and change its appearance using the Character formatting buttons in the Font group.

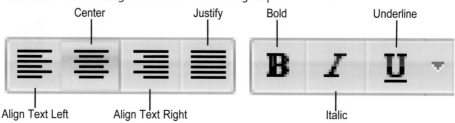

Center     Justify     Bold     Underline

Align Text Left     Align Text Right     Italic

○ With the cursor still somewhere in the heading, click the Center button. It will appear orange when selected, as in the screenshot on the previous page.

○ Select the heading and click the Bold button to make the heading bold. Now make it underlined and italic as well by clicking the relevant buttons.

The text under the heading is currently left-justified. This means that it is all lined up against the left-hand margin, and the text does not make a straight edge against the right-hand margin. You can make it do so by justifying the text.

○ Select all the text except the title by dragging the mouse across it with the left button held down.

○ Click the Justify button.

You can experiment with the other alignment buttons to see what the text looks like when it is centred or right-aligned.

You should always use these buttons to align text rather than insert spaces. The word processor software will take account of word lengths and size of characters, and adjust the word spacing correctly.

## The Undo and Redo commands                              Syllabus 3.2.2.8

You can use the Undo button on the Quick Access Toolbar to undo the last action. Clicking Undo three times, for example, will undo the last three actions.

Click the Redo button to redo the last action that you undid.

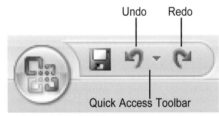

Return to justified text when you are satisfied you know what each of these buttons does.

Tip:

If you are unsure of what any ribbon button does, simply move the pointer over it and a tip will appear informing you of its function.

## Setting text colours                     Syllabus 3.3.1.4

To change the colour of text, you must first select the text and then click the Font Color button in the Font group on the Home ribbon.

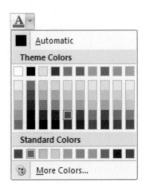

○ Select the title Itinerary and click the down-arrow next to the Font Color button. This opens a colour palette.

○ Select the red colour.

◐ Click in the left margin beside Day 1 to select the line.

◐ With the heading selected, click the Font Color button and select blue from the colour palette which appears.

Now you can make the other headings for Day 2, Day 3 etc. the same style and colour. To do this you will practise using the Repeat command.

◐ Select the heading Day 2.

◐ Select Heading 2 from the Styles group.

◐ Select the heading Day 3.

◐ Click the Repeat button on the Quick Access Toolbar.

Repeat

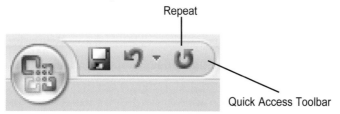

Quick Access Toolbar

◐ Do this again for each of the other Day headings.

◐ Now colour each Day heading the same blue as the heading Day 1, using the Font Color button and the Repeat button.

## Applying case changes and other formats          Syllabus 3.3.1.2–3/3.3.1.5

You can apply formatting or case changes (e.g. make all letters uppercase) to any selected text using the Change Case button in the Font group on the Home ribbon.

Suppose you want to change the case of the words Day 1.

◐ Select the text Day 1.

◐ Click the Change Case button.

◐ In the Change Case menu, click the case you want to apply to the text. Try selecting the option UPPERCASE.

◐ It looked better in Sentence case, so click the Undo button.

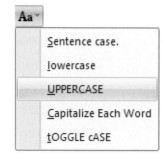

Note:

You can often access more commands and features by clicking the **Dialogue Launcher** that might appear at the bottom right-hand side of a ribbon group.

Dialogue Launcher

113

Now suppose you want to give the heading Itinerary a double underline.

- ◑ Select the word Itinerary.

- ◑ Click the down-arrow next to the Underline button.

- ◑ Choose a double underline style.

- ◑ You can either leave this format or undo it by clicking the Undo button.

**Note:**

The **Font** group on the **Home** ribbon provides other options for text formatting, such as **subscript** and **superscript**.

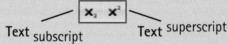

Text $_{subscript}$    Text $^{superscript}$

- ◑ Change the case of the heading Itinerary to UPPERCASE.

## Changing paragraph and line spacing                     Syllabus 3.3.2.7–8

The document looks rather cramped and the lines need to be spaced out. One way of spacing out the text would be to insert a blank line between paragraphs but it is better practice to apply spacing between paragraphs and between lines automatically. This ensures that the formatting is consistent throughout the document.

First increase the space after each paragraph.

- ◑ Click in the first paragraph.

- ◑ Click the Dialogue Launcher on the Paragraph group on the Home ribbon to display the Paragraph dialogue box as shown on the following page.

- ◑ In the Spacing group, change the After: setting to 12 pt, and click the OK button.

- ◑ Repeat for all the paragraphs.

You can add single, 1.5 or double spacing between lines. Double spacing is very useful when you are creating a draft of a document which will be checked or edited by someone else because it allows space for corrections to be made by hand on the printed document. Try it now.

- ◑ Select all the text under the title.

- ◑ Open the Paragraph dialogue box again and change the setting in the Line spacing: list box to Double.

- ◑ Click OK.

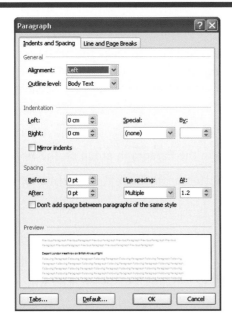

**Tip:**

You can set paragraph spacing and indentation in the **Paragraph** group on the **Page Layout** ribbon.

|  | Indent |  |  | Spacing |  |
|--|--------|--|--|---------|--|
| ⬛ Left: | 0 cm | | ⬛ Before: | 0 pt | |
| ⬛ Right: | 0 cm | | ⬛ After: | 12 pt | |
| | | Paragraph | | | ⬛ |

○ Examine the effect on the text. It is not quite what you want, so click the Undo button until the text is restored to how it was.

Try an alternative, which is to put some space before each of the 'Day' headings.

○ Select the heading Day 1, then open the Paragraph dialogue box again.

○ Click the up-arrow in the Spacing, After: box to select 6 pt and click OK.

○ Make this heading Italic.

## Copying a format                                    Syllabus 3.3.3.2–3

⬛ Format Painter — You can now copy this format to other paragraphs using the Format Painter button in the Clipboard group on the Home ribbon. To use this tool once, you select the text which has the formatting you want to copy, click Format Painter and then you select the text you want to copy the format onto. Try it like this:

○ With Day 1 selected, click the Format Painter button once.

○ Select the heading Day 2. Both the character format (italic) and paragraph format (6 pt spacing) is copied to Day 2.

To copy the same format to several different bits of text, you must first select the text which has the formatting you want to copy, then double-click the Format Painter button. Then you can select as many bits of text as you like. Try it now.

○ With either Day 1 or Day 2 selected, double-click the Format Painter button.

○ Select Day 3, Day 4 and Day 5 in turn to change the formatting of these lines.

○ Now click the Format Painter button again to turn it off.

## Indenting paragraphs                      Syllabus 3.3.2.3/5

You can indent all the text under the Day headings to make the headings stand out more. Again, you can do this by inserting spaces using the keyboard, but it is good practice to set the indentation as a paragraph format so that your document will look neat because of consistent formatting.

- ● Select the paragraph under Day 1.
- ● Click the Increase Indent button in the Paragraph group on the Home ribbon.
- ● Use either the Increase Indent button or the Format Painter to apply the same indent to the other paragraphs.

**Tip:**

> You can accurately set indentations using the **Left:** and **Right:** indentation list boxes in the **Paragraph** dialogue box, or by using the **Indent** boxes in the **Paragraph** group on the **Page Layout** ribbon (see the tip on page 115).

- ● Your text should now look like this:

---

# *ITINERARY*

*Day 1*

> Depart London Heathrow on British Airways flight

*Day 2*

> Arrive at Dar es Salaam Airport. Our representative will meet and transfer the group to the hotel. The morning will be at leisure to rest after the overnight flight. After lunch our representative will meet and escort you to the GEA offices. The Country Representative, Dr David Moshi, will give a presentation and brief you on the GEA projects in Tanzania.

*Day 3*

> After breakfast your guide will meet you for the transfer to Mikumi Kiboga Camp.
> Dinner and Overnight – Mikumi Kiboga Camp

*Day 4*

> You will be met and escorted for an early morning game drive through the Mikumi Park.
> Return to your accommodation for breakfast.
> Following breakfast your guide will escort you on the transfer to Udzungwa Mountain National Park.
> Followed by an accompanied late afternoon walk in the forest

*Day 5*

> The day includes trekking and sightseeing in the area.
> After breakfast your guide will escort the group on a leisurely walk to Sanje Falls, with a chance to take a refreshing swim in the falls. A picnic lunch will be provided.

---

### More on indents

One of the options in the Paragraph dialogue box (shown on page 115), under Indentation in the box labelled Special:, is Hanging. A hanging indent means that first line of the paragraph is not indented but all the subsequent lines in the paragraph are.

If you are writing a letter or story, you might want to set a first line indent to indent only the first line of each paragraph. You would do this by selecting First line in the Special: box.

◉ Save and close your document.

◉ If you are finished for now, exit Word.

## Exercise

In this exercise you will format the job advertisement you created in the exercise at the end of Chapter 11.

1. Open the file Job advert.docx. Save the file as Job advert1.docx.

2. Format the heading Clerical Assistant to size 18, Times New Roman, bold.

3. Now format the heading dark blue and double-underlined.

4. Delete the blank lines between paragraphs.

5. Insert spacing of 6 pt before the first four paragraphs.

6. Insert the following text on a line beneath the main heading:

    Ipswich £12k–£13.5k pro rata

7. Format this text Times New Roman, bold, size 12, dark blue and right-aligned.

8. Format the word essential in the third paragraph italic and bold.

9. Insert a superscript number 1 after the word hours in the first sentence.

10. Insert the following text on a new line at the end of the advert.

    [1]hours per week

11. Finally indent all paragraphs by 1 cm on the left and 2 cm on the right.

12. Save your work. It should look something like this:

---

## Clerical Assistant

**Ipswich £12k–13.5k pro rata**

This is a part-time position (18.5 hours[1]) and is temporary for six months.

A small insurance broker requires an experienced person to join the team and assist in the delivery of a wide range of duties to help maintain this busy office. Regular duties will include word processing documents, dealing with queries from the public and from staff, and maintaining records.

Experience of working in a team is *essential*, as is a good working knowledge of Microsoft Office. Experience of working in a personnel environment is preferable, although training will be provided.

Closing date: 18th July
Contact: Jane Hall on 01578 23455
[1]hours per week

---

## Ask yourself

❷     Can I save an existing file with a new name?

❷     Can I apply an existing style to a character, word, line or paragraph?

❷     Can I change font size, text colour and cases?

❷     Can I change line spacing before, after and within a paragraph?

❷     Do I know how to copy a format?

❷     Do I know how to undo an action?

In this chapter you should have created and saved the following files:
Job advert1.doc
NewItinerary.docx

In this chapter you have been introduced to the following buttons:

Format Painter
in the Clipboard group on the Home ribbon

Change Case
Character formatting: Bold, Italic, Underline
Font
Font Color
Font Size
in the Font group on the Home ribbon

Increase Indent
Paragraph formatting: Align Text Left, Center, Align Text Right, Justify
in the Paragraph group on the Home ribbon

The Style gallery in the Styles group on the Home ribbon

# Basic Operations

In this chapter you will find out:

- ❶ how to select, copy and move text
- ❶ how to find and replace text
- ❶ more about the ribbon
- ❶ how to draw a line
- ❶ how to check spelling.

## Ribbon groups used in this chapter

In this chapter you will use the following buttons and features in the Clipboard group and in the Editing group on the Home ribbon:

this button in the Proofing group on the Review ribbon:

this button in the Illustrations group on the Insert ribbon:

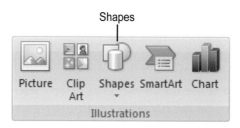

and this button in the Shape Styles group on the Drawing Tools Format ribbon:

Shape Outline

🅾 Load Word. A new blank document will appear on your screen.

**Tip:**

If Word is already running, click **New** on the **Office button** menu. Then select **Blank document** on the **New Document** window, and click the **Create** button.

Type the first five lines of the first verse from Old MacDonald. Remember to press Enter at the end of each line.

---

Old MacDonald

Old MacDonald had a farm, E-I-E-I-O
And on his farm he had a cow, E-I-E-I-O
With a "moo moo" here and a "moo moo" there
Here a "moo", there a "moo"
Everywhere a "moo moo"

---

**Tip:**

Use the double-quote marks above the 2 on the keyboard. "Straight quotes" will be replaced with "smart quotes" (i.e. opening and closing quotes) if the options are set to do this under **Office button, Word Options, Proofing, AutoCorrect Options, AutoFormat**.

## Selecting text                                   Syllabus 3.2.2.2

There are many ways to select text. It is well worth getting to know them. You have already practised selecting text by holding down the left mouse button and dragging across the text. This method applies to any amount of text, from a single character to a whole document. Here are some quicker ways.

When selected, text appears on a blue background.

🅾 **To select a word:** Double-click anywhere in the word.

🅾 **To select one or more lines:** Click in the left margin beside the line to select a line. Drag down the left margin to select several lines.

🅾 **To select a sentence:** Hold down Ctrl and then click anywhere in the sentence.

🅾 **To select a paragraph:** Triple-click anywhere in the paragraph.

🅾 **To select an entire document:** Click Select, Select All in the Editing group on the Home ribbon. Or triple-click in the left margin, or you can use the shortcut key combination Ctrl-A.

❶ **To select a large block of text:** Click the mouse at the beginning of the text you want to select. Then scroll to the end of the text and hold down Shift while you click again.

❶ **To select non-adjacent text:** Select the first bit of text, then hold down Ctrl while you select another piece of text.

You can try out some of these techniques on the text you have just typed:

▶ Select all the text and change the font to Comic Sans MS, Bold, size 13.5.

▶ Select the heading and make it size 18.

▶ Select both the occurrences of E-I-E-I-O. Then make this text blue.

## Copying text                                                 Syllabus 3.2.2.6

The last line of the verse is missing. It is a repetition of the first line.

You are going to use the Copy and Paste buttons to save yourself the trouble of having to write out the same line again.

▶ Select the line Old MacDonald had a farm, E-I-E-I-O by clicking in the left-hand margin next to the line.

 ▶ Click the Copy button in the Clipboard group on the Home ribbon.

▶ Place the text insertion point at the end of the last line and press Enter.

▶ Click the Paste button in the Clipboard group on the Home ribbon. The line will be copied into the text.

**Tip:**

 You will see an icon which looks like the Paste button appearing under your text. This is the **Paste Options** button. It allows you to change the formatting of the text you have copied.

▶ Now type in the first five lines of the next two verses, leaving a blank line between each verse.

▶ Use the Format Painter to copy the formatting – make each E-I-E-I-O blue.

> Old MacDonald had a farm, E-I-E-I-O
> And on his farm he had a horse, E-I-E-I-O
> With a "neigh neigh" here and a "neigh neigh" there
> Here a "neigh", there a "neigh"
> Everywhere a "neigh neigh"
>
> Old MacDonald had a farm, E-I-E-I-O
> And on his farm he had a pig, E-I-E-I-O
> With a (snort) here and a (snort) there
> Here a (snort), there a (snort)
> Everywhere a (snort)

## Cutting and pasting

Syllabus 3.2.2.6

Suppose you've made a mistake and Old MacDonald had a pig *before* he had a horse!

You can move the third verse back to become the second verse using the Cut button.

> ◉ Select the verse you have just typed (about the pig) by clicking in the margin to its left and dragging down.

> ◉ Click the Cut button in the Clipboard group on the Home ribbon. The selected text will disappear, but it is not lost completely: it is being stored for you on the clipboard.

> ◉ Now click immediately before the first line in the second verse (about the horse) and click the Paste button. The verse is now pasted from the clipboard into the text exactly where you want it.

> ◉ Press Enter after your pasted verse if you need to insert another blank line.

You have been using the ribbon buttons to Cut, Copy and Paste. However, if you prefer, you can use these keyboard shortcuts: for Cut, press Ctrl-X; for Copy, press Ctrl-C; for Paste, press Ctrl-V (i.e. press the Ctrl key and the letter key together on the keyboard).

> ◉ Now use the Copy and Paste buttons again to duplicate the parts of the rhyme that repeat (i.e. lines 3–5 from each verse and the last line). The completed rhyme should look something like this:

---

**Old MacDonald**

Old MacDonald had a farm, E-I-E-I-O
And on his farm he had a cow, E-I-E-I-O
With a "moo moo" here and a "moo moo" there
Here a "moo", there a "moo"
Everywhere a "moo moo"
Old MacDonald had a farm, E-I-E-I-O

Old MacDonald had a farm, E-I-E-I-O
And on his farm he had a pig, E-I-E-I-O
With a (snort) here and a (snort) there
Here a (snort), there a (snort)
Everywhere a (snort)
With a "moo moo" here and a "moo moo" there
Here a "moo", there a "moo"
Everywhere a "moo moo"
Old MacDonald had a farm, E-I-E-I-O

Old MacDonald had a farm, E-I-E-I-O
And on his farm he had a horse, E-I-E-I-O
With a "neigh, neigh" here and a "neigh neigh" there
Here a "neigh", there a "neigh"
Everywhere a "neigh neigh"
With a (snort) here and a (snort) there
Here a (snort), there a (snort)
Everywhere a (snort)
With a "moo moo" here and a "moo moo" there
Here a "moo", there a "moo"
Everywhere a "moo moo"
Old MacDonald had a farm, E-I-E-I-O

---

## Finding and replacing text                         Syllabus 3.2.2.4–5

Suppose that after completing your lyrics, you decide that you would prefer the pig in the rhyme to grunt rather than snort.

As you can see this word appears many times and you need a quick way of changing each occurrence.

○ Click at the start of the first line.

○ Click Replace `ab Replace` in the Editing group on the Home ribbon (or press Ctrl-H on the keyboard).

You will see a dialogue box and you can type the word or phrase you want to replace, and the word or phrase to replace it with.

You can get the computer to replace all occurrences, or search for them one at a time so that you can decide whether or not to replace each one. In this case you want them all replaced.

○ Click the button marked Replace All. Word tells you how many words have been replaced. Click OK and close the Find and Replace dialogue box.

○ Save your document as Old Macdonald.docx.

Note that if you simply want to find a specific word or phrase you should select Find `Find ▾` in the Editing group on the Home ribbon.

## Minimising and restoring the ribbon                 Syllabus 3.1.2.4

Sometimes you might want to increase the working area where you type. You can minimise (hide) the ribbon so only the ribbon tabs are displayed. If the ribbon is minimised, you need to know how to get it back!

○ Right-click anywhere in the line containing the ribbon tabs, on the Office button, on the Quick Access Toolbar, or on a ribbon group name.

○ Click Minimize the Ribbon on the shortcut menu that is displayed.

> To restore the ribbon, right-click in one of the same places as before to un-tick Minimize the Ribbon on the shortcut menu.

**Tip:**

> Use **Ctrl-F1** (i.e. press at the same time the **Control** key and the **F1** key on the keyboard) or double-click a ribbon tab to toggle between minimising and maximising the ribbon. At any time when the ribbon is minimised, simply click a ribbon tab to show the ribbon temporarily when you need it.

## Drawing a horizontal line                                         Syllabus 3.4.3.1

You are going to add a line between the first and second verse of the Old MacDonald poem.

> Click the Insert ribbon tab, and click Shapes in the Illustrations group. This will display a menu of drawing shapes you can use in your documents.

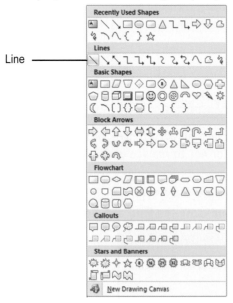

Line

**Tip:**

The same drawing shapes are also available in the **Insert Shapes** group on the **Drawing Tools Format** ribbon.

> Select the Line shape from the Lines group.

> Click the page where you want to start the line and drag the mouse to its end position. Do not release the mouse button.

> Press the Shift key to ensure that the line is horizontal, and release the mouse button.

> Drag and drop the line to position it exactly where you want it.

> With the line still selected, click the Shape Outline button in the Shape Styles group that has been displayed on the Drawing Tools Format ribbon.

> Click Weight and select 1½ pt.

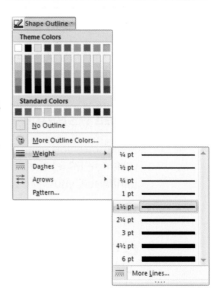

- Now comes the clever bit! Press both Shift and Ctrl and keep them pressed down while you drag and drop the line down to between the second and third verses. Then drag again to the end of the third verse.

---

**Old MacDonald**

Old MacDonald had a farm, E-I-E-I-O
And on his farm he had a cow, E-I-E-I-O
With a "moo moo" here and a "moo moo" there
Here a "moo", there a "moo"
Everywhere a "moo moo"
Old MacDonald had a farm, E-I-E-I-O

---

Old MacDonald had a farm, E-I-E-I-O
And on his farm he had a pig, E-I-E-I-O
With a (grunt) here and a (grunt) there
Here a (grunt), there a (grunt)
Everywhere a (grunt)
With a "moo moo" here and a "moo moo" there
Here a "moo", there a "moo"
Everywhere a "moo moo"
Old MacDonald had a farm, E-I-E-I-O

---

Old MacDonald had a farm, E-I-E-I-O
And on his farm he had a horse, E-I-E-I-O
With a "neigh, neigh" here and a "neigh neigh" there
Here a "neigh", there a "neigh"
Everywhere a "neigh neigh"
With a (grunt) here and a (grunt) there
Here a (grunt), there a (grunt)
Everywhere a (grunt)
With a "moo moo" here and a "moo moo" there
Here a "moo", there a "moo"
Everywhere a "moo moo"
Old MacDonald had a farm, E-I-E-I-O

---

You should have three identical lines. Keeping a finger on Ctrl copies, rather than moves, an object. Keeping a finger on Shift means that the object can only move vertically while you drag down, which ensures that all the lines will be perfectly lined up.

## Spell-checking                                   Syllabus 3.6.2.1–2

Before you print a document you should check it carefully. Check the spelling and grammar and then check for errors of layout and presentation, including appropriate margins, font sizes and formats.

Word has a built-in spell-checker so that when you type a document, any words that Word does not recognise are underlined with a red squiggle.

It will also red underline repeated words, so if for example you write 'I went to the the cinema', the second occurrence of 'the' will be underlined in red.

If the grammar checker is switched on, then parts of the text that Word thinks are not grammatical will be underlined in green, though you may disagree. You will also see a green wavy line if you leave two spaces rather than one between words.

Word cannot know when you have simply typed the wrong word, like 'widow' instead of 'window' or 'their' instead of 'there', so you still need to check your own spelling carefully even if nothing is underlined in red.

To try out Word's spell-checker manually, put some errors in Old Macdonald.

○ Delete the h in everywhere in the first verse. Replace every other occurrence of everywhere with this misspelt word.

○ Replace the first occurrence of there with their.

○ Now position the pointer at the start of the document and click the Review ribbon tab.

○ Click the Spelling & Grammar button in the Proofing group.

A window opens offering you suggestions for the first misspelling:

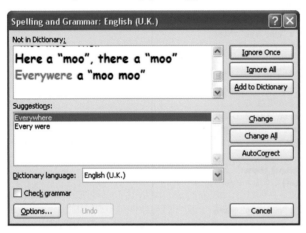

○ Click the Check grammar tick box to remove the tick and turn off grammar checking if it is on.

○ You can accept the first suggestion, which looks correct, and change every occurrence. Click Change All.

Word does not find the misspelling of there. You will have to correct that yourself.

**Tip:**

Make sure that you are using the correct dictionary for your country, otherwise the spell-checker will highlight words as being incorrectly spelt even though they are correct.

○ Put one more misspelling in so that you can try out the shortcut menu. Change Old to Oold.

○ As soon as you click away from the word it will be underlined in red. Right-click the word and a shortcut menu appears.

○ Click the correct spelling and the word will be corrected.

If Word does not recognise a word that you know is correctly spelled, you can add it to the dictionary by clicking Add to Dictionary. Alternatively, if you have a word or an abbreviation that you want to use frequently in your current document, but you do not want to add it to the dictionary, you can click Ignore All. The word will only be ignored in the current document.

Tip:
> If you are working on a network, you may not be able to add words to the dictionary.

◉     Save your document.

When you have carefully checked your document you should preview it before printing it (see page 104). Make any corrections that are needed before you print.

◉     Close your document, saving again if you have made any changes. Close Word.

## Exercise

You have been asked to produce a match report for a school football match.

1.     Enter the following text as a new word-processed document. Use Arial, size 11 font.

Year 7 Football Barksfield vs Holdbrook, Thursday 25 February

There was plenty of action in both halves during the first period of the game, with both goalies having plenty to do. The finest save of the match came from the brilliant Jamie Dereham in the Barksfield goal. As a shot came in from the edge of the area, flying into the bottom corner of the net, Jamie leapt up to punch it deftly away. A fleet Holdbrook forward picked up the rebound and before Jamie was back on his feet the opposition had netted their first. The score remained the same until half time.

In the second half Barksfield rallied well with both Doug Glere and Chris Holmes creating some good runs and direct passes to feet. The visitors won a corner which was fired onto the head of a Holdbrook player, but the shot was superbly cleared off the line by Alex Beardshaw. Holdbrook maintained the pressure and won another corner. This time Barksfield were not so lucky and a superb goal was scored directly from the corner flag. This was a closely fought game between two well-matched sides. Full time score: Barksfield 0 Holdbrook 2.

2.     Run the spell-checker and correct any typing errors.

3.  Make the heading Arial, size 14 and bold.

4.  Cut the complete sentence This was a closely fought... in the last paragraph and paste it at the beginning of the first paragraph.

5.  The visiting team is called Holdbroom, not Holdbrook. Use the Find and Replace feature to replace all occurrences of the word Holdbrook with Holdbroom.

6.  This may be used as an article in the school newsletter. As such it will require a horizontal line beneath the article. Draw a short thick line, centred beneath the text.

7.  Check the document carefully for errors before you save it as Football report.docx.

8.  Check the document in Print Preview before printing it.

## Ask yourself

❷  Do I know the ways to select different parts of a text document?

❷  Can I copy and paste text within a document?

❷  Can I cut and paste text within a document?

❷  Can I find text within a document, replacing occurrences as required?

❷  Do I know how to minimise and restore the ribbon?

❷  Can I use a spell-checker to find and correct incorrectly spelt words?

❷  Do I know how to add words to a custom dictionary so they are recognised in future spell-checks?

In this chapter you should have created and saved the following files:
Football report.docx          Old Macdonald.docx

In this chapter you have been introduced to the following buttons:

Copy, Cut and Paste in the Clipboard group on the Home ribbon
Find, Replace and Select in the Editing group of the Home ribbon

Spelling & Grammar in the Proofing group on the Review ribbon

Shapes in the Illustrations group on the Insert ribbon

Shape Outline in the Shapes Style group on the Drawing Tools Format ribbon

# Working with Templates

**In this chapter you will find out:**

- ❶ about templates and how to use them
- ❶ more about styles
- ❶ how to copy and move text between documents
- ❶ how to insert symbols that are not on the keyboard.

In this chapter you will be doing some more work on the travel itinerary that you started in Chapter 12.

Imagine that you want to write some more information about the places that the tourists will visit. However, you want to check your facts first by sending a fax to someone in Tanzania to cast an eye over them for accuracy.

Templates are useful because they allow you to keep the 'look' of a document consistent every time you use it. Word has many different templates which are used for different types of document such as a letter, fax, memo, formal report or web page. In fact, every time you open a new document you are using a template, probably without realising it.

(Note: It is possible that the templates used in this chapter are not installed on your computer. If this is the case, you can use and adapt one of the alternatives that is installed.)

## Ribbon group used in this chapter

In this chapter you will use the following button in the Symbols group on the Insert ribbon:

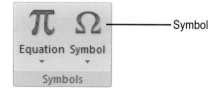
————Symbol

## Using a template

Syllabus 3.1.1.2

- ▶ Load Word.
- ▶ Click New on the Office button menu to display the New Document window.

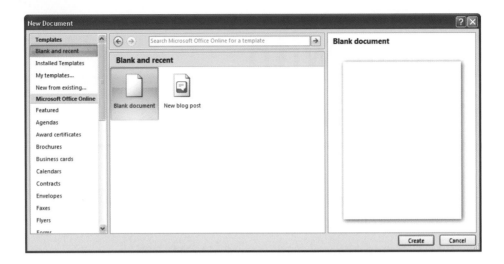

If you wanted to create a plain page blank document, you would click Blank document under Blank and recent in the template list. This creates a new document using Word's default template called the Normal template.

This time, however, you are going to select a template that will be suitable for writing a fax.

◉   Click Installed Templates in the template list. You will see that there are several different templates for you to choose from.

◉   Select the Origin Fax template and click Create.

The document shown on the next page will open:

▶**Fax**

[Pick a date]

| | |
|---|---|
| From: | Axel Seraph |
| Phone: | [Type the sender phone number] |
| Fax: | [Type the sender fax number] |
| Company Name: | [Type the sender company name] |
| | |
| To: | [Type the recipient name] |
| Phone: | [Type the recipient phone number] |
| Fax: | [Type the recipient fax number] |
| Company Name: | [Type the recipient company name] |

**Comments:**

[Type comments]

**Tip:**

cc stands for **carbon copy**. Use this if you are sending a copy of the fax to a second person.

You can use this template to insert your details including a message. You might find that Word has automatically inserted a name in the From: field, but you can change this if you need to. Read the instructions in square brackets. You can save your changed document as a customised template by clicking Save As, Word Template on the Office button menu. The next time you want to use it, the name you selected (e.g. GEAFaxForm) will appear in the list of templates.

- Fill in the company name Global Environment Association and all the other items above the main fax message – make them up or use those shown on page 132).

- Save your fax as a document with the name FaxTanzania, but do not close it yet.

- Delete the heading Comments:

- Type the following text in the [Type comments] field:

> Henry:
> Could you please check these paragraphs and make sure I have got all the facts right?

- Under this text type the paragraphs shown on the next page.

Dar es Salaam is the largest city in Tanzania with an estimated 3.0 million people. It is the gateway to Zanzibar, a 75-minute ferry ride away and a starting point to the Northern and Southern safari circuit.

Mikumi National Park covers an area of 3230 sq km and is the third largest park in Tanzania. It is one of the most popular parks in Tanzania and is an important centre for education, where students go to study ecology and conservation. It contains a wide range of wildlife.

Yours, Brian

## Using styles                                    Syllabus 3.3.3.2

You can change this style to give the text more emphasis as follows:

- Select the last two paragraphs of the message text by dragging down the left margin.

- Move the mouse over the styles in the Styles gallery on the Home ribbon and watch the text formatting change. Click the Emphasis style.

Your fax will look similar to this:

- Save this document and close it.

## Copying text between documents                              Syllabus 3.2.2.6

Now suppose that the content of the fax message has been confirmed by Henry and you are ready to insert it into your travel itinerary.

You are going to copy the text from the document FaxTanzania.doc into the itinerary document.

- ▶ Open the document NewItinerary.doc that you created in Chapter 12.

- ▶ Open the document FaxTanzania.doc.

- ▶ Select the paragraph about Dar es Salaam and copy it to the clipboard by pressing Ctrl-C.

- ▶ Click NewItinerary.doc on the taskbar to display it.

- ▶ At the end of the paragraph under Day 2 (just before Day 3), press Enter to insert a new paragraph.

- ▶ Press Ctrl-V to insert the text that you just copied.

- ▶ If it is in a different font, use the Format Painter to make it look the same as the rest of the text, as described in the paragraph Copying a Format on page 115.

- ▶ Indent the new paragraph 0.5 cm as described on page 116.

 ▶ Similarly, insert the paragraph about Mikumi National Park under Day 3. This time, format it by selecting Match Destination Formatting from the Paste Options button which appeared when you pasted the paragraph.

- ▶ Delete any extra blank lines at the end of the new paragraphs by clicking on the blank line and pressing Backspace.

## Deleting text                                              Syllabus 3.2.2.7

 To delete text, first select it and then select Cut in the Clipboard group of the Home ribbon. Alternatively, press Ctrl-X on the keyboard.

You can delete text by pressing the Delete key on the keyboard but do not do this if you want to keep a copy for pasting elsewhere.

## Moving text between open documents                         Syllabus 3.2.2.6

 To move text between open documents, you can first cut it from the original document by one of the methods described above. Then click in the second document where you want the text to appear, and select Paste in the Clipboard group of the Home ribbon or press Ctrl-V.

## Inserting special symbols

You will now put an aeroplane symbol before and after the sentence Depart London Heathrow on British Airways flight in the NewItinerary document.

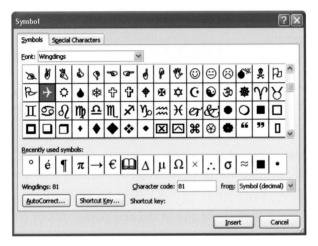

▶ Open the document NewItinerary.doc if it is not already open, and click at the start of the sentence.

▶ Click the Insert ribbon tab, and click Symbol in the Symbols group.

▶ Click More Symbols... Ω More Symbols... on the menu that is displayed to show the Symbol window.

▶ Select the Wingdings font.

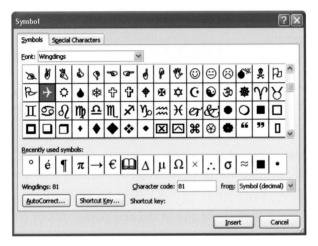

▶ Find the aeroplane symbol and click Insert and then Close.

▶ Now insert a second aeroplane symbol at the end of the sentence.

You can also insert special characters that are not on the keyboard, such as ©, ® etc. To do this click the Special Characters tab in the Symbol window shown above. The following screen appears:

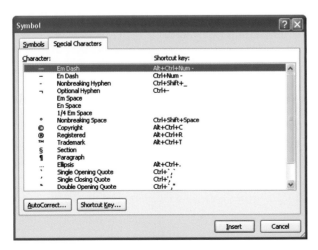

You don't need any of these characters in this document so you can close this window.

Your itinerary should look like this:

---

# *ITINERARY*

*Day 1*

✈ Depart London Heathrow on British Airways flight ✈

*Day 2*

Arrive at Dar es Salaam Airport. Our representative will meet and transfer the group to the hotel. The morning will be at leisure to rest after the overnight flight. After lunch our representative will meet and escort you to the GEA offices. The Country Representative, Dr David Moshi, will give a presentation and brief you on the GEA projects in Tanzania.

Dar es Salaam is the largest city in Tanzania with an estimated 3.0 million people. It is the gateway to Zanzibar, a 75-minute ferry ride away and a starting point to the Northern and Southern safari circuit.

*Day 3*

After breakfast your guide will meet you for the transfer to Mikumi Kiboga Camp.
Dinner and Overnight – Mikumi Kiboga Camp

Mikumi National Park covers an area of 3230 sq km and is the third largest park in Tanzania. It is one of the most popular parks in Tanzania and is an important centre for education, where students got to study ecology and conservation. It contains a wide range of wildlife.

*Day 4*

You will be met and escorted for an early morning game drive through the Mikumi Park.
Return to your accommodation for breakfast.
Following breakfast your guide will escort you on the transfer to Udzungwa Mountain National Park.
Followed by an accompanied late afternoon walk in the forest

*Day 5*

The day includes trekking and sightseeing in the area.
After breakfast your guide will escort the group on a leisurely walk to Sanje Falls, with a chance to take a refreshing swim in the falls. A picnic lunch will be provided.

---

▶ Save your work, close all your documents and exit Word!

## Exercise

As a Home Watch coordinator you need to prepare a letter to send to homes in your local area about a special crime awareness initiative.

1. Open the Urban Letter template provided with Microsoft Word and use it to create the following letter. Save the file as Letter.docx.

John Ruddick
Home Watch Coordinator
26 The Gardens
DARKSHAM
Hampshire
TY5 4RF

☎ 01543 672345

Mr and Mrs K Hills
The White House
Belvedere Road
DARKSHAM
Hampshire
TY5 23RF

30 June 2008

Dear Mr and Mrs Hills

As we enter the holiday season the local police have asked Home Watch coordinators to remind people about the increased risk of burglary. If you are planning to go away this summer, please ensure that your home is secure. A home that looks unoccupied is more likely to be targeted than one that is secure.

Make your house look as though someone is living there:

Install automated / programmable light switches.

Ask a neighbour to regularly clear your letter box and doorstep.

Ask a neighbour to park on your drive.

Cancel regular deliveries.

Do not advertise that you are going away and do not show your address on your luggage for the outward journey.

Yours sincerely

John Ruddick
Home Watch Coordinator

2. Right-align the date and left-align the closing text as shown.

3. Double-line space the list of security measures and insert the telephone symbol as shown.

4. Click each section of text and count the number of different styles used.

5. Save the document.

6. Copy and paste the list of security measures into a new document and save as Poster.docx. You will use this at the end of the next chapter.

## Ask yourself

❷    Do I know what templates are and why they are useful?

❷    Can I copy text between documents?

❷    Can I move text between documents?

❷    Can I insert special character symbols in a document?

In this chapter you should have created and saved the following files:
FaxTanzania.docx
Letter.docx
NewItinerary.docx
Poster.docx

In this chapter you have been introduced to the following button:

Symbol in the Symbols group on the Insert ribbon

# 15 Tabs, Borders and Lists

**In this chapter you will find out:**

- ❶ about tabs and how to use them
- ❶ about non-printing characters and how to display them
- ❶ how to add a border around text and a page
- ❶ how to adjust page orientation, size and margins
- ❶ about lists
- ❶ about spacing and indenting paragraphs
- ❶ how to add background colour
- ❶ about automatic hyphenation.

## Ribbon groups used in this chapter

In this chapter you will use the following buttons and features in the Paragraph group on the Home ribbon:

Bullets Numbering

Borders

and these buttons in the Page Setup group on the Page Layout ribbon:

Margins  Orientation    Size

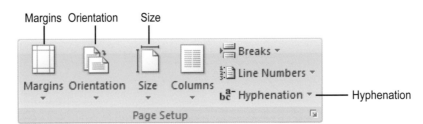

Hyphenation

# Introduction to tabs

You will now learn how to make neat lists – such as price lists, lists of travel times, numbered steps in instructions, or any other list you can think of.

When you want items to line up neatly in columns, it is good practice to use the Tab key – you won't be able to align text accurately by using spaces. Pressing the Tab key will advance the cursor to the next preset tab stop. In the list below, the first column is left-aligned, the second is centre-aligned, the third is aligned on the decimal point and the last column is right-aligned. This is achieved by setting different tab stops, which appear as marks on the ruler underneath the ribbon.

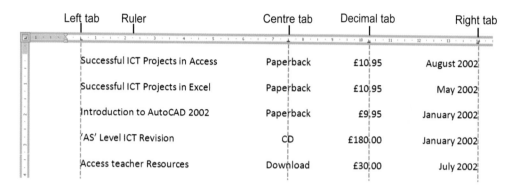

Before you set any tab stops, Microsoft Word has default tab positions which appear as faint marks below the ruler.

Tip:

If the ruler is not displayed at the top and left-hand side of the document page, click the **View Ruler** button at the top right of the document area above the vertical scroll bar.

The following assumes that Word is configured for centimetres. You can check and change this by selecting Office button, Word Options, Advanced, Display, Show measurements in units of:

● Open a new document and look at the ruler line at the top of the screen. The default tab positions are probably set at intervals of 1.27 cm (which is 0.5 in).

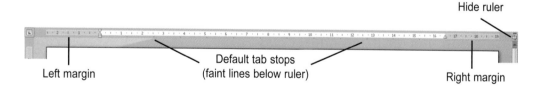

You are going to produce a price list for a company selling stationery items, similar to the one on the next page.

## Setting default tab stops                                    Syllabus 3.3.2.6

You will start by changing the default tab positions.

● Click the Dialogue Launcher on the Paragraph group on the Home ribbon to display the Paragraph dialogue box.

● Click the Tabs... button to display the Tabs dialogue box.

● Click the up-arrow on the right-hand side of the Default tab stops: box until it is set at 3 cm. Then click OK. The position of the default tab marks will move on the ruler.

### Typing the price list

Type the following list, pressing the tab key between each entry. You will need to press it twice after the word Description.

ECONOMY SQUARE-CUT FOLDERS

| Product Code | Description | Qty | Price per pack |
|---|---|---|---|
| ESF151 | Coloured folders | 100 | £12.99 |
| ESF152 | Buff folders | 50 | £4.49 |
| ESF003 | Assorted coloured folders | 100 | £11.99 |
| ESF004 | Assorted coloured folders | 10 | £6.99 |

## Displaying non-printing characters                           Syllabus 3.2.2.1

Although the list looks quite neat, it would be better if the quantities were right-aligned, and the prices lined up on the decimal point.

Many of the characters that Word stores in your document are 'non-printing' and do not normally show on the screen. These characters include Tab, Enter and even spaces between words.

Sometimes it is useful to be able to see these characters and you can display them by clicking the Show/Hide ¶ icon that you first met in Chapter 11 on page 104.

¶ ────○ Click the Show/Hide ¶ icon.

Your document will now look like this:

ECONOMY·SQUARE-CUT·FOLDERS¶
¶
Product·Code → Description → → Qty → Price·per·pack¶
ESF151 → Coloured·folders→ → 100 → £12.99¶
ESF152 → Buff·folders → → 50 → £4.49¶
ESF003 → Assorted·coloured·folders → 100 → £11.99¶
ESF004 → Assorted·coloured·folders → 10 → £6.99¶

**Note:**

The different symbols which appear are for a **Space** (·), **Enter** (¶) and **Tab** (→). Wherever the **Enter** key has been pressed to create a new paragraph, a sign like a backwards **P** appears. This is a pilcrow.

You can see that you have two **Tab** characters in some places, for example between Description and Qty.

○ Click Show/Hide ¶ again to hide the non-printing characters.

## Setting custom tabs                          Syllabus 3.3.2.6

You will now set your own tab positions.

○ Select your list and column headings, starting at Product Code.

○ Open the Tabs dialogue box once again.

○ In the Tab stop position: box, type 3 and then click the Set button.

The next tab position needs to be right-aligned at approximately 9.5 cm.

○ In the Tab stop position: box, type 9.5. Under Alignment, click Right. Then click the Set button.

○ In the Tab stop position: box, type 14.5. Under Alignment, click Decimal. Then click the Set button.

○ Click OK.

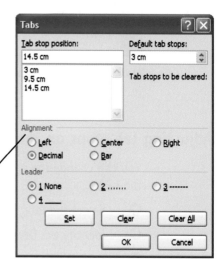

```
ECONOMY SQUARE-CUT FOLDERS

Product Code      Description                                          Qty    Price per
pack
ESF151            Coloured folders                                     100    £12.99
ESF152            Buff folders                                          50    £4.49
ESF003            Assorted coloured folders            100            £11.99
ESF004            Assorted coloured folders             10            £6.99
```

Your previously neat layout has gone wrong! The problem is that when you set custom tabs, the default tabs disappear. Remember that you pressed the tab key twice after some words. Now you have only one tab stop where previously there were two.

Luckily this is easy to fix. You need to delete the extra Tab characters.

❿  Click Show/Hide ¶ again to display the hidden Tab characters.

❿  Click just before the word Qty and press the Backspace key.

❿  Click just before 100 on the next line and press the Backspace key.

❿  Delete the other extra tab on the next line.

❿  Hide the non-printing characters again.

Now everything is looking pretty good except that the prices are too far to the right.

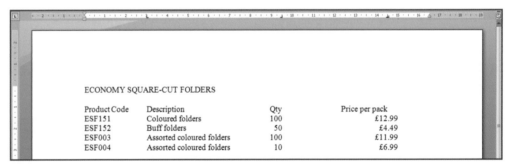

Notice the position and type of the tab markers on the ruler match those you selected in the Tab dialogue box.

## Adjusting tab stops on the ruler                      Syllabus 3.3.2.6

You can change the position of tab stops by dragging the tab markers left or right on the ruler.

❿  Select the four lines of the list (i.e. excluding the column headers).

❿  Identify the Decimal tab marker at the far right of the ruler (at 14.5 cm).

❿  Drag the Decimal tab marker to 13.5 cm on the ruler.

## Setting and removing tab markers                    Syllabus 3.3.2.6

At the left of the ruler you will see the tab alignment button.

Tab alignment
button currently
set to left tab

To set a left, centre, right or decimal tab, you click this button repeatedly until the tab type that you want is shown. Then click in the ruler line at the position where you want the tab stop.

Here are the button symbols for the Left, Center, Right and Decimal Tabs:

Left tab          Centre tab          Right tab          Decimal tab

You can delete an unwanted tab stop by dragging it off the ruler.

## Adding a border                                      Syllabus 3.3.2.10

Now you will add a border to the list.

○    Select the whole list and the headings.

○    Click the Borders button in the Paragraph group on the Home menu. (Note that the icon on this button changes depending on the border selection last made. However, the button is always located in the same place in the group.)

○    Click Outside Borders on the menu of border options that appears.

Note that you would click the appropriate menu item to set borders at other places around selected text.

A box will appear around the price list. You can make the headings bold and increase the font size of the main heading if you want to.

○    Save your list as Price List.docx.

| Bottom Border |
| Top Border |
| Left Border |
| Right Border |
| No Border |
| All Borders |
| Outside Borders |
| Inside Borders |
| Inside Horizontal Border |
| Inside Vertical Border |
| Diagonal Down Border |
| Diagonal Up Border |
| Horizontal Line |
| Draw Table |
| View Gridlines |
| Borders and Shading... |

**ECONOMY SQUARE-CUT FOLDERS**

| Product Code | Description | Qty | Price per pack |
|---|---|---|---|
| ESF151 | Coloured folders | 100 | £12.99 |
| ESF152 | Buff folders | 50 | £4.49 |
| ESF003 | Assorted coloured folders | 100 | £11.99 |
| ESF004 | Assorted coloured folders | 10 | £6.99 |

You are going to create a poster to help with a typical office problem – working the coffee machine.

> ## Using the Coffee Machine
>
> ➢ Put a sheet of filter paper into the coffee compartment (The filter papers are in the drawer under the counter)
>
> ➢ Measure coffee into the filter paper – one tablespoon of coffee for each cup your are making
>
> ➢ Fill the jug with the required amount of water – use the scale marked on the side of the jug to measure the amount
>
> ➢ Pour the water into the top compartment, then place the jug on the base of the machine
>
> ➢ Turn on the machine and wait for the coffee to filter through it

## Modifying the document setup                          Syllabus 3.6.1.1–2

When you open a new document the page size, orientation (portrait or landscape) and margins are set to default values for the Normal template. You can change any of these attributes.

⚫   Open a new document.

⚫   Click Size in the Page Setup group on the Page Layout ribbon, and select A5 from the menu of standard page sizes that is displayed. You might not see the page size change, but the ruler will show that it has.

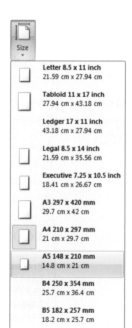

### Note:
You can also set non-standard page sizes by choosing **More Paper Sizes...** from the menu and specifying the paper dimensions you want in the **Page Setup** dialogue box that is displayed.

Size

Letter 8.5 x 11 inch
21.59 cm x 27.94 cm

Tabloid 11 x 17 inch
27.94 cm x 43.18 cm

Ledger 17 x 11 inch
43.18 cm x 27.94 cm

Legal 8.5 x 14 inch
21.59 cm x 35.56 cm

Executive 7.25 x 10.5 inch
18.41 cm x 26.67 cm

A3 297 x 420 mm
29.7 cm x 42 cm

A4 210 x 297 mm
21 cm x 29.7 cm

A5 148 x 210 mm
14.8 cm x 21 cm

B4 250 x 354 mm
25.7 cm x 36.4 cm

B5 182 x 257 mm
18.2 cm x 25.7 cm

○ Click Margins in the Page Setup group on the Page Layout ribbon, and select Narrow from the menu of preset margins that is displayed. The ruler will show the new margin settings.

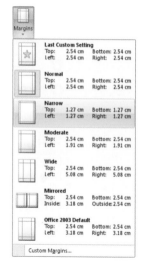

**Note:**

You can also set custom margins by choosing **Custom Margins...** from the menu and specifying them in the **Page Setup** dialogue box that is displayed.

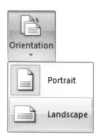

○ Click Orientation in the Page Setup group on the Page Layout ribbon, and select Landscape from the menu that is displayed.

**Tip:**

Use **Landscape** orientation when you want the page to be wider than it is long.

○ Select a suitable font for the title. The one shown on the previous page is Verdana, size 36.

○ Type the heading and make sure that it is Center-aligned.

○ Press Enter and left-align the text.

○ Change to a different font – the one shown in the example is Arial, size 18 and press Enter again.

## Making bullets                                             Syllabus 3.3.2.9

 ○ Click the Bullets button in the Paragraph group on the Home ribbon.

○ Type the instructions listed in the figure on the previous page. Each time you press Enter, a bullet will automatically appear on the next line.

○ After typing the last item in the list, press Enter once more.

○ Turn off the bullets by clicking the Bullets button again.

**Tip:**

You can add bullets after typing a list, rather than before. Just select the items you want to bullet, and then click the **Bullets** button.

## Customising bullets

You can alter the appearance of bullets.

○ Select the list.

 ○ Click the down-arrow on the Bullets button in the Paragraph group on the Home ribbon to display a menu of alternative bullet styles.

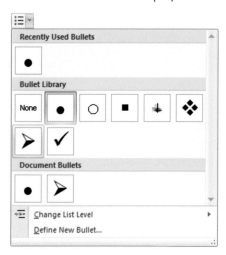

**Tip:**
To remove bullets, select the bulleted list and then click the **Bullets** button, which acts as a 'toggle'.

○ Select a different style of bullet, and click OK.

## A numbered list

Instead of using bullets, sometimes you may want to number your steps (usually to indicate importance or a sequence of steps in an instruction list).

○ Select the list.

 ○ Click the Numbering button in the Paragraph group on the Home ribbon.

Your list will appear with numbers instead of bullets. Note that you can customise numbers in the similar ways as you customised the bullets. Sometimes you may want a list that uses Roman numerals, or maybe one that has some unnumbered text in the middle of the list. To do this, click the down-arrow by the Numbering button and choose from the options displayed.

○ Click the Numbering button again to remove the numbers and leave the list as a bulleted list for the purposes of this exercise.

## Spacing paragraphs

Every time you press Enter, you create a new paragraph. So, in your list, Word treats each separate bullet point as a separate paragraph. You can put extra space between each bullet point so that the list fills the page more neatly. You were shown how to space paragraphs on page 114, and this is another way of applying the good practice rather than using the Enter key.

◑ If the list is not already selected, select it now.

◑ Right-click the list to display a shortcut menu.

◑ Select **Paragraph...** to display the paragraph dialogue box shown on page 115.

◑ Set the **Spacing** list boxes as shown in the following diagram, making sure that the **Don't add space between paragraphs of the same style** check box is unticked.

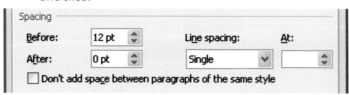

◑ If that is not enough spacing to fill your page comfortably, try again. You could try increasing the **Spacing Before:** to size 18, or alternatively you could insert some spacing after each paragraph using the **Spacing After:** box. Experiment until you are happy with the layout.

## Inserting a soft carriage return                 Syllabus 3.3.2.2

Sometimes you want to have a second paragraph under a bullet point, that does not have its own bullet. You can insert a soft carriage return (line break) by holding down **Shift** and pressing **Enter**.

◑ Try pressing **Shift** and **Enter** at the end of the first paragraph and inserting the words:

(The filter papers are in the drawer under the counter)

**Tip:**

You can remove a soft carriage return by clicking the **Show/Hide ¶** button ¶ in the **Paragraph** group of the **Home** ribbon to display the hidden character that has been inserted ↵. Place the text insert cursor between the character and the last letter of the list item and press the **Delete** key. Click the **Show/Hide ¶** button again to hide the hidden characters.

## Placing a border around the page

You can put a border round the whole page.

○ Click the Borders button in the Paragraph group on the Home ribbon (see page 143) and select the Borders and Shading... option on the menu that is displayed.

○ Click the Page Border tab on the Borders and Shading dialogue box.

○ Click the Box icon, select the border attributes (e.g. colour, style, width etc.) you want, and then click OK.

## Shading the title                                                    Syllabus 3.3.2.10

The notice heading needs to have a yellow heading on a blue background.

○ Select the title by clicking in the left margin next to it.

 ○ Click the arrow next to the Font Color button in the Font group of the Home ribbon, and select Yellow from the palette for your title.

○ Now, keeping the heading selected, click the Borders button in the Paragraph group on the Home menu and select the Borders and Shading... option on the menu that is displayed.

○ Click the Shading tab on the Borders and Shading dialogue box.

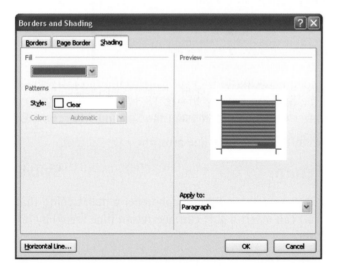

○ Choose a Blue shade to go behind your heading by selecting it from the Fill box palette, and click OK.

○ When you are happy with your poster, save it as Coffee.docx and print it.

○ Close your document.

## Automatic hyphenation                              Syllabus 3.3.1.6

If a word is too long to fit on the end of a line, by default Microsoft Word moves the word to the beginning of the next line instead of hyphenating it. However, you can turn on automatic hyphenation from the Page Setup group on the Page Layout ribbon by clicking the Hyphenation button and then selecting Automatic.

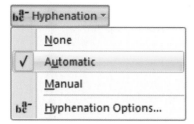

Hyphenation is useful to eliminate gaps in justified text or to maintain even line lengths in very narrow columns of text.

You can turn off automatic hyphenation by clicking the None on the same menu.

## Exercise

This exercise develops the poster that you began at the end of the previous chapter.

1. Open the file Poster.docx and change the page orientation to Landscape.

2. Insert and centrally align a heading Going on holiday? in Comic Sans MS, size 24, bold.

3. Colour the text and shade the title in colours of your choice.

4. Change the remainder of the text to Comic Sans MS, size 16, single line-spaced.

5. Add eye-catching bullets to the list of security measures.

6. Insert paragraph spacing before and after the list and between each bullet point.

7. Add the following text on a new line after the existing text.

   For more advice contact Darksham Police station on 01543 587435 or talk to one of your local Home Watch co-ordinators:

8. Change the font size of the new text to 14, and increase the line spacing before and after it.

9. Set up custom tab stops at 3.5 cm and 11 cm. Select leader dots for the second tab stop. Enter the following details:

   Stanley Smith        01543 723433
   Samir Dall           01543 423788
   John Ruddick         01543 672345

10. Insert a decorative border around the page.

11. Adjust the paragraph spacing if needed so that the poster fits neatly on the page.

12. Save your work. Your poster will look similar to that shown on the next page.

**Going on holiday?**

Make your house look as though someone is living there:

❖ Install automated / programmable light switches.

❖ Ask a neighbour to regularly clear your letter box and doorstep.

❖ Ask a neighbour to park on your drive.

❖ Cancel regular deliveries.

Do not advertise that you are going away and do not show your address on your luggage for the outward journey.

For more advice contact Darksham Police station on 01543 587435 or talk to one of your local Home Watch co-ordinators:

Stanley Smith ...............................01543 723433
Samir Dall ....................................01543 423788
John Ruddick................................01543 672345

## Ask yourself

❓ Do I know what the different tabs are and what they are used for?

❓ Can I set tabs for different purposes?

❓ Do I know what non-printing characters are and how you can view them?

❓ Can I add borders and shading to different document features?

❓ Can I create bullet and number lists, and do I know why they might be used?

❓ Do I know how to set up pages sizes, margins and page orientation?

❓ Can I change paragraph spacing?

❓ Can I indent paragraphs?

❓ Can I change the hyphenation settings for a document?

In this chapter you should have created and saved the following files:

Coffee.docx          Poster.docx          Price List.docx

In this chapter you have been introduced to the following buttons:

Borders, Bullets and Numbering in the Paragraph group on the Home ribbon

Hyphenation, Margins, Orientation and Size in the Page Setup group on the Page Layout ribbon

# Using Tables

In this chapter you will find out:

- ❶ how to add a table to a document
- ❶ how to select table cells
- ❶ how to change row height and column width
- ❶ how to merge cells
- ❶ how to format a table and its contents
- ❶ how to add and delete rows and columns
- ❶ how to sort text in a table.

In this chapter, you will insert a table into a document and type out a timetable or itinerary like the one shown below.

## Programme for Winter Sports Holiday

|  | Monday | Tuesday | Wednesday | Thursday | Friday | Saturday |
|---|---|---|---|---|---|---|
| 10-12 | Snowboarding | Snowboarding | Beginners Skiing | Snowboarding | Snowboarding | Beginners Skiing |
| 12-2 | LUNCH BREAK | | | | | |
| 2-4 | Beginners Skiing | Tobogganing | Experienced Skiing | Skidoo | Tobogganing | Experienced Skiing |
| 4-6 | Experienced Skiing | Skidoo | Ice Skating | Skidoo | Tobogganing | Snowboarding |
| 6-8 | DINNER | | | | | |
| 8-late | Apres-Ski | Karaoke | Late-night Skiing | Apres-Ski | Ice Skating | Leaving Party |

## Ribbon groups used in this chapter

In this chapter you will use this button in the Tables group on the Insert ribbon:

these buttons and features in the Table, Cell Size, Merge, Rows & Columns, Data and Alignment groups on the Table Tools Layout ribbon:

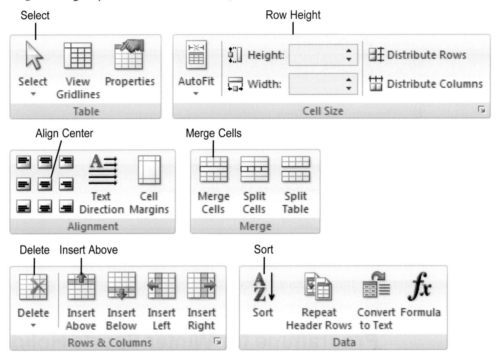

and these buttons in the Table Styles group on the Table Tools Design ribbon:

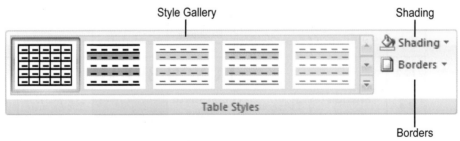

- ○ Begin by opening a new document.

- ○ Type the heading **Programme for Winter Sports Holiday.**

- ○ Make the heading **Arial**, size **20**, **Bold** and **Center-aligned**.

- ○ Press **Enter** twice and change the font back to **Times New Roman**, size **10**, left aligned and not bold.

- ○ Save the files as **Winter Hols.docx** and remember to save it often as you work on it.

## Inserting a table

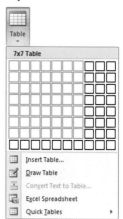

> ◗ Click the Table button in the Tables group on the Insert ribbon to display a menu of table options.

> ◗ Move the mouse pointer over the grid of squares, then click when you have dragged out a 7 × 7 table.

**Tip:**

> If you want a table greater than 10 × 8 cells, or want to set other table attributes, then click **Insert Table...** on the menu and set your requirements in the **Insert Table** dialogue box that is displayed.

A table will be inserted into your document like this:

| Programme for Winter Sports Holiday | | | | | | |
|---|---|---|---|---|---|---|
| | | | | | | |
| | | | | | | |
| | | | | | | |
| | | | | | | |
| | | | | | | |

> ◗ The cursor will be flashing in the first cell, which is the rectangle at the top left-hand corner of the table.

> ◗ The first cell is going to remain blank. Press the Tab key to move one cell to the right.

> ◗ Type Monday and then tab to the next cell.

> ◗ Type Tuesday, Wednesday etc. in the cells across the top row.

> ◗ Press the Tab key to go to the first cell of the second row.

> ◗ Now fill in the rest of the programme so that it looks like the one below.

## Programme for Winter Sports Holiday

| | Monday | Tuesday | Wednesday | Thursday | Friday | Saturday |
|---|---|---|---|---|---|---|
| 10-12 | Snowboarding | Snowboarding | Beginners Skiing | Snowboarding | Snowboarding | Beginners Skiing |
| 12-2 | LUNCH BREAK | | | | | |
| 2-4 | Beginners Skiing | Tobogganing | Experienced Skiing | Skidoo | Tobogganing | Experienced Skiing |
| 4-6 | Experienced Skiing | Skidoo | Ice Skating | Skidoo | Tobogganing | Snowboarding |
| 6-8 | DINNER | | | | | |
| 8-late | Apres-Ski | Karaoke | Late-night Skiing | Apres-Ski | Ice Skating | Leaving Party |

## Selecting cells                                    Syllabus 3.4.1.3

When you want to change the format of one or more cells, for example to change the font or shading, you first have to select the cells to change. Here are some of the ways of selecting cells:

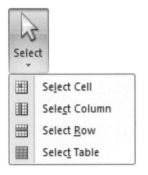

ⓘ   To select a cell, column, row or the entire table, click the I-beam cursor in the cell, column, row or anywhere in the table, respectively. Click Select in the Table group on the Table Tools Layout ribbon, and click the relevant option on the menu.

ⓘ   To select a row, click next to the row in the left margin.

ⓘ   To select a column, move the I-beam cursor above the column till it turns into a black down-arrow, then click.

ⓘ   To select a cell, move the I-beam cursor to the left of the cell until it turns into a right up-slanting black arrow, then click (or simply triple-click in the cell).

ⓘ   You can also select cells by dragging the I-beam cursor across them while you click the left button on the mouse.

**Tip:**

You may have noticed a small four-pointed arrow in a box over the top left-hand corner of your table. By clicking on it you can select the whole table. This is quicker and more convenient than using the ribbon.

## Modifying row height/column width precisely        Syllabus 3.4.2.1

The programme looks rather cramped. It would look better if it was more spread out.

▶   Select the whole table.

▶   Set the row height to 1 cm using the Height: box in the Cell Size group on the Table Tools Layout ribbon.

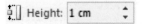

You can set column widths in the same way by using the Width: box in the same group.

▶   Click the Align Center button ▤ in the Alignment group on the Table Tools Layout ribbon to align text centrally in all the cells both vertically and horizontally.

## Merging cells in a table

If you look at your programme, you will see that the breaks for lunch and dinner occur at the same time every day. You are able to spread the words LUNCH BREAK and DINNER across several cells to make your table look more balanced.

- ▶ Drag across the row of cells for the LUNCH BREAK period.
- ▶ Click Merge Cells in the Merge group on the Table Tools Layout ribbon.
- ▶ Increase the font size to 20 pt and make it bold.
- ▶ Repeat this process for the DINNER period of your table.

## Formatting text in cells

You have already centred all the text in the cells.

- ▶ Select the top row and click the Bold button to make the heading row stand out.
- ▶ Do the same for the first column of times.

## Shading                                        Syllabus 3.4.2.3

You can shade any of the cells in the table.

- ▶ Click in the left margin beside the top row to select it.
- ▶ Click the Shading button ⟨Shading ▾⟩ in the Table Styles group on the Table Tools Design ribbon.
- ▶ Click a light red colour on the colour palette then click OK.
- ▶ Select and shade the Skidoo cells green.

Tip:

> The **Style Gallery** in the **Table Styles** group on the **Table Tools Design** ribbon provides many preset table styles for you to choose from.

## Changing cell borders                          Syllabus 3.4.2.2

You can set the borders of any cell, or the whole table, to a specified width and style.

- ▶ Click anywhere in the table.
- ▶ Click the Borders button ⟨Borders ▾⟩ in the Table Styles group on the Table Tools Design ribbon, and select Borders and Shading... from the menu that is displayed.
- ▶ The Borders and Shading dialogue box shown on the next page appears. Click the Borders tab.
- ▶ Make sure Setting: is set to All. Scroll down the styles in the Style box to select a different style or leave the style as it is. Change the width to 1 pt. Notice that this border style in the Apply to: box is set to Table.

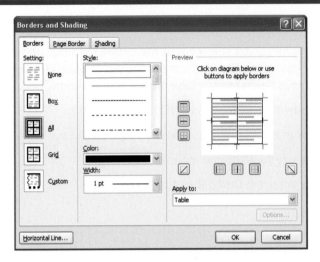

**Tip:**

Notice that you can change the colour of the borders in this dialogue box by clicking the down-arrow in the **Color:** box and selecting a colour.

▶ Click OK.

**Tip:**

You can also directly apply borders using the options on the **Borders** button on the ribbon, however you will need to use dialogue box to set colours and widths.

## Inserting and deleting rows and columns          Syllabus 3.4.1.4

Suppose you want to insert an extra row above the row for 2–4.

▶ Click anywhere in the row for 2–4, then click the Insert Above button in the Rows & Columns group on the Table Tools Layout ribbon.

▶ Delete the row again by clicking the Delete button in the Rows & Columns group on the Table Tools Layout ribbon, and then choosing Delete Rows from the menu.

If you want to insert an extra row at the end of a table, click in the very last cell (at the bottom right of the table) and press the Tab key. You can delete this row again if you wish.

You can use the Rows & Columns group buttons in a similar way to insert rows below a selected row, insert columns to the left or right of a selected column, or delete them.

## Changing row height/column width with the mouse  Syllabus 3.4.2.1

On page 154 you learnt how to set row heights and column widths precisely. If you are not worried about exact dimensions, you can change these properties by using the mouse to drag the cell borders.

▶ To change the width of a column, put the pointer over one of the boundary lines separating the cells. When the pointer changes to a double-headed arrow, you can drag the boundary line either way to make the column wider or narrower.

| | Monday |
|---|---|
| 10-12 | Snowboarding |
| 12-2 | |
| 2-4 | Beginners |

▶ Save your document, and preview it before printing it.

## Sorting table data

Now create a new table with 2 columns and 10 rows. Fill it in with the information below from a garden bird survey. Do not worry about formatting it (unless you want the practice) and save it as Garden Birds.docx.

| Bird | Number seen in 1 hour |
|---|---|
| Blackbird | 2 |
| Blue tit | 20 |
| Chaffinch | 11 |
| Dunnock | 3 |
| Great tit | 14 |
| House sparrow | 4 |
| Robin | 2 |
| Siskin | 4 |
| Song thrush | 0 |

The person who watched the birds listed them in alphabetical order to make it easier to tick them off as they were counted. However, you now want to see the birds listed in numerical order, with the most seen in the top row and the least seen in the bottom row.

▶ Select the table and click the Sort button in the Data group on the Table Tools Layout ribbon to display the Sort dialogue box.

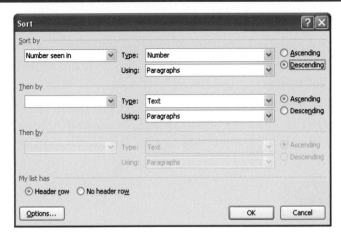

● You want to list the data sorted by the number of birds seen, so change the Sort by box to Number seen in and change the Type: box to Number (if it does not do this automatically.

● Finally, you want the highest number seen at the top of the list, so click Descending to make the number order decrease as you go down the rows.

● Click OK, to reorder the table and save the changes.

## Exercise

You have been asked to produce a programme of events for an agricultural show.

1.   In a new Word document create a table with 3 columns and 12 rows.

2.   Enter the following information:

| Barksfield Show 2008 | | |
|---|---|---|
| Day 1 – Wed 28 May | | |
| Time | Event | Venue |
| 9 am | Judging – Dairy goats | President's ring |
| 9 am | Judging – Flower arranging | Main marquee |
| 10 am | Competition – Horse shoeing | Heavy horse arena |
| 10 am | Demonstration – Sheep shearing | Sheep ring |
| Noon | Demonstration – Birds of prey | President's ring |
| Noon | Competition – Sheepdogs | Sheep ring |
| 3 pm | Judging – Commercial pigs | Ring 9 |
| 3 pm | Exhibition – Rare breeds | Cattle ring |
| 3 pm | Exhibition – Vintage tractors | President's ring |

3.   Sort the data by venue Z to A. (Make sure you do not include the top three rows in your selection).

4.   Make the heading in the first cell Arial size 20, bold and dark green.

5.  Merge and centre the cells in the top row.

6.  Make the remaining text in the table Arial, size 12. Adjust the column widths to fit the text on single lines.

7.  Insert blank rows to separate the different venues.

8.  Insert line spacing of 3 pt Before and 3 pt After in all cells.

9.  Embolden, merge and shade cells as shown in the finished programme below which shows the events listed by venue.

| Barksfield Show 2008 | | |
|---|---|---|
| Day 1 – Wed 28 May | | |
| **Time** | **Event** | **Venue** |
| | | |
| 10 am | Demonstration – Sheep shearing | Sheep ring |
| Noon | Competition – Sheepdogs | Sheep ring |
| | | |
| 3 pm | Judging – Commercial pigs | Ring 9 |
| | | |
| 9 am | Judging – Dairy goats | President's ring |
| Noon | Demonstration – Birds of prey | President's ring |
| 3 pm | Exhibition – Vintage tractors | President's ring |
| | | |
| 9 am | Judging – Flower arranging | Main marquee |
| | | |
| 10 am | Competition – Horse shoeing | Heavy horse arena |
| | | |
| 3 pm | Exhibition – Rare breeds | Cattle ring |

10. Save the document as Programme.docx.

## Ask yourself

❷ Can I create a new table?

❷ Do I know how to select cells, rows, columns and whole tables?

❷ Can I change table row heights and table column widths?

❷ Do I know how to merge table cells?

❷ Can I format table cells and the text within a table?

❷ Can I sort data on a single criterion?

In this chapter you should have created and saved the following files:
Garden Birds.docx
Programme.docx
Winter Hols.docx

In this chapter you have been introduced to the following buttons and features:

Table in the Tables group on the Insert ribbon

Select in the Table group on the Table Tools Layout ribbon
Row Height in the Cell Size group on the Table Tools Layout ribbon
Align Center in the Alignment group on the Table Tools Layout ribbon
Merge Cells in the Merge group on the Table Tools Layout ribbon
Delete and Insert Above in the Rows & Columns group on the Table Tools Layout ribbon
Sort in the Data group on the Table Tools Layout ribbon

Borders, Shading and the table Style Gallery in the Table Styles group on the Table Tools Design ribbon

# Headers, Footers and Objects

In this chapter you will find out:

- ❶ about headers and footers, and how to add them to a document
- ❶ how to insert a page break
- ❶ how to change the screen view by zooming in and out
- ❶ about the different display modes in Microsoft Word
- ❶ about objects, such as graphics and charts, and how to manipulate them
- ❶ how to get help.

## Ribbon groups used in this chapter

In this chapter you will use these buttons in the Header & Footer, Pages, Illustrations and Text groups on the Insert ribbon:

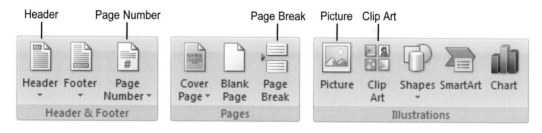

these buttons in the Insert and Close groups on the Header & Footer Tools Design ribbon:

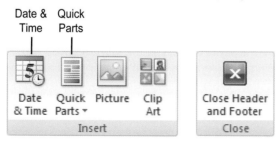

these buttons in the Zoom and Document Views groups on the View ribbon:

and these buttons in the Arrange group on the Picture Tools Format ribbon:

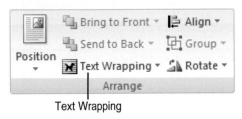

## Headers and footers

In this chapter you will create a report with a header and footer. You will also import a graphic to insert in the report.

Headers and footers are used to display text that is to appear on every page of a document. A header appears at the top of a page and a footer at the bottom. Either may contain information such as the page number, date, author, file name etc.

For this exercise, there is no need to type an enormous amount of text to illustrate the use of headers and footers. You will type only a heading and one or two sentences on each of two pages.

○ Open a new blank document.

○ Type the following text, using Heading 1 style for the headings and Normal style for the text. Save the document as Chairman's Report.docx.

### Letter from the Chairman

This year marks our fortieth anniversary – a milestone of which we can be proud. GEA has come a long way during this time, and the journey has been both challenging and fruitful.

### Our work

All GEA's work has a global impact. Although it is best known for its work protecting endangered species, this is merely a part of what it does.

**Tip:**

Either select the style from the **Style Gallery** in the **Styles** group on the **Home** ribbon before you start typing, or select the text after typing it and apply the style afterwards.

## Inserting a header and footer

Syllabus 3.6.1.5–7

You are going to insert a header that contains the file name and date, and a footer that contains the page number.

○ Click the Header button in the Header & Footer group on the Insert ribbon. A gallery of built-in header styles is displayed. You can choose from the header options to add things like document titles and the date, but here you are going to add the file name and date as fields.

○ Click the Blank (Three Columns) built-in header style.

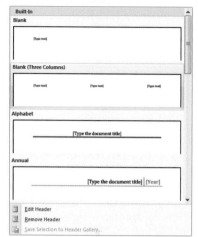

The cursor will be positioned in the header ready for you to enter something, and the text in the rest of the document will appear faded.

○ Click middle of the three [Type text] placement markers, and press the Delete key to remove it.

○ Click the right [Type text] placement marker to select it.

○ Click the Date & Time button in the Insert group of the Header & Footer Tools Design ribbon to display the Date and Time dialogue box which shows a selection of date and time formats.

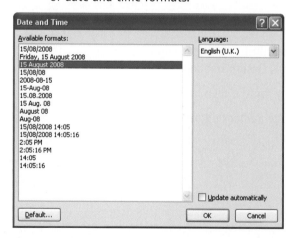

**Tip:**

In this example you have inserted fields in the **[Type text]** placement markers. However, you can show any text you want by typing it in these places.

○ Check the Language: box is set to English (U.K.), select a date-only format, and click OK. Today's date will be automatically inserted.

○ Now click the left [Type text] placement marker to select it.

○ Click the Quick Parts button in the Insert group of the Header & Footer Tools Design ribbon and choose Field... from the menu that is displayed. The Field dialogue box appears.

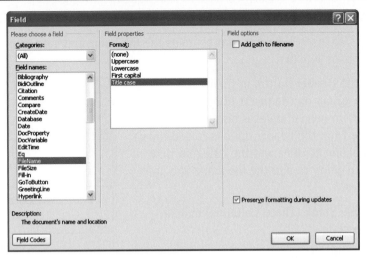

○ Select the field name FileName and the format Title case. Click OK. The filename is automatically inserted.

Your header will look similar to this.

You are now going to add automatic page numbers to the document footer.

○ Click the Page Number button in the Navigation group on either the Insert or the Header & Footer Tools Design ribbon.

○ Select Bottom of Page on the menu of position options.

○ Select the built-in page number option Plain Number 2 to place the page number centrally in the footer.

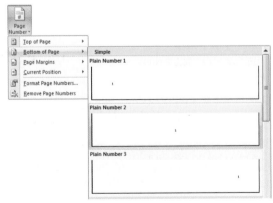

○ Click the Close Header and Footer button in Close group on the Header & Footer Tools Design ribbon.

You can easily format the text in a header or footer. First select the text and then apply the formatting in the usual way.

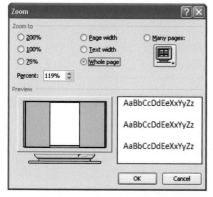

> Save the document.

## Inserting a page break                                    Syllabus 3.6.1.3–4

At the moment, the document comprises only one page so you cannot see the headers and footers repeating. The second paragraph of the Chairman's report needs to be on a new page. You could repeatedly press the Return key to move the paragraph down, but it is good practice to insert a page break to 'force' the text onto a new page. This means that if any new text is added to the first page, the text on the second page is not moved down.

> Click just before the second heading, and then click the Page Break button in the Pages group on the Insert ribbon.

You can also insert a page break by clicking where you want the break, then holding down Ctrl while you press Enter.

> **Tip:**
>
> Click **Show/Hide ¶** to display the page break in the document. If you want to delete the page break, simply position the insertion point before the break and press the **Delete** key.

The footer on the new page shows 2 because you have created a second page. The filename and date appear in the header on page 2 exactly the same as on page 1.

## Using the Zoom tool                                        Syllabus 3.1.2.3

You will probably not be able to see the whole page on the screen. You can 'zoom out' using the Zoom tool to display the whole page.

> Click the Zoom button in the Zoom group on the View ribbon to display the Zoom dialogue box.

Here you can set the magnification your document is displayed at. This can be useful when you are working with graphics ... or if your eyesight is poor.

## Changing the page display mode
Syllabus 3.2.1.1

- It can be useful to view your text in a different layout, especially now it is on two pages. Word provides five views in the Document Views group on the View ribbon: Print Layout, Full Screen Reading, Web Layout, Outline and Draft. You have been using the Print Layout view so far in this book.

- Full Screen Reading – This maximises the use of space on your computer's screen by showing the document with all the Word ribbons and ribbon tabs etc. removed.

- Web Layout – This shows the document as it might appear on a website.

- Outline – This shows how the document is organised.

- Draft – This shows the document without headers, footers and margins.

- Look at your document in the different views, then return to the Print Layout view. Save your document.

## Importing objects
Syllabus 3.4.3.1–2

You can place file types into Word that have not been created in Word, for example graphics (including clip art) and charts. These are called objects, and the process of putting them in Word is called importing.

You will now import a graphics file to put in the report. The graphics file is called fishcage.jpg and can be downloaded into your computer from the website at www.payne-gallway.co.uk. See page 93 for instructions on how to do this.

First of all, add a bit more text to the end of your document.

- Type the following text, using style Heading 3 for the heading and Normal for the rest of the text:

> ### Marine Conservation
>
> The goal of our marine programme is to improve nature conservation, resource management and pollution prevention. We work with people whose livelihoods depend on the seas to secure the long-term health of marine ecosystems.

- Make sure you have pressed Enter at the end of the text so that the cursor is on a new line. Press Enter again to leave a blank line.

- Select Picture in the Illustrations group on the Insert ribbon.

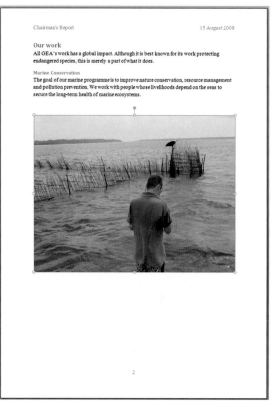

○ Navigate to the picture fishcage.jpg which you downloaded, and select it.

○ Click the Insert button. The graphic will now appear underneath the text (see opposite).

○ Click the graphic to select it. Small circles and squares (called handles) will appear around it.

## Resizing a graphics object                                   Syllabus 3.4.3.4

Once a graphic is selected you can drag any of the corner handles to make it bigger or smaller. If you drag one of the handles in the middle of a side you will change the proportions of the picture and it will appear distorted.

○ Drag the bottom right-hand handle upwards and inwards to make the picture about one quarter the area of the original. (The pointer changes to a diagonal double-headed arrow when you click and hold over a corner handle.)

○ Making sure that the picture is still selected, centre it using the Center button in the Paragraph group of the Home ribbon.

## Moving a graphics object                                     Syllabus 3.4.3.3

When a selected graphic has handles around it, it is embedded in the text. You can move it within the existing text by clicking it and dragging it to a new position. Placing it like this will break up the text as it effectively forms part of it – it is in line with the text. You cannot move it to a location out of the text. (Show the ¶ symbols to see the extent of the area in which you can move the graphic.)

If you want to move it anywhere on the page without breaking up the text, you must change the wrapping style.

○ With the graphic selected, select Text Wrapping in the Arrange group on the Picture Tools Format ribbon, and click Tight from the menu that appears.

You can now drag the picture into the text or anywhere on the page.

◉ Position the graphic to the right of the text. Resize it if necessary.

**Our work**

All <u>GEA</u>'s work has a global impact. Although it is best known for its work protecting endangered species, this is merely a part of what it does.

Marine Conservation

The goal of our marine programme is to improve nature conservation, resource management and pollution prevention. We work with people whose livelihoods depend on the seas to secure the long-term health of marine ecosystems.

## Copying or deleting a graphics object    Syllabus 3.4.3.3/3.4.3.4

Once the image is selected, you can delete it simply by pressing the Delete key. You can also cut or copy it onto the clipboard and then paste it to another part of your document or into another document.

◉ Try copying the graphic to the first page of the document by clicking the Copy button while the graphic is selected. Move to the first page and click the Paste button.

◉ Undo the paste, as you do not need two copies of the image.

◉ Save and close the document.

## Inserting and manipulating other types of object

The techniques for importing and manipulating graphics objects also apply to other types of object. For example, a chart created in Microsoft Excel can be placed in a Word document and moved, resized, copied or deleted in exactly the same way as a picture or image.

In this exercise you will insert a chart from a spreadsheet called Birdschart.xlsx. You can download this from the website www.payne-gallway.co.uk.

◉ Open a new document in Word.

○ Click Object in the Text group on the Insert ribbon, and select Object... from the menu that appears.

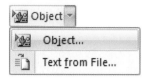

○ The Object dialogue box is displayed.

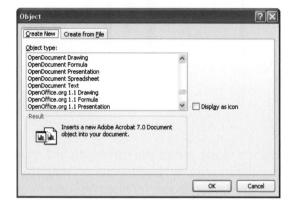

○ You are going to open a file that already exists, so click the Create from File tab.

○ Click the Browse button and navigate to the Birdchart.xls spreadsheet.

○ Click the Insert button.

You now have three options:

ℹ To insert the file as an image – the image is embedded.

ℹ To insert the file so that it is linked to the original – this means that any changes in the original are shown in the imported version by updating it in Word.

ℹ To display the file as an icon rather than an image.

○ Choose the first option (that is, to embed the file by leaving the check boxes unticked). Click OK.

The image of the spreadsheet is imported onto the Word page.

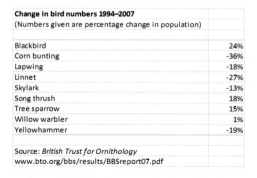

Of course, if you only want to show an image of the chart, then you will have to open the source file (the Excel spreadsheet in this case) and then Copy the chart and Paste it into Word. You have now duplicated the chart between a spreadsheet and a document – it is exactly the same technique that you used to copy a picture or image to another open document.

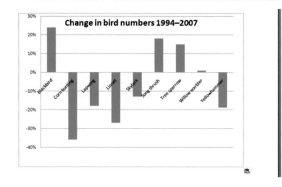

Clip Art is another type of graphics object and so you can import and manipulate these images in similar ways as other objects. You can insert a clip art image by clicking Clip Art in the Illustrations group on the Insert ribbon. Try inserting some suitable clip art images of birds in your document.

⚫ Close the document. You do not need to save it unless you want to keep a copy.

**Tip:**

While you practise inserting objects, you might find it helpful to save the different versions. You can switch between open documents by clicking the open Word file buttons on the taskbar (**Syllabus 3.1.1.5**).

## Getting help                                           Syllabus 3.1.2.2

If you want to perform a particular function and are uncertain how to do it, you can use the Microsoft Office Word Help system. This takes two forms: online and offline, depending on whether or not your computer has Internet access.

⚫ Click the Help icon 🔘 that is located near the top right of the Word screen (or simply press the F1 function key on the keyboard) to open the Word Help window.

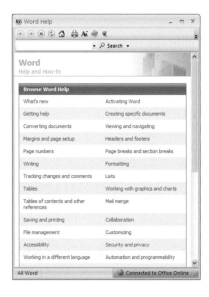

Suppose you want help with inserting a page number.

- Type some appropriate words, such as add a page number in the search text box as shown, and click the Search button to display a list of items about new pages.

> add a page number            ▾  🔎 Search ▾

- Look at the list of results to see if there are any that might help you insert a page number. Insert or remove page numbers is probably the most relevant.

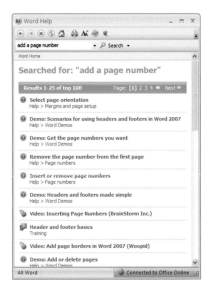

- Click Insert page numbers to display the help instructions.

## Exercise

In this exercise you will develop the programme for the local agricultural show (that you began at the end of the end of the last chapter) into a multi-page document.

1. Open the file Programme.docx.

2. Insert a page break before the table. On this first page enter a large heading Barksfield Show 2008 Programme of Events. Enter a sub-heading in a smaller font Organised by Barksfield Town Council.

3. Insert an appropriate piece of clip art onto this front cover.

4. Add a decorative border to this page.

5. Copy the table (now on page 2) and paste it onto pages 3 and 4 of the document.

6. Edit the contents of the table on the two new pages to show events taking place on days 2 and 3 of the show.

7. Insert a footer (on all pages except page 1) that displays the page number in the centre and the text Barksfield Show 2008 on the right.

8. Save the document as Complete Programme.docx and print.

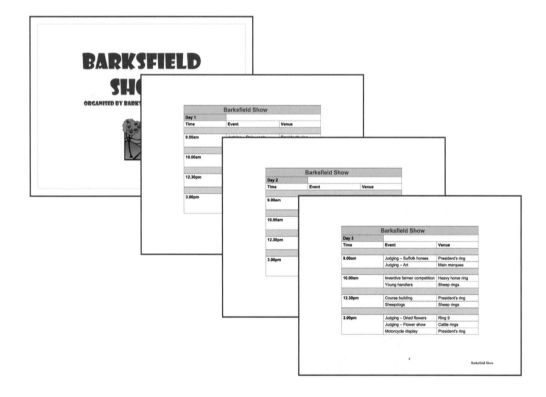

## Ask yourself

❷ Do I know what headers and footers are, and can I add them to a document?

❷ Can I insert a page break into a document?

❷ Do I know what the different views available in Word are for?

❷ Can I insert an object into a document, and then manipulate it?

❷ Do I know where I can get help if I need to?

In this chapter you should have created and saved the following files:
Chairman's Report.docx
Complete Programme.docx

In this chapter you have been introduced to the following buttons and features:

Header and Page Number in the Header & Footer group on the Insert ribbon
Page Break in the Pages group on the Insert ribbon
Picture and Clip Art in the Illustrations group on the Insert ribbon
Object in the Text group on the Insert ribbon

Date & Time and Quick Parts in the Insert group on the Header & Footer Tools Design ribbon
Close Header and Footer in the Close group on the Header & Footer Tools Design ribbon

Text Wrapping in the Arrange group on the Picture Tools Format ribbon

In this chapter you will find out:

- about mail merge in Microsoft Word
- how to create a document for mail merge
- how to set up a list of recipients for mail merge
- how to create mail labels.

Word's mail merge feature is very useful when you want to send the same letter to a number of different people. You can personalise each letter by inserting the correct name, address and other details from a database or other data file.

You will edit the letter that you created in Chapter 11 and prepare a personalised version to send out to several recipients, and also create address labels for the envelopes.

## Ribbon group used in this chapter

In this chapter you will use this button in the Start Mail Merge group on the Mailings ribbon:

Start Mail
Merge

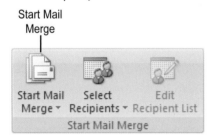

## Creating the letters                                    Syllabus 3.5.1.1–3/3.5.2.1–2

There are six steps involved in setting up a mail merge.

**Step 1:** Selecting the type of document you are working on.

**Step 2:** Setting up and displaying your document.

**Step 3:** Selecting recipients – opening or creating the list of names and addresses to whom the document is being sent.

**Step 4:** Writing or amending your letter for mail merge.

**Step 5:** Previewing the letters.

**Step 6:** Completing the merge.

### Step 1: Selecting the type of document you are working on

▶ Open the letter you created and saved as TanzaniaLetter.docx in Chapter 11.

▶ Select Start Mail Merge in the Start Mail Merge group on the Mailings ribbon, and select Step by Step Mail Merge Wizard... from the menu that appears. The Mail Merge task pane appears on the right of the screen.

▶ Select Letters as the document type you are working with.

▶ Now click Next: Starting document at the bottom of the task pane. This will take you on to Step 2.

### Step 2: Setting up and displaying your document

▶ You already have the letter open that you want to work on, so select Use the current document.

▶ Click Next: Select recipients to move on to Step 3.

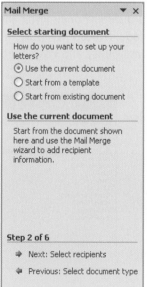

## Step 3: Selecting recipients

You now have the choice of using an existing data file, such as a database table or a spreadsheet, or creating a new list. If you select Use an existing list, you will be able to browse through the files on your computer until you find the file you want to use. The data will appear in a Mail Merge Recipients box exactly as described near the end of this step on page 177.

- You do not currently have any lists or contacts, so you need to create your own. Select the Type a new list option and click Create in the section that appears. The New Address List dialogue box will appear.

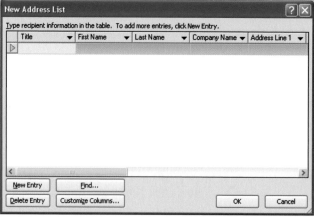

**Tip:**

You can press the Tab key to move from one box to the next.

- Enter a name and address. (You can use the name and address from the letter that you have on-screen if you like, or use a different one.) Enter the postcode of the address in the box that is entitled ZIP Code. (Note: City, State and Zip code are simply the American equivalents of Town, County and Postcode).

You will have left a lot of blank fields in the dialogue box – for example Company Name. You can delete these unneeded boxes from your records.

- Click the Customize Columns... button on the dialogue box. The Customize Address List dialogue box will appear.

- Click the first field name that you do not need – Company Name. With this selected, click the Delete button, then click Yes to confirm. Repeat this for the other field names that you do not need for your address list.

(You might wish to keep Address Line 2 because some addresses may be longer than the one used in this example.) Click OK.

● Now you are back in the New Address List box. Click New Entry and a new address record line will appear. You can now enter the name and address of a second person to whom you want to send the letter.

● Fill in the details for your second person and click New Entry. Repeat this until you have entered 5 or 6 addresses for your list.

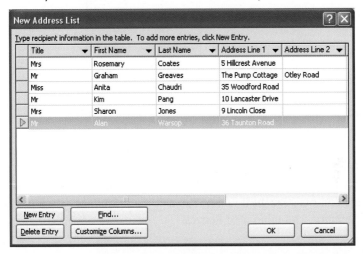

● Click OK when you have finished. The Save Address List dialogue box will appear.

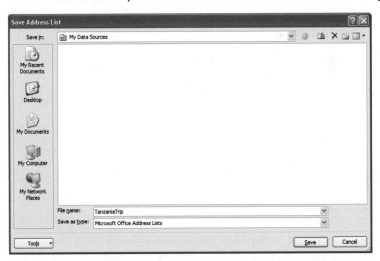

Your address list will automatically be saved as a Microsoft Access database file in the My Data Sources area of your computer.

● Save your address list as TanzaniaTrip.

When you have saved your address list, a further box will appear – the Mail Merge Recipients box. This allows you to view your completed list of names and addresses and make any amendments – for example you may want to arrange them in a particular order, or perhaps change one of the addresses.

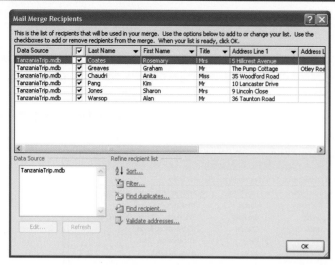

Suppose in the example above you wanted to change Greaves to Reeves.

▶ Select the TanzaniaTrip data source, then click the Edit... button.

▶ The Edit Data Source window that appears is similar to the original New Address List box, except it is now full of the information you stored in it. Now edit the name, changing it to Reeves.

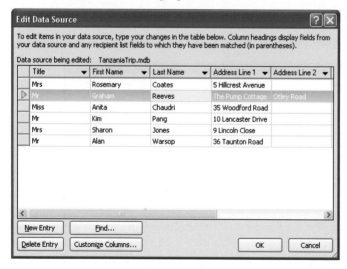

▶ Click OK to return to the Mail Merge Recipients box, in which the amended name now appears. Now click OK and you are ready to move on to Step 4 of your mail merge.

▶ At the bottom of the task pane, click Next: Write your letter.

If at any point you wish to return to a previous step of your mail merge, you can do so by clicking Previous at the bottom of the task pane and it will take you back to the last step that you completed.

◀ Previous: Select recipients

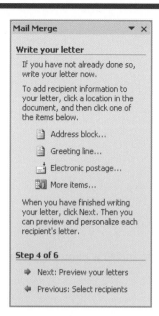

## Step 4: Writing or amending your letter for mail merge

You have already written your letter to Mrs Coates. However, you now want to amend it so you can use the names and addresses you saved in the previous step. Also, you want to add a greeting line so that all of your letters do not say Dear Mrs Coates like the original letter.

▶ In your original letter, delete the name and address you entered beginning Mrs R. Coates and ending with the postcode.

▶ Now click Address Block... on the task pane to display the Insert Address Block dialogue box.

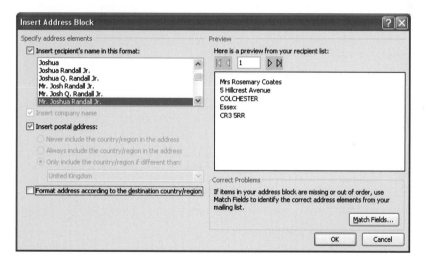

▶ Choose a suitable format for the recipient's name and set the other options as above. Click OK.

▶ The text <<AddressBlock>> is inserted in the document.

You can carry out many of these tasks using buttons in the Mailings ribbon groups; however, it is much easier if you follow the steps through using the Mail Merge Wizard, as you have been doing in this chapter.

▶ Now highlight the first line of the letter – Dear Mrs Coates, – and click Greeting line... on the task pane to open the Greeting Line dialogue box.

> Select the Greeting line format that uses just the first name, and then click OK. The text <<GreetingLine>> is placed in your letter.

The screen should look similar to this:

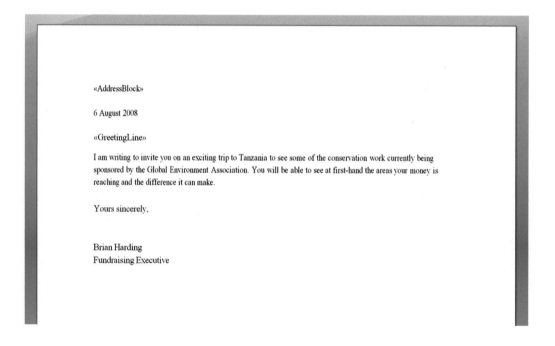

«AddressBlock»

6 August 2008

«GreetingLine»

I am writing to invite you on an exciting trip to Tanzania to see some of the conservation work currently being sponsored by the Global Environment Association. You will be able to see at first-hand the areas your money is reaching and the difference it can make.

Yours sincerely,

Brian Harding
Fundraising Executive

Your mail merge letter is now complete. You can now preview and personalise each recipient's letter.

> Click Next: Preview your letters at the bottom of the task pane.

## Step 5: Previewing your letters

○ You will see the preview of the first of your letters, with the address block and the greeting line inserted as you selected. Click the arrow button to the right of Recipient: 1 to preview the other letters.

○ Click Next: Complete the merge to move on to the last step.

## Step 6: Completing the merge

You are now ready to complete the merge and produce your letters. However, you might first need to edit your individual letters to ensure that everything is correctly placed.

○ If you do need to make changes, click Edit individual letters... .

○ In the Merge to New Document dialogue box select All and click OK.

○ A new document automatically opens containing all your letters. This document will be called Letters1, and you can now scroll down through each letter individually and make any necessary changes.

○ Save the file. You have now completed your mail merge.

○ Click Print... .

## Creating mailing labels
3.5.1.3/3.5.2.2

You can now create the labels to stick on the envelopes. For this, you can use the same name and address data that you have already stored as TanzaniaTrip.mdb and choose to create labels instead of letters.

○ Create a new Blank Document.

○ Select Start Mail Merge in the Start Mail Merge group on the Mailings ribbon, and select Step by Step Mail Merge Wizard... from the menu that appears. The Mail Merge task pane appears on the right of the screen.

○ Select the Labels option before clicking Next: Starting document.

○ With Change document layout selected, click Label options... to open the Label Options dialogue box where you can choose the size of your labels.

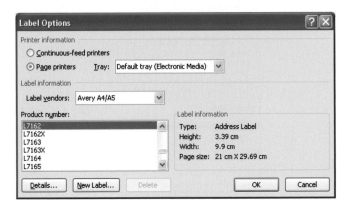

**Tip:**

If you want a specific type of label that does not appear as an option in the dialogue box, you can create your own custom labels by clicking **New Label...** and entering your own specifications.

○ Select your label size from the options shown and click OK. The blank page will be configured as a grid – show hidden characters to see this.

○ Click Next: Select recipients at the bottom of the task pane.

○ You want to use the same list of data that you used previously in setting up your mail merge. With Use an existing list selected, click Browse... to open the Select Data Source dialogue box.

> Select the TanzaniaTrip.mdb file that you created earlier in the chapter and click Open. The Mail Merge Recipients box will open showing the information you saved earlier. Click OK.

> With the insertion point in the first box in your grid, you are ready to begin putting your data onto the labels. Click Next: Arrange your labels at the bottom of the task pane.

When performing the actual mail merge, you inserted an Address block into your letter. This time you are going to insert the data fields manually.

> Click the More items... option to open the Insert Merge Field dialogue box. The dialogue box below will appear:

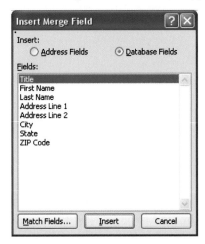

The Insert Merge Fields box presents you with the fields that you had previously saved in your database when performing the mail merge. You want to insert the name and address fields into your labels.

> With Title selected, click Insert to insert the field into the first label. Select and insert, in order, all the other fields. When you have inserted them all, click Close (which once you have inserted the first field replaces the Cancel button in the figure above).

Your fields currently have no spacing between them, so if you tried to preview your labels now they would look like the one below.

> MrsRosemaryCoates5 Hillcrest
> AvenueColchesterEssexCR3 5RR

> The parts of the name should appear spaced on one line, with the other parts of the address on separate lines. Use the space bar and Enter key to layout the label correctly.

> Once you have arranged your data fields correctly, click the Update all labels button [ Update all labels ] on the side bar to ensure that all of your labels have the same format.

○ Now you are ready to preview your labels. Click Next: Preview your labels at the bottom of the task pane. They should look something like this, although you may only see one label at this stage, and the actual layout will depend on which label you chose and the font.

| | |
|---|---|
| Mrs Rosemary Coates<br>5 Hillcrest Avenue<br>COLCHESTER<br>Essex<br>CR3 5RR | Mr Graham Reeves<br>The Pump Cottage<br>Otley Road<br>FRAMLINGTON<br>Suffolk<br>FR6 4ER |
| Miss Anita Chaudri<br>35 Woodford Road<br>WICKFORD<br>Essex<br>CH6 7YL | Mr Kim Pang<br>10 Lancaster Drive<br>BIRMINGHAM<br>BR5 3DN |
| Mrs Sharon Jones<br>9 Lincoln Close<br>LOUGHBOROUGH<br>Leicestershire<br>LE5 8HF | Mr Alan Warsop<br>36 Taunton Road<br>EXETER<br>Devon<br>EX3 1LK |

○ Click Next: Complete the merge to go to the final stage of creating your labels.

○ Now click Edit individual labels… . In the Merge to New Document dialogue box that appears, make sure All is selected before clicking OK. This creates a new document with the names and addresses on. You can now make any changes you think need making before saving the labels.

○ Save your labels as TanzaniaLabels.docx. If you want to print labels, you should make sure that you have the correct label stationery loaded in the printer.

○ You can save the document which contains the label format as Labels.docx.

○ Close both documents.

## Exercise

In this exercise you will create a list of names and addresses to receive the letter created at the end of Chapter 14. You will use the letter produced at the end of that chapter to perform a mail merge.

1.    Open the file Letter.docx.

2.    Delete the addressee details.

3.    Use this letter as your starting document in the mail merge.

4.    Enter a new list of six contacts that are to receive the letter.

5.    Produce the merged letters.

6.    Create mailing labels for the envelopes.

7.    Save and close your work.

## Ask yourself

❓    Can I use mail merge to create a series of documents for several recipients?

❓    Can I create labels using mail merge?

In this chapter you should have created and saved the following files:
Labels.docx
Letter.docx
Letters1.docx
TanzaniaLabels.docx
TanzaniaTrip.mdb

In this chapter you have been introduced to the following button:

Start Mail Merge in the Start Mail Merge group on the Mailings ribbon

# Module 4

## Spreadsheets

In this module you will learn the basic concepts of spreadsheets and how to use a spreadsheet application on a computer. You will learn how to:

- create a spreadsheet
- format a spreadsheet
- edit a spreadsheet
- generate and apply standard formulae and functions
- create graphs and charts
- format graphs and charts
- recognise good practice in creating lists
- recognise good practice in naming worksheets
- recognise good practice in formula creation.

This training, which has been approved by the ECDL Foundation, includes exercise items intended to assist Candidates in their training for an ECDL Certification Programme. These exercises are not ECDL Foundation certification tests. For information about authorised ECDL Test Centres in different national territories, please refer to the ECDL Foundation website at www.ecdl.org

# Module **4**

# Contents

# What is a Spreadsheet?

**In this chapter you will find out:**

- how to run and close Microsoft Excel
- about the Excel screen and how to move around a worksheet
- how to enter and edit data
- how to insert and delete rows and columns
- how to change the screen view by zooming in and out
- about the Excel ribbons and how to minimise/restore them
- how to open, save and close your spreadsheets
- how to change some of the Excel defaults and preferences
- how to get help.

## Getting started

Syllabus 4.1.1.1–2

Spreadsheet software is a very useful and is mainly used for working with numbers. Spreadsheets are used in thousands of different applications which involve doing calculations or drawing charts.

Spreadsheets are often used for planning budgets and working with financial data. Different figures can be entered and the effect of the changes will be calculated automatically.

Microsoft Excel is one of many different spreadsheet packages. In Excel, spreadsheets are referred to as workbooks. Just to make it even more confusing, a workbook can contain several worksheets.

In this chapter you will learn how to move around a worksheet and enter text and numbers.

- Load Microsoft Excel. You can do this in one of two ways:
- *Either* double-click the Excel icon (if it is on your desktop)
- *Or* click Start, All Programs, then click Microsoft Office Excel 2007. (Note: depending on how your computer is set up, you might need to click Start, All Programs, Microsoft Office, Microsoft Office Excel 2007.)

# Module 4 Spreadsheets

## The opening screen

Excel's opening screen will look something like this:

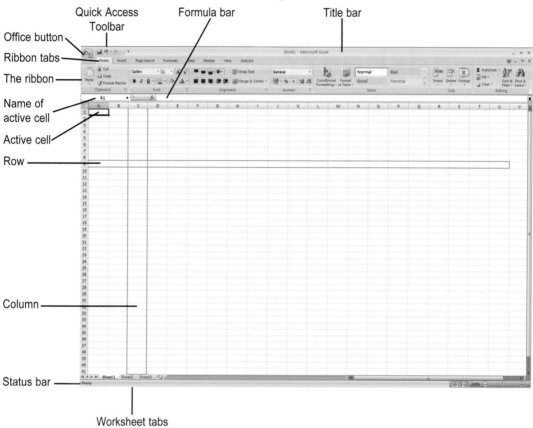

Quick Access Toolbar · Formula bar · Title bar · Office button · Ribbon tabs · The ribbon · Name of active cell · Active cell · Row · Column · Status bar · Worksheet tabs

### Features of the Excel screen

- The Title bar shows the name of your workbook. If you have only just opened Excel or have not yet given your file a name, it will say Book1. It will say Book2 if this is your second file since you started Microsoft Excel in this chapter.

- The Office button has options for you to choose from. You'll be using it when you need to open, close, print or save your workbook.

- The Ribbon is where you can find all the functions you will need to create and edit your workbook. The functions are shown as buttons with pictures called icons. They are grouped by related commands. The functions available on the ribbons can also change according to what you are currently working on. In this way they can be thought of as being context-sensitive toolbars. A ribbon is displayed by selecting its Ribbon tab.

- The grid area represents the worksheet into which you type.

- The Quick Access Toolbar provides some more useful commands.

- Sometimes a context-sensitive task pane is displayed at the side of the screen (not shown in the figure above). This lets you choose further options related to the task in hand.

### More on the worksheet

- A worksheet contains 16,384 columns and 1,048,576 rows – you can see only a few of these on the screen.

- The columns are labelled A, B, C and so on. The rows are labelled 1, 2, 3 etc.

- The worksheet is divided into cells in which you can type a number, a label or a formula. In the example, the address of the active (selected) cell is A1, because it is in column A and row 1.

- A workbook contains several worksheets, initially named Sheet1, Sheet2, Sheet3 etc. These names are on the worksheet tabs.

## Moving around a worksheet

When you open a new workbook, cell A1 is highlighted, showing that it is the active cell. When you start typing, the letters or numbers will appear in this cell.

You can move around the worksheet to make a cell active by:

- moving the cross-shaped cursor using the mouse and clicking the left mouse button in the cell you want

- using one of the arrow keys on the keyboard to go up, down, left or right

- using the Page Up or Page Down keys on the keyboard

- pressing the Tab key on the keyboard.

### Experiment!

- Try moving around the worksheet using the arrow keys and Page Up, Page Down keys.

- Try holding down the Ctrl key while you use any of the arrow keys. What happens?

- What is the name (i.e. address or cell reference) of the very last cell in the worksheet?

- With the active cell somewhere in the middle of the worksheet, try pressing Ctrl+Home. Where does this take you?

## Ribbon group used in this chapter

In this chapter you will use this button in the Zoom group on the View ribbon:

Zoom

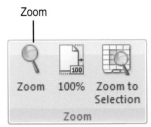

## The Zoom tool
Syllabus 4.1.2.3

You can easily change the size of the worksheet on your screen.

▶ Click the View ribbon tab, and then click the Zoom button in the Zoom group on the View ribbon. The Zoom dialogue box is displayed.

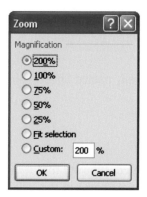

▶ Select a higher percentage to make the sheet bigger or a smaller percentage to make the sheet smaller and view more of the page on the screen.

Tip:

Use the Zoom tool to the right of the Status bar to zoom in or out of a worksheet – click the Zoom level percentage to open the Zoom dialogue box, or draw the slider/click the +/– buttons to change the magnification.

## Minimising and restoring the ribbon
Syllabus 4.1.2.4

Sometimes you might want to increase the working area where you type. You can minimise (hide) the ribbon so only the ribbon tabs are displayed. If the ribbon is minimised, you need to know how to get it back!

▶ Right-click anywhere in the line containing the ribbon tabs, on the Office button, on the Quick Access Toolbar, or on a ribbon group name.

▶ Click Minimize the Ribbon on the shortcut menu that is displayed.

▶ To restore the ribbon, right-click in one of the same places as before to un-tick Minimize the Ribbon on the shortcut menu.

Tip:

Use Ctrl-F1 (i.e. press at the same time the Control key and the F1 key on the keyboard) or double-click a ribbon tab to toggle between minimising and maximising the ribbon. At any time when the ribbon is minimised, simply click a ribbon tab to show the ribbon temporarily when you need it.

## Changing defaults and preferences
Syllabus 4.1.2.1

By default (i.e. unless you tell it otherwise) Excel saves your documents in a folder called My Documents on the C: drive. You can change this default as well as many other preferences.

○ Click the Office button, and then click Excel Options on the window that appears.

You will now be able to change the default directory for opening and saving files. You can also change the user name, the standard font and how many sheets a new workbook should have.

○ Click the Save option.

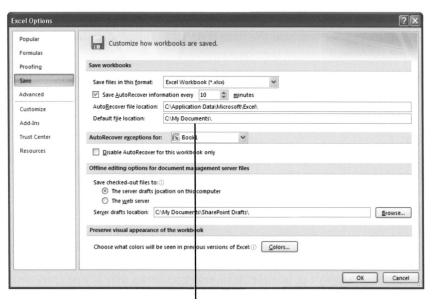

Here you can change the default folder for opening and saving files.

You can also change various other default settings such as how frequently your document is automatically saved.

Clicking Popular on the menu will open a window in which you can change the name of the author of workbooks you write. This name appears in a 'tip' as you hover over a file name in Windows Explorer or when opening a file.

## Getting help                                                    Syllabus 4.1.2.2

If at any time you're unsure of how to do something in Excel, you can search the Microsoft Office Excel Help system. You use this in exactly the same way as the Word help system described on page 170.

## Entering data                                                 Syllabus 4.2.1.1–3

Suppose that you have to produce a list of all the employees in an office along with the number of holiday days they have taken so far this year. The list might look like this:

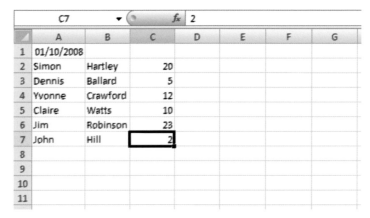

- ▶ Click cell A1 and type the date (e.g. 01/10/08). You will learn how to change the date format later in the chapter.

- ▶ Copy the rest of the list. Do not worry if you make any mistakes because you can correct them easily. Move from active cell to active cell using the techniques you practised on page 191.

Tip:

Notice that when you type data into a cell a ✗ and ✓ symbol appear in the formula bar. You can click ✓ to register the data or click ✗ to clear it.

Tip:

If you start to type another name beginning with, say S in cell A8, Excel will guess that you are going to type Simon again and enter the letters for you. If you were going to type Simon, you can just tab out of the cell or press Enter. If you were going to type Stuart or some other name beginning with S, just carry on typing.

## Good practice when entering data

There are some good practices that you should use when entering data so that you will find it easier to understand your spreadsheet when you use it and so that you don't get unexpected or incorrect results.

ⓘ    It is important to ensure that you have only a single element of data in a cell. This means that you can use the spreadsheet features to process the data. In this example the names are split into forenames and surnames rather than the whole name being in one cell.

ⓘ    Do not leave any blank rows or columns when you enter a data list as this can affect the results of some spreadsheet functions.

ⓘ    It is also a good idea to lay out calculations in a similar way as you would on paper. For example, you should leave a blank row or column before a cell that calculates a total.

ⓘ    Make sure that cells bordering a list are left blank so that it is clear what the list comprises.

## Editing data                                                    Syllabus 4.2.2.1

One name has been spelt wrongly. It should be Clare, not Claire. There are several ways of putting it right.

### First way

▶    Click cell A5 containing the name Claire. You will see that the name appears in the Formula bar, as shown below:

| | A | B | C | D | E | F |
|---|---|---|---|---|---|---|
| 1 | 01/10/2008 | | | | | |
| 2 | Simon | Hartley | 20 | | | |
| 3 | Dennis | Ballard | 5 | | | |
| 4 | Yvonne | Crawford | 12 | | | |
| 5 | Claire | Watts | 10 | | | |
| 6 | Jim | Robinson | 23 | | | |
| 7 | John | Hill | 2 | | | |
| 8 | | | | | | |
| 9 | | | | | | |
| 10 | | | | | | |

A5 — *fx* Claire ——— Formula bar

Click in the Formula bar. Use the arrow keys to move the insertion point between i and r, and then press the Backspace key. You will see that the change is made in cell A5 at the same time as you edit the name in the Formula bar.

▶    Press Enter to register the change.

### Second way

Another way to edit a cell is simply to type over the text in the cell. Suppose Simon's surname is actually Hemmings, not Hartley.

▶ Click cell B2 containing the surname Hartley.

▶ Type Hemmings.

▶ Press Enter.

## Deleting the contents of a cell                    Syllabus 4.2.3.4

To delete the contents of a cell, click the cell and then press the Delete key.

▶ Delete the surname Robinson.

## Inserting and deleting rows and columns           Syllabus 4.3.1.3

You will now delete the whole of row 6 so that no gap is left between Clare's and John's records.

▶ Right-click the row header for row 6 (the row headers are the boxes containing the row numbers to the left of the worksheet – see the figure below).

▶ Click Delete from the shortcut menu which appears.

The entry for John moves up to row 6.

The numbers 1, 2, 3, ... down the side of the worksheet are called the row headers

The letters A, B, C, ... across the top of the worksheet are called the column headers

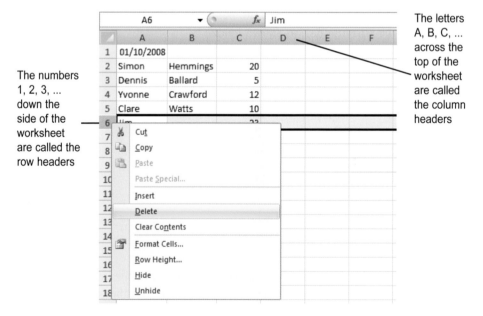

Tip:

You delete columns in a similar way: right-click the column header and select Delete from the shortcut menu.

Now suppose you want to put a heading at the top of the worksheet, above the date. You need to insert a new row.

▶ Right-click the header for row 1.

▶ Select Insert from the shortcut menu. A new row appears.

▶ Select cell A1 and type Holiday Days Taken. Press Enter.

▶ Insert another blank line below the date in the same way.

| | A | B | C | D | E | F |
|---|---|---|---|---|---|---|
| 1 | Holiday Days Taken | | | | | |
| 2 | 01/10/2008 | | | | | |
| 3 | | | | | | |
| 4 | Simon | Hemmings | 20 | | | |
| 5 | Dennis | Ballard | 5 | | | |
| 6 | Yvonne | Crawford | 12 | | | |
| 7 | Clare | Watts | 10 | | | |
| 8 | John | Hill | 2 | | | |
| 9 | | | | | | |
| 10 | | | | | | |

**Tip:**

Insert columns in a similar way: right-click the column header immediately to the right of where you want to insert the new column. Select Insert from the shortcut menu.

 Insert

 Delete

**Tip:**

You can insert rows or columns by clicking the Insert button in the Cells group on the Home ribbon and selecting Insert Sheet Rows or Insert Sheet Columns, respectively, from the menu of options that is displayed.
If you want to delete a row or column, select a cell in the relevant row or column and click the bottom half (i.e. the down-arrow) of the Delete button in the Cells group on the Home ribbon, and select Delete Sheet Rows or Delete Sheet Columns, respectively, from the menu of options that is displayed.

## Saving your work                                              Syllabus 4.1.1.3

 ▶ Click the Office button, and then click Save on the menu that appears.

The Save As dialogue box is displayed. Excel gives your workbook a default name such as Book1.xlsx or Book2.xlsx The name appears in the File name box.

Folder name

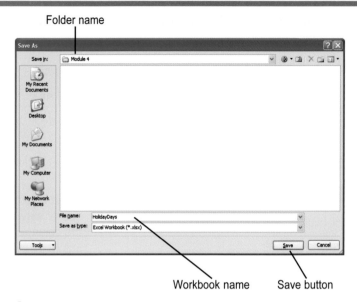

Workbook name     Save button

○ Make sure the folder you want is displayed in the Save in: box, then type the name HolidayDays in the File name: box.

○ Click the Save button to save the workbook.

○ Close the workbook by selecting Close from the Office button menu.

X Exit Excel ─○ Close Excel by clicking the Exit Excel button on the Office button menu.

Tip:

X─── You can close a workbook by clicking the Close icon in the top right of the window.

## Exercise

Suppose you want to find out how much it will cost to host a children's birthday party. You can safely accommodate 20 children. Create a spreadsheet to calculate the cost.

1. Open a Microsoft Excel worksheet and type a main title Cost of Party.

2. In three adjacent cells below the main title enter three headings: Item, Cost and Total Cost, respectively, where Cost is the unit cost for that item and Total Cost is the total cost for that item for all the children attending.

3. Enter the data shown below:

| Item | Cost | Total Cost |
|------|------|------------|
| Catering | 3 | |
| Magician | 60 | |
| Party bag | 1 | |
| Balloons | 10 | |
| Cake | 15 | |

4.  Edit the last two column headings to read as follows:

    Cost (£)                    Total Cost (£)

5.  Insert a blank row after the main title and another after the column headings.

6.  Insert a new column between Item and Cost to show the number of items:

| Number |
|--------|
| 20 |
| 1 |
| 20 |
| 1 |
| 1 |

7.  Save your file as Birthday1 and close Excel.

## Ask yourself

❓   Do I know what spreadsheets are used for?

❓   Can I run and close Microsoft Excel?

❓   Can I minimise and restore the ribbon?

❓   Do I know how to move around within a worksheet and select cells?

❓   Can I create a new worksheet and enter simple data?

❓   Can I edit data in a spreadsheet?

❓   Can I insert and delete rows and columns?

❓   Do I know how to set Excel's defaults and preferences?

❓   Do I know how to get help?

❓   Can I save a worksheet?

In this chapter you should have created and saved the following files:

Birthday1.xlsx                    HolidayDays.xlsx

In this chapter you have been introduced to the following button:

Zoom in the Zoom group on the View ribbon

# 20 Formulae

In this chapter you will find out:

- ❶ how to use formulae in a spreadsheet
- ❶ how to select cells
- ❶ how to format cell contents
- ❶ how to insert a border around cells
- ❶ about standard error values and how to correct them
- ❶ how to format numbers.

## Ribbon groups used in this chapter

In this chapter you will use these buttons in the Font group and in the Number group on the Home ribbon:

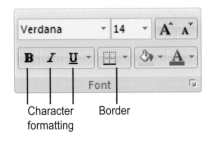

Character    Border
formatting

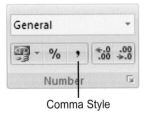

Comma Style

## Using formulae

Formulae are the really useful part of spreadsheets. Excel uses them to perform calculations automatically.

To see how formulae work in Excel, you'll start by doing a page of 'sums'. Excel uses the following arithmetical symbols:

+ add       – subtract       * multiply       / divide       ( ) brackets

Your first task is to set out a worksheet to demonstrate how to use these symbols.

### Project: Create a worksheet to do simple calculations

▷ Open Excel. A new blank workbook will automatically be created.

| | A | B | C | D | E | F | G |
|---|---|---|---|---|---|---|---|
| 1 | ADD | | SUBTRACT | | MULTIPLY | | DIVIDE |
| 2 | 100 | | 100 | | 5 | | 250 |
| 3 | 400 | | 60 | | 6 | | 10 |

▷ Type the text and numbers into the cells as shown above. They will be easy sums.

## Selecting cells                                            Syllabus 4.2.1.4

Before you enter some formulae in the worksheet, you will format the text in certain cells by making it bold or changing the font. To do this the cells first have to be selected. Try these ways to select a range of cells. Selected cells appear highlighted and a new selection replaces a previous one.

ⓘ Click the intersection of the row and column headers to select every cell in the worksheet. The cells appear highlighted.

Click here to
select the whole
worksheet

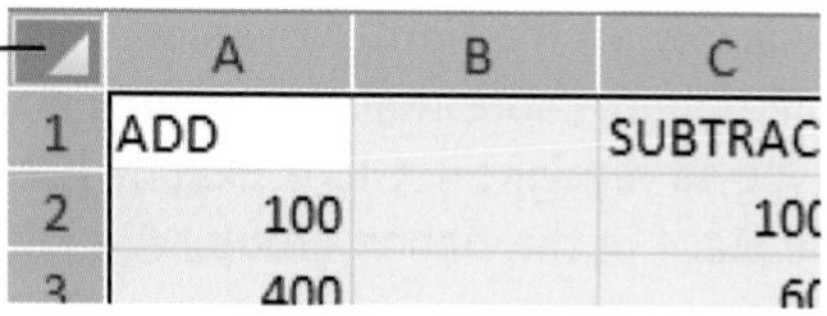

| | A | B | C |
|---|---|---|---|
| 1 | ADD | | SUBTRAC |
| 2 | 100 | | 10( |
| 3 | 400 | | 6( |

ⓘ Click a row or column header to select a row or column, respectively.

ⓘ To select adjacent columns or rows, click the first header and hold down the button while you drag the mouse across adjacent headers.

ⓘ To select a block of cells, click in the first cell and hold down the button while you drag the mouse across adjacent cells. Alternatively, press the Shift key while you click the last cell in the block.

ⓘ To select non-adjacent cells, click the first and then hold down the Ctrl key while you click each of the other cells.

You can use different combinations of these techniques, for example to select non-adjacent columns or to select non-adjacent blocks of cells. Try them out.

## Formatting cell contents                                  Syllabus 4.5.2.2–3

You can format text and numbers in a worksheet by selecting the appropriate cells and then using buttons in the Font group on the Home ribbon.

**B** ─── ⓘ Embolden cell contents using the Bold button.

*I* ─── ⓘ Italicise cell contents using the Italic button.

U̲ ─── ⓘ Underline cell contents using the Underline button.

Try making the headings bold.

◉      Make sure cells A1 to G1 are selected.

◉      Click the Bold button in the Font group on the Home ribbon.

**Tip:**

You can double underline text by clicking the arrow on the right-hand side of the Underline button in the Font group and choosing Double Underline from the menu that is displayed.
The Font group button will now look like this: **D̲** . To change back to single underlining, click the arrow to the right of the Double Underline button and choose Underline from the menu.

## Inserting a border

Syllabus 4.5.3.4

You are now going to add borders to cells A4, C4, E4 and G4 to make them look more like sums.

◉      Click cell A4. Hold down Ctrl while you click each of the other cells listed above to select them.

 ◉      Click the arrow on the right-hand side of the Border button in the Font group on the Home ribbon. (Note that the image on the button displays the last selected border type so it might not look exactly like this. However, it will be located in the same place in the ribbon group.) A menu of border options is displayed.

◉      Click Top and Thick Bottom Border from the menu list.

You are now going to change the colour of the border lines.

◉      Reselect the cells listed above if you have deselected them.

◉      Click the arrow on the right-hand side of the Border button again, and this time choose More Borders... from the menu of border options. The Format Cells dialogue box is displayed with the Border tab selected.

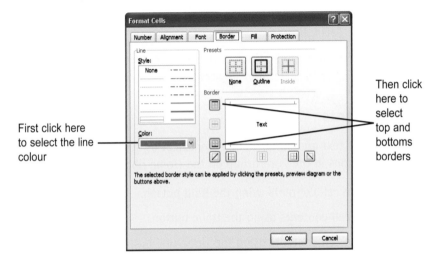

▶ Change the border colour by clicking the down-arrow on the right-hand side of the Color: box and choosing a red colour from the palette displayed.

▶ Click the top and bottom Border boxes as shown in the screenshot.

▶ Click OK.

▶ Click away from the cells and you will see that all the cells you selected now have a top and bottom red border.

|   | A | B | C | D | E | F | G |
|---|---|---|---|---|---|---|---|
| 1 | ADD | | SUBTRACT | | MULTIPLY | | DIVIDE |
| 2 | 100 | | 100 | | 5 | | 250 |
| 3 | 400 | | 60 | | 6 | | 10 |
| 4 | | | | | | | |
| 5 | | | | | | | |

Tip:

The features of the **Format Cells** dialogue box let you format your worksheet cells in many different ways without using the ribbon buttons. You can display the **Format Cells** dialogue box at any time by clicking the **Dialogue Launcher** located on some groups on the **Home** ribbon.

Dialogue Launcher

▶ Before you do any more work, save the workbook, naming it Sums.

Tip:

You can save your workbook by doing any of the following:

ⓘ Click **Save** on the Office button menu.

ⓘ Click the **Save** button 🖫 on the **Quick Access Toolbar**.

ⓘ Press the **Ctrl** and **S** keys at the same time.

If it is the first time you have saved a particular workbook, you can specify the location and file name in the **Save As** dialogue box (see page 197).

If you have already named and saved the file, simply save any changes you might have made by clicking the **Save** button on the **Quick Access Toolbar** or pressing Ctrl+S.

## Entering formulae

Syllabus 4.4.1.1–2

Formulae are entered using cell references. They always start with an equals sign (=).

▶ Click cell A4.

▶ Type = to tell Excel that you are about to enter a formula.

▶ You want to add 100 (in cell A2) to 400 (in cell A3), so type a2+a3 so that the formula appears as shown on below:

| SUM | ▼ | ● ✗ ✓ *fx* | =a2+a3 |

|   | A | B | C | D |
|---|---|---|---|---|
| 1 | ADD | | SUBTRACT | MUl |
| 2 | 100 | | 100 | |
| 3 | 400 | | 60 | |
| 4 | =a2+a3 | | | |
| 5 | | | | |

Note the word 'SUM'. It is the last Excel function that was used. It is likely to show something else on your system. You will meet functions in Chapter 22.

▶ Press Enter. The answer appears!

▶ Type =c2–c3 in cell C4, and press Enter.

▶ Type =e2*e3 in cell E4, and press Enter.

▶ Type =g2/g3 in cell G4, and press Enter.

Tip:
Don't forget to type the equals (=) sign!

Now your worksheet should look like this:

|   | A | B | C | D | E | F | G |
|---|---|---|---|---|---|---|---|
| 1 | ADD | | SUBTRACT | | MULTIPLY | | DIVIDE |
| 2 | 100 | | 100 | | 5 | | 250 |
| 3 | 400 | | 60 | | 6 | | 10 |
| 4 | 500 | | 40 | | 30 | | 25 |
| 5 | | | | | | | |

## Automatic recalculation

You should always apply good practice and use cell references when you use formulae. The great thing about a spreadsheet is that once you have entered the formula, when you change the contents of cells, the answers to formulae will automatically be recalculated.

▶ Change cell A2 to 75. What is the answer now?

## Entering formulae by pointing

Instead of typing in a formula such as =a2+a3 you can use the mouse to point to the cells in the formula.

▶ Restore the worksheet to how it looks on the previous page. Delete all the formulae in row 4.

▶ Type = in cell A4, and then click cell A2.

▶ Type + and then click cell A3.

- ▶ Press Enter.

- ▶ Try entering the other formulae in the same way.

- ▶ When you have finished experimenting, save your workbook.

## Standard error values and correction actions     Syllabus 4.2.2.2/4.4.1.3

- ▶ Delete the contents of cells C2 by selecting the cell and then pressing the Delete key. What is the answer in cell C4?

If you try and make Excel do a formula it cannot calculate, the error #VALUE! will appear.

Another error will occur if you try to divide a number by zero. Whenever Excel returns #DIV/0! as the answer to a formula, it is because it is trying to divide by zero. The answer when you divide anything by zero is infinity so Excel shows the error.

- ▶ Replace the contents of the cell G3 with 0 and click Enter. Now Excel will try and divide 250 by 0.

- ⓘ If you ask Excel to do a calculation on a non-numeric value, it will give the error message #VALUE!.

|   | A | B | C | D | E | F | G |
|---|---|---|---|---|---|---|---|
| 1 | ADD | | SUBTRACT | | MULTIPLY | | DIVIDE |
| 2 | 75 | | | | 5 | | 250 |
| 3 | 400 | | 60 | | 6 | | 0 |
| 4 | 475 | | #VALUE! | | 30 | | #DIV/0! |
| 5 | | | | | | | |

Tip:

You can undo your last action by clicking the **Undo** button and redo an action by clicking the **Redo** button. Both buttons are on the **Quick Access Toolbar**. If the last action cannot be undone or redone, the button will appear faded.

Undo  Redo

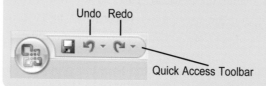

Quick Access Toolbar

Tip:

A Space is a text (non-numeric) character even though it is invisible!

Tip:

Some other standard error values include:

| ##### | This indicates that the cell contents cannot be displayed because the column is too narrow. |
|---|---|
| #NAME? | This is displayed if Excel does not recognise text in a formula. |
| #NUM! | This is displayed if invalid numeric values are used in a formula. |
| #REF! | This is displayed if a cell referred to in a formula has been deleted. |

## Formatting numbers

Notice that when you type data starting with a letter it is automatically left-justified in a cell. Numeric data on the other hand is automatically right-justified.

Numbers can be formatted in several ways. For example it is sometimes neater to have a comma to indicate thousands: 1,532,000 is easier to read than 1532000.

You'll format the cells in this spreadsheet to do this.

▶ Click cell A2 and drag across to cell G4. Right-click the selection and select Format Cells... from the shortcut menu to open the Format Cells dialogue box.

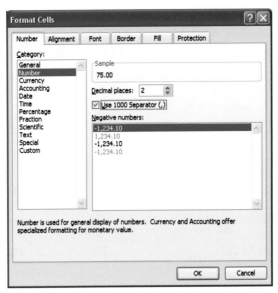

▶ Click the Number tab and select Number from the Category: list.

▶ Click the checkbox for Use 1000 Separator (,).

▶ Click OK. Try entering a value greater than 1000 to see how it is displayed.

▶ Save and close the Sums workbook.

Tip:
You can also use the **Comma Style** button in the **Number** group on the **Home** ribbon to format numbers with a thousand separator.

Tip:
You can also use the features in the **Format Cells** dialogue box to format numbers as currency or percentage if you do not use the ribbon buttons.

Tip:
You can use the **Decimal places:** box to set how many decimal places numbers are displayed to.

## Exercise

In the exercise at the end of Chapter 19 you entered the costs for a children's birthday party. You will now perform some calculations on the data and format the spreadsheet.

1. Open the file Birthday1.xlsx. Your spreadsheet should look similar to this:

| | A | B | C | D |
|---|---|---|---|---|
| 1 | Cost of Party | | | |
| 2 | | | | |
| 3 | Item | Number | Cost (£) | Total Cost (£) |
| 4 | | | | |
| 5 | Catering | 20 | 3 | |
| 6 | Magician | 1 | 60 | |
| 7 | Party Bag | 20 | 1 | |
| 8 | Balloons | 1 | 10 | |
| 9 | Cake | 1 | 15 | |
| 10 | | | | |

2. Make the main title in row 1 and the column headings in row 3 bold.

3. Format cells C5 to C9 and cells D5 to D11 to two decimal places.

4. In cell D10 create a thick top and bottom border.

5. In cell D5 enter a formula to calculate the total cost for catering (i.e. the number × cost).

6. Insert similar formulae to calculate the total cost for the other items.

7. Enter a label Total in cell C10. Make it bold.

8. In cell D10 insert a formula to find the grand total.

9. In cell C11 enter a label Per child. Make it bold.

10. In cell D11 enter a formula to divide the grand total by 20.

    Your spreadsheet should now look similar to this:

| | A | B | C | D |
|---|---|---|---|---|
| 1 | **Cost of Party** | | | |
| 2 | | | | |
| 3 | **Item** | **Number** | **Cost (£)** | **Total Cost (£)** |
| 4 | | | | |
| 5 | Catering | 20 | 3.00 | 60.00 |
| 6 | Magician | 1 | 60.00 | 60.00 |
| 7 | Party Bag | 20 | 1.00 | 20.00 |
| 8 | Balloons | 1 | 10.00 | 10.00 |
| 9 | Cake | 1 | 15.00 | 15.00 |
| 10 | | | **Total** | 165.00 |
| 11 | | | **Per child** | 8.25 |
| 12 | | | | |

11. Save the file as Birthday2.xlsx.

## Ask yourself

❷     Do I know what an Excel formula is?

❷     Do I know the basic arithmetic symbols used by Excel formulae?

❷     Can I enter a formula in a worksheet cell?

❷     Do I know the different ways to select cells in a worksheet?

❷     Can I apply simple formatting to a worksheet cell?

❷     Can I add borders to a worksheet cell?

❷     Do I know what Excel's standard error values mean?

❷     Can I apply different formats to numbers and do I know what they mean?

In this chapter you should have created and saved the following files:
Birthday2.xlsx
Sums.xlsx

In this chapter you have been introduced to the following buttons:

Bold
Border
Italic
Underline
in the Font group on the Home ribbon

Comma Style
in the Number group on the Home ribbon

# Columns of Data

# CHAPTER 21

In this chapter you will find out:

- how to work with columns of data
- how to change column width
- how to format data as decimals
- how to sum a column of data
- how to insert, delete, select, rename, copy and move worksheets.

## Ribbon groups used in this chapter

In this chapter you will use these buttons in the Number group and in the Editing group on the Home ribbon:

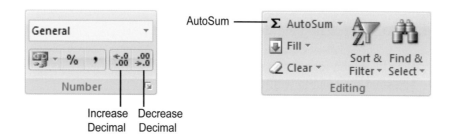

Increase Decimal   Decrease Decimal

AutoSum

### Project: Create a spreadsheet to hold data on baby statistics

You are going to create a spreadsheet to hold data about the weights and lengths of newly born babies on a maternity ward.

○ Open a new Excel workbook.

> **Tip:**
>
> 4.1.1.2 Excel automatically creates a new workbook when you run it. However, if you want to create a new workbook when Excel is already running, click New on the Office button list, and choose Blank Workbook from the Blank and Recent template list. Then click the Create button.

    ◉    Type the title BABY STATISTICS in cell A1. It will overflow the cell, but that's OK. Press Enter.

**B** ──── ◉    Select cell A1 again and make it bold by clicking the Bold button in the Font group on the Home ribbon.

    ◉    Now add the title SOMERVILLE WARD in cell E1. Make it Bold.

## Changing column widths                 Syllabus 4.3.1.4

You can change the width of column A so that the title BABY STATISTICS fits into cell A1.

    ◉    Position the pointer so that it is on the line between column headers A and B. The pointer will change to a double-headed arrow.

    ◉    Press the left mouse button and hold it down while you drag to the right. The column will widen. Make it wide enough to contain the whole title.

Now try a second way of widening a column.

    ◉    Position the pointer between the column headers of columns E and F containing the words SOMERVILLE WARD, so the double-headed arrow appears once again.

    ◉    Double-click the left mouse button. The column automatically widens to fit the heading.

Tip:

This is called **autosizing** the cell width.

    ◉    Now fill in and format the rest of the headings, months and numbers as shown, adjusting the column widths if you need to.

    ◉    Save your workbook, calling it Stats.

| | A | B | C | D | E |
|---|---|---|---|---|---|
| 1 | BABY STATISTICS | | | | SOMERVILLE WARD |
| 2 | | | | | |
| 3 | First name | Surname | Weight (kg) | Length (cm) | |
| 4 | Anthony | Goddard | 3.5 | 50 | |
| 5 | Timothy | Salter | 3 | 47.5 | |
| 6 | Kerry | Meredith | 4.1 | 52.9 | |
| 7 | Deborah | Roberts | 2.9 | 48.8 | |
| 8 | Omar | Iqbal | 4 | 52 | |
| 9 | Victoria | King | 3.3 | 51.6 | |
| 10 | | | | | |
| 11 | TOTAL | | | | |
| 12 | | | | | |
| 13 | AVERAGE | | | | |
| 14 | | | | | |
| 15 | MAXIMUM | | | | |
| 16 | | | | | |
| 17 | MINIMUM | | | | |
| 18 | | | | | |
| 19 | COUNT | | | | |
| 20 | | | | | |
| 21 | | | | | |

## Formatting decimals

Syllabus 4.5.1.1

The measurements would look much better if they were all shown to two decimal places. At the moment, if a measurement is entered as 3.0, Excel automatically shortens this to 3. You were shown one way of doing this on page 206. Here is a quick way that uses a ribbon button.

▷  Select cells C4 to D19 by dragging across them.

▷  Click the Increase Decimal button in the Number group on the Home ribbon once to show another decimal place.

All the measurements should now be shown to two decimal places, as shown in the next screenshot.

|  | A | B | C | D | E |
|---|---|---|---|---|---|
| 1 | BABY STATISTICS |  |  |  | SOMERVILLE WARD |
| 2 |  |  |  |  |  |
| 3 | First name | Surname | Weight (kg) | Length (cm) |  |
| 4 | Anthony | Goddard | 3.50 | 50.00 |  |
| 5 | Timothy | Salter | 3.00 | 47.50 |  |
| 6 | Kerry | Meredith | 4.10 | 52.90 |  |
| 7 | Deborah | Roberts | 2.90 | 48.80 |  |
| 8 | Omar | Iqbal | 4.00 | 52.00 |  |
| 9 | Victoria | King | 3.30 | 51.60 |  |
| 10 |  |  |  |  |  |
| 11 | TOTAL |  |  |  |  |
| 12 |  |  |  |  |  |
| 13 | AVERAGE |  |  |  |  |
| 14 |  |  |  |  |  |
| 15 | MAXIMUM |  |  |  |  |
| 16 |  |  |  |  |  |
| 17 | MINIMUM |  |  |  |  |
| 18 |  |  |  |  |  |
| 19 | COUNT |  |  |  |  |

Tip:

Use the Decrease Decimal button to hide the number of decimal places that are shown.

## Summing a column of numbers

Syllabus 4.4.2.1

You will now add up each of the baby's weights to get the total weight of all the babies on the ward.

▷  Click cell C11 to make it the active cell.

▷  Click the AutoSum button in the Editing group on the Home ribbon.

Excel guesses which cells you want to add up. Your screen will look like the one on the next page.

The text =SUM(C4:C10) appears in cell C11. The = sign shows that the cell is to perform a calculation. SUM is a function. It tells Excel to add all the cells in column C from row 4 to row 10. You will find out more about functions in the next chapter.

You could, of course, type the function rather than use the ribbon button.

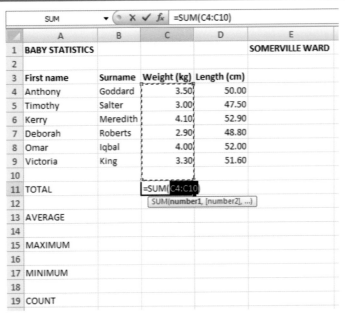

- Press Enter. The answer appears.
- Now find the total Length of all the babies on the ward.
- Save your workbook.

## Selecting and renaming worksheets

Syllabus 4.3.2.1/3–4

You can switch between worksheets by clicking the worksheet tabs.

You will now change the names of the worksheets to something more meaningful than Sheet1, Sheet2 and Sheet3.

Insert Worksheet

- Right-click the Sheet1 sheet tab.
- Select Rename from the shortcut menu that appears. The text on the sheet tab is now selected.

**Tip:**
You can also rename a sheet by double-clicking the sheet tab then typing a new name. Always use a name that is meaningful so you know what the worksheet is for.

- Type Birth Stats. The text will appear on the sheet tab. Just click away from the sheet tab when you have finished typing.
- Repeat this for Sheet2, renaming it Daily Weights.

## Inserting and deleting sheets

▶ To delete Sheet3, right-click the sheet tab then select Delete from the shortcut menu that appears.

▶ Click the Insert Worksheet tab to insert a new sheet.

Tip:

You can insert a new worksheet by clicking the arrow on the **Insert** button in the **Home** ribbon **Cells** group and selecting **Insert Sheet** from the menu of options. The new worksheet is placed immediately to the left of the selected current worksheet as the new current worksheet.

You can delete a selected current worksheet by clicking the arrow on the **Delete** button in the **Home** ribbon **Cells** group and selecting **Delete Sheet** on the menu of options. If you wish to continue, click the **Delete** button on the warning that is displayed.

## Moving and copying a worksheet within a workbook

You can move or copy a worksheet within a workbook. Suppose you want to move the new worksheet (Sheet4) to be the second of the three worksheets in your Stats workbook.

▶ Click the Sheet4 tab and drag and drop it to the new position.

Tip:

Copy a worksheet in a similar way, but press the **Ctrl** key as you drag the tab to its new position. A small **+** will appear on the pointer to show that you are making a copy.

▶ Delete Sheet4.

▶ Save the Stats workbook. You will need it again in the next chapter so you do not need to close it.

Tip:

You can use the **Organize Sheets** options on the **Home** ribbon **Cells** group **Format** button menu to rename, copy or move worksheets.

## Exercise

This exercise continues with the spreadsheet you created at the end of Chapter 20. You have decided that it might be a good idea to hold the party at a theme park so you now need to find out how much it will cost so you can make a comparison. In this case only 10 children can be accommodated because of transport limitations.

1. Open the spreadsheet Birthday2.xlsx.

2. Widen the columns so that everything fits in neatly.

3. Centre the contents of cells A3 to D3. (Use the Center button in the Alignment group of the Home ribbon to do this.)

4. Remove the formula in cell D10 and replace it with a formula using the AutoSum button.

5. Rename the worksheet Home.

6. Make a copy of worksheet Home and rename it Trip.

7. If you need to, move the worksheet Trip before Sheet2.

8. Edit the formula in Trip cell D11 to divide by 10 (there are now only 10 children).

9. Edit the data in columns A, B and C on the Trip worksheet so that it looks like this:

| | A | B | C | D |
|---|---|---|---|---|
| 1 | Cost of Party | | | |
| 2 | | | | |
| 3 | Item | Number | Cost (£) | Total Cost (£) |
| 4 | | | | |
| 5 | Minibus | 1 | 50.00 | 50.00 |
| 6 | Entrance fee | 10 | 10.00 | 100.00 |
| 7 | Lunch | 10 | 4.00 | 40.00 |
| 8 | Drinks | 10 | 2.00 | 20.00 |
| 9 | Cake | 1 | 15.00 | 15.00 |
| 10 | | | Total | 225.00 |
| 11 | | | Per child | 22.50 |

10. Save the spreadsheet as Birthday3.xlsx.

## Ask yourself

❓ Can I change column widths and row heights?

❓ Can I format a cell to show different numbers of decimal places?

❓ Can I find the total of a column or row of numbers?

❓ Can I rename worksheets?

❓ Can I insert new worksheets and delete worksheets?

❓ Can I copy and move worksheets within a workbook?

In this chapter you should have created and saved the following files:
Birthday3.xlsx          Stats.xlsx

In this chapter you have been introduced to the following buttons:
AutoSum                                    in the Editing group on the Home ribbon
Decrease Decimal and Increase Decimal      in the Number group on the Home ribbon

# Functions

In this chapter you will find out:

- ❗ about functions
- ❗ about Excel's SUM, AVERAGE, MIN, MAX, COUNT and ROUND functions, and how to use them
- ❗ how to add a new record into a worksheet
- ❗ how to copy data between worksheets
- ❗ how to automatically fill a series of cells with data
- ❗ how to freeze row and column titles
- ❗ how to switch between open workbooks
- ❗ how to save a spreadsheet as a different file type.

In this chapter you will continue to work on the Stats spreadsheet of baby weights and lengths that you started in the last chapter.

## Ribbon group used in this chapter

In this chapter you will use these buttons in the Clipboard group on the Home ribbon:

Paste — Cut
Copy

and these buttons in the Window group on the View ribbon:

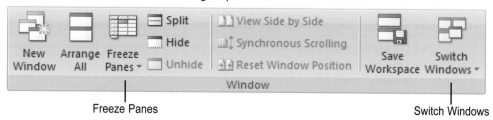

Freeze Panes

Switch Windows

## What is a function?

A function is a pre-defined formula used in a calculation. Excel provides over 300 functions to help with business, scientific and engineering applications. Do not worry, you only need a few of them at this stage!

► Load the workbook Stats that you created in the last chapter, if it is not already open. It should look similar to this.

| | A | B | C | D | E |
|---|---|---|---|---|---|
| 1 | BABY STATISTICS | | | | SOMERVILLE WARD |
| 2 | | | | | |
| 3 | First name | Surname | Weight (kg) | Length (cm) | |
| 4 | Anthony | Goddard | 3.50 | 50.00 | |
| 5 | Timothy | Salter | 3.00 | 47.50 | |
| 6 | Kerry | Meredith | 4.10 | 52.90 | |
| 7 | Deborah | Roberts | 2.90 | 48.80 | |
| 8 | Omar | Iqbal | 4.00 | 52.00 | |
| 9 | Victoria | King | 3.30 | 51.60 | |
| 10 | | | | | |
| 11 | TOTAL | | 20.80 | 302.80 | |
| 12 | | | | | |
| 13 | AVERAGE | | | | |
| 14 | | | | | |
| 15 | MAXIMUM | | | | |
| 16 | | | | | |
| 17 | MINIMUM | | | | |
| 18 | | | | | |
| 19 | COUNT | | | | |
| 20 | | | | | |

## The SUM function

Syllabus 4.4.2.1

You have already used one of Excel's built-in functions – the SUM function (see page 211).

► Click cell C11 or D11 and you will see the function displayed in the Formula bar.

**Σ AutoSum** You entered the SUM function by clicking the AutoSum button. Adding up a row or column of numbers is such a common task in spreadsheet work that this special shortcut button is provided.

You can also enter a function by typing it into the cell.

► Click cell C11 and then press the Delete key to delete the formula in the cell.

► Type =sum( in the cell (including the open bracket).

► Now click cell C4 and hold the left mouse button down while you drag down to cell C10. Notice that Excel is automatically filling in the formula as you do this in both the cell and the Formula bar.

► Type ) to finish the formula.

► Press Enter. Click cell C11 again to see the formula in the Formula bar.

**Tip:**
You don't need to type the closing bracket. Excel will add it when you press Enter.

You'll find out why you included the blank cell C10 on page 219.

Note:

Instead of using the **SUM** function you could have typed a formula =B4+B5+B6+B7+B8+B9+B10.

## The AVERAGE function

Syllabus 4.4.2.1

Using the AVERAGE function is similar to the SUM function.

**Σ AutoSum**—○  Click cell C13 and then click the arrow on the right-hand side of the AutoSum button in the Editing group on the Home ribbon.

○  Select Average from the list that is displayed. Excel tries to guess which cells you want to use, but this time it is wrong!

○  Click cell C4 and drag down to cell C10.

○  Press Enter. The answer, 3.47, appears in the cell.

○  In cell D13, find the average length of all the babies (it should be 50.47).

Notice that although you included seven cells in the range, Excel has calculated the average of only the six cells that contain data. It ignores blank cells.

Tip:

You can type directly into the cell in a similar way as described on the previous page for the **SUM** function. This time, type =average(). You can type any function directly into a cell but some are provided on the **AutoSum** button for quick access.

## The MAX and MIN functions

Syllabus 4.4.2.1

You need to use the MAX function to find the maximum number in a selected range.

**Σ AutoSum**—○  Click cell C15 and then click the arrow on the right-hand side of the AutoSum button in the Editing group on the Home ribbon.

○  Select Max from the list that is displayed. Excel again tries to guess which cells you want to use. You will need to select the cell range yourself so the correct cells are included in the function calculation.

○  Click cell C4 and drag down to cell C10.

○  Press Enter. The answer, 4.10, appears in the cell.

○  Now do the same for the maximum length.

○  Use the MIN function to find the minimum weight and the minimum length.

Your spreadsheet should look similar to that shown on the next page.

| | A | B | C | D | E |
|---|---|---|---|---|---|
| 1 | BABY STATISTICS | | | | SOMERVILLE WARD |
| 2 | | | | | |
| 3 | First name | Surname | Weight (kg) | Length (cm) | |
| 4 | Anthony | Goddard | 3.50 | 50.00 | |
| 5 | Timothy | Salter | 3.00 | 47.50 | |
| 6 | Kerry | Meredith | 4.10 | 52.90 | |
| 7 | Deborah | Roberts | 2.90 | 48.80 | |
| 8 | Omar | Iqbal | 4.00 | 52.00 | |
| 9 | Victoria | King | 3.30 | 51.60 | |
| 10 | | | | | |
| 11 | TOTAL | | 20.80 | 302.80 | |
| 12 | | | | | |
| 13 | AVERAGE | | 3.47 | 50.47 | |
| 14 | | | | | |
| 15 | MAXIMUM | | 4.10 | 52.90 | |
| 16 | | | | | |
| 17 | MINIMUM | | 2.90 | 47.50 | |
| 18 | | | | | |
| 19 | COUNT | | | | |
| 20 | | | | | |

## The COUNT function Syllabus 4.4.2.1

You will need to use the COUNT function to count the number of babies.

▶ You could use the Count Numbers option on the AutoSum button in the Editing group on the Home ribbon, but this time you are going to practise typing the function directly into the cell.

▶ Click cell C19 to select it.

▶ Type =count(. Click cell C4, then drag down to cell C10. Press Enter.

Excel automatically adds the closing bracket for you. The answer 6.00 should appear in the cell. Notice that although you included seven rows in the COUNT formula, Excel has only counted those cells rows that contain a number.

▶ Repeat this for the Length column.

Note:
> COUNT ignores cells that do not contain numerical data. If you want to include all cells (other than blank cells), then use the COUNTA function.

▶ Highlight cells C19 and D19, then click the Decrease Decimal button twice. You can only have whole numbers of babies so you don't need any decimal points!

## The ROUND function Syllabus 4.4.2.1

You have decided that you don't need to know the total weight and length accurately – a rounded figure is sufficient. The ROUND function rounds the value in a cell for you.

▶ Type ROUND in cell A21.

- Type =round(C11,0) in cell C21. This means that the value in cell C11 is rounded to a whole number. You can change the number of digits the number is rounded to by changing the 0 to another number.

- In cell D21, round the total length to the nearest whole number.

## Adding another record

Suppose another baby is born on the ward and his measurements have to be recorded on the worksheet.

- Right-click the row header for row 10 and insert a new row using the shortcut menu that appears (see page 196).

- In the new row, enter the data for Jacob Walton, who weighs 3.7 kg and is 51 cm long.

- Click cell C12 and look at the formula in the Formula bar. It has automatically adjusted to include the new row, which saves you having to change it! Excel has adjusted the other formulae similarly.

### Tip:

When you typed the functions in the worksheet you included row 10. When you insert a new row above row 10 the Sum formula is still correct!

Your worksheet will now look similar to this:

|    | A | B | C | D | E |
|----|---|---|---|---|---|
| 1 | BABY STATISTICS | | | | SOMERVILLE WARD |
| 2 | | | | | |
| 3 | First name | Surname | Weight (kg) | Length (cm) | |
| 4 | Anthony | Goddard | 3.50 | 50.00 | |
| 5 | Timothy | Salter | 3.00 | 47.50 | |
| 6 | Kerry | Meredith | 4.10 | 52.90 | |
| 7 | Deborah | Roberts | 2.90 | 48.80 | |
| 8 | Omar | Iqbal | 4.00 | 52.00 | |
| 9 | Victoria | King | 3.30 | 51.60 | |
| 10 | Jacob | Walton | 3.70 | 51.00 | |
| 11 | | | | | |
| 12 | TOTAL | | 24.50 | 353.80 | |
| 13 | | | | | |
| 14 | AVERAGE | | 3.50 | 50.54 | |
| 15 | | | | | |
| 16 | MAXIMUM | | 4.10 | 52.90 | |
| 17 | | | | | |
| 18 | MINIMUM | | 2.90 | 47.50 | |
| 19 | | | | | |
| 20 | COUNT | | 7 | 7 | |
| 21 | | | | | |
| 22 | ROUND | | 25.00 | 354.00 | |
| 23 | | | | | |

Check the formulae if it looks different. If you had not included row 10 in your formulae originally, the formulae would not have adjusted when you entered a new row. That's because the new row would be outside the range specified in the formulae.

 ◉  Save your spreadsheet.

## Copying data between sheets                                    Syllabus 4.2.3.1/3

On the Daily Weights worksheet you created in the last chapter (on page 212) you want to show the weights of all the babies over the first five days. You can copy the titles and names of all the babies to save us typing them in again.

◉  Make sure the Birth Stats worksheet tab is selected. Select cells A1 to E10.

 ◉  Click Copy in the Clipboard group on the Home ribbon.

◉  Click the Daily Weights worksheet tab to go to the second sheet.

◉  Click cell A1 to make it the active cell.

 ◉  Click Paste in the Clipboard group on the Home ribbon.

◉  Widen the column widths so the data is clear.

◉  In cell C3, type Day 1, replacing the text already there.

◉  Select cells D3 to D10 and press Delete.

Now your worksheet should look similar to this.

|   | A | B | C | D | E |
|---|---|---|---|---|---|
| 1 | BABY STATISTICS | | | | SOMERVILLE WARD |
| 2 | | | | | |
| 3 | First name | Surname | Day 1 | | |
| 4 | Anthony | Goddard | 3.50 | | |
| 5 | Timothy | Salter | 3.00 | | |
| 6 | Kerry | Meredith | 4.10 | | |
| 7 | Deborah | Roberts | 2.90 | | |
| 8 | Omar | Iqbal | 4.00 | | |
| 9 | Victoria | King | 3.30 | | |
| 10 | Jacob | Walton | 3.70 | | |

Tips:

You can copy a single cell or a range of cells within a worksheet and between open workbooks in the same way.

 ❶  To move a single cell or a range of cells within a worksheet, between worksheets or open workbooks use the **Cut** button instead of **Copy**.

❶  To copy or move a row or column, right-click in the relevant row or column header and choose either **Copy** or **Cut** from the shortcut menu. Select the destination row or column and then **Paste**.

## Filling a series

Excel has a very useful feature that allows you to fill automatically a series of cells based on the first or first few cells in the series. You can use it to copy formulae as well. Instead of typing all the other days, Day 2, Day 3 etc. in cells D3 to G3, you can let Excel do it for you.

- ▶ Click cell C3.

- ▶ Click and drag the small black square at the bottom right-hand corner of the cell. This is called the Fill handle. Drag it to cell G3 and release the mouse button. As you drag the handle a small box appears showing the contents of the cells as you auto-fill them. This lets you check that Excel has 'guessed' the series correctly.

| | A | B | C | D | E | F | G | H |
|---|---|---|---|---|---|---|---|---|
| 1 | BABY STATISTICS | | | | SOMERVILLE WARD | | | |
| 2 | | | | | | | | |
| 3 | First name | Surname | Day 1 | | | | | |
| 4 | Anthony | Goddard | 3.50 | | | Day 5 | | + |
| 5 | Timothy | Salter | 3.00 | | | | | |
| 6 | Kerry | Meredith | 4.10 | | | | | |

Your headings should look like this:

| | A | B | C | D | E | F | G |
|---|---|---|---|---|---|---|---|
| 1 | BABY STATISTICS | | | | SOMERVILLE WARD | | |
| 2 | | | | | | | |
| 3 | First name | Surname | Day 1 | Day 2 | Day 3 | Day 4 | Day 5 |
| 4 | Anthony | Goddard | 3.50 | | | | |
| 5 | Timothy | Salter | 3.00 | | | | |

- ▶ Save your workbook.

**Tip:**

> If the first cell is not numeric or part of a series, dragging the **Fill handle** will copy the data rather than increment.

## Freezing row and column titles

In a big spreadsheet, it is useful to have the row and column titles frozen so that no matter where you scroll in the spreadsheet you can see them.

You'll extend the Daily Weight worksheet so you can see how 'freezing' helps.

- ▶ Make Daily Weights the active sheet.

- ▶ Click cell G3. Use the Fill Handle to extend the headings to Day 50.

- ▶ Click cell A11 and type Baby. Use the fill handle to extend to row 63.

- ▶ Type 8 in cell B11, and 9 in cell B12.

- ▶ Select cells B11 and B12. Use the fill handle for this range to extend the number series to 60.

Freeze
Panes ▾

▶ To freeze the row and column titles, place the cursor in the nearest cell to A1 that you do not want frozen. That sounds like a bit of a mouthful! Basically, you need columns A and B frozen, and row 3 frozen. For this you need to make cell C4 the active cell.

▶ Click Freeze Panes in the Window group on the View ribbon, and choose Freeze Panes from the menu that appears. Black lines will appear below the frozen rows 1, 2 and 3 and to the right of the frozen columns A and B.

| | A | B | C | D | E | F | G | H |
|---|---|---|---|---|---|---|---|---|
| 1 | BABY STATISTICS | | | | SOMERVILLE WARD | | | |
| 2 | | | | | | | | |
| 3 | First name | Surname | Day 1 | Day 2 | Day 3 | Day 4 | Day 5 | Day 6 |
| 4 | Anthony | Goddard | 3.50 | | | | | |
| 5 | Timothy | Salter | 3.00 | | | | | |
| 6 | Kerry | Meredith | 4.10 | | | | | |
| 7 | Deborah | Roberts | 2.90 | | | | | |
| 8 | Omar | Iqbal | 4.00 | | | | | |
| 9 | Victoria | King | 3.30 | | | | | |
| 10 | Jacob | Walton | 3.70 | | | | | |
| 11 | Baby | 8 | | | | | | |
| 12 | Baby | 9 | | | | | | |
| 13 | Baby | 10 | | | | | | |
| 14 | Baby | 11 | | | | | | |
| 15 | Baby | 12 | | | | | | |
| 16 | Baby | 13 | | | | | | |
| 17 | Baby | 14 | | | | | | |
| 18 | Baby | 15 | | | | | | |

▶ Scroll across to Day 50. The baby names will stay visible. Freezing panes like this is invaluable for anyone entering data because it means they do not have to scroll left to see which baby was in each row before entering the data.

▶ Now try scrolling down to Baby 50 to see the effect of the frozen column headings.

Tip:

ⓘ To freeze just a column, or several columns, select the column to the right of where you want the split to appear and then select Freeze Panes.

ⓘ To freeze just a row, or several rows, select the row below where you want the split to appear and then select Freeze Panes.

To unfreeze columns and rows, click Freeze Panes in the Window group on the View ribbon, and choose Unfreeze Panes from the menu that appears. It doesn't matter which cell is the active cell. The black lines will disappear.

## Switching between open workbooks                    Syllabus 4.1.1.5

You can open a second workbook in just the same way you did the first (see page 209). It will contain its own worksheets (which are different ones to those in the other open workbooks).

Switch
Windows ▾

ⓘ To switch between workbooks, *either* select Switch Windows in the Window group on the View ribbon, and then choose the workbook you want from the displayed list of open workbooks

ⓘ *or* use the taskbar buttons at the bottom of the desktop.

## Saving as a different file type                                      Syllabus 4.1.1.4

By default, Excel will save your workbooks as .xlsx files, but you can choose from many other file types (some similar to those mentioned for Word on page 100). Some of the other formats specific to spreadsheets are listed here.

ⓘ  Saving a workbook in Text format allows it to be imported easily into spreadsheets from other manufacturers and databases and across operating systems.

ⓘ  You can also save a workbook in formats used by earlier versions of Excel or in a different software format (e.g. Lotus 1-2-3).

ⓘ  Saving a workbook as a template lets you create a file that you can use to keep consistency of design when you use a spreadsheet layout frequently.

◯  To save a file in a format other than the Excel default, click Save As on the Office button menu to display the Save As dialogue box.

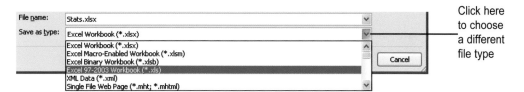

Click here to choose a different file type

◯  Type a name for the file in the File name: box, and choose a folder location for the file, in the same way as you would when saving any file.

◯  Click the down-arrow in the Save as type: box to view all the different file types. Select the one you want, then click the Save button.

◯  Close the Stats workbook.

## Exercise

A local Scout troop has organised a Quiz Night to raise funds. Ten teams have entered and the organisers want a spreadsheet to enter the scores and quickly calculate the winners of particular rounds, the overall champions and the winner of the 'wooden spoon' award. Teams can nominate a Joker round for which they are awarded double points.

1. Enter the following data into a new worksheet and save it as Quiz.xlsx.

| | A | B | C | D | E | F | G | H | I | J | K |
|---|---|---|---|---|---|---|---|---|---|---|---|
| 1 | **QUIZ NIGHT** | | | | | | | | | | |
| 2 | | | | | Round | | | | | | |
| 3 | | 1 | 2 | 3 | 4 | 5 | 6 | | | | |
| 4 | | History | TV | Music | General knowledge | Geography | Film | Joker round | Total points | Joker points | Grand Total |
| 5 | | | | | | | | | | | |
| 6 | Team 1 | 18 | 10 | 15 | 10 | 19 | 16 | 1 | | | |
| 7 | Team 2 | 15 | 8 | 13 | 8 | 17 | 14 | 2 | | | |
| 8 | Team 3 | 8 | 10 | 9 | 12 | 9 | 11 | 2 | | | |
| 9 | Team 4 | 17 | 15 | 14 | 17 | 19 | 18 | 4 | | | |
| 10 | Team 5 | 12 | 15 | 10 | 13 | 10 | 18 | 4 | | | |
| 11 | Team 6 | 7 | 9 | 9 | 9 | 10 | 11 | 4 | | | |
| 12 | Team 7 | 12 | 14 | 13 | 15 | 13 | 16 | 6 | | | |
| 13 | Team 8 | 19 | 17 | 14 | 18 | 13 | 15 | 1 | | | |
| 14 | Team 9 | 12 | 13 | 16 | 17 | 12 | 19 | 6 | | | |
| 15 | Team 10 | 10 | 11 | 15 | 12 | 11 | 12 | 4 | | | |
| 16 | | | | | | | | | | | |
| 17 | Average score | | | | | | | | | Champions | |
| 18 | | | | | | | | | | Wooden spoon | |

2. Insert a formula in cell I6 that uses the SUM function to add up the points that Team 1 has scored over the 6 rounds (excluding extra Joker points).

3. Fill this formula down to cell I15.

4. Team 1 nominate round 1 to play their Joker. Insert a formula in cell J6 that enters the number of extra points for Team 1's Joker round (i.e. contents of cell B6).

5. Enter a similar formula into cells J7 to J15. Note that the teams do not all nominate the same round in which to play their Joker.

6. In cell K6 enter a formula to add up the total points and the Joker points.

7. Fill this fomula down to cell K15.

8. Insert a formula in cell K17 that uses the MAX function to find the highest Grand Total.

9. Insert a formula in cell K18 that uses the MIN function to find the lowest Grand Total.

10. Insert a formula in cell B17 that uses the AVERAGE function to find the average score for round 1.

11. Fill this formula across to cell G17. Were any rounds particularly difficult?

12. Save and Close the workbook.

## Ask yourself

❷ Do I know what a function is?

❷ Do I know what the SUM, AVERAGE, MAX, MIN, COUNT, COUNTA and ROUND functions are used for?

❷ Can I use the functions listed in the previous question?

❷ Can I copy and move single cells and ranges of cells?

❷ Can I copy and move rows and columns?

❷ Can I use auto-fill to create series and copy data/formulae?

❷ Do I know how to freeze rows and columns?

❷ Do I know how to save spreadsheets in different formats?

In this chapter you should have created and saved the following files:
Quiz.xlsx
Stats.xlsx

In this chapter you have been introduced to the following buttons:

Copy
Cut
Paste
in the Clipboard group on the Home ribbon

Freeze Panes
Switch Windows
in the Window group on the View ribbon

# 23 Charts

In this chapter you will find out:

- about displaying data in charts
- how to sort data
- how to draw bar, pie and other charts, and how to change between them
- how to move and size a chart
- how to change the appearance of a chart.

## Ribbon groups used in this chapter

In this chapter you will use this button in the Sort & Filter group on the Data ribbon:

Sort A to Z ———

and these buttons in the Charts group on the Insert ribbon:

Column          Pie

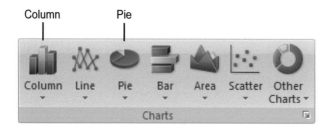

### Project: Draw charts relating to the number of birds in England

Charts are a very good way of presenting information in a way that is easy to grasp immediately. In this chapter you'll look at how the numbers of some birds in the UK have changed as estimated in RSPB reports in 2002 and 2006.

| Bird populations (2002 and 2006) | | |
| --- | --- | --- |
| (Estimated numbers given in millions) | | |
| | 2002 | 2006 |
| Corn bunting | 0.020 | 0.010 |
| Turtle dove | 0.075 | 0.044 |
| Spotted flycatcher | 0.130 | 0.064 |
| Grey partridge | 0.150 | 0.073 |
| Bullfinch | 0.200 | 0.166 |
| Reed bunting | 0.240 | 0.202 |
| Linnet | 0.540 | 0.556 |
| Skylark | 1.000 | 1.785 |
| Song thrush | 1.100 | 1.144 |

*Source: RSPB – The state of the UK's birds 2002 and 2006*
*http://www.rspb.org.uk/Images/State%20of%20UK%20Birds%202002_tcm9-133195.pdf*
*http://www.rspb.org.uk/Images/soukb06_tcm9-167697.pdf*

- Open a new workbook.

- Type the headings and the names of the birds in the survey as shown below:

| | A | B | C | D | E |
| --- | --- | --- | --- | --- | --- |
| 1 | Bird Populations in the UK (2002 and 2006) | | | | |
| 2 | (Estimated numbers given in millions) | | | | |
| 3 | | | | | |
| 4 | | 2002 | 2006 | | |
| 5 | Bullfinch | | | | |
| 6 | Corn bunting | | | | |
| 7 | Grey partridge | | | | |
| 8 | Linnet | | | | |
| 9 | Reed bunting | | | | |
| 10 | Skylark | | | | |
| 11 | Song thrush | | | | |
| 12 | Spotted flycatcher | | | | |
| 13 | Turtle dove | | | | |
| 14 | | | | | |
| 15 | Source: RSPB | | | | |

- Position the pointer between the column headers A and B. Drag to the right to widen column A so it fully contains the names of the birds.

- Click row header 1, and hold down the Ctrl key while you click row headers 4 and 15. This selects all three rows.

- Click the Bold button to make these rows bold.

- Click cell A15 and click the Italic button to make it italic.

- Type the data given in the table at the top of this page.

When you have done that, your worksheet will look similar to the screenshot shown overleaf:

| | A | B | C | D |
|---|---|---|---|---|
| 1 | **Bird Populations in the UK (2002 and 2006)** | | | |
| 2 | (Estimated numbers given in millions) | | | |
| 3 | | | | |
| 4 | | **2002** | **2006** | |
| 5 | Corn bunting | 0.02 | 0.01 | |
| 6 | Turtle dove | 0.075 | 0.044 | |
| 7 | Spotted flycatcher | 0.13 | 0.064 | |
| 8 | Grey partridge | 0.15 | 0.073 | |
| 9 | Bullfinch | 0.2 | 0.166 | |
| 10 | Reed bunting | 0.24 | 0.202 | |
| 11 | Linnet | 0.54 | 0.556 | |
| 12 | Skylark | 1 | 1.785 | |
| 13 | Song thrush | 1.1 | 1.144 | |
| 14 | | | | |
| 15 | *Source: RSPB* | | | |

◉ Save your workbook, naming it Birds.xlsx.

## Sorting data

Syllabus 4.2.2.5

It would be neater if the birds were sorted in alphabetical order.

◉ First you need to select the data you want to sort. Click to select cell A5 and drag to cell C13.

◉ Click the Sort A to Z button in the Sort & Filter group on the Data ribbon.

The rows are sorted in bird alphabetical order.

| | A | B | C | D |
|---|---|---|---|---|
| 1 | **Bird Populations in the UK (2002 and 2006)** | | | |
| 2 | (Estimated numbers given in millions) | | | |
| 3 | | | | |
| 4 | | **2002** | **2006** | |
| 5 | Bullfinch | 0.2 | 0.166 | |
| 6 | Corn bunting | 0.02 | 0.01 | |
| 7 | Grey partridge | 0.15 | 0.073 | |
| 8 | Linnet | 0.54 | 0.556 | |
| 9 | Reed bunting | 0.24 | 0.202 | |
| 10 | Skylark | 1 | 1.785 | |
| 11 | Song thrush | 1.1 | 0.044 | |
| 12 | Spotted flycatcher | 0.13 | 0.064 | |
| 13 | Turtle dove | 0.075 | 0.044 | |
| 14 | | | | |
| 15 | *Source: RSPB* | | | |

◉ Deselect the cells by clicking anywhere on the worksheet.

**Tip:**

You can sort in descending alphabetical order by selecting the **Sort Z to A** option in the **Sort & Filter** group.

You sort numbers in ascending or descending order in a similar way.

## Drawing a bar chart

Now you are going to draw a vertical bar chart to show this data. Excel calls this type of chart a Column chart.

▶ Click A4 and drag diagonally through to C13 to select the cells to be charted.

▶ Click the Column button in the Charts group on the Insert ribbon to display a gallery of column chart options.

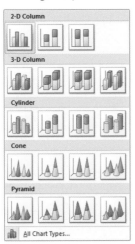

**Tip:**

Click **All Chart Types...** on the chart gallery or click other **Charts** group buttons to explore the different chart types available. You can create bar charts, line charts and pie charts, as well as other types. Pie charts are covered more thoroughly on page 234.

▶ Click the Clustered Column option in the 2–D Column group. The chart is placed on your worksheet.

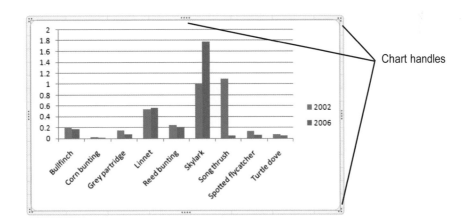

Chart handles

**Note:**

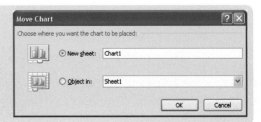

Click the **Move Chart** button in the **Location** group on the **Chart Tools Design** ribbon, and select **New sheet** in the **Move Chart** dialogue box if you want to create the chart on its own without showing the source data.

## Adding a chart title

Syllabus 4.6.2.1

The chart needs a title so anybody looking at it knows what the data shows.

- ⓞ If the chart is not already selected, then click it to select it. A selected chart has a border with handles as shown in the screenshot on the previous page. The Chart Tools ribbon appears.

- ⓞ Click the Chart Tools Layout ribbon tab.

- ⓞ Click the Chart title button in the Labels group, and choose Above Chart from the menu that appears. A chart title placeholder is displayed on the chart as shown below.

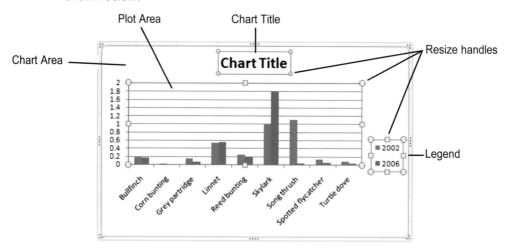

- ⓞ Click in the Chart Title text box and type UK bird populations (2002 and 2006).

**Tip:**

To edit a chart title, click the title placeholder to select it (the resize handles will appear around the text). Then click the text again to position the text insertion point. You can now edit the text.
Delete a selected chart title by pressing the Delete key.

## Moving, sizing and deleting a chart

Syllabus 4.6.1.2/4

You can move the chart so that it is positioned exactly where you want it on a worksheet.

- ⓞ Move the mouse pointer around the selected chart, letting it rest for a few seconds in different places. Notice that a tool tip tells you what each part of the chart is called. Some of these are identified in the screenshot above.

- ⓞ See if you can identify parts of the chart called Chart Area, Plot Area, Horizontal (Category) Axis, Vertical (Value) Axis, Series "2002"..., Series "2006"... .

- ⓞ Click in the Chart Area and drag and drop the chart below the data.

- ⓞ Drag the bottom right-hand corner handle of the chart to resize it.

**Tip:**

To resize a chart without distorting the shape of the graph, press the **Shift** key whilst dragging the handle.

**Tip:**

To delete a chart, first select it, then press the **Delete** key.

## Adding axis titles                                                  Syllabus 4.6.2.5

It would be nice to have a data label on the *y*–axis, to make it clear that the figures are in millions.

▶  If the chart is not already selected, then click it to select it. The Chart Tools ribbon appears.

▶  Click the Chart Tools Layout ribbon tab.

▶  Click the Axis Titles button in the Labels group, and choose Primary Vertical Axis from the menu that appears, and then choose Rotated Title from the sub-menu. An axis title placeholder is displayed on the chart.

**Tip:**

The *x*-axis is self-explanatory in this example; however, you can add a horizontal axis label in a similar way to adding a *y*-axis label by choosing the appropriate option after clicking the **Axis Titles** button.

▶  Click the new axis placeholder to select it, and then click the label text to place the text insertion cursor.

▶  Change the text Axis Title to Millions.

**Tip:**

You can delete an axis title by clicking to select it, then pressing the **Delete** key.

▶  Select the *y*-axis label and right-click it to display a shortcut menu and toolbar.

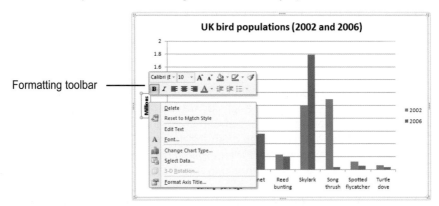

Formatting toolbar

▶  Use the buttons on the Formatting toolbar to change the font size, the text colour and other attributes of the label.

**Tip:**

You can format chart labels (such as the legend, title etc.) in a similar way by using the **Formatting** toolbar that appears when you right-click the chart text.

## Changing the background colour                    Syllabus 4.6.2.3/5

▶ Right-click the Plot Area. If you're not sure which is the Plot Area, just leave the mouse pointer over different parts of the selected chart for a few seconds and a tool tip will tell you.

▶ Select Format Plot Area... from the shortcut menu to open the Format Plot Area window.

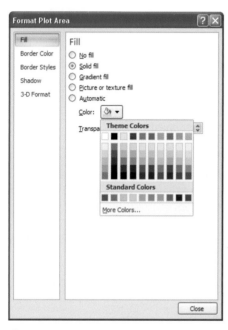

▶ Click Fill in the left-hand pane, and click the Solid fill option.

▶ Click the Color: button and choose a colour from the palette that is displayed.

▶ You can change other formatting options, such as the border style and colour by choosing from the options available in the Format Plot Area window. Try some, and then click Close when you have finished.

**Tip:**

You can change the formatting of other areas of a chart, such as the **Chart Area**, the **Legend** etc. in a similar way to that described above. Simply right-click the feature you want to format and choose the **Format...** option from the shortcut menu. Note that this option changes its name slightly depending on which chart feature you right-clicked, for example it might be shown as **Format Legend...** or **Format Data Series...**. Choosing the **Format...** option displays a **Format...** window similar to the **Format Plot Area** window shown above, where you can select the formatting options you want to use. For example, changing the colour of the columns is described in the next section.

## Changing the colour of the columns                 Syllabus 4.6.2.4

The bird population chart shows two data series. You have to change the colour of the 2002 columns separately from the 2006 series. Start by changing the 2002 series.

Tip:
Don't forget to click **Undo** if you don't like the changes you make!

▶ Rest the mouse pointer over any bar in the 2002 series. A tool tip will appear identifying the bar as Series "2002" followed by the bird name and population number of the particular bar you are on.

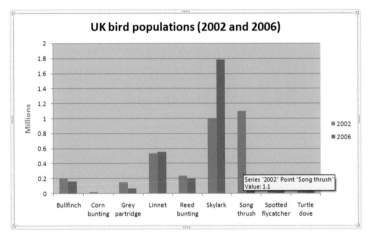

▶ Right-click the bar to show a shortcut menu, and choose Format Data Series... from the options.

The Format Data Series window appears. Here you can change the border around each bar (by selecting from the Border Color and Border Styles options) and the fill colour of the bars (by selecting from the Fill options).

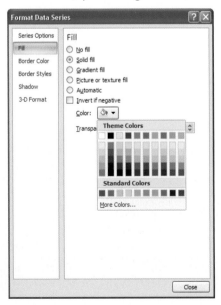

◐ Now repeat this for the 2002 series. Follow exactly the same method, but make sure that you right-click a 2002 series bar to start.

Your chart will now look something like this depending on how you've formatted the different features.

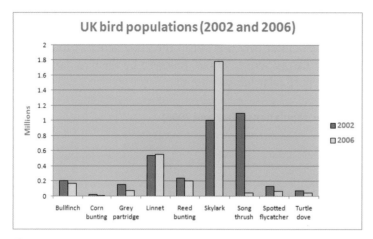

◐ When you are happy with the way the chart looks, save and close your worksheet.

## Creating a pie chart                    Syllabus 4.6.1.1/4.6.2.1–5

You will now use another sheet in the same workbook to enter some data from the RSPB 2007 Garden Bird Watch Survey (www.rspb.org.uk/birdwatch). You will then use this data to practise creating a pie chart.

◐ Make sure the Birds workbook is open.

◐ Click the tab for Sheet2.

◐ Enter the following data and format the title and column headings.

| | A | B |
|---|---|---|
| 1 | 2007 Garden Bird Watch Survey – England | |
| 2 | | |
| 3 | Species | Average per garden |
| 4 | House sparrow | 4.27 |
| 5 | Starling | 3.58 |
| 6 | Blue tit | 2.75 |
| 7 | Blackbird | 2.25 |
| 8 | Woodpigeon | 1.63 |
| 9 | Collared dove | 1.61 |
| 10 | Chaffinch | 1.56 |
| 11 | Great tit | 1.33 |
| 12 | Robin | 1.24 |
| 13 | Greenfinch | 1.17 |

Pie

○ Drag across cells A4 to B13 to select them.

○ Click the Pie button in the Charts group on the Insert ribbon to display a gallery of pie chart options.

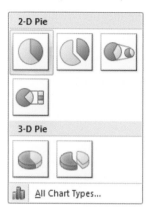

○ Click the Pie option in the 2–D Pie group. The chart is placed on your worksheet.

○ Use the techniques you practised when creating a bar chart (page 230) to add the chart title Garden Birds in England 2007.

You are going to add labels to the pie chart to show the percentage found of each bird listed in the table.

○ Select the chart and click anywhere in the circle to select it.

○ Right-click the selected circle and select Add Data Labels from the shortcut menu. The data values are displayed.

○ Right-click the circle again and select Format Data Labels... from the shortcut menu. The Format Data Labels window is displayed.

○ Select Label Options in the left-hand pane.

○ Deselect Value and then select Category Name and Percentage in the Label Contains group of tick boxes.

○ Click Close.

**Tip:**

To change the pie slice colours, click a slice to select the whole circle. Click it again to select just that slice. Right-click the selected slice and click **Format Data Point...** on the shortcut menu that is displayed. Select the **Fill** option in the left-hand pane and then choose a colour or fill effect.

You don't really need a legend on this pie chart because it has labels near each slice.

○ Right-click the legend and select Delete from the shortcut menu.

ⓘ To reinstate the legend, click the Legend button in the Labels group on the Chart Tools Layout ribbon, and then choose from the location menu that is displayed.

Your pie chart will look similar to this:

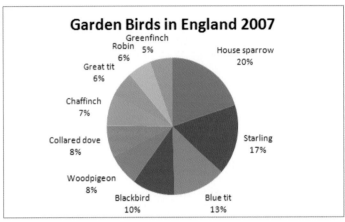

○ Save your workbook.

## Changing the chart type                                    Syllabus 4.6.1.3

It's easy to change the chart type, for example from a pie chart to a bar or line chart, even after you have created it.

○ With the Birds workbook open, make sure the pie chart is displayed and selected. Right-click the Chart Area. A shortcut menu appears.

○ Select Change Chart Type... to display the Change Chart Type window.

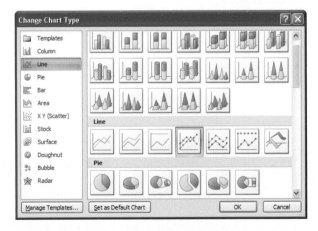

○ Here all you need to do is choose another chart type. Although it doesn't make much sense to display percentages of different items as a line, practise with a different type of chart by choosing the Line with Markers option from the chart gallery. Click OK.

A line chart can be formatted in a similar way to a bar chart or a pie chart. For example try changing the colour of the lines or other feature in a similar way to when you formatted the column chart on page 233.

▶ You decide that line chart is an unsuitable way to display the bird data. Change the chart type to a column chart.

▶ Delete the labels above each column by right-clicking on a column and selecting Format Data Labels... from the shortcut menu to show the Format Data Labels window.

▶ Select Label Options and untick all the Label Contains boxes.

▶ Click Close and save your workbook.

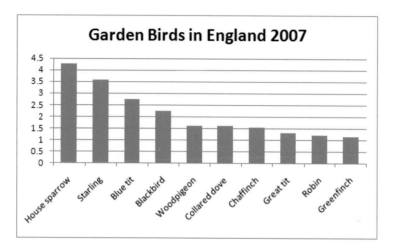

## Exercise

In this exercise you are asked to produce and format a column chart to show these population estimates for the UK for a ten-year period.

1. Enter the following data into a new worksheet and save it as Population.xlsx. Use the auto-fill feature to enter the Years.

|  | A | B |
|---|---|---|
| 1 | UK Population Estimates | |
| 2 | | |
| 3 | Year | Population (thousands) |
| 4 | 1998 | 58,475 |
| 5 | 1999 | 58,684 |
| 6 | 2000 | 58,886 |
| 7 | 2001 | 59,113 |
| 8 | 2002 | 59,324 |
| 9 | 2003 | 59,557 |
| 10 | 2004 | 59,846 |
| 11 | 2005 | 60,238 |
| 12 | 2006 | 60,587 |
| 13 | 2007 | 60,975 |

2. Use the Chart Wizard to create a column chart to represent this data. Use cells A4 to A13 as the *x*-axis labels.

Tip:

- ▶ Select the range A3 to B13.
- ▶ Select the chart type you want.
- ▶ Right-click the chart area and click Select Data... from the shortcut menu to display the Select Data Source dialogue box.
- ▶ In the Legend Entries (Series) pane, select Year, then click the Remove button.
- ▶ In the Horizontal (Category) Axis Labels pane, click Edit, then click cell A4 and drag the mouse to cell A13 and release the mouse button. Click OK.
- ▶ Click OK on the Select Data Source dialogue box.

3. Change the chart title to UK Population Estimates.

4. Label the *x*-axis and the *y*-axis appropriately and delete the legend.

5. Insert the chart alongside the spreadsheet data.

6. Change the colour of the text (i.e. headings, labels etc.) to blue and change the colour of the columns to yellow.

Your chart should look something like this:

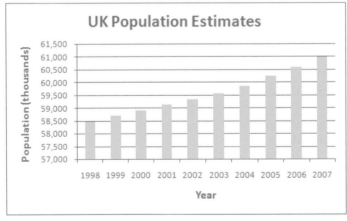

7. Save and close your work.

Statistics are also produced that break down the figures into age groups. You are now asked to create a pie chart to show the age distribution of the UK population.

8.    Enter the following data onto a new worksheet.

|   | A | B | C |
|---|---|---|---|
| 1 | UK Population by age group | | |
| 2 | | | |
| 3 | Age | Percentage | |
| 4 | 0–4 | 5.9 | |
| 5 | 5–15 | 14.2 | |
| 6 | 16–44 | 40.1 | |
| 7 | 45–64M/59F | 21.3 | |
| 8 | 65M/60F–74 | 10.9 | |
| 9 | 75 and over | 7.6 | |

9.    Create a pie chart to represent this data.

10.   Insert a main chart title UK population by age group.

11.   Display the legend.

12.   Add data labels as percentages.

13.   Display the chart in a separate worksheet.

Your pie chart should look similar to this:

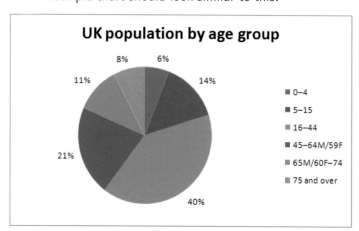

14.   Change the pie chart into a column chart and remove any unwanted labels

15.   Save and close your work.

## Ask yourself

- ❓ Can I sort spreadsheet data in ascending/descending order?

- ❓ Can I create different types of chart from spreadsheet data?

- ❓ Can I move and resize a chart?

- ❓ Can I add and delete a chart title?

- ❓ Can I change how a chart is formatted, for example change background colour, column colour?

- ❓ Can I change one type of chart into another?

In this chapter you should have created and saved the following files:
Birds.xlsx
Population.xlsx

In this chapter you have been introduced to the following buttons:

Sort A to Z
in the Sort & Filter group on the Data ribbon

Column
Pie
in the Charts group on the Insert ribbon

# Printing

**CHAPTER 24**

In this chapter you will find out:

- how to print an entire worksheet and workbook
- how to print a specified range of cells
- how to print a selected chart
- how to print row and column headings
- how to print title rows and columns
- how to fit the contents of a worksheet onto a specified number of pages
- how to hide and show gridlines on a printout
- how to change paper orientation, size and margins.

## Ribbon groups used in this chapter

In this chapter you will use this button in the Preview group on the Print Preview ribbon:

these buttons in the Print group on the Print Preview ribbon:

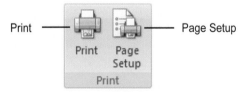

and these buttons in the Page Setup group on the Page Layout ribbon:

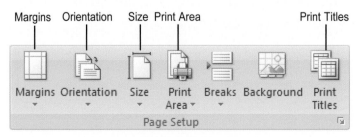

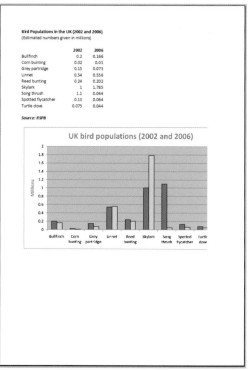

▶ Open the Birds workbook.

▶ Click the Sheet1 tab to select it.

▶ Click Print on the Office button menu, and then select Print Preview.

This is how your worksheet will look when it is printed. Depending on how large you resized your chart, and depending on the paper size set, you might find that the print preview shows the worksheet spread over several pages (as in the example).

▶ Close the print preview by clicking the Close Print Preview button in the Preview group on the Print Preview ribbon.

You will see dashed lines on your spreadsheet that indicate the page size.

▶ Resize the chart so that it fits neatly on one page, as in the example on the right.

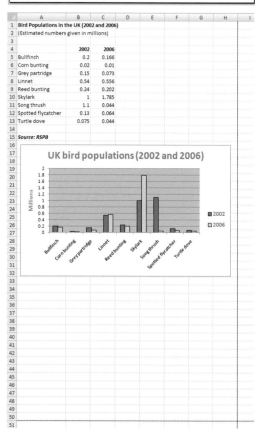

▶ Return to Print Preview to check the layout, and if you are happy with it, click Print on the Office button menu, and then select Print to display the Print dialogue box.

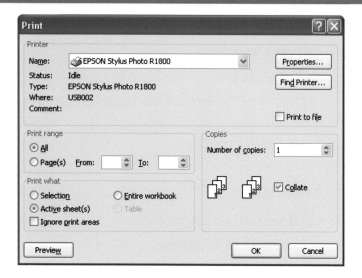

Here you can change various options such as the number of copies and which printer to use.

◉ Select All for the print range, and Active sheet(s).

◉ Check and change the other options as necessary, and click OK to print.

## Printing a cell range                                         Syllabus 4.7.2.5

You can specify the cell range that you want to print. You'll use this method to print only the figures on Sheet1, without the chart.

◉ Select cells A1 to F15 – these are the cells you want to print.

◉ Open the Print dialogue box and select Selection in the Print what section.

◉ Now click Preview. Only the selected cells are shown.

◉ Click the Print button in the Print group on the Print Preview ribbon.

◉ Close the print preview.

## Printing an entire workbook                                   Syllabus 4.7.2.5

You can print all the sheets in a workbook.

◉ Open the Print dialogue box.

◉ Select Entire workbook in the Print what section.

◉ Click OK.

## Printing a selected chart
Syllabus 4.7.2.5

You can print only a chart on a worksheet.

▶ Select the chart you want to print.

▶ Open the Print dialogue box. The Selected chart option in the Print what section is automatically selected.

▶ Click OK to print the selected chart.

## Printing row and column headings
Syllabus 4.7.2.2

▶ Make sure Sheet1 is selected, but not the chart.

▶ Display the print preview of the worksheet.

▶ Click the Page Setup button in the Print group on the Print Preview ribbon to display the Page Setup dialogue box.

▶ Click the Sheet tab.

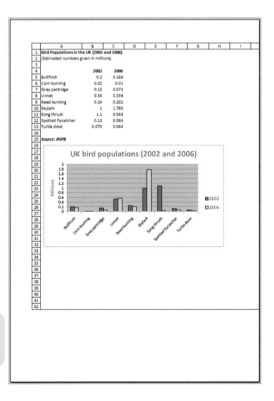

▶ Select Row and column headings in the Print section.

▶ The print preview on the right shows the effect this has.

▶ Close the print preview.

**Tip:**
It is good practice to preview a worksheet before printing it so that you can see what it will look like on paper before potentially wasting any.

## Printing title rows and columns

Syllabus 4.7.2.3

Print Titles

If you have a very large worksheet that spans several pages, it is useful to have the title printed on all the pages. You can do this in the Page Setup dialogue box.

○ Open the Page Setup dialogue box on the Sheet tab – this time by clicking the Print Titles button in the Page Setup group on the Page Layout ribbon.

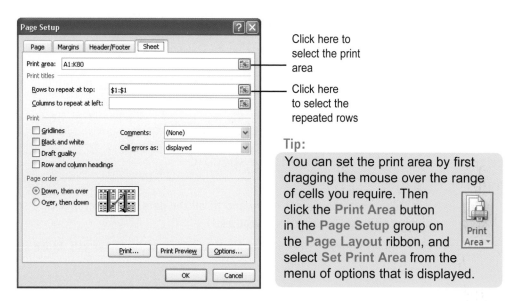

Click here to select the print area

Click here to select the repeated rows

**Tip:**

You can set the print area by first dragging the mouse over the range of cells you require. Then click the **Print Area** button in the **Page Setup** group on the **Page Layout** ribbon, and select **Set Print Area** from the menu of options that is displayed.

Sheet1 of the Birds worksheet is only 1 page, so to demonstrate title rows and columns appearing on more than one sheet you will need to set a print area that extends beyond the single page. If a worksheet already extends to more than one page, you won't need to set the print area. *Either*

○ type the print area, say A1 to K80, in the Print area: box

○ *or* you can select the cells by clicking the icon on the right-hand side of the Print area: box. The dialogue box will collapse to show only the relevant box. Use the mouse to drag out the area on the worksheet that you want to print.

Click here once you've selected the print area you want

○ When you have selected the print area you require, click the icon on the right-hand side of the box to expand the dialogue box once again.

Now you need to set the row(s) that you want to appear as the title row. *Either*

○ type $1:$1 in the Rows to repeat at top: box to specify row 1 as the repeated row

○ *or* you can select the cells by clicking the icon on the right of the Rows to repeat at top: box. The dialogue box will collapse to show only the relevant box and the cursor will become a small horizontal arrow, with which you should point and click row 1.

Click here once you've
selected the row(s) you
want repeated

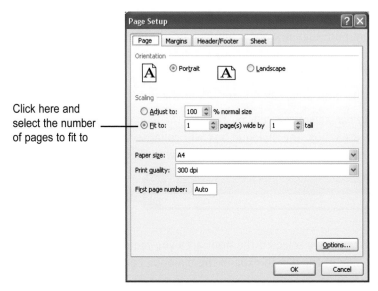

◉ When you have selected row 1, click the icon in the right of the box to expand the dialogue box again.

◉ You also have the option of repeating a column, which you do in exactly the same way as rows. Try repeating column A, using the same method as for repeating row 1.

◉ Print preview the worksheet.

Although they're not very neat, the title row and column are repeated in print preview and when you print.

◉ Close the print preview.

## Fitting worksheet contents onto a specific number of pages
**Syllabus 4.7.1.3**

It is sometimes convenient to try and fit all the data onto one page or a specific number of pages for printing purposes.

◉ Open the Page Setup dialogue box and click the Sheet tab. Make sure the print area is still selected.

◉ Click the Page tab.

Click here and
select the number
of pages to fit to

◉ Click the Fit to: option in the Scaling section and set the other options as 1 page wide by 1 page tall.

◉ Click Print Preview.

The print area range is the same as before, but now there is only one page.

◉ Close the print preview.

## Hiding/unhiding gridlines on printouts

Excel automatically prints without gridlines, but sometimes it can be useful to see them on paper.

▶   Open the Page Setup dialogue box and click the Sheet tab.

▶   Click the Gridlines box in the Print section. (You can click it again to remove the tick and turn off gridline printing.)

▶   Now go to Print Preview to see what it will look like.

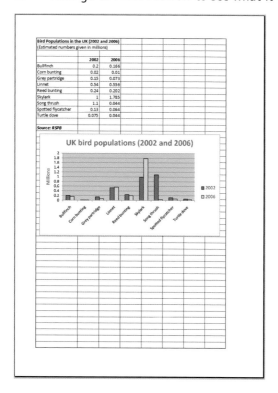

## Paper orientation and size Syllabus 4.7.1.2

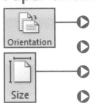

- ▶ Click the Orientation button in the Page Setup group on the Page Layout ribbon.
- ▶ Select Portrait or Landscape from the menu that appears.
- ▶ Click the Size button in the Page Setup group on the Page Layout ribbon.
- ▶ Select the paper size you want from the list displayed on the menu that appears.

> **Tip:**
> You can also set the orientation and page size on the **Page** tab of the **Page Setup** dialogue box.

## Changing the margins Syllabus 4.7.1.1

- ▶ Click the Margins button in the Page Setup group on the Page Layout ribbon.
- ▶ Select the margin arrangement you want from the list displayed on the menu that appears.

> **Tip:**
> You can set custom margins on the **Margins** tab of the **Page Setup** dialogue box.

## Preparation Syllabus 4.7.2.1

You have looked at a number of ways to set up your worksheet before printing it. Print Preview is a useful tool for checking your work, but you should also check all text in a worksheet for spelling errors, make a rough check that the calculations are as you intended, and check for formula errors (see page 254).

> **Tip:**
> Click the **Spelling** button in the **Proofing** group on the **Review** ribbon to run the spell-checker. You use this in a similar way to the spell-checker in Microsoft Word (see Module 3, page 125).

## Exercises

Now you will print parts of the worksheets you created in previous practice exercises.

1.  Open Population.xlsx.
2.  Select the column chart only and print it.
3.  Click away from the chart and print the whole worksheet.
4.  Use the Print Area command to print only the figures, without the chart.
5.  Close the workbook.

6.  Open Birthday3.xlsx and print the entire workbook.
7.  Print the worksheet Home to show the row and column headings.
8.  Close the workbook.

9.  Open Quiz.xlsx.
10. Print the worksheet in landscape orientation.
11. Print the worksheet with gridlines.
12. Close the workbook.

## Ask yourself

- ❷ Can I print an entire worksheet?

- ❷ Can I print an entire workbook?

- ❷ Can I print a range of cells?

- ❷ Can I print a selected chart?

- ❷ Can I print row and column headings?

- ❷ Can I print gridlines?

- ❷ Can I print title rows/columns?

- ❷ Can I fit a printout of a worksheet onto a specified number of pages?

- ❷ Can I set paper orientation and size, and change the margins?

In this chapter you should have created and saved the following files:
Birds.xlsx
Birthday3.xlsx
Population.xlsx
Quiz.xlsx

In this chapter you have been introduced to the following buttons:

Close Print Preview
in the Preview group on the Print Preview ribbon

Page Setup
Print
in the Print group on the Print Preview ribbon

Margins
Orientation
Print Area
Print Titles
Size
in the Page Setup group on the Page Layout ribbon

# Cell Referencing

In this chapter you will find out:

- about relative and absolute cell referencing
- more about formulae and the importance of checking results
- how to calculate a percentage
- how to format data as currency
- how to merge and centre cell contents
- how to add a date
- about text wrapping and how to use it
- how to find and replace data
- how to add a header and footer, and use special fields in them.

## Ribbon groups used in this chapter

In this chapter you will use these buttons in the Alignment group on the Home ribbon:

this button in the Number group on the Home ribbon:

and this button in the Editing group on the Home ribbon:

There are two different ways of referencing a particular cell in a formula: relative and absolute. You'll work on a project about car imports to learn about their different uses.

## Relative cell referencing                                    Syllabus 4.4.1.4

This is the default setting in Excel. If you take the example in the following screenshot, Excel actually remembers the formula as =the cell 3 above and one to the left. This means that when you copy the formula to a different cell, the formula will no longer say =A1.

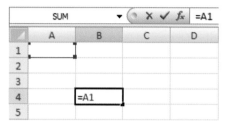

For example, if you copy cell B4 to cell C4, the formula becomes =B1, because B1 is the cell 3 above and 1 to the left of cell C4!

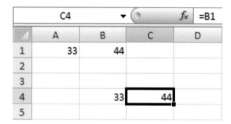

▶ Create a worksheet like the one above and try copying and pasting cells and formulae. Close the workbook when you have finished without saving it.

## Absolute cell referencing                                    Syllabus 4.4.1.4

Absolute cell referencing is used when you always want to refer to the same cell. You'll work through the following project to demonstrate when to use absolute cell referencing.

▶ Open a new workbook. Copy the data in the screenshot below, entering all the cell contents and replicating the formatting.

| | A | B | C | D | E | F |
|---|---|---|---|---|---|---|
| 1 | | | | | | |
| 2 | Current exchange rate: | 1.55 | euros to the pound | | | |
| 3 | | | | | | |
| 4 | | | | | | |
| 5 | Car make & model | UK price (pounds) | Imported price (euros) | Imported price (pounds) | £Saving | %Saving |
| 6 | Peugeot 206 Coupe Cabriolet | 15370 | 20723.5 | | | |
| 7 | VW Golf GTi | 18330 | 24792.25 | | | |
| 8 | Mini 16V Cooper | 15465 | 21583.75 | | | |
| 9 | BMW 5 Series SE | 33060 | 44942.25 | | | |
| 10 | VW Passat SE | 17120 | 21692.25 | | | |
| 11 | Alfa Romeo T Spark Selespeed Lusso | 18750 | 24025 | | | |
| 12 | Toyota Yaris 16V | 11470 | 13942.25 | | | |

**Tip:**

The text has been right-aligned so that it lines up with the numbers below. To do this just highlight the text cells and click the **Align Right** button in the **Alignment** group on the **Home** ribbon.

First you need to enter a formula to calculate the price of the imported cars in pounds. The price will be calculated using the current exchange rate which is entered at the top of the sheet.

▶ Click cell D6. Enter the formula =C6/B2. (To convert euros to pounds, you need to divide the euro amount by the exchange rate.) Press Enter.

You need the same formula in all the cells in that column, from D6 to D12. Let's see what happens when you copy the formula down.

▶ Click in cell D6. Click and drag the small handle at the bottom right of the cell down to cell D12.

| | D6 | ▼ | | *fx* =C6/B2 | | |
|---|---|---|---|---|---|---|
| | A | B | C | D | E | F |
| 1 | | | | | | |
| 2 | Current exchange rate: | 1.55 | euros to the pound | | | |
| 3 | | | | | | |
| 4 | | | | | | |
| 5 | Car make & model | UK price (pounds) | Imported price (euros) | Imported price (pounds) | £Saving | %Saving |
| 6 | Peugeot 206 Coupe Cabriolet | 15370 | 20723.5 | 13370 | | |
| 7 | VW Golf GTi | 18330 | 24792.25 | #DIV/0! | | |
| 8 | Mini 16V Cooper | 15465 | 21583.75 | #VALUE! | | |
| 9 | BMW 5 Series SE | 33060 | 44942.25 | #VALUE! | | |
| 10 | VW Passat SE | 17120 | 21692.25 | 1.41133702 | | |
| 11 | Alfa Romeo T Spark Selespeed Lusso | 18750 | 24025 | 1.310692853 | | |
| 12 | Toyota Yaris 16V | 11470 | 13942.25 | 0.901535726 | | |
| 13 | | | | | | |

Excel has automatically used relative cell referencing, and as you can see, it hasn't worked!

▶ Click cell D8 to see what formula is there.

The Formula bar shows =C8/B4. What is in cell B4? Nothing! Take a look at the other formulae in the column. Can you see what has happened?

You should have used absolute cell referencing, as you want the formula to always refer to cell B2 where the exchange rate is.

▶ Select cells D6 to D12 and press the Delete key.

▶ Click in cell D6. You need to alter the formula to make B2 an absolute cell reference.

For absolute cell referencing, all you do is add a $ symbol in front of the column letter AND row number. You can put the symbol in front of the column only, but this will mean that when you copy the formula, only the column part of the formula will be kept constant. The same principle applies to rows. This is called mixed cell referencing.

▶ Change the formula in cell D6 to =C6/$B$2.

▶ Now copy the formula to the other cells in the column.

| D6 | | ▾ | $f_x$ =C6/$B$2 | | | | |

| | A | B | C | D | E | F |
|---|---|---|---|---|---|---|
| 1 | | | | | | |
| 2 | Current exchange rate: | 1.26 | euros to the pound | | | |
| 3 | | | | | | |
| 4 | | | | | | |
| 5 | Car make & model | UK price (pounds) | Imported price (euros) | Imported price (pounds) | £Saving | %Saving |
| 6 | Peugeot 206 Coupe Cabriolet | 15370 | 20723.5 | 13370 | | |
| 7 | VW Golf GTi | 18330 | 24792.25 | 15995 | | |
| 8 | Mini 16V Cooper | 15465 | 21583.75 | 13925 | | |
| 9 | BMW 5 Series SE | 33060 | 44942.25 | 28995 | | |
| 10 | VW Passat SE | 17120 | 21692.25 | 13995 | | |
| 11 | Alfa Romeo T Spark Selespeed Lusso | 18750 | 24025 | 15500 | | |
| 12 | Toyota Yaris 16V | 11470 | 13942.25 | 8995 | | |
| 13 | | | | | | |

◉ Change the imported price to display two decimal places (see page 211)

◉ Save the worksheet as Cars.xlsx.

## Entering and checking formulae Syllabus 4.7.2.1

◉ You need to enter a formula for the £Saving column. For this, use the formula:

UK price (pounds) – Imported price (pounds)

◉ Copy the formula down the whole column. Do you need relative or absolute cell referencing for this?

Always check that the results look correct. The spreadsheet should look similar to this:

| E6 | | ▾ | $f_x$ =B6-D6 | | | | |

| | A | B | C | D | E | F |
|---|---|---|---|---|---|---|
| 1 | | | | | | |
| 2 | Current exchange rate: | 1.55 | euros to the pound | | | |
| 3 | | | | | | |
| 4 | | | | | | |
| 5 | Car make & model | UK price (pounds) | Imported price (euros) | Imported price (pounds) | £Saving | %Saving |
| 6 | Peugeot 206 Coupe Cabriolet | 15370 | 20723.5 | 13370.00 | 2000.00 | |
| 7 | VW Golf GTi | 18330 | 24792.25 | 15995.00 | 2335.00 | |
| 8 | Mini 16V Cooper | 15465 | 21583.75 | 13925.00 | 1540.00 | |
| 9 | BMW 5 Series SE | 33060 | 44942.25 | 28995.00 | 4065.00 | |
| 10 | VW Passat SE | 17120 | 21692.25 | 13995.00 | 3125.00 | |
| 11 | Alfa Romeo T Spark Selespeed Lusso | 18750 | 24025 | 15500.00 | 3250.00 | |
| 12 | Toyota Yaris 16V | 11470 | 13942.25 | 8995.00 | 2475.00 | |
| 13 | | | | | | |

**Tip:**

If you want to check for formula errors, or if you see an error (such as those explained on page 205), click the **Error Checking** button in the **Formula Auditing** group on the **Formulas** ribbon. You can trace and correct errors in the **Error Checking** dialogue box that is displayed.

## Calculating a percentage                    Syllabus 4.5.1.3

You will now include formulae in the %Saving column.

○ Enter the formula for this calculation in cell F6:

£Saving / UK price (pounds)

○ Adjust the cell formatting to show two decimal places.

○ Copy the formula down for all the cars.

○ Select cells F6 to F12 and then click the Percent Style button in the Number group on the Home ribbon. This changes the answers into percentages.

○ Now change the exchange rate in cell B2. At what exchange rate does the %Saving become zero for the Mini?

## The currency format                    Syllabus 4.5.1.2

The table will look a lot better if the prices are displayed with currency symbols. You will now change the format of some of the columns to give them the Currency number type.

○ Select cells B6 to B12 and right-click anywhere within the selected cells to bring up a shortcut menu.

○ Select Format Cells....

○ Select Currency from the Category: list (having made sure that the Number tab is selected). Set the Decimal places to 0. Excel should choose the £ symbol by default, which is fine.

○ Click OK.

○ Repeat this for the euro column. Remember to choose the euro symbol from the Symbol list.

○ Format all the other currency columns correctly.

Your spreadsheet should now look similar to this:

| | A | B | C | D | E | F |
|---|---|---|---|---|---|---|
| 1 | | | | | | |
| 2 | **Current exchange rate:** | 1.55 | euros to the pound | | | |
| 3 | | | | | | |
| 4 | | | | | | |
| 5 | **Car make & model** | **UK price (pounds)** | **Imported price (euros)** | **Imported price (pounds)** | **£Saving** | **%Saving** |
| 6 | Peugeot 206 Coupe Cabriolet | £15,370 | € 20,724 | £13,370 | £2,000 | 13% |
| 7 | VW Golf GTi | £18,330 | € 24,792 | £15,995 | £2,335 | 13% |
| 8 | Mini 16V Cooper | £15,465 | € 21,584 | £13,925 | £1,540 | 10% |
| 9 | BMW 5 Series SE | £33,060 | € 44,942 | £28,995 | £4,065 | 12% |
| 10 | VW Passat SE | £17,120 | € 21,692 | £13,995 | £3,125 | 18% |
| 11 | Alfa Romeo T Spark Selespeed Lusso | £18,750 | € 24,025 | £15,500 | £3,250 | 17% |
| 12 | Toyota Yaris 16V | £11,470 | € 13,942 | £8,995 | £2,475 | 22% |

## Merge and centre cell contents                    Syllabus 4.5.3.3

You can easily merge and centre cell contents using the button in the Alignment group. This is particularly useful for titles. First change the heading for the price columns.

- ◉ Type UK Price in cell B4 and Imported Price in cell C4.

- ◉ Replace the contents of cells B5 and D5 with Price in pounds and the content of cell C5 with Price in euros.

- ◉ Format the new text as bold and aligned right.

- [Merge & Center] ◉ Select cells C4 and D4. Click the Merge & Center button.

This makes it a bit clearer which the imported prices are.

## Adding a date field                    Syllabus 4.5.1.2

A quick way to enter today's date is to press Ctrl+; (Ctrl and ; together) on the keyboard. Alternatively you can type a date (separated with either hyphens or slashes) into a cell and then format it.

You need to add a date to show when the exchange rate was last updated.

- ◉ Add the text and date in cells D2 and E2 as shown in the next screenshot.

| | A | B | C | D | E | F |
|---|---|---|---|---|---|---|
| 1 | | | | | | |
| 2 | **Current exchange rate:** | 1.55 | euros to the pound | **Updated:** | 09/10/2008 | |
| 3 | | | | | | |
| 4 | | **UK Price** | **Imported Price** | | | |
| 5 | **Car make & model** | **Price in pounds** | **Price in euros** | **Price in pounds** | **£Saving** | **%Saving** |
| 6 | Peugeot 206 Coupe Cabriolet | £15,370 | € 20,724 | £13,370 | £2,000 | 13% |
| 7 | VW Golf GTi | £18,330 | € 24,792 | £15,995 | £2,335 | 13% |
| 8 | Mini 16V Cooper | £15,465 | € 21,584 | £13,925 | £1,540 | 10% |
| 9 | BMW 5 Series SE | £33,060 | € 44,942 | £28,995 | £4,065 | 12% |
| 10 | VW Passat SE | £17,120 | € 21,692 | £13,995 | £3,125 | 18% |
| 11 | Alfa Romeo T Spark Selespeed Lusso | £18,750 | € 24,025 | £15,500 | £3,250 | 17% |
| 12 | Toyota Yaris 16V | £11,470 | € 13,942 | £8,995 | £2,475 | 22% |

- ◉ Now right-click in the date field, and select Format Cells... from the shortcut menu that appears.

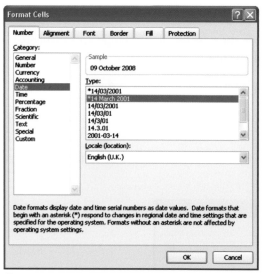

○ Excel has already guessed that you want the Date category. Pick a date Type from the right-hand list.

○ You might need to widen column E to display the whole date.

Note:

Make sure that the **Locale (location):** box is set for your country. Different countries express dates in different formats.

## Wrapping cell content                                    Syllabus 4.5.3.1

Some of the car makes and models are quite long. It would look neater if the longer descriptions ran onto two lines, rather than making the column extra wide to fit them.

 ○ Select cell A11, and click the Wrap Text button in the Alignment group on the Home ribbon.

○ Now resize column A so that it is too small to fit all the words on one line (be careful to keep the content of cell A6 still fully visible!).

○ If the row height does not automatically adjust, increase it for row 11 by clicking and dragging between the row headers of row 11 and row 12.

The text fills onto the next line!

○ Repeat this for some of the other cells where the Car make & model description is long.

○ Now make the column headings in row 6 wrap over two lines.

## Find and replace

There aren't many records in this spreadsheet, but in larger spreadsheets it is useful to be able to search for a particular value.

### Finding a cell containing a particular word or value

○ Click Find & Select in the Editing group on the Home ribbon to show a menu of options.

○ Select the Find... option on the menu to display the Find and Replace dialogue box on the Find tab.

○ Type VW in the Find what: box.

○ Click the Find Next button.

○ Excel makes the cell containing VW the active cell. Click Find Next again. Excel moves to the second cell containing VW.

### Replacing a word or value

If you have spelt a name wrongly in several different places in a spreadsheet, it is useful to find and replace each instance of the word. For practice, replace the word VW with Volkswagen.

○ Click Find & Select in the Editing group on the Home ribbon to show a menu of options.

○ Select the Replace... option on the menu to display the Find and Replace dialogue box on the Replace tab.

○ Check that VW is still showing in the Find what: box, and type Volkswagen in the Replace with: box.

○ Click the Replace All button.

▶ Click OK. Notice that VW has now become Volkswagen. Click Close.

## Adding headers and footers
Syllabus 4.7.1.4

Headers and footers are useful for automatically inserting information such as the current date and page numbers on large documents.

▶ Open the Page Setup dialogue box and select the Header/Footer tab.

**Tip:**
You can also add header and footer text by clicking the **Header & Footer** button in the **Text** group on the **Insert** ribbon. The **Header & Footer Tools Design** ribbon appears. You can use the buttons in the groups to add the features described here to worksheets.

▶ Click the Custom Header... button.

▶ Click in the Center Section: box and type Car Import Savings Sheet.

Now you are going to change the text to 12 point and bold.

▶ Highlight the text you have just written, then click the Format Text button to display the Font dialogue box.

Format Text button —

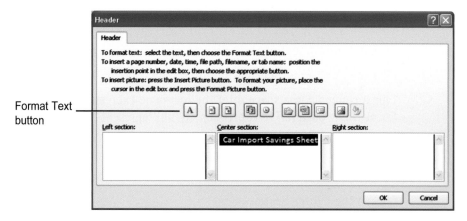

- ▶ Change the text to Arial 12 point and bold.

- ▶ Click OK to close the Font dialogue box.

- ▶ Click OK to close the Header dialogue box. Notice the header is not visible on the worksheet. You will, however, be able to see it in print preview when you close the Page Setup dialogue box.

Now you'll insert some fields into the Footer.

- ▶ Open the Page Setup Header/Footer tab again if you closed it, and click the Custom Footer... button. You can enter text here just the same as you did in the Header. This time you won't enter any text, you'll just insert fields using the buttons provided.

- ⓘ You can modify and delete text in the header and footer by using the Page Setup dialogue box in a similar way as you entered it in the first place. Remove all headers and footers from the worksheet by selecting (none) in both the Header: and the Footer: drop-down lists in the Page Setup dialogue box.

## Header and footer fields                            Syllabus 4.7.1.5

You'll have noticed that there are quite a few buttons on the header and the footer dialogue boxes. You use these to enter fields that automatically include information such as page numbers, filenames and the date/time.

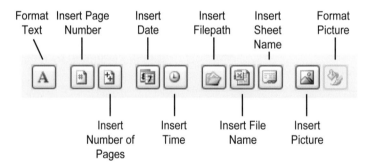

- ▶ If not already open, click the Custom Footer... button on the Header/Footer tab of the Page Setup dialogue box to display the Footer dialogue box.

### Inserting the file name and worksheet name

- ▶ Click in the Left section: box.

- ▶ Click the Insert File Name button. The expression &[File] represents the file name.

- ▶ Type a comma and a space after the file name expression, then click the Insert Sheet Name button. The expression &[Tab] represents the worksheet name.

### Inserting the page number

A page number is useful in longer documents. Add it here for practice.

- ▶ Click in the Center Section: box.

- Click the Insert Page Number button. The expression &[Page] represents the page number.

- Type a space followed by the word of and then another space.

- Click the Insert Number of Pages button. The expression &[Pages] represents the total number of pages in the worksheet.

### Inserting the date and time

- Click in the Right Section: box.

- Click the Insert Date button. The expression &[Date] represents today's date.

- Type a comma and a space after the date, then click the Insert Time button. The expression &[Time] represents the current time.

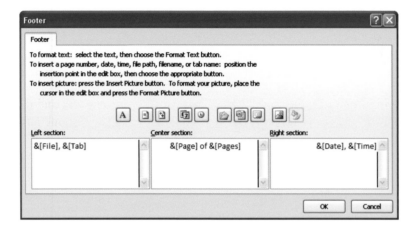

- Click OK. You can see what the headers and footers will look like in the Page Setup dialogue box.

- Click OK to see the header and footer in print preview (see overleaf).

**Car Import Savings Sheet**

| | | euros to the | | | |
|---|---|---|---|---|---|
| Current exchange rate: | | 1.55 pound | Updated: | 09 October 2008 | |

| Car make & model | UK Price Price in pounds | Imported Price Price in euros | Price in pounds | £Saving | %Saving |
|---|---|---|---|---|---|
| Peugeot 206 Coupe Cabriolet | £15,370 | € 20,724 | £13,370 | £2,000 | 13% |
| Volkswagen Golf GTi | £18,330 | € 24,792 | £15,995 | £2,335 | 13% |
| Mini 16V Cooper | £15,465 | € 21,584 | £13,925 | £1,540 | 10% |
| BMW 5 Series SE | £33,060 | € 44,942 | £28,995 | £4,065 | 12% |
| Volkswagen Passat SE | £17,120 | € 21,692 | £13,995 | £3,125 | 18% |
| Alfa Romeo T Spark Selespeed Lusso | £18,750 | € 24,025 | £15,500 | £3,250 | 17% |
| Toyota Yaris 16V | £11,470 | € 13,942 | £8,995 | £2,475 | 22% |

cars.xlsx, Sheet1      1 of 1      10/10/2008, 10:09

▶ Print the spreadsheet if you want to.

▶ Save and close the worksheet.

## Exercise

In this exercise you will create a worksheet that uses absolute cell referencing.

A company has decided to introduce a commission scheme. The management want some idea how much this will cost. They want to see the effect of different commission levels for each product group.

| | A | B | C | D | E | F | G | H |
|---|---|---|---|---|---|---|---|---|
| 1 | **Anglebar Tools – Commission Tracker** | | | | | | | |
| 2 | 10 October 2008 | | | | | | | |
| 3 | | | | | | | | |
| 4 | Commission Rate A | 5% | | | | | | |
| 5 | Commission Rate B | 10% | | | | | | |
| 6 | Commission Rate C | 15% | | | Items sold | | | |
| 7 | | | Tools | Commission (Rate A) | Accessories | Commission (Rate B) | Consumables | Commission (Rate C) |
| 8 | Salesperson 1 | | £1,300.00 | | £ 582.00 | | £ 317.00 | |
| 9 | Salesperson 2 | | £1,224.00 | | £ 280.00 | | £ 289.00 | |
| 10 | Salesperson 3 | | £1,026.00 | | £ 332.00 | | £ 297.00 | |
| 11 | Salesperson 4 | | £1,670.00 | | £ 620.00 | | £ 124.00 | |
| 12 | Salesperson 5 | | £1,488.00 | | £ 719.00 | | £ 188.00 | |

1.  Enter the data shown at the top of the next page into a new Excel worksheet and save the file as Commission.xlsx. Format cell A2 as a date field. Format cells C8 to H12 as currency and cells B4 to B6 as percentage. Merge and centre cells C6 to H6.

2.  Enter a formula in cell D8 that calculates the commission for the tools that Salesperson 1 has sold. Use the commission rate from cell B4 (absolute address) in the formula.

3.  Fill the formula down to cell D12.

4.  Enter a similar formula in cells F8 to F12 and H8 to H12 using the relevant commission rates.

5.  Enter a label Total Commission in cell A14.

6.  Enter a formula in cell B14 to calculate the total commission payable to all salespersons for all items sold.

7.  Shade cell B14 in red and make the font colour white. Draw a thick border around the cell.

8.  If the company want to reduce the total commission payment by 10 per cent by adjusting the commission rate for consumables only, what would commission rate C have to be reduced to?

9.  Insert a footer with your name and print out the worksheet in landscape format.

10.  Save and close your work.

## Ask yourself

- ❓ Do I know the difference between relative and absolute cell addressing?

- ❓ Do I know how to insert absolute addressing into a spreadsheet cell?

- ❓ Can I calculate a percentage using a spreadsheet?

- ❓ Can I format cells for currency?

- ❓ Do I know how to merge and centre cells?

- ❓ Do I know how to apply wrapping to cell content?

- ❓ Can I add borders to cells?

- ❓ Can I find and replace text?

- ❓ Can I add headers and footers?

- ❓ Can I insert fields into headers and footers?

In this chapter you should have created and saved the following files:
Cars.xlsx
Commission.xlsx

In this chapter you have been introduced to the following buttons:

Merge & Center
Text Align
Wrap Text
in the Alignment group on the Home ribbon

Percent Style
in the Number group on the Home ribbon

Find & Select
in the Editing group on the Home ribbon

# If...Then...Else

In this chapter you will find out:

- ❗ how to change font style and size
- ❗ about IF statements and how to use them
- ❗ how to change font and background colour
- ❗ how to align contents within a cell.

## Ribbon groups used in this chapter

In this chapter you will use these buttons in the Font group on the Home ribbon:

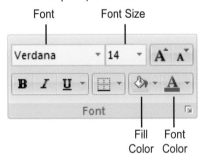

and this button in the Clipboard group on the Home ribbon:

Project: Create a spreadsheet to produce instant quotes

In this chapter you'll create a worksheet for a shop that sells mirrors. It offers cut-to-size mirrors, and they need a worksheet that will give an instant quote to a customer.

The shop offers only one thickness of glass, 6 mm. It offers a choice of polished, or polished and bevelled edges.

The price of the mirror is dependent on the surface area and the perimeter length.

These are the prices:

£32 per square metre of surface area

£1.70 per linear metre of perimeter for polished edges

£2.10 per linear metre of perimeter for polished and bevelled edges

▶ Open a new workbook, type in the text, format it and add the borders so that your worksheet looks like this:

| | A | B | C | D | E |
|---|---|---|---|---|---|
| 1 | Mirror, Mirror! | Cut to Size Mirrors | | | |
| 2 | | | | | |
| 3 | | | | | |
| 4 | Price per square metre | 32 | | | |
| 5 | Price per linear metre for polished edges | 1.7 | | | |
| 6 | Price per linear metre for polished and bevelled edges | 2.1 | | | |
| 7 | | | | | |
| 8 | Requested mirror size | | | | |
| 9 | Width (m) | | Type of edges (enter P or PB) | P = polished | |
| 10 | Height (m) | | | PB = polished and bevelled | |
| 11 | | | | | |
| 12 | Total surface area (square metres) | | Price for surface area | | |
| 13 | Total perimeter length (m) | | Price for edges | | |
| 14 | | | | | |
| 15 | Instant quote | | | | |

## Changing font style and size                  Syllabus 4.5.2.1–2/4.5.2.4

You need to give the title and some of the other headings a bit of a makeover.

▶ Select cell A1.

▶ Change the font size to size 26 by clicking the down arrow on the right-hand side of the Font Size list box in the Font group on the Home ribbon, and selecting the size from the displayed list.

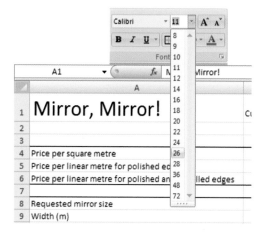

▶ Now change the font. Click the down arrow on the right-hand side of the Font list box in the Font group on the Home ribbon, and choose one you like the look of from the displayed list.

**B** ▶ Make the text in cell A1 bold by clicking the Bold button in the Font group on the Home ribbon.

- ▶ You need to move the contents of cell B1 to cell D1. Make sure cell B1 is selected, then click the black border and drag over to cell D1.

- ▶ Change some more of the headings and formats to look similar to this:

| | A | B | C | D | E | F |
|---|---|---|---|---|---|---|
| 1 | Mirror, Mirror! | | | | Cut to Size Mirrors | |
| 2 | | | | | | |
| 3 | | | | | | |
| 4 | Price per square metre | 32 | | | | |
| 5 | Price per linear metre for polished edges | 1.7 | | | | |
| 6 | Price per linear metre for polished and bevelled edges | 2.1 | | | | |
| 7 | | | | | | |
| 8 | Requested mirror size | | | | | |
| 9 | Width (m) | | Type of edges (enter P or PB) | | P = polished | |
| 10 | Height (m) | | | | PB = polished and bevelled | |
| 11 | | | | | | |
| 12 | Total surface area (square metres) | | Price for surface area | | | |
| 13 | Total perimeter length (m) | | Price for edges | | | |
| 14 | | | | | | |
| 15 | Instant quote | | | | | |
| 16 | | | | | | |

**Tip:**

To copy the formatting from a cell or cell range, select the cell(s) containing the formatting you want to copy. Click the **Format Painter** button in the **Clipboard** group on the **Home** ribbon. Click in the cell(s) you want to format. **All** the original cell's formatting is copied.

## Adding the formulae

You'll do some more formatting in a minute. First you need to type the formulae.

- ▶ The calculation for Total surface area is Width × Height. Type the formula =B9*B10 in cell B12.

- ▶ The calculation for Total perimeter length is 2 × (Width + Height). Type the formula =2*(B9+B10) in cell B13. You will need the brackets in the formula.

- ▶ Type the formula for Cost for surface area in cell D12. It is =B12*B4.

- ▶ Save the workbook as Mirrors.xlsx.

Now you can enter some data.

- ▶ Try out your formulae by typing the length and width of a mirror in cells B9 and B10, respectively.

## IF statements                                          Syllabus 4.4.2.2

- ▶ Now type either P or PB in cell D9 to specify the mirror's edges.

The calculation for the Price for edges has to include an IF statement because it is conditional on whether they are polished, or polished and bevelled.

IF the edges are polished THEN the price for edges = perimeter length × polished price

IF the edges are bevelled THEN the price for edges = perimeter length × bevelled price

Breaking these statements down further:

IF cell D9 = P THEN cell D13 = B13*B5

IF cell D9 = PB THEN cell D13 = B13*B6

▶ Select cell D13. Click the Insert Function button to the left of the Formula bar.

▶ The Insert Function dialogue box is displayed. Select IF from the Select a function: list. If you cannot see it in the list, change the category to Logical.

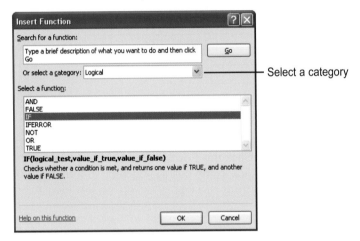

Select a category

▶ Click OK.

▶ The Function Arguments dialogue box is displayed. Complete the three IF fields as shown.

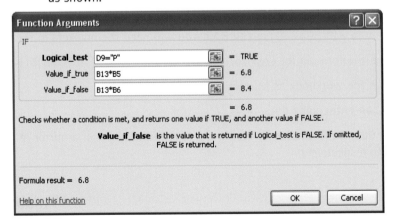

**Tip:**

If you're confused about how this function works, try clicking the **Help on this function** link at the bottom of the window. This gives an explanation and some more examples.

▶ Click OK.

▶ Fill in the last formula for the total price, next to the Instant Quote heading in cell B15. It should be =SUM(D12:D13).

| | A | B | C | D | E | F |
|---|---|---|---|---|---|---|
| 1 | Mirror, Mirror! | | | | Cut to Size Mirrors | |
| 2 | | | | | | |
| 3 | | | | | | |
| 4 | Price per square metre | £32.00 | | | | |
| 5 | Price per linear metre for polished edges | £1.70 | | | | |
| 6 | Price per linear metre for polished and bevelled edges | £2.10 | | | | |
| 7 | | | | | | |
| 8 | Requested mirror size | | | | | |
| 9 | Width (m) | | 0.5 Type of edges (enter P or PB) | P | P = polished | |
| 10 | Height (m) | | 1.2 | | PB = polished and bevelled | |
| 11 | | | | | | |
| 12 | Total surface area (square metres) | | 0.6 Price for surface area | 19.20 | | |
| 13 | Total perimeter length (m) | | 3.4 Price for edges | 5.78 | | |
| 14 | | | | | | |
| 15 | Instant quote | £24.98 | | | | |
| 16 | | | | | | |

Now you are gong to apply a 10 per cent discount if the quote is £100 or more.

▶ Type and format the cells A16 and A17, and change the border around the quote as shown in the screenshot.

| | A | B | C | D | E | F |
|---|---|---|---|---|---|---|
| 1 | Mirror, Mirror! | | | | Cut to Size Mirrors | |
| 2 | | | | | | |
| 3 | | | | | | |
| 4 | Price per square metre | £32.00 | | | | |
| 5 | Price per linear metre for polished edges | £1.70 | | | | |
| 6 | Price per linear metre for polished and bevelled edges | £2.10 | | | | |
| 7 | | | | | | |
| 8 | Requested mirror size | | | | | |
| 9 | Width (m) | | 0.5 Type of edges (enter P or PB) | P | P = polished | |
| 10 | Height (m) | | 1.2 | | PB = polished and bevelled | |
| 11 | | | | | | |
| 12 | Total surface area (square metres) | | 0.6 Price for surface area | £19.20 | | |
| 13 | Total perimeter length (m) | | 3.4 Price for edges | £5.78 | | |
| 14 | | | | | | |
| 15 | Instant quote | £24.98 | | | | |
| 16 | Discount | | | | | |
| 17 | Final price | | | | | |

You will use the IF statement as before, but this time you need the formula to recognise when the price quoted in cell B15 is more than £99.99. To do this you will use the > operator.

Tip:

Use the < operator if you want to find out if something is less than another.

The calculation for the Discount is conditional on whether the quoted price is more than £99.99.

IF the instant quote is more than £99.99 THEN the discount = instant quote × 10%, OTHERWISE the discount = 0.

Breaking these statements down further:

IF cell B15 > 99.99 THEN cell B16 = B15*10% OTHERWISE cell B16 = B15*0

▶ Click cell B16 and open the Function Arguments dialogue box as described earlier.

▶ Complete the three IF fields using the > operator as shown.

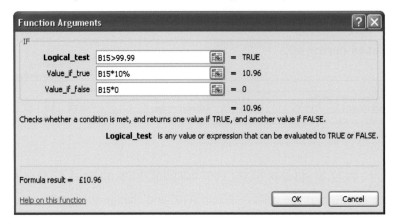

▶ Type the formula =B15–B16 in cell B17 to calculate the final price.

▶ Try typing different lengths and widths, and different types of mirror into the worksheet to see the effect on the final price.

▶ Finally, format all the currency cells to show pound signs, and set as two decimal places if you haven't done so already.

| | A | B | C | D | E | F |
|---|---|---|---|---|---|---|
| 1 | Mirror, Mirror! | | | | Cut to Size Mirrors | |
| 2 | | | | | | |
| 3 | | | | | | |
| 4 | Price per square metre | £32.00 | | | | |
| 5 | Price per linear metre for polished edges | £1.70 | | | | |
| 6 | Price per linear metre for polished and bevelled edges | £2.10 | | | | |
| 7 | | | | | | |
| 8 | Requested mirror size | | | | | |
| 9 | Width (m) | 3 | Type of edges (enter P or PB) | PB | P = polished | |
| 10 | Height (m) | 2 | | | PB = polished and bevelled | |
| 11 | | | | | | |
| 12 | Total surface area (square metres) | 6 | Price for surface area | £192.00 | | |
| 13 | Total perimeter length (m) | 10 | Price for edges | £21.00 | | |
| 14 | | | | | | |
| 15 | Instant quote | £213.00 | | | | |
| 16 | Discount | £21.30 | | | | |
| 17 | Final price | £191.70 | | | | |

## Adding some colour                                         Syllabus 4.5.2.3

The quote worksheet might look better if it was a bit more colourful. You can do this by changing the font colour and the background fill colour.

### Changing the font colour

▶ Select cell A1.

Click the down-arrow on the Font Color button in the Font group on the Home ribbon, and select a colour.

### Changing the background fill colour

With cell A1 still selected, click the down-arrow on the Fill Color button in the Font group on the Home ribbon, and select a colour.

## Aligning cell content                                    Syllabus 4.5.3.2

You can set where the text appears in a cell – left, right, top, bottom or centre. Use the Align Right, Align Left and Center buttons, and the Top, Middle and Bottom buttons, in the Alignment group on the Home ribbon (page 251) to align the cell content horizontally and vertically, respectively. You can also use the Format Cells dialogue box, which allows you more alignment options (e.g. slanting).

- Widen row 1 by clicking and dragging between the row selectors of row 1 and row 2.

- Select cells A1 and D1 and click the Middle Align button.

### Cell content orientation

You can change the orientation of the text in the cells using the Format Cells dialogue box.

- Right-click cell A1 and select Format Cells... from the shortcut menu.

- Select the Alignment tab on the Format Cell dialogue box.

- Change the orientation of the text by dragging the red dot on the Orientation dial so that the text is slightly slanting.

- Click OK.

Add some more colours, and try different formatting so that your spreadsheet looks something like the one below.

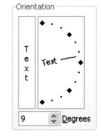

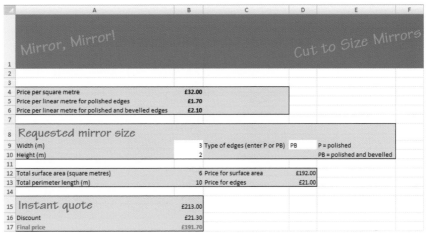

> ◉ Enter some different values for the width and height of the mirror. You can also change the prices.

> ◉ Save and close the worksheet when you're happy with it.

## Exercise

In this exercise you will create a worksheet to record the times of athletes in a particular race. It will automatically indicate if the competitor has broken their personal best record.

1. Enter the following data into a new Excel worksheet. Format it as shown.

|   | A | B | C | D | E | F |
|---|---|---|---|---|---|---|
| 1 | The Annual Ashfield Athletics Meeting | | | | | |
| 2 | | | | | | |
| 3 | Event | Surname | Forename | Club | Personal Best | Result |
| 4 | | | | | | |
| 5 | 100 m | Baptist | Kyle | Hilcrest | 10.99 | 11.01 |
| 6 | | Carr | Lee | Drayton | 10.54 | 10.55 |
| 7 | | Coya | Paul | C&C | 10.80 | 10.80 |
| 8 | | Hills | Saleem | Wilton | 10.75 | 10.95 |
| 9 | | Nield | Conrad | Raylor | 11.20 | 10.95 |
| 10 | | Njerba | James | Grenfer | 10.94 | 10.87 |
| 11 | | Raman | Sherif | Fielden | 10.80 | 10.99 |
| 12 | | Seth | Marcus | Merses | 10.79 | 10.53 |
| 13 | | Williams | Odette | V&V | 11.10 | 11.00 |

2. Enter a formula in cell G5 that checks to see if the competitor's result is less than their current personal best. If it is, then the letters PB are inserted. If it is not, the cell is left blank.

3. Copy this formula in column G for all the runners.

4. Format the cells in column G to be centred, blue and bold.

5. Sort the competitors into descending order of result.

6. Change the background colour of cells B5 to F13 to a pale blue.

Your worksheet should look similar to this:

|   | A | B | C | D | E | F | G |
|---|---|---|---|---|---|---|---|
| 1 | The Annual Ashfield Athletics Meeting | | | | | | |
| 2 | | | | | | | |
| 3 | Event | Surname | Forename | Club | Personal Best | Result | |
| 4 | | | | | | | |
| 5 | 100 m | Baptist | Kyle | Hilcrest | 10.99 | 11.01 | |
| 6 | | Williams | Odette | V&V | 11.10 | 11.00 | PB |
| 7 | | Raman | Sherif | Fielden | 10.80 | 10.99 | |
| 8 | | Hills | Saleem | Wilton | 10.75 | 10.95 | |
| 9 | | Nield | Conrad | Raylor | 11.20 | 10.95 | PB |
| 10 | | Njerba | James | Grenfer | 10.94 | 10.87 | PB |
| 11 | | Coya | Paul | C&C | 10.80 | 10.80 | |
| 12 | | Carr | Lee | Drayton | 10.54 | 10.55 | |
| 13 | | Seth | Marcus | Merses | 10.79 | 10.53 | PB |

7. Save your worksheet as Results.xlsx and close your work.

## Ask yourself

❓ Do I know how to change font type and size?

❓ Can I use IF statements to determine the result value in a cell?

❓ Can I change font and background colours?

❓ Can I align text horizontally and vertically in cells?

In this chapter you should have created and saved the following files:
Mirrors.xlsx
Results.xlsx

In this chapter you have been introduced to the following buttons:

Fill Color
Font
Font Color
Font Size
in the Font group on the Home ribbon

Format Painter
in the Clipboard group on the Home ribbon

# Module 5
## Database

In this module you will learn some of the main concepts of databases and how to use a database on a computer. You will learn how to:

- create and modify tables
- create and modify queries
- create and modify forms
- create and modify reports
- relate tables
- manipulate data and retrieve information using queries
- manipulate data and retrieve information using sort tools.

This training, which has been approved by the ECDL Foundation, includes exercise items intended to assist Candidates in their training for an ECDL Certification Programme. These exercises are not ECDL Foundation certification tests. For information about authorised ECDL Test Centres in different national territories, please refer to the ECDL Foundation website at www.ecdl.org

# Module **5**

# Contents

# Introduction to Databases

# CHAPTER 27

In this chapter you will find out:

- ❗ about databases and Microsoft Access
- ❗ about planning and operating a database
- ❗ about the differences between flat-file and relational databases
- ❗ about the primary key
- ❗ about data types
- ❗ about field properties
- ❗ about database structure
- ❗ about naming conventions.

## What is a Microsoft Access database?　Syllabus 5.1.1.1–4/5.1.2.1–4

Microsoft Access is one of the most widely used database packages. Databases are used to store large amounts of related data and allow you to sort and filter it to give information in the form of useful reports.

A database is based on tables of data, and each table contains many fields.

This is an example of how an art collection might look in a table of data:

| Name of Painting | Artist | Gallery |
|---|---|---|
| Acuminatus | Mark Johnston | CCA Galleries |
| The North Unfolds | Neil Canning | Martin Tinney Gallery |
| Heat of the Day | Claire Blois | Kilmorack Gallery |
| Two Birches | James Hawkins | Rhue Studio |

**Questions:**　How many columns are there in the table?

How many rows are there in the table?

**Answers:**　There are three columns. The column headings are the fields, so there are three fields in the table.

There are four rows. The rows are the records. There are four records in this table.

Each time the art collector purchases a new painting, he can catalogue it by adding a new record to the table.

In itself the table doesn't help the collector. It simply records the data in an organised way. However, the data can provide a lot of information, if the right questions are asked.

The art collector can use the database to find out information such as:

- which paintings he owns by a particular artist
- which gallery a particular painting came from
- how many paintings he has from a particular gallery
- the artist of a particular painting.

Databases are not often used for such small amounts of data because the answers to the above questions can be easily answered just by looking at the table. However, if a gallery had thousands of paintings there would be thousands of rows, and the table would be so big it would take hours to answer the questions. This is an example of where a database becomes very useful.

Databases are common in business. Some large-scale databases include:

- airline booking systems
- government records
- bank account records
- hospital patient records.

## Running a database                                    Syllabus 5.1.4.1–4

As you can imagine, databases such as those listed above, need to be carefully managed. There may be one user, or many users, entering data and other users retrieving information. Those entering data and those retrieving information could be the same people (for example, a telesales person may create a new record for a customer, update fields for an existing customer, or retrieve price and availability information for a potential customer). Several people may use the database at the same time, as is likely to be the case in a booking system.

In some databases, it is not appropriate for all the users to be able to enter or retrieve data. A database administrator allocates access rights to users so records can be seen or changed only by authorised people. For example, a hospital porter might be authorised to view a patient's location in a ward, but would not be able to change any personal or medication data.

The database administrator is usually responsible for the seamless recovery of a database in the event of a system failure. Some important databases rely on duplication of systems, so in the event of one system failure, the duplicate system can be used immediately without loss of data and the need for using backups.

It is important that the data held and information retrieved is accurate, so databases are designed and maintained by specialists.

## Planning a database                                    Syllabus 5.1.3.1

Before creating a database on the computer it is important to plan. You need to think about the answers to these questions:

- ⓘ What is the purpose of the database?
- ⓘ What information will you want to look up in the database?
- ⓘ What data will you store in the database?

### Letting Agency Database

During the course of this module you'll build up a database for a letting agency, Hemlets Ltd. Hemlets rents properties on behalf of private landlords in Ipswich.

### Purpose of the database

Hemlets needs the database to store information about the properties it manages and the landlords it deals with. The staff need to be able to find out quickly and easily:

- ⓘ which properties are available to let
- ⓘ how many bedrooms each property has
- ⓘ which properties are available for a particular monthly rent
- ⓘ whether a property is a flat, terraced, semi-detached or detached
- ⓘ when the lease runs out, if the property is let
- ⓘ the landlord of a particular property
- ⓘ contact details of a particular landlord.

Each property is owned by just one landlord. Each landlord may own one or more properties.

Your database should contain details on each property and each landlord. The next step is to decide which fields you need.

Based on the information given above, the table must contain the following data about each property:

- ⓘ Style (flat, terraced, semi, detached)
- ⓘ Bedrooms (1, 2, 3, 4, 5 or 6)
- ⓘ Rent (monthly)
- ⓘ Rented? (Y/N)
- ⓘ Lease expiry date
- ⓘ Landlord name

In addition, the following data needs to be held about each landlord:

- ⓘ Title
- ⓘ Initials
- ⓘ Surname
- ⓘ Contact number

Each of these pieces of data will be held in one field in your table.

Note that it is important that each field should contain only one element of data, otherwise the powerful filters and queries that provide information will not be so useful. For example, if a single field contained the title, initials and surname of a landlord, you would not be able to sort the data by only the surname.

It is also good practice to group fields related to a single subject in only one table. This avoids duplication of data, thereby keeping the size of the database more manageable. Fields in different subject tables can be related (see page 281).

Tip:

Remember that the **fields** in the table are the **column headings**.

## A flat-file database

A flat-file database is a database with just one table in it. If the Hemlets database was designed as a flat-file database, the table of data might look something like this:

| PropertyRef | Style | Bedrooms | Rent | Rented | Lease Expiry | Landlord Title | Landlord Initials | Landlord Surname | Contact No |
|---|---|---|---|---|---|---|---|---|---|
| P1 | Semi | 3 | 800 | Y | 1/6/2009 | Mrs | J | Welsh | 01474 276499 |
| P2 | Flat | 2 | 650 | Y | 5/12/2009 | Mr | S | Hemmings | 01474 572772 |
| P3 | Detached | 4 | 1050 | N | | Mr | S | Hemmings | 01474 572772 |
| P4 | Terraced | 2 | 700 | Y | 15/8/2009 | Mr | S | Hemmings | 01474 572772 |
| P5 | Semi | 3 | 850 | N | | Mr | M | Jenkins | 01474 387465 |
| etc. | | | | | | | | | |

Tip:

The **PropertyRef** field has been added because you need one field in each record that is unique. This will be explained in more detail later.

### Problems with a flat-file database

It is a common problem with many flat-file databases that the same data is duplicated several times. To find out why, look again at the example of the property table.

Look at the different landlords who own the various properties; notice that Mr S Hemmings owns three of the properties. This means that the data for Mr Hemmings had to be entered three different times, and if he changed his telephone number, you would have to be careful to change it in all three rows of the table, for every property he owns.

This is not only a waste of time, but it can introduce a lot of errors in a database. It would be easy to make a spelling mistake when entering Mr Hemmings' details, for example entering Hennings instead of Hemmings. If Hemlets searched to see which properties were owned by Hemmings, the one with the spelling mistake wouldn't be listed, and the staff at Hemlets would be none the wiser.

## A relational database                                        Syllabus 5.1.3.2

The solution to this problem is to hold the data in separate tables. You need a table for the properties and a different table for the landlords. The two tables will need to be linked. A database that contains two or more linked tables is called a relational database. Before you learn how to design this sort of database you need to learn some new vocabulary.

- ⓘ An entity is a person or thing about which data is held. In our example there are two entities, Property and Landlord.

- ⓘ An attribute is a piece of data about the entity. For example the attributes belonging to the entity Landlord are Title, Initials, Surname and Contact No.

**Question:** What attributes belong to the entity Property shown in the previous table?

**Answer:** PropertyRef, Style, Bedrooms, Rent, Rented and Lease Expiry. There is also one other attribute – Landlord. (You will need to know who the property belongs to.)

### Relationships

There are three different types of relationship between entities:

- ⓘ One-to-one E.g. Husband and wife. A husband can have one wife and a wife can have one husband.

- ⓘ One-to-many E.g. Football team and player. A football team has many players, but a player belongs to only one team.

- ⓘ Many-to-many E.g. Student and subject. A student studies many subjects and a subject is studied by many students.

**Question:** Which of these relationships applies to Landlord and Property in the example?

**Answer:** One-to-many: A property is owned by one landlord, but a landlord can own many properties.

## Entity-relationship diagrams

Each of these relationships can be shown in an Entity-Relationship (E-R) diagram, as shown below:

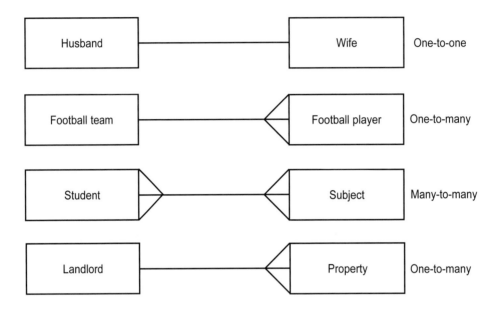

## The primary key

Syllabus 5.1.2.5

Each entity needs its own table containing its own attributes. In addition each record in a table must have a field which uniquely identifies that record, the primary key.

You will use PropertyRef as the key field for the Property table. Each landlord will also be given a unique reference number, LandlordRef, which you can use as the key field for the Landlord table. You cannot use Surname as the key field because there may be more than one landlord with the same surname.

Don't forget – although you will put the landlords' details in a separate table, you still need to know which landlord owns which property. For this, all you need to do is have an extra field in the Property table that contains LandlordRef for the landlord who owns the property.

Now the two tables look like this:

Property table

| PropertyRef | Style | Bedrooms | Rent | Rented | LeaseExpiry | LandlordRef |
|---|---|---|---|---|---|---|
| P1 | Semi | 3 | 800 | Y | 1/6/2009 | L1 |
| P2 | Flat | 2 | 650 | Y | 5/12/2009 | L2 |
| P3 | Detached | 4 | 1050 | N | | L2 |
| P4 | Terraced | 2 | 700 | Y | 15/8/2009 | L2 |
| P5 | Semi | 3 | 850 | N | | L3 |
| P6 | Detached | 5 | 1200 | Y | 25/7/2009 | L4 |
| P7 | Flat | 1 | 500 | N | | L5 |
| P8 | Flat | 2 | 600 | N | | L5 |
| P9 | Terraced | 3 | 750 | Y | 3/9/2009 | L5 |
| P10 | Semi | 3 | 900 | N | | L6 |

Landlord table

| LandlordRef | Title | Initials | Surname | ContactNo |
|---|---|---|---|---|
| L1 | Mrs | J | Welsh | 01474 276499 |
| L2 | Mr | S | Hemmings | 01474 572772 |
| L3 | Mr | M | Jenkins | 01474 387465 |
| L4 | Mr | M | Stevenson | 01474 783748 |
| L5 | Miss | L | Vacher | 01474 583689 |
| L6 | Mrs | J | Hemmings | 01474 856683 |

**Question:**

From the two tables above, find the name of the landlord of property P7.

**Answer:**

From the Property table you can see it's owned by the landlord with LandlordRef L5. The Landlord table shows that Landlord L5 is Miss L Vacher.

## Data types

Before you can enter these fields into your database, you need to think about what format the data will be in. Access has many different data types, which are explained in the table below:

| Text | Letters, symbols and numbers, i.e. alphanumeric data. |
|------|-------------------------------------------------------|
| Number | Numbers only (no letters). Includes numbers with decimal points. |
| Date/Time | Dates and times. |
| Currency | For all monetary data. Access will insert a currency symbol before the amount (such as £ or $ etc.) |
| Yes/No | Used wherever the field can be one of only two values, Yes/No, True/False, Male/Female etc. |
| AutoNumber | This is a unique value generated by Access for each record. |

You will have to choose a data type for each field from the table given above. For example, should you hold a telephone number as a Text field or a Number field? At first you may think that a Number field would be better, but in practice this is a bad idea for two reasons:

ⓘ    Access will not record leading zeros in a number field. So if the telephone number is 01473874512 it will be recorded as 1473874512 which is incorrect.

ⓘ    Access will not allow you to put a space, bracket or hyphen in a number field. Therefore, you should use a text field for a telephone number so you can record it as, for example, 01473 874512.

## Field properties

When you enter the field names used in each table into Access, you can specify the properties associated with the field or you can use the defaults provided. If you want a field to always contain specific data, such as the current date, you can set this as a Default Value.

It is good practice to change the default field length for Text fields (255 characters) because it means that Access will not create excessively large fields when you create forms and other database objects. It can also act as a type of data validation, as Access won't let you enter anything in a field that has more characters than the specified field length.

For Date/Time fields you can specify the format of the date (e.g. dd/mm/yy or mm/dd/yy etc.).

For Currency fields you can specify the number of decimal places.

## The database structure

The structure of the database can be thought of as what the table will look like without any data in (i.e. the design of the table). To describe the structure you need to know:

- how many fields the table will have (the columns in the table)
- what the field names will be (the column headings)
- what data type will be held in each field.

The number of rows will change as the user enters more data, and is not part of the database structure.

It is important to know the difference between the database structure (think of the empty table) and the data held in the database (the data that you put into the table).

### Questions:

For each of the following changes to the Painting database on page 277, will you need to change the database structure or edit the data?

- You decide to add a new field name, Price, to the database.
- The painting Two Birches was actually purchased from Kilmorack Gallery.

### Answers:

If you add a new field name, you are changing the database structure.

If you are changing the Two Birches record, you are only editing the data.

## Naming conventions

You will use a common convention when naming tables and fields. This means putting tbl in front of the table names, and not using any spaces in any of the names. Use capital letters in the middle of a field name to make the words easier to read. Look at the table below to see examples:

tblProperty

| Field Name | Data Type | Field Length/Type |
|---|---|---|
| PropertyRef | AutoNumber | |
| Style | Text | 15 |
| Bedrooms | Number | Long Integer |
| Rent | Currency | 0 decimal places |
| Rented | Y/N | - |
| LeaseExpiry | Date/Time | - |
| LandlordRef | Text | 4 |

tblLandlord

| Field Name | Data Type | Field Length/Type |
|---|---|---|
| LandlordRef | Text | 4 |
| Title | Text | 4 |
| Initials | Text | 4 |
| Surname | Text | 20 |
| ContactNo | Text | 15 |

This will be the structure of the tblProperty and tblLandlord tables.

Notice that PropertyRef and LandlordRef have been underlined. This is because they are both primary keys.

In text fields, you should set the field length to be the length of the longest word you expect to be entered. You wouldn't expect a Surname to be longer than 20 letters.

## Exercises

1. What is the difference between data and information?

2. A library wants to keep a database to record the books borrowed by library users. Each library user has their own unique ID, and can take out up to six books at a time. Each book has its own unique book number. The database designer has decided that three tables will be needed, called tblBook, tblLibraryUser and tblLoan. The tblLoan table will hold details of who has which books out on loan. Once a book is returned to the library, the loan record is deleted, so that there is never more than one loan record in tblLoan table for a given book.

   (a) What is the relationship between tblBook and tblLoan?

   (b) What is the relationship between tblLibraryUser and tblLoan?
   Label the following entity-relationship diagram.

   (c) What is an attribute?

3. A database is to be constructed to help a school keep track of who has been entered for each examination. Each pupil may be entered for several examinations.

   (a) Name two entities in the database. Suggest a primary key for each entity.

   (b) What is the relationship between the two entities?

4. A hospital database is to hold details of which patients and which nursing staff are assigned to each ward. Each nurse may be assigned to a single ward, but each ward may have several nurses. A patient is assigned to a single ward.

   (a) What is the relationship between tblWard and tblPatient?

   (b) Name one other entity in this database.

   (c) Design the structure of each of the tblWard and tblPatient tables. Show suitable field names. Show data types and field lengths for each field.

   (d) Make up three data records for each table.

5. A Sports Competition database is created showing all the competitors and events, and who entered which event. Some of the data is shown below:

tblCompetitor

| CompetitorID | Surname | Firstname | Date of Birth | Sex |
|---|---|---|---|---|
| C1 | Grand | Jane | 01/04/88 | F |
| C2 | Keino | Michael | 14/02/89 | M |
| C3 | Dowsett | Robert | 12/04/88 | M |
| C4 | Perez | Juanita | 31/07/89 | F |

tblEvent

| EventID | EventName | Men/Women |
|---|---|---|
| E1 | Long Jump | M |
| E2 | Long Jump | W |
| E3 | 100m | M |
| E4 | 100m | W |
| E5 | 100m Hurdles | M |

Michael Keino entered the long jump and the 100m hurdles events for men.

Robert Dowsett entered the men's 100m race.

Jane Grand and Juanita Perez entered the women's 100m.

Fill in the data in table tblEventEntry. (The column headings are given below.)

tblEventEntry

| EventID | CompetitorID |
|---|---|
| ... | ... |

# Module 5 Database

## Ask yourself

- ❓ Do I understand how columns and rows can be used to record data?

- ❓ Do I know what a database field is?

- ❓ Do I know what a database record is?

- ❓ Can I explain the limitations of a flat-file database?

- ❓ Can I explain how a relational database overcomes the limitations of a flat-file database?

- ❓ Do I understand the different relationships that are possible in a relational database?

- ❓ Can I draw and interpret entity-relationship diagrams?

- ❓ Do I know what a primary key is?

- ❓ Do I know how different data types are used?

- ❓ Do I know what a field type is and how it can be used?

- ❓ Do I understand the structure of a simple relational database and the naming conventions used?

# Creating a New Database

In this chapter you will find out:

- ❗ how to open and close Microsoft Access
- ❗ about the database window
- ❗ how to hide and restore the ribbon
- ❗ how to create a new table
- ❗ how to define a primary key
- ❗ how to edit and save a database structure
- ❗ how to edit field size attributes
- ❗ about indexing
- ❗ how to get help.

▶ Log on to the Payne-Gallway website www.payne-gallway.co.uk and download the files for Module 5 (see page 93 for how to do this).

## Ribbon groups used in this chapter

In this chapter you will use:
this button in the Views group on the Datasheet or Home ribbon:

this button in the Tables group on the Create ribbon:

Table ———

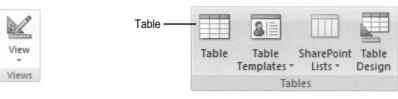

and these buttons in the Tools group on the Table Tools Design ribbon:

Primary Key

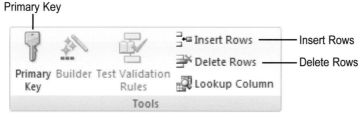

Insert Rows ——— Insert Rows

Delete Rows ——— Delete Rows

## Opening Microsoft Access

You can open Microsoft Access in one of two ways:

▶ *Either* double-click the Access icon (if it is on your desktop)

▶ *Or* click the Start, All Programs, then click Microsoft Office Access 2007. (Note: depending on how your computer is set up, you might need to click Start, All Programs, Microsoft Office, Microsoft Office Access 2007.)

Your screen will look like this:

Click to create a
new database

Existing databases
will be shown here

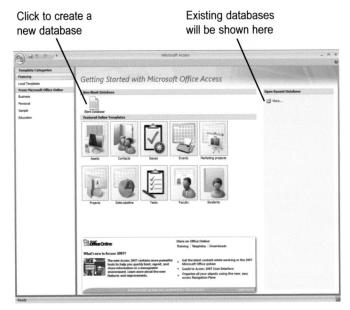

You now have the option of either opening an existing database or creating a new one. Here you will create a new database from scratch.

▶ Click the Blank Database button in the New Blank Database section of the opening screen.

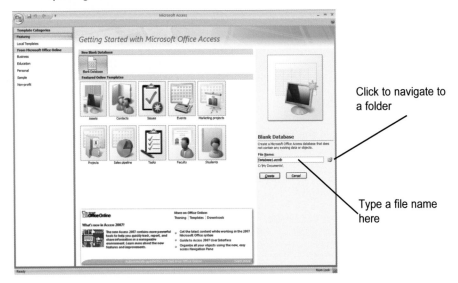

Click to navigate to
a folder

Type a file name
here

The right-hand side of the opening screen changes to show the Blank Database task pane as shown in the previous screenshot.

◗ Click the folder button 🖿 to open the File New Database window where you can select a folder and a name for your new database.

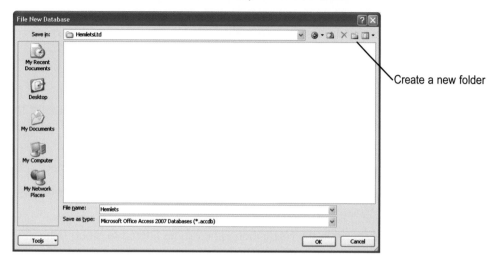

Create a new folder

◗ Click the Create New Folder button and create a new folder named HemletsLtd.

◗ In the File name: box, type the name Hemlets.

◗ Click the OK button. Access will automatically add the file extension .accdb.

◗ Click the Create button on the task pane of the opening screen.

Tip:

It is a good idea to keep each Access database in its own folder.

The database will open showing a window similar to this:

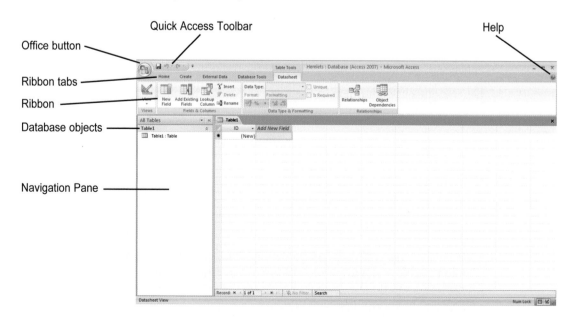

## The database structure

The next thing to do is set up the database structure. As you learned in the last chapter, all data in an Access database is stored in tables. Each table has a row for each record and a column for each field. All you have to do is tell Access exactly what fields you want in each record, and what data type each field is. After this has been done and the structure is saved, you can start adding data to the database.

### The Navigation Pane

Access databases are made up of objects. Database objects are displayed in the Navigation Pane. A table is an object, and it is the only object you have met so far. Other objects, which you will come across in this module, include Queries, Forms and Reports.

This is a new database, so the Navigation Pane shows only one object – Table1.

This Navigation Pane is a sort of central menu for your database, from which you can open the objects in your database.

The objects shown in the Navigation Pane can be filtered to group them in different ways (e.g. grouped by tables with objects related to those tables, or grouped by object type).

Click to display the
Navigation Pane menu

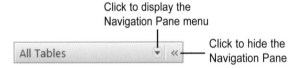

Click to hide the
Navigation Pane

## Minimising and restoring the ribbon                    Syllabus 5.2.1.4

You will learn about what individual ribbon buttons do as they become relevant whilst you are creating your database. Here are a few tips that apply to all Office ribbons. You may find that you already know most of this – it is exactly the same as you have experienced in other Microsoft applications such as Word or Excel.

Sometimes you might want to increase the working area where you type. You can minimise (hide) the ribbon so only the ribbon tabs are displayed. If the ribbon is minimised, you need to know how to get it back!

▶  Right-click anywhere in the line containing the ribbon tabs, on the Office button, on the Quick Access Toolbar, or on a ribbon group name.

▶  Click Minimize the Ribbon on the shortcut menu that is displayed.

▶  To restore the ribbon, right-click in one of the same places as before to un-tick Minimize the Ribbon on the shortcut menu.

Tip:

Use **Ctrl-F1** (i.e. press at the same time the **Control** key and the **F1** key on the keyboard) or double-click a ribbon tab to toggle between minimising and maximising the ribbon. At any time when the ribbon is minimised, simply click a ribbon tab to show the ribbon temporarily when you need it.

## Getting help

If at any time you're unsure about how to do something in Access, you can search the Microsoft Office Access Help system for instructions on your chosen subject. You use this in exactly the same way as the Word help system described on page 170.

## Creating a new table

Access provides different ways of looking at your database objects. The Hemlets database you have just created is shown in the Datasheet View (note that the Datasheet ribbon tab is selected) and you can enter data directly into the grid if you want to. However you will have much more control over how this data is presented if you use the Design View. See page 307 to read more about these views.

▶ Click the down arrow on the View button in the Views group on the Datasheet ribbon to display a menu of view options.

▶ Click Design View to display the Save As dialogue box.

▶ Type the name tblProperty and click OK.

**Tip:**
Click the views buttons located on the Status bar in the bottom right of the Access window to switch between object views. Rest the mouse pointer over a button to see a screen tip telling you what it is for.

The Table Design view and Table Tools Design ribbon are displayed. The table name also appears in the Navigation Pane.

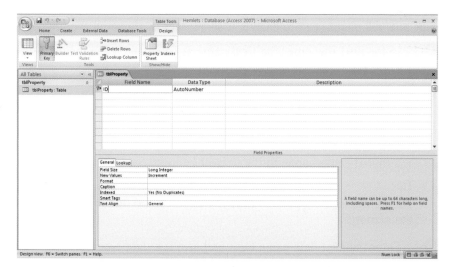

Look back at the structure of the tblProperty table on page 285. You need to type all these fields into the new table.

Access has entered the first field name for you. It has called it ID and applied good practice by assigning it as a primary key (see page 282 and below) with the AutoNumber data type. You need to replace the default name that Access has provided with the primary key text for this table in your database.

▶ Replace the Field Name ID with the first field name, PropertyRef.

▶ Press the tab key to move the insertion point to the Data Type box. You do not need to change the data type, so press tab again to move to the Description box.

> **Note:**
> If you want a field to always contain specific data, such as the current date, you can set this as a Default Value.

▶ Type This is the Key field.

▶ Leave the Field Size as Long Integer (the default) in Field Properties.

## Defining the primary key                                    Syllabus 5.3.2.5

Every table in an Access database must have a primary key (also known as the key field). The field which you specify for the primary key must have a different value for each record. The primary key in this example was set by default, but you need to know how to define a field as the primary key or change the default if another field holds unique data.

Primary Key

▶ Click the field name you want to set as the primary key.

▶ Click the Primary Key button in the Tools group on the Table Tools Design ribbon.

A key symbol 🔑 to the left of the Field Name shows which field is set as the primary key.

## Entering the other fields

Now you can enter all the other fields. Access will automatically provide a default data type and you might need to change it sometimes as shown in the following steps.

▶ In the next row enter the field name as Style and leave the data type as Text. Enter the Field Size as 15.

▶ In the third row enter Bedrooms as the field name. Tab to the Data Type column and click the small down-arrow on the right-hand side of the box. Select Number from the list of data types. Notice that in Field Properties the Field Size will automatically change to the default Long Integer.

| Text |
| Memo |
| **Number** |
| Date/Time |
| Currency |
| AutoNumber |
| Yes/No |
| OLE Object |
| Hyperlink |
| Attachment |
| Lookup Wizard... |

> **Tip:**
> Note that Field Properties always appear at the bottom of the screen.

▶ Enter the next field name Rent and give it a data type Currency. Click below in the Field Properties. Notice that in Field Properties the Decimal Places is set by default to Auto. You don't want any decimal places, as the rent will always be in whole pounds. Click where it says Auto then click the small down-arrow on the right; select 0 from the drop-down list.

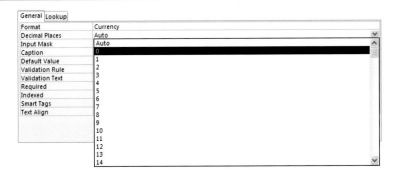

● On the next row enter the field name Rented and give it a data type Yes/No. Click below in Field Properties – notice that there are different types of Yes/No fields available – you can also choose True/False or On/Off. Leave it as Yes/No.

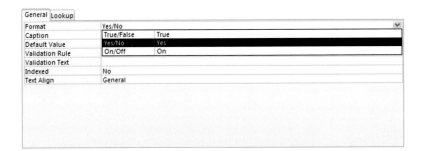

● Next, enter the field name LeaseExpiry (one word) and change the default data type to Date/Time. Again, there are several formats available to choose from in Field Properties. Click on the down-arrow next to the Format row and choose Short Date from the list.

● Finally enter the field name LandlordRef with the default data type Text. In Field Properties, set the Field size to 4.

Your table design view should now look like this:

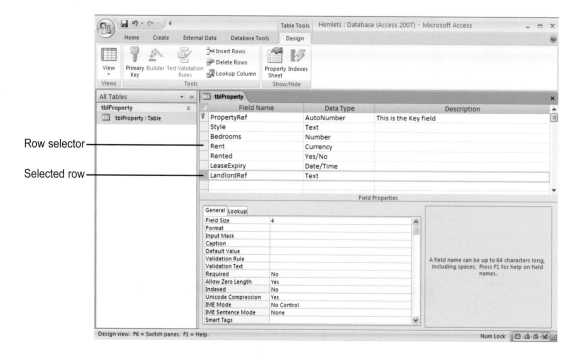

## Tip:

It is good practice to take care when setting up field names and data types, but don't worry too much if you make a few mistakes – when you've entered all the fields, you will learn how to move fields around, delete them or insert new fields. You can correct any mistakes at that point.

## Saving the table structure

Save the table structure by clicking the Save icon on the Quick Access Toolbar.

You have already given the table the name tblProperty so you won't be asked to name it again.

## Tip:

You can also save a table by clicking Save on the Office button menu.

## Tip:

If you have named the table wrongly, or made a spelling mistake, right-click the name in the Navigation Pane and select Rename from the shortcut menu. Then type in the correct name. To delete a table, select it and press the Delete key on the keyboard.

## Editing a table structure

- Open the tblProperty table in Design View if it is not already.

### Inserting a field

To insert a new row for a TotalRooms column just above Rent:

- Click the row selector (see the figure on the previous page) for Rent.

- Press the Insert key on the keyboard or click the Insert Rows button in the Tools group on the Table Tools Design ribbon.

- Enter the new field name TotalRooms, data type Number.

### Deleting a field

To delete the field you have just inserted:

- Select the field by clicking in its row selector.

- Press the Delete key on the keyboard or click the Delete Rows button in the Tools group on the Table Tools Design ribbon.

**Tip:**

> If you make a mistake, you can undo your last action by clicking the **Undo** button and redo an action by clicking the **Redo** button. Both buttons are on the **Quick Access Toolbar**. If the last action cannot be undone or redone, the button will appear faded.
>
> Undo  Redo
>
> Quick Access Toolbar

### Moving a field

- Click the row selector to the left of the field name to select the field.

- Click again and drag to where you want the field to be. You will see the cursor change and a line appear between fields as you drag over them to indicate where the field will be placed.

| Field Name | Data Type |
|---|---|
| PropertyRef | AutoNumber |
| Style | Text |
| Bedrooms | Number |
| Rent | Currency |
| Rented | Yes/No |
| LeaseExpiry | Date/Time |
| LandlordRef | Text |

**Tip:**

The row selector is the square to the left of the field name.

- Move the fields back so that your table looks like the one on the previous page when you have finished experimenting.

- Save the tblProperty table.

### Creating the tblLandlord table

Table

▶ Create a new table by clicking the Table button in the Tables group on the Create ribbon. The new table, Table1, appears in the Navigation Pane.

▶ Change to the table design view and save the table as tblLandlord when asked to do so.

▶ Change the primary field name ID to LandlordRef and give it a data type Text. Later you will link the two tables using this field and the LandlordRef field in the tblProperty table. It is very important that the two fields have the same data type and field properties or you won't be able to link the tables.

▶ Give LandlordRef a field length of 4 just as you did in the tblProperty table.

▶ Enter the other field names, data types and field properties just as they were defined on page 283. Don't forget to enter the correct field lengths!

Your table should now look like this:

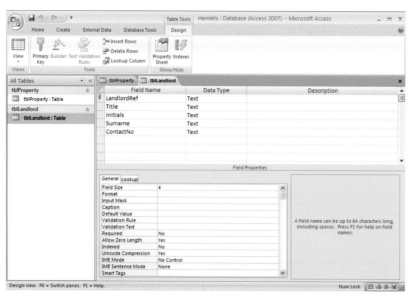

▶ Save the tblProperty table.

### Editing field size attributes                                        Syllabus 5.3.2.4

If you have made any mistakes in field names or field sizes, you can edit them now. Remember, it is easy to make changes to the table structure BEFORE you enter any data. If you change field size attributes AFTER data has been entered, this may cause problems. For example:

ⓘ If you change the field size of the LandlordRef field in this table, it may no longer link correctly to another table.

ⓘ If you change the field size of Surname from 20 to 15, some surnames already in the database may be truncated if they are longer than 15 characters.

## Indexing Syllabus 5.1.2.6/5.3.2.6

When a field is defined as a primary key, it is automatically indexed by Access. For example in tblLandlord, if you click in the LandlordRef row, you will see that the Indexed property in the list of Field Properties is set to Yes (No Duplicates).

Any other field can also be indexed simply by changing its Indexed property to Yes.

Access keeps a separate Index table with the record number for each field that you index, rather like index entries in a book. When data is entered into the table, all the indexes have to be updated as well. (This happens automatically – you don't have to worry about it!)

Indexing on the Surname field, for example, will make it quicker to search a very large database for everyone with a particular surname. On a small database it is not worth doing.

### Indexing with and without duplicates allowed

When you index on a key field, Access automatically sets the Indexed property to Yes (No Duplicates). This is because there cannot be two records with the same value in the key field. However, if you choose to index on a field such as Surname, you would have to set the Indexed property to Yes (Duplicates OK) to allow for the fact that more than one customer may have the same surname.

## Closing the database application Syllabus 5.2.1.1

 Close the database by clicking Close Database on the Office button menu. If you have any unsaved objects you will be asked to save them now.

 Close Access (the application) by clicking Exit Access on the Office button menu.

## Exercise

This exercise is based on creating a new database table/file for an examining board. Part of the file creation is the appropriate design of the fields, including the type and size of fields.

1. Open your database application. Open a new blank database and save as ExamBoard.accdb.

2. Design a table with three fields using the appropriate data types and field sizes. The following fields must be created for the table: CandidateID, Surname, Initials.

3. Save the table as tblCandidate.

4. Save and close the database.

5. Close Access.

## Ask yourself

❷      Do I know how to run and close Microsoft Access?

❷      Can I create a new database file?

❷      Do I know how to hide and restore ribbons?

❷      Do I know how to use the Microsoft Access Help facility?

❷      Can I create a new table?

❷      Can I set data types for fields?

❷      Can I set field properties?

❷      Can I set a primary key and do I know why it is used?

❷      Can I save a table structure?

❷      Can I edit a table structure and do I understand the limitations of doing it?

❷      Do I know what indexing does?


In this chapter you should have created and saved the following files:
ExamBoard.accdb
Hemlets.accdb


In this chapter you have been introduced to the following buttons:

View
in the Views group on the Datasheet or Home ribbon

Table
in the Tables group on the Create ribbon

Delete Rows
Insert Rows
Primary Key
in the Tools group on the Table Tools Design ribbon

# Setting up Relationships

In this chapter you will find out:

- how to open an existing database
- about the relationships window
- how to create, delete and save a relationship.

You looked at the relationships between the tables in Chapter 27, and drew entity-relationship diagrams to represent the relationships. You created two tables in Chapter 28 and you will now link them.

## Ribbon groups used in this chapter

In this chapter you will use this button in the Show/Hide group on the Database Tools ribbon:

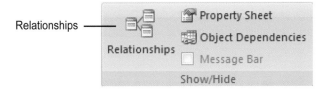

this button in the Relationships group on the Relationship Tools Design ribbon:

## Opening an existing database

○ Open Microsoft Access and click Open on the Office button menu.

○ Navigate to where you saved the Hemlets database and open it.

### Note:
If you see a warning, do not worry. Click the Options... button and select Enable this content and OK to continue.

### Tip:
Alternatively, after starting Access you can click a file in the Open Recent Database list on the opening screen. If Access is already running, select a file from the Recent Documents list that is displayed when you click the Office button. However, be careful that you open your version of a file if you use this method on a networked PC!

## Relationships window

○ Click Relationships in the Show/Hide group on the Database Tools ribbon to display the Show Table window.

You want to form relationships between the two tables, so you need to add both to the Relationships window that has appeared behind the Show Table window.

○ Highlight each in turn and click Add. Then click Close.

The two tables will now appear in the relationships window.

○ If you need to, click and drag the field lists so that you can clearly see all the field names.

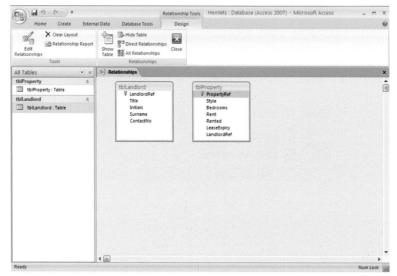

## Creating a relationship

Syllabus 5.1.3.3

You will recall from page 281 that you want a one-to-many relationship between tblLandlord and tblProperty.

▶ Click and drag the field LandlordRef from tblLandlord and drop it onto the field LandlordRef at the bottom of tblProperty. Always drag from the one side to the many side of the relationship.

The Edit Relationships window will appear.

ⓘ tblLandlord is the table on the one side of the relationship.

ⓘ tblProperty is the table on the many side of the relationship.

ⓘ LandlordRef is the field which links the two tables.

### Enforce referential integrity

You can enforce referential integrity if:

ⓘ the table on the one side of the relationship has a field containing unique data. In this example the table on the one side is the tblLandlord table, which does have a field containing unique data – LandlordRef – a primary key.

ⓘ the link fields have the same data type and length. In this example the link field is LandlordRef; you have given this field the same data type Text, length 4, in both tables.

If you enforce referential integrity, the following rules apply:

ⓘ You cannot enter a value into the many side of the relationship that does not exist in the one side. In this example, you must enter the landlord's details into tblLandlord before you can enter the properties that the landlord owns into tblProperty.

ⓘ You cannot delete a record from a table in the one side of a relationship if related records exist in the many table. This means that you cannot delete a landlord's details in tblLandlord if there are properties in tblProperty that the landlord owns. If you want to be able to delete a landlord and automatically delete the properties that the landlord owns at the same time you would use Cascade Delete, which is explained below.

If you choose Enforce Referential Integrity, you are given the option of Cascade Update Related Fields and Cascade Delete Related Fields.

### Cascade Update Related Fields

Cascade Update means that if you change the related field (in our case the related field is LandlordRef) in the one side of the relationship, Access will automatically update related fields in the many side. This means that if you change a Landlord's LandlordRef in tblLandlord, the LandlordRef will automatically be changed in all related records in tblProperty.

### Cascade Delete Related Fields

Choosing Cascade Delete means that if you delete a record from a table on the one side of a relationship, all related records on the many side will automatically be deleted. For example, if you delete a landlord in tblLandlord, all properties that the landlord owns will automatically be deleted from tblProperty.

That's a lot of information! Don't worry too much if you can't take it all in at once. If you ever need a recap you can always just type referential integrity into the Access Help System (see page 293).

### Creating the relationship

◉ First create the relationship without enforcing referential integrity. Click Create without checking any of the boxes.

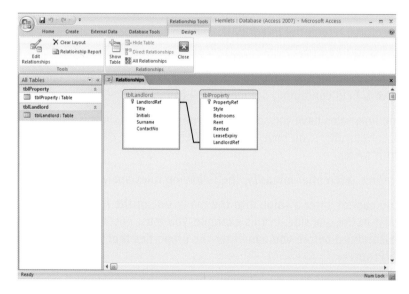

Notice that there is now a black line between the tables to represent the relationship. Because you didn't enforce referential integrity, Access has created a one-to-one relationship.

### Deleting relationships

You want a one-to-many relationship with enforced referential integrity, so delete the relationship you just created then create a new one.

◉ Right-click the black line between the tables and select Delete from the shortcut menu that appears.

● Click Yes when asked to confirm the delete.

Now create the new relationship.

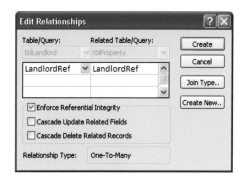

● Once again, click and drag the field LandlordRef from tblLandlord onto LandlordRef in tblProperty.

● This time, click in the box in the Edit Relationships window to Enforce Referential Integrity.

● Click the Create button.

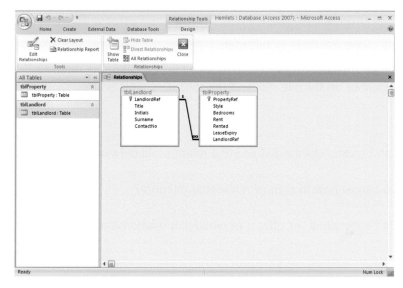

Notice that there is now a black line representing a one-to-many relationship between the two tables.

## Word of warning!

When there is no data in the database it is very easy to edit the relationships. Once you have entered data, it will still be possible to edit the relationships but this is not advisable. If you change a relationship after data has been entered, Access may get confused, and you could find error messages appearing at inconvenient moments.

## Saving the relationships

When you are satisfied that the relationships are correct, click the Close icon in the Relationships group on the Relationship Tools Design ribbon to close the Relationships window. The relationships are automatically saved.

● Close the database.

● Close Access by clicking its Close icon.

## Exercise

In this exercise you will create a database for a book shop. Part of the file creation is the appropriate design of the fields, including the type and size of fields.

1.   Create a new database and save it as Customer.accdb.

2.   Design two tables with 4 fields using the appropriate data types, distinguishing between text, numeric, currency etc., and with appropriate field sizes.

    (a)   The following fields must be created for the first table:
       CustomerID, Surname, Initials, ContactNumber.

    (b)   Save the table as tblCustomer.

    (c)   The following fields must be created for the second table:
       OrderNumber, Date, Price, Description, CustomerID.

    (d)   Save the table as tblOrders.

3.   Relate the tables using a one-to-many relationship. The tblCustomer table should be on the one side and the tblOrders table on the many.

## Ask yourself

❓   Can I create, change and delete a relationship between two tables?

❓   Do I know how to enforce referential integrity?

❓   Do I understand the effects of modifying relationships?

In this chapter you should have created and saved the following files:
Customer.accdb
Hemlets.accdb

In this chapter you have been introduced to the following buttons:

Relationships
in the Show/Hide group on the Database Tools ribbon

Close
in the Relationships group on the Relationship Tools Design ribbon

# Datasheet View

In this chapter you will find out:

- how to open an existing Access table
- how to enter data
- how to search for a record in a table
- how to modify data and records.

## Ribbon groups used in this chapter

In this chapter you will use this button in the Find group on the Home ribbon:

Find ———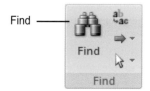

## Opening existing tables

Syllabus 5.2.2.1–2

There are two view modes to choose from when making changes to your database.

- Design View is used for making changes to the database structure, for example adding a field or changing a field name. This is the view that you used to set up the database structure of the Hemlets database.

- Datasheet View is used for entering and editing the data held in the database. In this chapter you will use Datasheet View to enter data about the properties and landlords into the tblProperty and tblLandlord tables.

You learnt how to switch between the two views on page 293.

## Entering data

▶ Open the Hemlets database.

Because of the referential integrity rules, you will enter the data into the one side of the relationship first, that is the tblLandlord table.

▶ Open the tblLandlord table by double clicking on its name in the Navigation Pane.

The table now appears in Datasheet view as shown.

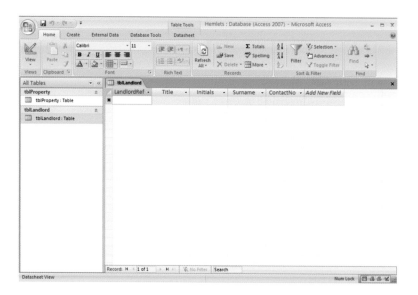

▶ You can drag the border between column headers (the field names) to alter the column widths. Drag the borders so that the whole row easily fits on the screen.

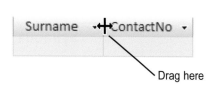

Drag here

**Tip:**

Right click a column header and select **Column Width...** from the menu that is displayed. You can set a precise width or set a best-fit width in the **Column Width** dialogue box.

▶ Click in the first row of the LandlordRef column and type L1.

▶ Tab to Title and type Mrs.

▶ Tab across and type the initial J.

▶ Go to the Surname field and type Welsh.

▶ Type 01474 276499 as the ContactNo.

▶ Your table should now look similar to the one at the top of the next page.

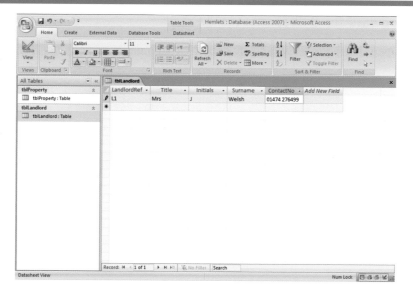

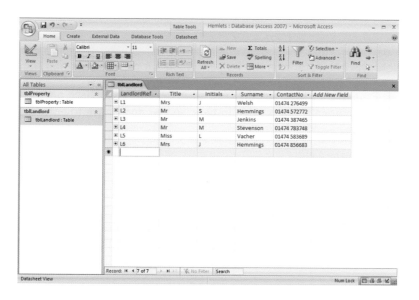

Now enter the rest of the data from the Landlord table on page 283.

When you have entered all the data, right click the
tblLandlord tab and select Close from the shortcut
menu that is displayed.

If you have changed the column widths, you will be
asked if you want to save the changes you made to
the layout.

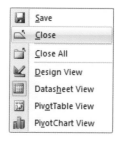

### Entering data for tblProperty

▶ Open the tblProperty table by double clicking on its name in the Navigation Pane.

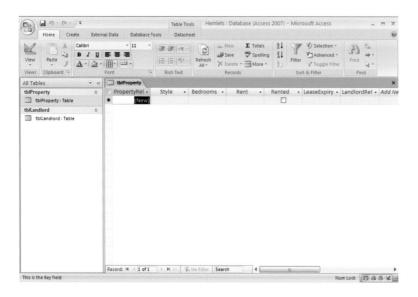

▶ Now type the data from the Property table on page 283, noting the following:

ℹ The PropertyRef field has the (AutoNumber) data type (see page 294). Access will automatically put a value in here, so you don't have to enter anything.

ℹ You don't need to type the pound sign in the Rent field – it will appear when you leave the field.

ℹ Click in the tick box in the Rented column to indicate a Yes.

Tip:

> Pressing the **Space** bar in the **Rented** field has the same effect as ticking an empty checkbox. Pressing the Space bar again will remove a tick.

ℹ In the Lease Expiry column, when you type 1/6/09 it will automatically change to 01/06/2009 when you leave the cell.

ℹ Try typing L9 as a LandlordRef, and pressing the Enter key. You will get the following error message because there isn't a landlord with LandlordRef L9 entered in tblLandlord. Click OK and correct the reference.

⊙     When you have entered all the data, your property data table will look similar to this.

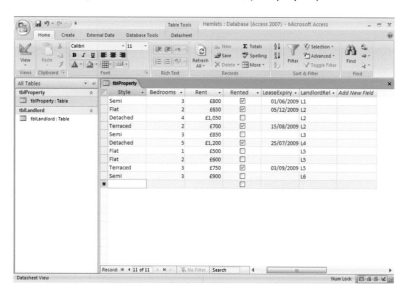

⊙     Close the table, saving any changes if you are asked to do so.

## Finding a record                                          Syllabus 5.2.2.4/5.4.1.1

### Using the record selector

You can navigate to the next or previous record in a table, query or form by using the record selector in Datasheet View. You can also move to the first or last record, or to a new record at the end of the database.

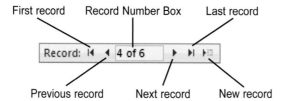

### Searching for a record

Sometimes you may want to search for a particular record, for example for a particular landlord. This method is most useful on a much larger database. Suppose you want to find the record for Mr Jenkins.

⊙     Open tblLandlord and click anywhere in the Surname column, except in Mr. Jenkins' record.

⊙     Click the Find button in the Find group on the Home ribbon to display the Find and Replace dialogue box.

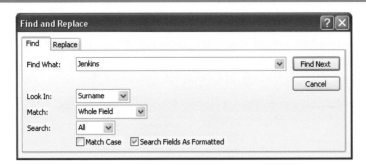

**Note:**

As well as searching for a specific word, you can search for a specific number or a specific date by typing it in the **Find What:** text box.

○ Type the name Jenkins in the Find What: text box, then click the Find Next button.

Mr Jenkins' record will now be highlighted.

○ You can use wildcards such as * in a search. Try searching for H*. This will find the next record starting with H each time you click Find Next.

○ Close the Find and Replace window by clicking its Close icon.

## Modifying data and records                    Syllabus 5.3.1.1

You can change the contents of any field (except an AutoNumber field, such as PropertyRef, which is set by Access) by clicking in the field and editing in the normal way. Use the Backspace or Delete key to delete unwanted text and type the corrections.

Remember you can undo changes using the Undo button on the Quick Access Toolbar, but only within the current record.

### Adding a new record

Suppose two new landlords have registered with Hemlets, and their details have to be added to the Hemlets database. Here are their details:

| LandlordRef | Title | Initials | Surname | ContactNo |
|---|---|---|---|---|
| L7 | Mr | I | Iqbal | 01474 733543 |
| L8 | Miss | E | Harrison | 01474 898398 |

There are two ways to add a new record:

○ *Either* click in the next blank line

○ *or* click the New Record button on the record selector (see the figure on the previous page).

○ Enter the details from the table above.

The first method is easy for such a small database, but if there were hundreds of landlords in the database you wouldn't want to scroll down to an empty row. For larger databases you would use the New Record button.

### Deleting a record

Suppose you entered Mr Iqbal's record by mistake and you want to delete it.

▶ Right-click the row selector for in Mr Iqbal's record.

▶ Click Delete Record on the shortcut menu that is
   displayed. You will see a message:

▶ Click Yes to delete the record.

▶ Close the table, then close the database.

## Exercise

1.  (a) Open the database ExamBoard.accdb that you created earlier.

    (b) Add the following records, save and close the database.

| CandidateID | Surname | Initials |
|-------------|---------|----------|
| 1 | Benaud | RJ |
| 2 | Matthews | SE |
| 3 | King | AE |
| 4 | Thompson | G |
| 5 | Adams | QH |
| 6 | Matthews | D |

2.  (a) Open the database Customer.accdb that you created earlier.

    (b) Enter four new customer records.

    (c) For each of these customers, enter two orders in the tblOrders table.

    (d) Save and close this database.

## Ask yourself

❓     Do I know how to open an existing table in Microsoft Access?

❓     Can I enter, edit and delete data in a table?

❓     Can I add and delete records in a table?

❓     Do I know how to navigate records in a table?

❓     Can I search for data in a table?


In this chapter you should have created and saved the following files:
Customer.accdb
ExamBoard.accdb
Hemlets.accdb


In this chapter you have been introduced to the following button:

Find
in the Find group on the Home ribbon

# Data Validation

In this chapter you will find out:

- ❶ about data validation
- ❶ how to set and test validation rules for different data types.

## Validation

Access can help to make sure that you have entered the data correctly into the database. If you make a mistake entering data, especially in very large databases, the error can be very difficult to trace. For example, if you entered Terrace instead of Terraced as the style for a property, then when you search the database for Terraced properties the record with the style Terrace won't be shown.

Although there are many errors which the database cannot detect (such as a misspelt name), there are many that it can.

You can write a set of rules which the data must abide by. For example:

- ❶ The style of a property can only be Flat, Terraced, Semi or Detached.

- ❶ The number of bedrooms must be between 1 and 9.

- ❶ The rent must be between £200 and £5000.

- ❶ The lease expiry date must be entered as a date later than today's date. The validation rule will only be applied when the date is entered – it doesn't matter if the date becomes invalid some months after it is has been entered.

The process of checking that the data meets various 'rules' is called validation. The rules themselves are called validation rules.

Alongside each rule, you can enter some text that Access will show to the user if they enter invalid data. This is called validation text.

## Comparison operators

There are several comparison operators that you can use, and they are listed in the table below:

| Operator | Meaning | Example |
|---|---|---|
| < | less than | <20 |
| <= | less than or equal to | <=20 |
| > | greater than | >0 |
| >= | greater than or equal to | >=0 |
| = | equal to | =20<br>="Flat" OR "Terraced" |
| <> | not equal to | <>"Semi" |
| BETWEEN | test for a range of values – must be two comparison values (a low & high value) separated by AND operator | BETWEEN 01/12/2002 AND 25/12/2002 |

## Entering the validation rules                              Syllabus 5.3.2.3

- ○ Open the Hemlets database.
- ○ Open the tblProperty table.
- ○ Open the table in Design View.

You are going to enter a validation rule for the Style field. The rule is: Style can only be Flat, Terraced, Semi or Detached.

- ○ Click in the Style field name.

Notice the two rows in the Field Properties at the bottom of the screen named Validation Rule and Validation Text. These are where you will enter the rules.

- ○ Click in the Validation Rule row.
- ○ Type Flat or Terraced or Semi or Detached and press Enter. Notice that Access adds quotes when you move the insertion point out of this field.
- ○ In the Validation Text row, type The Style must be Flat, Terraced, Semi or Detached.

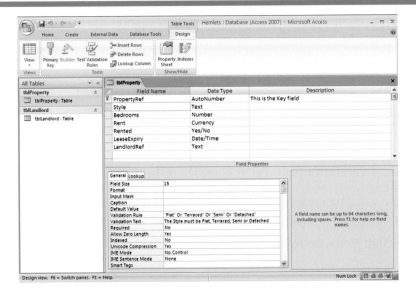

▶ Return to the Datasheet View.

▶ You will be asked to save the changes you have just made. Click Yes.

▶ Click Yes again when prompted about data integrity rules.

## Testing the validation rule

Test the validation rule by entering a new record that does not agree with it.

| Property Ref | Style | Bedrooms | Rent | Rented | Lease Expiry | Landlord Ref |
|---|---|---|---|---|---|---|
| (Auto Number) | Semi detached | 3 | 775 | N | | L3 |

▶ Click in the empty row below the last property. The PropertyRef will be entered automatically, so tab to the Style field and type Semi detached. Press Enter.

A message will appear on the screen containing the Validation Text that you entered:

○ Click OK. Re-type the style as Semi and press Enter. The validation rule will accept this.

○ Type the rest of the details for this property from the previous table.

Tip:

Access will not allow you to exit the field until the value in that field meets the validation rule.

## Entering a validation rule for a Number data type

Now set a validation rule for the Bedrooms field. The rule is: The number of bedrooms must be between 1 and 9.

○ Return to the Design View.

○ Click in the Bedrooms field.

○ Enter the Validation Rule and Validation Text as shown below:

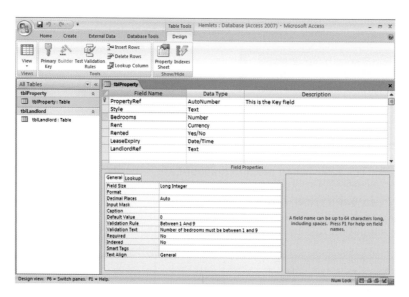

Tip:

Remember to press F1 for help if you get stuck!

## Entering a validation rule for a Currency data type

You can enter a validation rule for a Currency data type in just the same way as a Number data type.

○ With the cursor in the Rent row, enter Between 200 and 5000 as the validation rule.

○ Enter some suitable validation text.

## Entering a validation rule for a Date data type

This is also quite straightforward. Enter the following rule: the Lease Expiry must be between 1/1/2009 and 31/12/2012.

▶ Make sure the cursor is in the LeaseExpiry row of the tblProperty table.

▶ Enter the rule between #1/1/09# and #31/12/12# or is null as the validation rule. Enter some suitable validation text.

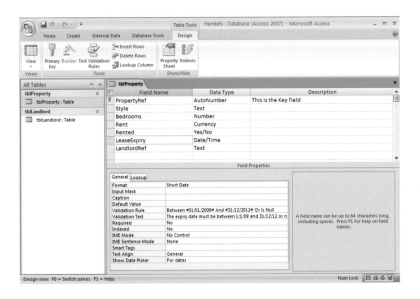

**Tip:**

You need to add the **or null** part because some of the date fields are blank.

ⓘ When using a date in a validation rule, you must put it between # marks, for example an ordinary date 1/1/09 becomes #1/1/09#. You don't need to remember all this – if you get stuck, just look up validation rule in the Access Help System, or press F1 when your cursor is in the Validation Rule row.

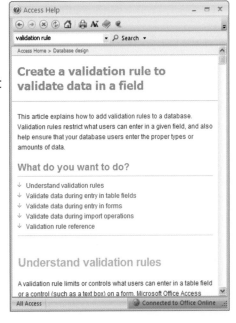

**More testing!**

▶ Return to the Datasheet View.

▶ Click Yes to save the changes and Yes to the prompt about data integrity rules.

▶ Enter the records below. Try entering invalid values to see the error messages.

**Tip:**

Always test your validation rules. Press Esc to cancel the record without saving it.

| PropertyRef | Style | Bed rooms | Rent | Rented | LeaseExpiry | LandlordRef |
|---|---|---|---|---|---|---|
| (Auto Number) | Detached | 4 | 950 | Y | 19/8/08 | L8 |
| (Auto Number) | Semi | 2 | 750 | N | | L4 |
| (Auto Number) | Terraced | 2 | 700 | Y | 5/1/10 | L5 |

▶ Close the table and database. Close Access if this is the end of a session.

## Exercise

In this exercise you will validate fields.

1. Open your database application Customer.accdb.

2. In the tblOrders table, set a validation rule so that the date entered cannot be earlier than 2008.

3. Set another rule so that the price cannot exceed £5,000.00 and warns the user with a suitable message if this happens.

4. Enter an order record and try out invalid values.

5. Save and close the database.

## Ask yourself

❓ Do I know what a validation rule is?

❓ Do I know what validation text is?

❓ Can I set validation rules and text for different data type fields in a table?

In this chapter you should have created and saved the following files:
Customer.accdb
Hemlets.accdb

# Sorting, Formatting and Printing

In this chapter you will find out:

- how to sort records
- how to format and print a data sheet
- how change page layout
- how to print selected records
- how to move columns.

## Ribbon groups used in this chapter

In this chapter you will use this button in the Sort & Filter group on the Home ribbon:

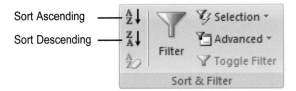

this button in the Close Preview group on the Print Preview ribbon:

this button in the Print group on the Print Preview ribbon:

and this button in the Page Layout group on the Print Preview ribbon:

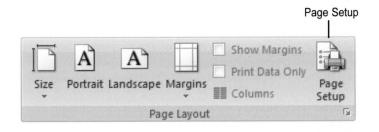

## Sorting records
Syllabus 5.2.2.5

- ● Open Access and the Hemlets database.

- ● Open the tblProperty table.

- ● If you need to, reduce the size of this window and drag it to one side so that you can see the database window.

- ● Open the tblLandlord table.

### Alphabetical sorts

You can perform a simple sort on one field by clicking anywhere in the column you want to sort on and clicking one of the two sort buttons (Sort Ascending and Sort Descending) in the Sort & Filter group on the Home ribbon.

For example, to sort the properties in the tblLandlord table by surname:

- ● Click in the Surname field and click sort Ascending. The records will now be sorted in ascending order of surname.

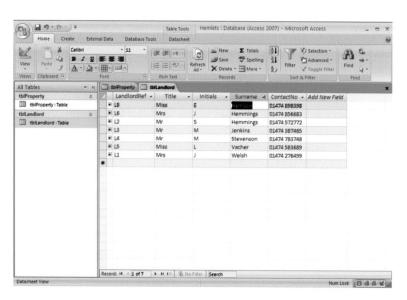

- ● Now click sort Descending.

The records will be re-sorted in descending alphabetical order.

### Numerical sorts

- ● Now click in the Bedrooms column of tblProperties.

- ● Click sort Descending.

The records will be sorted in descending order of the number of bedrooms. You can try re-sorting them in ascending order of Rent now!

- ● When you have finished experimenting, close tblProperties. You don't need to save the re-sorted table.

## Formatting and printing a datasheet
### Syllabus 5.6.2.1–2

You can print a datasheet just as it is, or you can format it first by hiding unwanted columns, changing the order of the columns and changing column widths.

◉ With tblLandlord open in Datasheet View, click Print on the Office button menu and then click Print Preview from the options provided. The data appears as shown below.

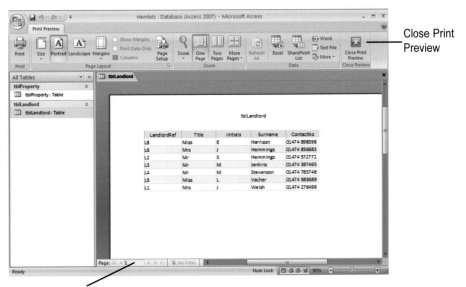

Close Print Preview

Page selector

A large datasheet may not fit on one page. You can use the page selector at the bottom of the screen to view the other pages and the zoom features to increase or decrease the preview area.

◉ Click the Close Print Preview button in the Close Preview group on the Print Preview ribbon to exit Print Preview.

## Changing the page layout
### Syllabus 5.6.2.1

The current page layout is in Portrait view. You can change this to Landscape view.

◉ Display the print preview once again.

◉ Click the Page Setup button in the Page Layout group on the Print Preview ribbon.

◉ Click the Page tab on the Page Setup dialogue box that is displayed.

◉ Click the Landscape radio button and then the OK button.

- ○ The change is shown immediately in the print preview.

- ○ Click the Print button in the Print group on the Print Preview ribbon to open the Print dialogue box.

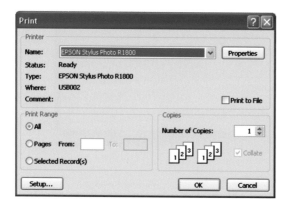

- ○ Choose which pages and how many copies to print, and select the printer you want to print to.

- ○ Click OK to print, otherwise click Cancel.

- ○ Close the print preview.

## Printing selected records                                    Syllabus 5.6.2.2

- ○ With the table in Datasheet View, select just a few records by clicking and dragging across the row selectors of the rows you require.

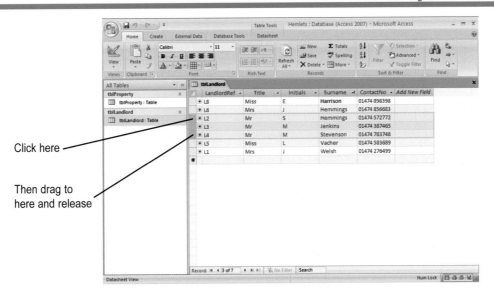

Click here

Then drag to
here and release

● This time, as an alternative to printing from the print preview, select the Print option for Print on the Office button menu.

● The Print dialogue box is displayed. Select Selected Record(s) in the Print Range section.

● Click OK to print only those records you highlighted.

## Moving columns

Suppose you want the Surname column to appear before the Title column.

● Click the Surname column header to select the column.

● Click again and hold down the mouse button, then drag the header to the left of the Title column. A thick line will show you where you have dragged the column.

This is the Surname column header

● Release the mouse button to drop the column in its new position. The table will now look similar to the screenshot on the next page.

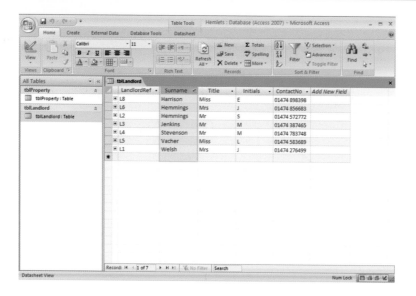

**Tip:**

You have already adjusted column widths by dragging the column header border (see page 308). If you double-click the border between headers, the column width is adjusted to just enclose the maximum width text in the column.

▶ Print preview that table again to see what the page will look like when printed.

▶ Close the print preview and the table, saving changes to the table layout.

## Exercise

1. Open the ExamBoard.accdb database.

2. Print the first four records of the tblCandidate table with fields in the order CandidateID, Surname, Initials.

3. Print all the records with fields in the order Surname, Initials, CandidateID.

4. Close the database.

## Ask yourself

❓ Do I know how to sort fields numerically and alphabetically in ascending and descending order?

❓ Do I know how to format and change the layout of a datasheet for printing?

❓ Do I know how to preview a datasheet before printing?

❓ Do I know how to print selected records?

❓ Can I move columns in a table?

In this chapter you should have created and saved the following files:
ExamBoard.accdb
Hemlets.accdb

In this chapter you have been introduced to the following buttons:

Sort Ascending
Sort Descending
in the Sort & Filter group on the Home ribbon

Close Print Preview
in the Close Preview group on the Print Preview ribbon

Print
in the Print group on the Print Preview ribbon

Page Setup
in the Page Layout group on the Print Preview ribbon

# 33 Forms

In this chapter you will find out:

- about how forms are used with a database
- how to create a new form
- how to add header and footer text to a form, and how to format it
- how to open and close a form
- how to enter, modify, sort and delete data and records using a form
- how to navigate tables using a form
- how to print a form.

## Ribbon groups used in this chapter

In this chapter you will use this button in the Forms group on the Create ribbon:

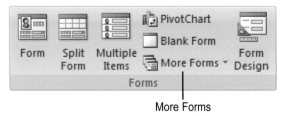

More Forms

these buttons in the Font group on the Form Design Tools Design ribbon:

Font Size  Font Color

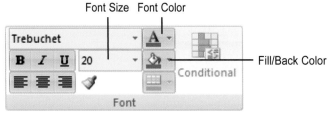

Fill/Back Color

and this button in the Controls group on the Form Design Tools Design ribbon:

Label

## User interface

You need to consider how the users interact with your database – how they choose what to do next, how they enter data and so on.

You will start by creating a form to allow the user to input data about landlords.

This form will be used to enter new landlords when they register with Hemlets.

## Creating a new form

○    Open the Hemlets database (if it is not open already).

 ─○    Click the More Forms button in the Forms group on the Create ribbon, and select Form Wizard from the menu that is displayed. The first step in the Wizard appears. Using the Wizard to create a form is usually the quickest method, and the one you normally use to create a simple form.

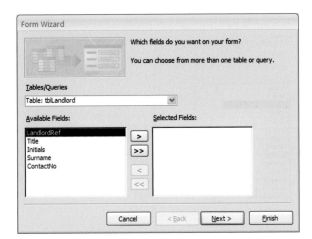

○    The first step in the Wizard (above) asks which fields you want to appear on your form. You want all the fields, so click ▶▶ . All the Available Fields will now appear in the Selected Fields pane.

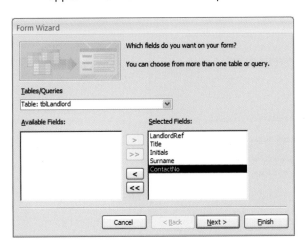

▶   Click Next to display the second step in the Wizard.

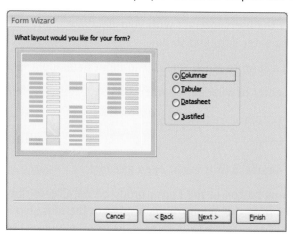

▶   Select the Columnar form layout.

▶   Click Next to display the third step in the Wizard.

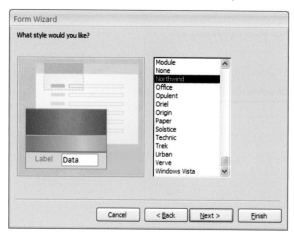

**Note:**
You can select another style if the one used in the example is unavailable on your computer.

▶   Select the Northwind style.

▶   Click Next to display the fourth step in the Wizard.

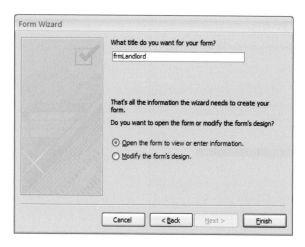

○ Type frmLandlord as the title of the form. You will change this title later, but you need to enter it here so that Access will save the form with that name.

○ Click Finish to create the form.

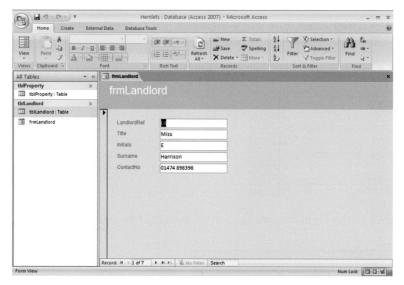

○ The form opens in Form View and the new object appears in the Navigation Pane. The record selector at the bottom of the form shows that records already exist in the form – these are all the records you entered directly into the tblLandlord table.

## Changing view mode

As with tables, you need to have the form open in Design View in order to modify it.

○ Click Design View to view the form in Design View.

○ If the Field List pane is showing, click the highlighted Add Existing Fields button in the Tools group on the Form Design Tools Design ribbon to close it. Your database form will look similar to this:

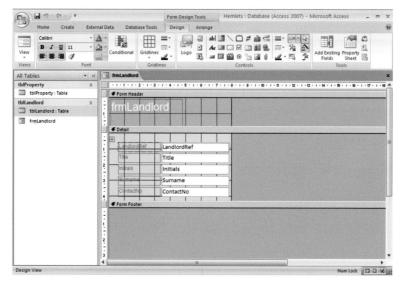

## Adding text to the header

Currently the title frmLandlord appears in the Form Header section at the top of the Design View. You need to change this to something more understandable.

It would be better if the form was a bit wider too, so there is more space for a title.

▷ Widen it by clicking and dragging the thin black line at the right-hand edge of the form. Drag it a couple of centimetres or so.

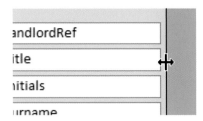

▷ Click in the Form Header section so the text box outline appears.

▷ Click in the text box to place the flashing text cursor.

▷ Delete the current title and type Landlord Details Form.

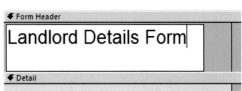

You will now change the font, the font size and formatting just as you would in Word or Excel – you will need to use the buttons in the Font group on the Form Design Tools Design ribbon.

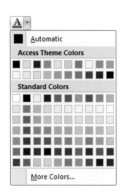

### Changing text size

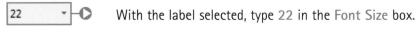 ▷ With the label selected, type 22 in the Font Size box.

### Changing text colour

▷ Click the small down-arrow on the Font Color button.

▷ Select a colour from the palette!

Now change the background colour, using the Fill/Back Color button.

If you need to, click and drag the handles so that the label box fills the whole Form Header.

Return to the Form View to see what your form looks like.

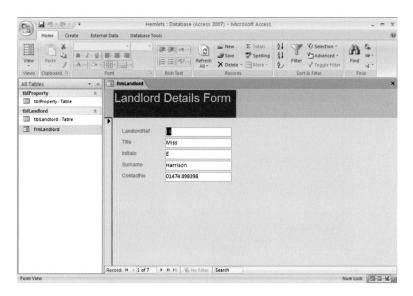

The form looks better, but if you're unhappy with it, just return to the Design View and use the Font group buttons to change the formatting.

 The data you enter into forms is automatically saved, but you have to remember to save any changes you make to the design. Save your form now by clicking the Save icon on the Quick Access Toolbar.

## Adding text to the footer

Adding text as a footer is done in a similar way as adding it to the header, except you will use the Form Footer section instead of the Form Header, and you will create a new text box rather than use one already provided.

Click Design View to view the form in Design View once again.

 Click the Label (Form Control) button in the Controls group on the Form Design Tools Design ribbon.

Click in the top left of the Form Footer section and drag out a rectangle as shown overleaf.

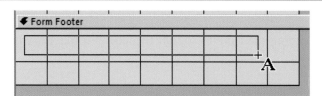

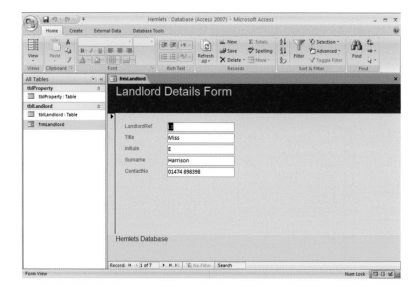

▶ Click in the text box and type the text Hemlets Database. Change the font size and colour, and the background colour until you are happy with the way it looks. You can also change the size of the text box if you need to. Go to Form View to see your handiwork!

▶ Try resizing the form by clicking and dragging its borders. You'll see that whatever size you make the form, the footer will remain at the bottom of the window.

## Closing and opening a form                          Syllabus 5.2.2.1/3

▶ Click the Close button on the top right of the form to close it. If you have made changes to the design of the form since you last saved, you will be asked if you want to save the changes.

The form name, frmLandlord, still appears in the Navigation Pane. If you want to delete the form for any reason, you can do so by right-clicking the form name and selecting Delete from the menu that appears. Don't delete it now – you're going to need it again.

▶ Open the frmLandlord again by double-clicking its name in the Navigation Pane.

Tip:

You can delete tables, forms, queries and reports by selecting them in the Navigation Pane, and then pressing the delete key.

## Entering data using a form

Now you'll use the form you've just created to enter some more landlord details into the table.

### The record selector

When using the form to enter or look up data, you will need to use the Record Selector. These are the buttons you can see at the bottom of your form. The record selector is exactly the same as the one you first met in Chapter 30 on page 311 for navigating through records – this time you will use it for navigating through the records in a form.

Tip:

> The **Previous record** button is not active at the moment because you are already on the first record – so you can't go back one.

ⓘ  Remember each record contains a different landlord.

You will now enter the following additional landlord details into the tblLandlord form.

| LandlordRef | Title | Initials | Surname | ContactNo |
|---|---|---|---|---|
| L9 | Mr | T | Hodson | 01474 243046 |
| L10 | Mr | P | Chisholm | 01474 384446 |
| L11 | Miss | F | Kennedy | 01474 558374 |

▶  Go to a new record using the New record button on the record selector.

▶  The cursor will now be in the LandlordRef box on the new record, so type L9.

▶  Either click in the Title box or just press tab. Enter Mr.

▶  Enter the remaining details for Mr Hodson.

▶  Click the New Record button and type the details for the next landlord.

▶  Repeat for the third new landlord in the table.

### Going to specific records

▶  You can use the record selector to find records in a form.

▶  Go through the form records using the Previous record and Next record buttons.

ⓘ  You can look up a specific record in the same way as you did in the table by using the Find button in the Find group on the Home ribbon (see page 311).

## Using a form to modify records                    Syllabus 5.5.1.3

Sometimes you may want to find a record in order to modify or delete it. For example, suppose you have made a mistake entering Mr Chisholm's telephone number – it should be 01474 384464, not 01474 384446.

○ Open the Find and Replace dialogue box as explained on page 311.

○ Type Chis in the Find What: box to find the landlord's surname.

○ Click the down-arrow next to the Look In: box and change the option to frmLandlord if it isn't already showing.

○ Click the down-arrow next to the Match box and change this option to Any Part of Field.

○ Click the Find Next button. Mr Chisholm's record will appear.

○ Close the Find and Replace dialogue box.

○ Click in the ContactNo field and edit the telephone number.

## Using a form to delete records                    Syllabus 5.5.1.4

You can delete a record from a form.

○ Display the record you want to delete.

○ Clicking the arrow on the Delete button in the Records group on the Home ribbon, and select Delete record from the menu that is displayed. You will see a message on the screen:

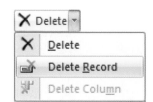

○ Click No for now as you do not want to delete any records.

## Printing the form                    Syllabus 5.6.2.1/5.6.2.3

It is a good idea to use Print Preview to check what the form will look like when it is printed, before you go ahead and print.

○ Make sure you're in Form View.

○ Click Print on the Office button menu and then click Print Preview from the options provided. The data appears as shown on the next page.

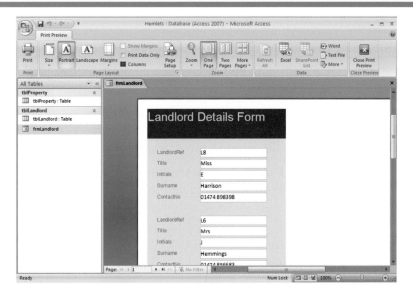

Tip:

If the form is too small to read, simply click it to enlarge it.

### Page setup

You can use Page Setup in exactly the same way as you did for the table on page 323. You can change the orientation of the paper and its size. If you want to print, click OK, otherwise click Cancel.

○ Close the print preview by clicking the Close Print Preview button on the Print Preview ribbon

○ Close the form.

○ You may be asked if you want to save changes to the design. Click Yes.

## The Property form

It would be useful to have a form to enter all the property details. Using exactly the same method you used for the frmLandlord form, try and create a form for the properties. Save it as frmProperty.

○ Try using the Find button to find all the two-bedroom properties. You can click the Find Next button in the Find and Replace window to scroll through them all.

○ You can also click in the LeaseExpiry field and find a record with a particular lease expiry date. Try finding the record with a lease expiry date of 05/12/2009.

## Sorting data in forms Syllabus 5.2.2.5

You can sort data in forms into ascending or descending numeric or alphabetical sequence. You have already practised sorting records in a table (see page 322) and the procedure is exactly the same.

▶ Click in the field for Rent and click the sort Descending button in the Sort & Filter group on the Home ribbon. This will sort the records in descending order of Rent. Scroll through the forms to satisfy yourself that this is so.

▶ Sort the records back to the original sequence by clicking in the PropertyRef field and clicking the sort Ascending button.

## Exporting from a database Syllabus 5.6.1.6

You can export a table or the result of a query in other file formats to other locations on a drive or network.

▶ Click the External Data ribbon tab.

The buttons in the Export group allow you to choose the file format you want to export to.

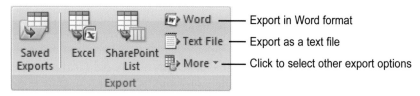

Access can export to many file formats, including those used by other database software. As well as different versions of Excel spreadsheets, common formats include Text, HTML and XML.

▶ To export, click the button for the file format you want and follow the on-screen instructions.

That's all you need to know about forms, so now you can close your database and have a break!

▶ Close your database and close Access.

## Exercises

1. (a) Open the ExamBoard.accdb database.

   (b) Create a simple form to input data into your tblCandidate table.

   (c) Save the form as frmCandidate.

   (d) Enter two new records using the form.

   (e) Close the database.

2.   (a)   Open the Customer.accdb database.

      (b)   Create a simple form to input data into your tblCustomer table.

            Make all the text labels font size 14. Include a heading in a larger font on a shaded background. In the Footer section, insert the text BetterBooks Ltd.

      (c)   Save the form as frmCustomer.

      (d)   Enter two new records using the form.

      (e)   Close the database.

## Ask yourself

❓   Do I know how to create a new form and switch between the Design and Form views?

❓   Can I use the form's header and footer, and apply simple formatting?

❓   Can I open, save and close a form?

❓   Can I enter data into a table using a form?

❓   Can I navigate records within a form?

❓   Can I add, edit and delete records within a form?

❓   Do I know how to print a form using different print options?

❓   Can I sort records within a form?

In this chapter you should have created and saved the following files:

Customer.accdb         ExamBoard.accb         Hemlets.accdb

In this chapter you have been introduced to the following buttons:

More Forms
in the Forms group on the Create ribbon

Fill/Back Color
Font Color
Font Size
in the Font group on the Form Design Tools Design ribbon

Label
in the Controls group on the Form Design Tools Design ribbon

# CHAPTER 34 Applying Filters

In this chapter you will find out:

- ❶ about filters
- ❶ how to use and remove a filter in a form and in a table
- ❶ how to filter by selection and by form.

## Ribbon group used in this chapter

In this chapter you will use these buttons in the Sort & Filter group on the Home ribbon:

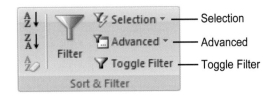

## Filters

Both filters and queries (which you'll meet in the next chapter) are used to select specific records (referred to as a subset of records) from a table of data.

- ❶ In general, you use a filter to view or edit a subset of records temporarily while you're in a table or form. Queries are similar to filters but they can perform more complicated tasks that cannot be done with a filter, and which need to be repeated. You'll understand more about which is more appropriate once you've used them.

## Using a filter in a form                                    Syllabus 5.4.1.2

You'll use a filter to select specific types of records in the frmLandlord form.

- ▶ Open the Hemlets database, then open the frmLandlord form in Form View.

The filter options are in the Sort & Filter group on the Home ribbon.

### Filter by selection

With filter by selection, all you need to do is find one instance of the value you are looking for in the form.

You'll use filter by selection to select only those records where the title is Miss.

▶ Use the record selector (or Find) to navigate to any record where the title is Miss. Click in the Title field so that the cursor is in the same field as the Miss entry.

▶ Click the Selection button and click the filter criterion you want from the menu of options – in this case click Equals "Miss".

▶ Use the record selector at the bottom of the form to go through the filtered records. There should only be three, each having the title Miss.

### Removing a filter

Syllabus 5.4.1.3

▶ To remove the filter temporarily, click the Toggle Filter button in the Sort & Filter group to display the whole table or form once again. (The button appears highlighted when a filter is applied.) The form returns to normal with all 10 records available.

▶ Click the (now unhighlighted) Toggle Filter button again to reapply the filter by selection.

▶ To remove the filter completely, click the Advanced button in the Sort & Filter group and select Clear All Filters from the menu that appears.

**Tip:**

A table or form that does not have a filter applied is shown by a faded No Filter button in the record navigation bar at the bottom of the Access screen. If a filter is defined, you can toggle between Filtered and Unfiltered by clicking the button.

## Filter by Form

To filter by form, you simply type in the value you are looking for into a blank form. You will look for landlords with the surname Hemmings.

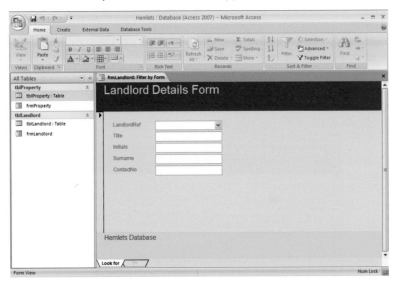

Make sure that the filter isn't currently applied. Click the Advanced button in the Sort & Filter group on the Home ribbon, and select Filter By Form from the menu of options. A blank form appears.

> Click in the Surname field.

> Click the arrow that appears at the right of the field.

This conveniently gives you a list of all the surnames entered in the database. You can either click a surname in the list or just type it in.

> Click Hemmings.

> Click the Advanced button again and select Apply Filter/Sort from the menu of options.

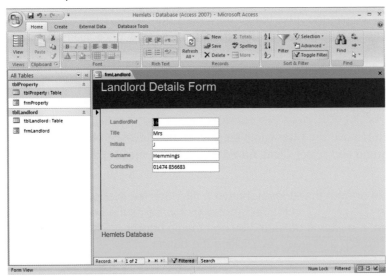

- Two records have been filtered. Check they both have the surname Hemmings.

- Remove the filter and close the frmLandlord form.

## Using a filter in a table                                    Syllabus 5.4.1.2–3

This is very similar to using a filter in a form, so the following runs though this briefly.

- Open the tblLandlord table in Datasheet View.

- The Field List pane that shows related fields in other tables might appear. Close it by clicking the Close button **X** on the pane.

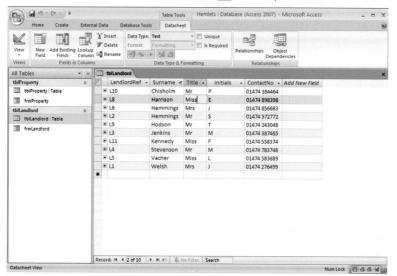

- Place the cursor in the Title column in a record that says Miss as shown in the previous screenshot.

- Click the Selection button in the Sort & Filter group on the Home ribbon and click the filter criterion you want from the menu of options – in this case click Equals "Miss".

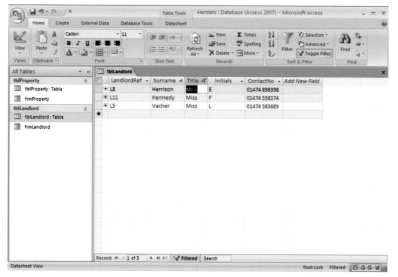

There are three records shown with the title Miss.

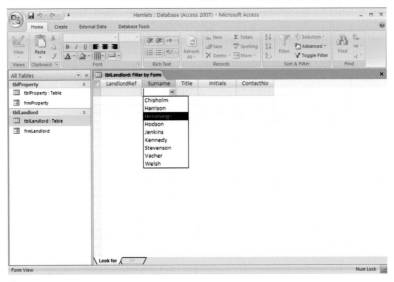

Remove the filter by clicking the Filtered button that appears highlighted next to the record selector at the bottom of the screen.

Now click the Advanced button in the Sort & Filter group on the Home ribbon, and select Filter By Form from the menu of options.

Click the Advanced button again and select Clear Grid from the menu of options.

Click in the Surname field then click the arrow to show the list of surnames.

Click Hemmings.

Click the Advanced button again and select Apply Filter/Sort from the menu of options.

Two records with the surname Hemmings have been filtered.

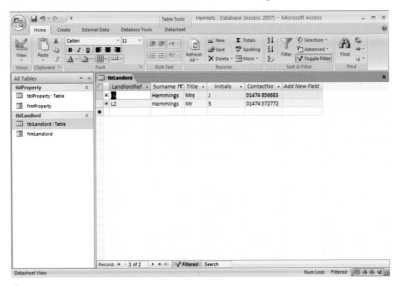

Remove the filter, save and close the table.

## Exercise

1.  Open the database Student.accdb. It contains details about 50 students applying to a college.

2.  Add another field named UCAS to the end of the student table. The new field is to be numeric and will hold students' UCAS points.

3.  Set a validation rule for the new field, specifying that the value entered must be between 0 and 480. Enter suitable validation text.

4.  Save the table structure.

5.  Create a simple form for the students table.

6.  Save the form as frmStudent.

7.  Write down the number of records in the database.

8.  Find the record for the student whose surname is Peterson.

9.  Change the name to Pedersen.

10. Filter the records to find all the students who come from Northcliff School. Write down the first names and surnames of students you found.

11. Filter the records to find all Male students from Eastcliff School. How many are there?

12. Remove the filter and save and close the database.

## Ask yourself

❓ Do I know what a filter is?

❓ Can I filter by selection to find all occurrences of a particular data entry in a table or in a form?

❓ Can I filter by form a table or a form?

In this chapter you should have created and saved the following file:
Hemlets.accdb
Student.accdb

In this chapter you have been introduced to the following buttons:
Advanced
Selection
Toggle Filter
in the Sort & Filter group on the Home ribbon

# CHAPTER 35

# Making Queries

In this chapter you will find out:

- ❗ about queries
- ❗ how to create a query by selecting fields from one and from two tables
- ❗ how to show, hide, remove and order fields in a query
- ❗ how to add and remove criteria
- ❗ how to save and run a query
- ❗ how to sort data in a query result, on one and two fields
- ❗ about comparison operators and how to use them in a query
- ❗ how print a query result.

## Ribbon groups used in this chapter

In this chapter you will use this button in the Other group on the Create ribbon:

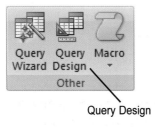

Query Design

this button in the Results group on the Query Tools Design ribbon:

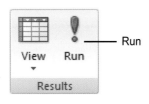

Run

and this button in the Query Setup group on the Query Tools Design ribbon:

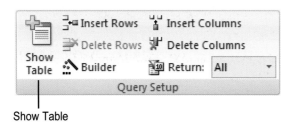

Show Table

One of the most useful things you can do with a database is to find all the records that satisfy a certain condition, such as "all properties that have 2 bedrooms". Queries are similar to filters, but they allow more scope for changing the format of the results. Queries are useful when you are likely to be searching the database repeatedly for the same thing, because you can easily save them. You can then run the saved query without first opening a table or form.

▶ Load Access and open the Hemlets database.

## Creating a new query                                                       Syllabus 5.4.2.1–2

You'll create a new query that finds all properties that are currently not rented. You can then add other criteria such as number of bedrooms and rent to narrow down the search for a prospective tenant.

▶ Click the Query Design button in the Other group on the Create ribbon.

A new tab, Query1, is created and the Show Table window is displayed.

▶ You are going to base the query on the tblProperty table, so click tblProperty to select it then click Add.

▶ Click Close to close the Show Table window.

An empty query grid appears. Now you need to add fields from the table to the grid.

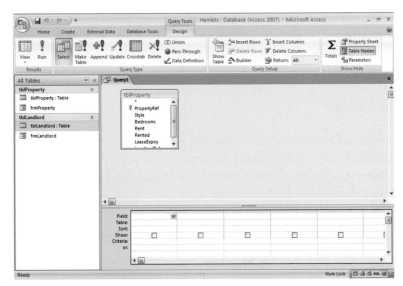

347

## Selecting fields to appear in the query

You need to add a field to the query grid if:

ⓘ   you want to specify a particular value for that field. In our case, you want to specify that the Rented field has a No value, so Rented will have to be put in the grid. You won't actually want to see this field with the results, as you already know that all records selected will not be rented.

ⓘ   you want the field to appear in the results table. You need to show property details like Style, Bedrooms and Rent so that anyone looking through can make a decision on which properties they might be interested in. The PropertyRef field should also be included.

▶   Double-click the PropertyRef field in the table representation to put it in the Query Builder grid.

▶   Double-click the fields Style, Bedrooms, Rent and Rented to add them to the grid.

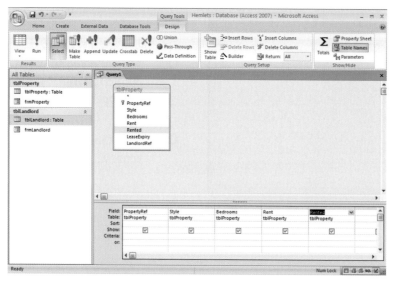

**Tip:**

You can drag a field from the table and drop it into the grid if you don't like double-clicking!

## Resizing columns

ⓘ   You can change the width of the columns in the query grid so that you can view them all without having to scroll across. Just place the cursor between two column headers so that it changes to a double-headed arrow, then either double-click the mouse or click and drag.

Double-headed arrow ———

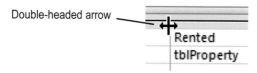

## Adding and removing fields from the grid

▶ Double-click the LeaseExpiry field to add it to the query grid.

▶ To delete the LeaseExpiry field, click in the column header for the LeaseExpiry field then press the Delete key.

## Adding and removing criteria

▶ Now you'll specify that the Rented field must have a No value.

▶ In the Criteria row under the Rented column, type No.

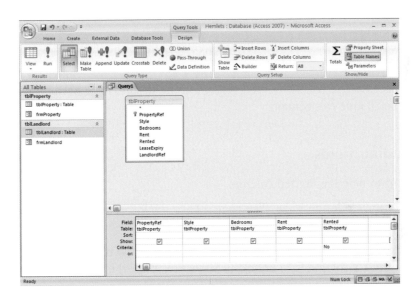

ℹ Removing a criterion is just as straightforward – just click the criterion you want to delete then press the Backspace or Delete key.

## Running a query

▶ Click the Run button in the Results group on the Query Tools Design ribbon.

You will get the Results table shown at the top of the next page.

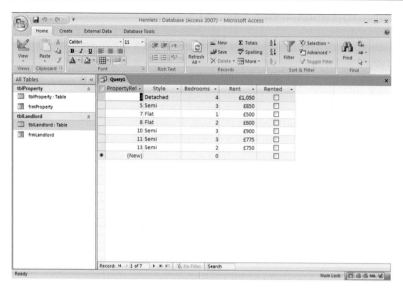

You can see that it has successfully selected only those properties that are not currently rented.

It isn't necessary to see the Rented column in the Results table because it will always be No. You'll hide this column.

## Hiding and unhiding fields                                    Syllabus 5.4.2.8

You want to hide the Rented column.

&#9673;   Return to Design View. (See page 293 to remind yourself how to switch between different views within Access.)

&#9673;   Notice that above the Criteria row there is a Show row. All you need to do to hide a column is to untick its Show box. Click the Show box in the Rented column to remove the tick.

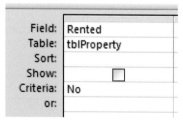

&#9673;   Run the query again to see that it has worked.

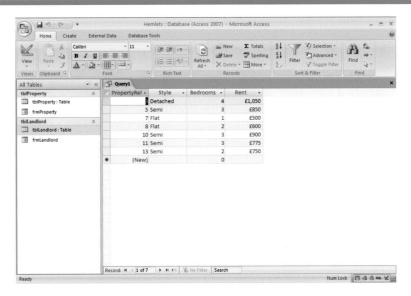

ⓘ    You can unhide fields simply by clicking the Show box again so that it is ticked.

## Saving a query                                              Syllabus 5.2.2.1

Before you do any more, save the query. You will now be able to run this query any time simply by double-clicking its name in the Database window.

Click the Save icon on the Quick Access Toolbar and type qryPropertyForRent as the query name. The tab on the Results table will change to show the new name, and the query will appear in the Navigation Pane so you can open it again in the future. (Delete a query by selecting it here and pressing the Delete key.)

## Sorting data in a query output                              Syllabus 5.2.2.5

Data in a query results table can be sorted in ascending or descending order in any field such as PropertyRef, Bedrooms or Rent in the example. The query results table is effectively the same as the original data table except that it shows only a subset of the data the original table holds. You sort data in the query results table in exactly the same way as you sorted data in the data table on page 322.

▶    Click anywhere in the Rent column.

Click the sort Ascending button. The records are reordered by rent from the cheapest to the most expensive.

You can also sort in ascending or descending alphabetical order in a text field such as Style.

▶    Click in the Style column.

▶    Click the sort Ascending button.

▶    Now try sorting in descending order of Bedrooms, so that the properties with the most bedrooms appear at the top of the list.

## Sorting on two fields

Sorting the query results table may be useful for a 'one-off' query but next time you run the saved query, the results will be in the original sequence.

You can specify a sort order in the actual query, so that the data will always appear in the desired sequence when you run the query. Also, you can sort by more than one field. (For example, a telephone directory is sorted by Surname and then by Initials, so that Smith, J.S. appears before Smith, R.A.)

In our query, it might be useful if the results were sorted by style and by number of bedrooms. When you want to sort by more than one field, Access has to prioritise which field it will sort by first. Access will sort first by the left-most field in the query builder.

At the moment, in the query qryPropertyForRent, the Style field is left of Bedrooms, so it will sort by Style then by Bedrooms.

▶ In Design View, click in the Sort row of the Style column then click the small down-arrow to show a menu of sort options.

▶ Click Ascending so that it sorts the house styles alphabetically from A to Z. Note that if you want to sort house styles from Z to A (Semi before Flat), you would select Descending.

▶ Repeat this for the Bedrooms field. Select Ascending to sort the properties in order of least to most bedrooms.

▶ Run the query.

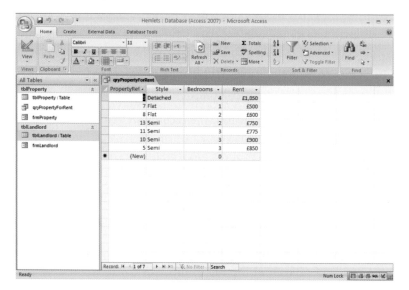

## Moving fields in the query builder

Suppose you now want to sort first by bedrooms, then house style.

You'll have to move the Bedrooms field to the left of the Style field so that Access will sort by Bedrooms first.

▶ Return to Design View.

▶ Move the mouse pointer over the Bedroom column header so that it appears as a black down-arrow, and click so that the whole column is selected.

▶ Click and drag the column to the left of the Style field. When you are dragging, you can tell where the column will be dropped by a black line that appears between the columns. Release the mouse button when the black line is to the left of the Style field (see below).

▶ Run the query.

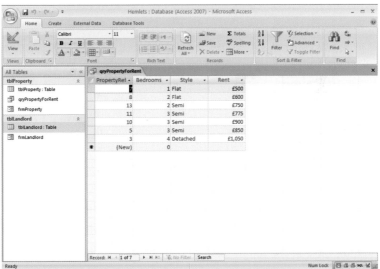

## Adding a second table to a query

Suppose you want to see who the landlord is for each of these properties. You would have to add the tblLandlord table to the query.

▶ Return to Design View.

▶ Click the Show Table button in the Query Setup group on the Query Tools Design ribbon to display the Show Table window.

> ▶ Make sure tblLandlord table is selected then click Add.

> ▶ Click Close.

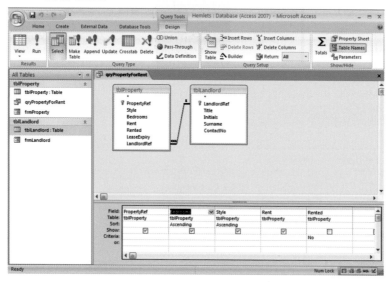

tblLandlord is added to the query. Now you want to add the fields Title, Initials and Surname from the tblLandlord table to the query grid.

> ▶ Double-click the fields Title, Initials and Surname in tblLandlord to add them.

> ▶ Run the query.

The query result table at the top of the next page now shows you who owns the properties.

**Tip:**

If you get repeated rows, check you haven't added any of the tables more than once. Do this by using the scroll bars in the top part of the query window in Design View to search for extra and unwanted tables.

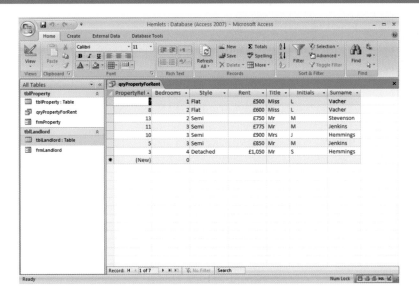

## Using operators

Syllabus 5.4.2.4–5

Sometimes you need to find all records with a field less than or greater than a particular value. In query criteria, you can use any of the comparison operators that you used for validating data. They are repeated here for reference. AND, OR and NOT are also operators used in queries.

| Operator | Meaning | Example |
|---|---|---|
| < | less than | <20 |
| <= | less than or equal to | <=20 |
| > | greater than | >0 |
| >= | greater than or equal to | >=0 |
| = | equal to | =20<br>="Flat" OR "Terraced" |
| <> | not equal to | <>"Semi" |
| BETWEEN | test for a range of values. Must be two comparison values (a low & high value) separated by AND operator | BETWEEN 01/12/2002 AND 25/12/2002 |
| AND | all criteria must be satisfied | Bedrooms>1 AND Rent<800 AND Rented="No" |
| OR | at least one of the criteria must be satisfied | ="Flat" OR "Semi" |
| NOT | all criteria are satisfied except for the ones specified | NOT "Flat" |

Add some more criteria to your query that specify the property must have more than one bedroom, and that the rent must be less than £800. The query builder will look similar to that shown on the next page.

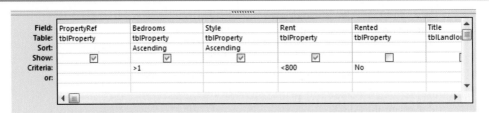

| Field: | PropertyRef | Bedrooms | Style | Rent | Rented | Title |
|---|---|---|---|---|---|---|
| Table: | tblProperty | tblProperty | tblProperty | tblProperty | tblProperty | tblLandlo |
| Sort: | | Ascending | Ascending | | | |
| Show: | ☑ | ☑ | ☑ | ☑ | ☐ | |
| Criteria: | | >1 | | <800 | No | |
| or: | | | | | | |

▶ Run the query.

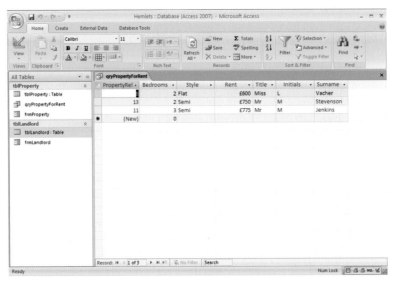

▶ Save the query.

Notice that when you place query criteria on the same line ALL have to be satisfied. This is equivalent to the "AND" condition in the Operator table on the previous page.

To enter criteria to find all properties which are EITHER a Flat "OR" a Semi, you could write the criteria as shown below:

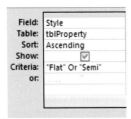

Alternatively, you can write the criteria one beneath the other:

You could find all properties which are EITHER one-bedroomed OR a Flat:

| Field: | Bedrooms | Style |
|---|---|---|
| Table: | tblProperty | tblProperty |
| Sort: | Ascending | Ascending |
| Show: | ☑ | ☑ |
| Criteria: | | "Flat" |
| or: | 1 | |

- Experiment with the different criteria in the query builder to see what effect there is on the results table. Do not save your results.

## Wildcards

You can use wildcards in Query or Find criteria. A wildcard represents a series of data. Here are the wildcards you need to know for Access databases with file extensions mdb or accdb:

- \* is used to represent a sequential series of characters in the position it is placed. Query (or Find) criterion examples: \*2009 in a field with a date property will return a result of all the dates in that year that are present in the database; Sh\* in a field containing surnames will return a result of all the surnames starting with Sh that are present in the database (e.g. Shar, Sharp, Sharpe etc.).

- ? is used to represent a single character in the position it is placed. Query (or Find) criterion example: T?m in a field containing names will return a result of all the matching names (e.g. Tim, Tom).

Note:

> You may come across a particular type of Access database called an **Access Project** (with a file extension **adp** or **accdp**). If you do you will need to use the wildcard **%** instead of \* and the wildcard _ instead of **?**.

## Printing the results of a query

All the options for printing a query are very similar to those for printing a table or form.

- In Datasheet View (the Results table), click Print on the Office button menu and then click Print Preview from the options provided.

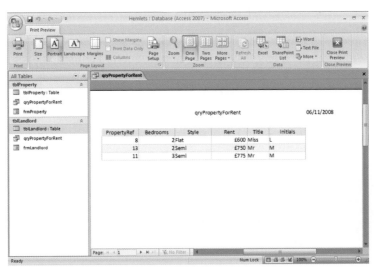

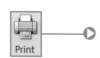

Print

○ Use the Page Layout group buttons on the Print Preview ribbon to change page orientation and paper size.

○ Click the Print button on the Print Preview ribbon to display the Print dialogue box where you can specify which pages to print and the number of copies. If you want to print, click OK, otherwise click Cancel.

○ Close the print preview and then close the database.

## Exercise

1.  (a)  Open the Student database that you downloaded earlier in this module.

    (b)  Create a query to select all records of students who come from Westcliff School. Display only the fields for Surname, Forename, Sex and School.

    (c)  Run the query.

    (d)  Sort the records in the results table so that all the records for male students appear before all female students.

    (e)  Save your query as qryWestcliff.

    (f)  Print the query results.

2.  (a)  Create a second query to select all records of students who were born before 01/09/1986.

    (b)  Sort the records into ascending order of Surname and Forename.

    (c)  Save your query as qryStudentAge.

    (d)  Run the query.

    (e)  Print out the query results on a single page in Landscape orientation.

## Ask yourself

❓ Do I know what a query is and how to create one?

❓ Can I select and remove fields in a query?

❓ Can I add and remove criteria in a query?

❓ Can I save and print a query?

❓ Can I sort data in a query output?

❓ Can I sort a query by two fields?

❓ Can I create a query based on two tables?

❓ Do I know how to use operators as query criteria?

In this chapter you should have created and saved the following files:
Hemlets.accdb          Student.accdb

In this chapter you have been introduced to the following buttons:

Query Design
in the Other group on the Create ribbon

Run
in the Results group on the Query Tools Design ribbon

Show Table
in the Query Setup group on the Query Tools Design ribbon

# CHAPTER 36  Reports

In this chapter you will find out:

- about reports
- how to create reports based on tables and on queries
- how to add header and footer text and fields
- how to add expressions to a report
- how to print a report.

## Ribbon groups used in this chapter

In this chapter you will use this button in the Report group on the Create ribbon:

Report Wizard

these buttons in the Clipboard group on the Home ribbon:

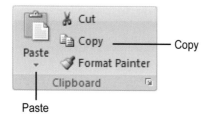

Copy

Paste

and this button in the Grouping & Totals group on the Report Design Tools Design ribbon:

Group & Sort

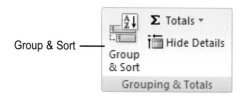

360

Suppose you want to present the data in a table or query in a neater way, for example perhaps by printing it with a proper title. For this you would use a Report. Reports allow you to present data in a wide variety of ways. They can be based on queries or on tables.

- ▶ Make sure the Hemlets database is open.

- ▶ Close any objects that are open.

## Reports based on tables                                              Syllabus 5.6.1.1–3

First you'll create a report based on the tblLandlord table which will simply list all the landlords and their contact details.

▶ Click the Report Wizard button in the Reports group on the Create ribbon to display the first step of the Report Wizard.

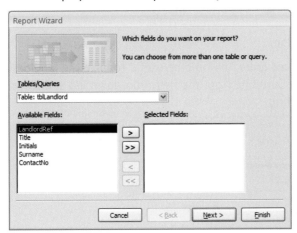

- ▶ Select tblLandlord from the Tables/Queries drop-down list if it isn't already showing.

- ▶ You want all the Available Fields to appear in the report, so click ⟩⟩ . The wizard screen will now look like the screenshot below.

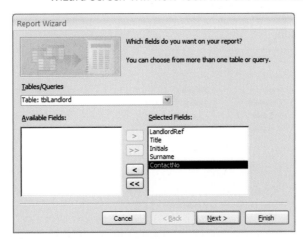

- ▶ Click the Next button.

▶ The next wizard screen asks about grouping levels. You won't need any for this report, so leave the settings as below:

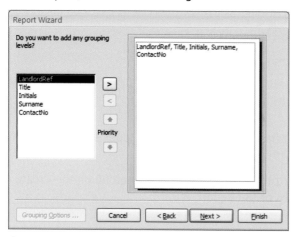

▶ Click the Next button.

▶ You can specify a sort order. It would be useful to have the landlords sorted by Surname, so select Surname from the first drop-down list and leave the button adjacent as Ascending.

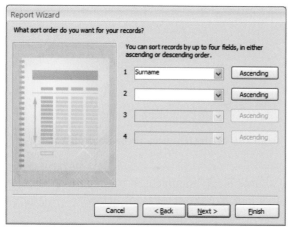

▶ Click the Next button.

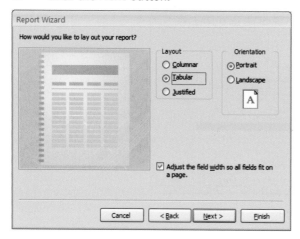

○ This screen lets you choose a layout for your report. Check that Tabular and Portrait are selected.

○ Click the Next button.

○ This screen lets you choose a style for your report. Select the Northwind style (or another if it isn't available on your computer).

○ Click the Next button.

○ Give the report the title rptLandlordDetails. This is what the report will then be saved as.

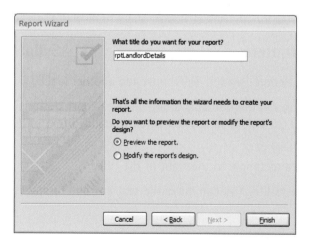

○ Click the Finish button to view the report. The report is displayed and its name appears in the Navigation Pane.

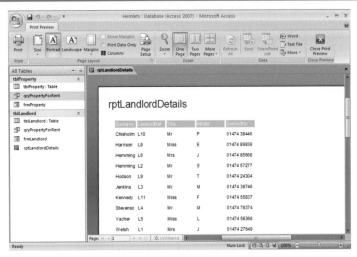

▶ Go to Design View.

▶ Now change the title of the report. First click where it says rptLandlordDetails so that handles appear around the title, and then click again in the title text. Now you can delete the text and type the new title, Landlord Details.

▶ The report will be more useful if the reference number comes before the names. Right click the report and select Layout View from the shortcut menu.

▶ Click in the Surname column and, holding down the mouse button, drag the column until the placement line is between the Initials and the ContactNo columns.

▶ Release the mouse button and select Report View to display the report.

## Adding text to headers and footers                    Syllabus 5.6.1.5

The title is already in the Report Header. You'll now add another label.

▶ Click the Label button in the Controls group on the Report Design Tools Design ribbon. You already used a similar button when you added text to a form on page 333.

▶ Click and drag out a rectangle to the right of the title.

▶ Type the text Hemlets Ltd. You can move the text box and format the text as you wish.

Now add some text in the Report Footer.

▶ Click and drag out a label rectangle at the bottom of the report under the Report Footer.

▶ Add the text Hemlets Database into a text box in the footer area.

Your report should look something like the screenshot on the next page.

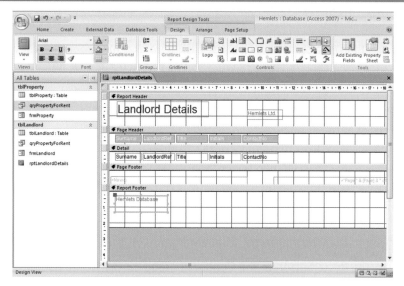

You can modify the footer text by clicking in the box and editing it.

▶ View the report by changing to the Report View.

**Tip:**

Remember that you can change the view of your database by either by clicking the View button in the Views group of the ribbon or clicking the View icons on the right of the status bar at the bottom of the Access screen (see page 293).

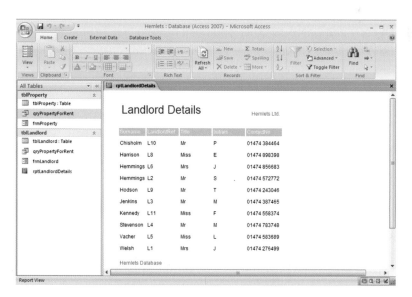

▶ Save and close your report.

**Tip:**

As with any object, once you have saved a report, you can open it again when you need it from the Navigation Pane.

## Reports based on queries

Hemlets would like a report that lists each landlord and the properties they own that are currently being rented. Hemlets will use this to calculate how much rent the landlord is earning every month.

This report will use data from both tblLandlord and tblProperty, and will use as its source a query that combines the fields from both tables.

You already have a query that contains the fields you need – qryPropertyForRent. You will copy the query then change the criteria to those you need for the report.

- ◯ Open the Hemlets database if it is closed.

- ◯ Click qryPropertyForRent query name in the Navigation Pane.

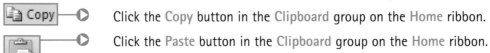 ◯ Click the Copy button in the Clipboard group on the Home ribbon.

◯ Click the Paste button in the Clipboard group on the Home ribbon.

**Tip:**

You can copy and paste all other database objects like Tables and Forms in just the same way.

You are asked to give a name to the new query.

- ◯ Type qryLandlordIncome and click OK.

- ◯ The new query name appears in the Navigation Pane – open it in Design View.

Now delete all the criteria currently in the query builder grid.

- ◯ Delete each criterion in turn by clicking it and then using either the Delete key or the Backspace key.

You also need to remove all the entries in the Sort row.

- ◯ Delete these in the same way as you did the criteria.

- ◯ Add the criterion Yes to the Rented column.

Your query should now look similar to the one on the next page.

○ It is a good idea to add the sorting rules in the query rather than the report. Give the Surname field an Ascending sort. This will sort the landlords alphabetically in the query.

○ Give the Rent column a Descending sort.

○ Save and close the query.

## Creating the report                                    Syllabus 5.6.1.3

Report Wizard ─○ Click the Report Wizard button in the Reports group on the Create ribbon to display the first step of the Report Wizard.

○ Make sure qryLandlordIncome is selected in the Tables/Queries box.

○ The fields and the order in which they appear in the final report is determined by which of the Available Fields you select and on the order you select them. You want all the fields in the query, except Style and Bedrooms, and you want them in the order Surname, Title, Initials, PropertyRef, Rent.

○ To do this, first click on Surname in the Available Fields: list, then click **>** to move the field to the Selected Fields: list.

○ Next select the Title, Initials, PropertyRef and Rent fields in turn.

○ Click the Next button.

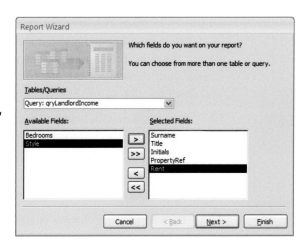

● You are now asked how you want to view the data. You want the results grouped by Landlord, so click to select tblLandlord.

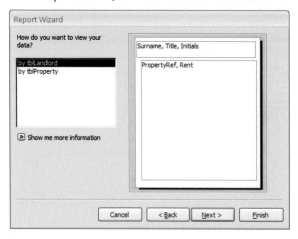

● Click the Next button to display the next step of the Report Wizard which allows you to create groups for the fields.

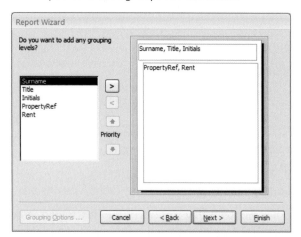

When creating a report you can show the field headings in any order to suit your purpose. In a letting agency you might be asked to put the landlord or property name first or alternatively to produce a report by landlord and then list the tenants who are renting from them. This is called grouping. You might want to present the landlords in alphabetical order and also list the tenants in alphabetical order or by the amount of rent they pay, or you might want to group the data by the type of property. If you change your mind about the order in which the groups appear, you can move them up and down by clicking the Priority arrows.

● You don't need to add any grouping levels, as the results are already grouped by tblLandlord, so just click the Next button.

● You can now specify which fields you want to sort by. You've already set the sorting rules in the underlying query so you don't need to specify them again here. Click the Next button.

● Click Next twice more – you don't need to change any of the presentation options.

▶ Give the report the title rptLandlordIncome; this is what it will be saved as and how it will appear in the Navigation Pane.

▶ Click the Finish button

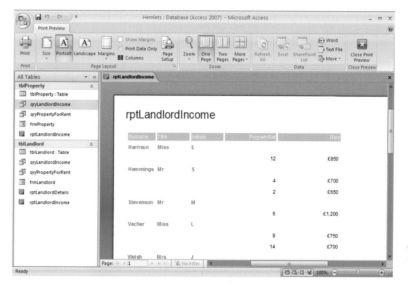

You need to make a few changes to it in Design View.

▶ Change to Design View.

## Adding a Sum field                                    Syllabus 5.6.1.4

You need the report to calculate the total income for each landlord by summing the rent for each of the properties that are rented.

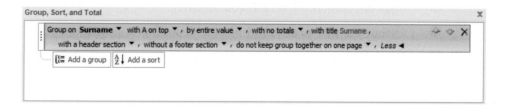

▶ Click the Group & Sort button in the Grouping & Totals group on the Report Design Tools Design ribbon to display the Group, Sort and Total pane.

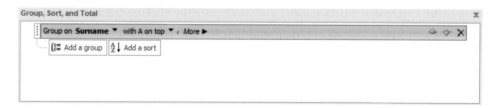

▶ Click More to display all the grouping, sorting and totalling options.

Group, Sort, and Total

Group on **Surname** ▼ with A on top ▼ , by entire value ▼ , with no totals ▼ , with title Surname ,
with a header section ▼ , without a footer section ▼ , do not keep group together on one page ▼ , Less ◀

[≡ Add a group   ᵃ↓ Add a sort

○ Click the down-arrow to the right of the with no totals option to display the Totals option box.

○ You want the total income for each landlord, so select Rent in the Total On drop-down list and Sum in the Type drop-down list.

○ Click Show in group footer to tick the check box.

○ Click away from the Group, Sort and Total pane. The Surname Footer containing the text =Sum(Rent) appears in the Design View.

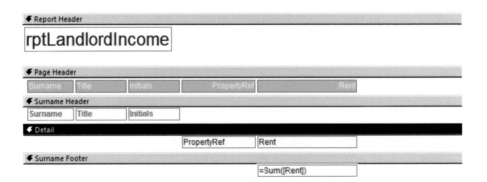

○ Close the Group, Sort and Total pane by clicking the Group & Sort button.

○ You have added a field that adds up the rents for each landlord, but you need to add a label to identify what the sum displayed means. Click the Label button in the Controls group on the Report Design Tools Design ribbon.

○ Drag out a text box to the left of the =Sum(Rent) field. You already used a similar button when you added text to a form on page 333.

○ Type the label text Total Rental Income.

○ Align and format the text as you require.

○ Change the title to Landlord Income Report.

○ Print preview the report. It should look similar to the one shown in the screenshot on the next page.

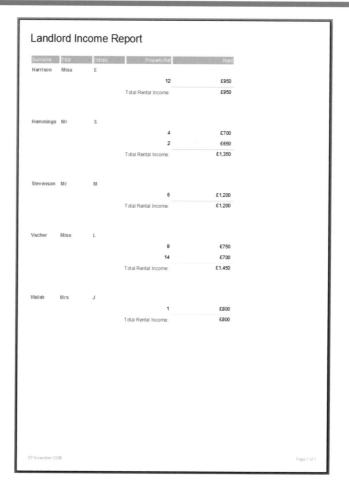

Landlord Income Report

| Surname | Title | Initials | Property Ref | Rent |
|---|---|---|---|---|
| Harrison | Miss | E | | |
| | | | 12 | £950 |
| | | | Total Rental Income: | £950 |
| Hemmings | Mr | S | | |
| | | | 4 | £700 |
| | | | 2 | £650 |
| | | | Total Rental Income: | £1,350 |
| Stevenson | Mr | M | | |
| | | | 6 | £1,200 |
| | | | Total Rental Income: | £1,200 |
| Vacher | Miss | L | | |
| | | | 9 | £750 |
| | | | 14 | £700 |
| | | | Total Rental Income: | £1,450 |
| Welsh | Mrs | J | | |
| | | | 1 | £800 |
| | | | Total Rental Income: | £800 |

07 November 2006                                         Page 1 of 1

## Adding a Count field

**Syllabus 5.6.1.4**

Now you'll add a field that totals the number of properties each landlord currently has rented. This time you'll copy the Sum expression you've just entered and change it to a Count expression to show the number of rented properties per landlord.

- Return to the report Design View.

- Click the Sum field you have just created so the border is highlighted.

- Right click it and select Copy from the shortcut menu that is displayed.

- Right-click in the Surname Footer section and select Paste from the shortcut menu.

- Click in the newly copied expression to place the text insertion cursor, and replace the word Sum with the word Count. Make sure you don't change the brackets or the word Rent in the brackets.

- Add a label Total Properties:.

- Drag the new label and expression to a suitable position below the Total Rental Income fields. The design view will look similar to the screenshot on the next page.

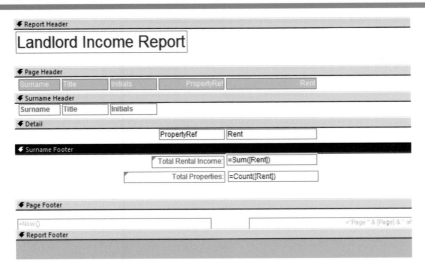

▶ The Count expression is currently a copy of the Sum expression and so will have a currency format. This is unsuitable for a field that shows a number of items. You need to change its properties so it has the General Number format.

▶ Click the Count expression box to highlight it.

▶ Right-click the box and select Properties from the shortcut menu.

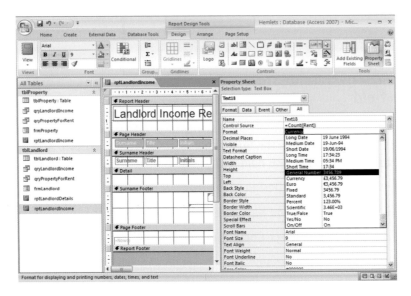

▶ The Property Sheet pane is displayed. Change the Format property to General Number, and Decimal Places to 0.

▶ Preview the report. You will now see the number of properties each landlord has rented as well as the total rental income for each landlord.

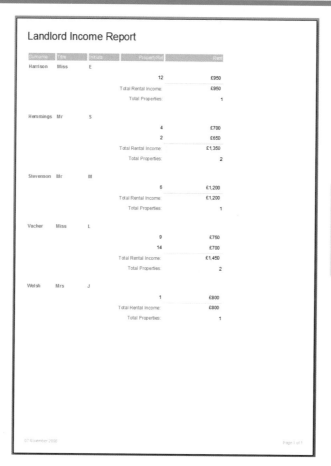

Landlord Income Report

| Surname | Title | Initials | Property/Ref | Rent |
|---------|-------|----------|--------------|------|
| Harrison | Miss | E | | |
| | | | 12 | £950 |
| | | | Total Rental Income: | £950 |
| | | | Total Properties: | 1 |
| Hemmings | Mr | S | | |
| | | | 4 | £700 |
| | | | 2 | £650 |
| | | | Total Rental Income: | £1,350 |
| | | | Total Properties: | 2 |
| Stevenson | Mr | M | | |
| | | | 6 | £1,200 |
| | | | Total Rental Income: | £1,200 |
| | | | Total Properties: | 1 |
| Vacher | Miss | L | | |
| | | | 9 | £750 |
| | | | 14 | £700 |
| | | | Total Rental Income: | £1,450 |
| | | | Total Properties: | 2 |
| Welsh | Mrs | J | | |
| | | | 1 | £800 |
| | | | Total Rental Income: | £800 |
| | | | Total Properties: | 1 |

07 November 2008                                                    Page 1 of 1

**Tip:**

You can include a **Count**, **Min**, **Max** or **Average** field in a similar way to that described for the **Sum** field within the **Group, Sort and Total** pane.

## Other useful expressions

Syllabus 5.6.1.4

So far you've used the **Sum** and **Count** expressions. Others which you can also use are:

- **Minimum:** gives the minimum value of all values in the group. In our example, where there was more than one property it would give the value of the smallest rent.

- **Maximum:** like minimum, except gives the maximum rent for a particular landlord's properties.

- **Average:** gives the average of all values in the group. In our example, where there is more than one property, it would give the average of all the rents for each landlord.

## Printing a report

Syllabus 5.6.2.1/5

This is very similar to printing tables, forms and queries.

- Click **Print** on the Office button menu and then click **Print Preview** from the options provided.

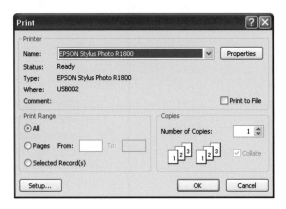

Click the Print button in the Print group on the Print Preview ribbon to open the Print dialogue box where you can select which pages of the report to print and how many copies you want.

**Tip:**

You can make changes to the orientation and paper size using the buttons in the Page Layout group on the Print Preview ribbon.

Click OK to print, otherwise click Cancel.

Save and close the report.

**Tip:**

You can delete an unwanted report by selecting it in the Navigation Pane and pressing the Delete key.

Close the database and Access. You've reached the end of the module!

## Exercise

The Softball database, which you downloaded earlier in this module, contains data on players and teams in a softball league. The database contains two tables, a Team table for team data such as coach name and contact number, and a Player table containing data on the players in each team, such as surname and position.

1. Open the Softball database.

2. Create a query using both tables and all fields.

3. Save the query as query1.

4. Create a report based on query1. Group the report by TeamName; sort the results by Surname.

5. Save the report as report1.

6. Add a Count field to count the players in each team.

7. Save and close the database.

## Ask yourself

❷ Can I create a report based on a table?

❷ Can I create a report based on a query?

❷ Can I add a header and a footer to a report?

❷ Can I add fields to a report?

❷ Can I print a report?

In this chapter you should have created and saved the following files:
Hemlets.accdb          Softball.accdb

In this chapter you have been introduced to the following buttons:

Report Wizard
in the Reports group on the Create ribbon

Copy
Paste
in the Clipboard group on the Home ribbon

Group & Sort
in the Grouping & Totals group on the Report Design Tools Design ribbon

# Module 6

## Presentation

In this module you will find out how to use presentation tools on a computer. You will learn how to:

- create a presentation using different slide layouts for display and printed distribution
- format and modify presentations
- insert images, charts and drawn objects into a presentation
- duplicate and move text, pictures, images and charts within a presentation
- duplicate and move text, pictures, images and charts between presentations
- use various slide show effects
- recognise good practice in adding slide titles
- recognise good practice in creating slide content.

# Module **6**

# Contents

# The Basics

**In this chapter you will find out:**

- how to run and close Microsoft PowerPoint
- about planning a presentation
- about the PowerPoint screen, ribbons, defaults and preferences
- how to start a blank presentation
- about the title slide and how to add, format and move text
- about placeholders and how to move and resize them
- about PowerPoint views
- how to save and close a presentation.

○ Log on to the Payne-Gallway website www.payne-gallway.co.uk and download the files for Module 6 (see page 93 for how to do this).

## What is Microsoft PowerPoint?

Microsoft PowerPoint is a widely used graphics presentation package. You can use it to create, design and organise professional presentations quickly and easily.

## Planning a presentation                      Syllabus 6.2.1.2/6.3.1.1

To deliver an effective presentation you need to consider who your audience is, and prepare your slides to suit them.

Whoever your presentation is for, here are a few basic guidelines:

- Start with a title screen showing what the presentation is about.
- Use lists – do not put more than four or five bulleted or numbered list items on each slide. People cannot concentrate on too much information at once.
- Keep each point short and simple. You may want to talk around each point to explain it in further detail.
- Sound, graphics and animation effects can add interest, but too many can distract from the message you are conveying.

# Module 6 Presentation

- ◉   Load Microsoft PowerPoint. You can do this in one of two ways:

- ◉   *Either* double-click the PowerPoint icon (if it is on your desktop)

- ◉   *Or* click Start, All Programs, then click Microsoft Office PowerPoint 2007. (Note: depending on how your computer is set up, you might need to click Start, All Programs, Microsoft Office, Microsoft Office PowerPoint 2007.)

The PowerPoint screen will look similar to the screenshot below:

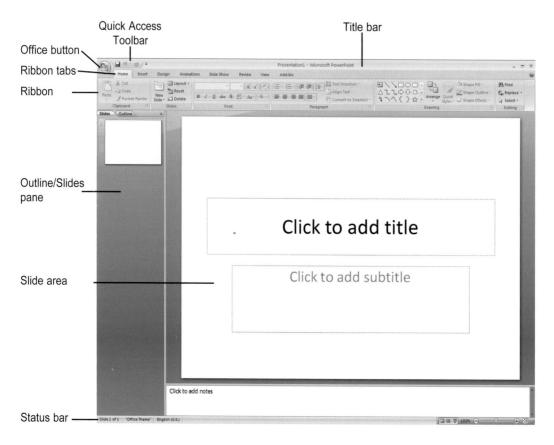

## Features of the PowerPoint screen

- ⓘ   The Title bar shows the name of your presentation. If you have only just opened PowerPoint or have not yet given your file a name, it will say Presentation1. It will say Presentation2 if this is your second file since you started Microsoft PowerPoint in this chapter.

- ⓘ   The Office button has options for you to choose from. You'll be using it when you need to open, close, print or save your presentation.

- ⓘ   The Ribbon is where you can find all the functions you will need to create and edit your presentation. The functions are shown as buttons with pictures called icons. They are grouped by related commands. The functions available on the ribbons can also change according to what you are currently working on. In this way they can be thought of as being context-sensitive toolbars. A ribbon is displayed by selecting its Ribbon tab.

- ❶ The Slide area represents the presentation pages into which you type. You can see the structure of you presentation and navigate through it by using the Slide/ Outlines pane.

- ❶ The Quick Access Toolbar provides some more useful commands.

- ❶ Sometimes a context-sensitive task pane is displayed at the side of the screen (not shown in the figure). This lets you choose further options related to the task in hand.

## Ribbon groups used in this chapter

In this chapter you will use these buttons and features in the Font group on the Home ribbon:

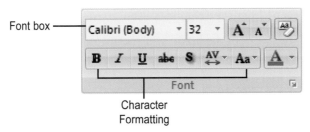

Font box

Character Formatting

these buttons in the Paragraph group on the Home ribbon:

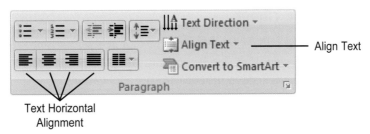

Align Text

Text Horizontal Alignment

and this button in the Zoom group on the View ribbon:

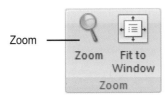

Zoom

## Starting a blank presentation · Syllabus 6.1.1.2/6.2.2.1/6.2.2.4

A blank slide that is ready for you to type in details of your presentation is displayed when you first start PowerPoint. However, at any time you can start a new blank presentation as follows:

- ▶ Click the New button on the Office button menu to display the New Presentation window.

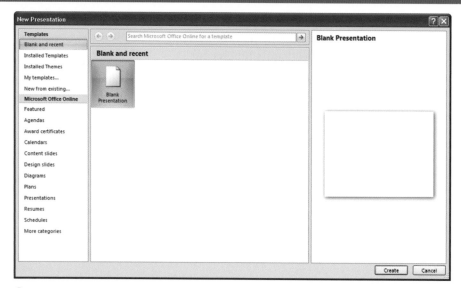

○ Click Blank and recent from the Templates list.

○ Click Blank Presentation from the Blank and recent templates that are displayed.

○ Click the Create button.

PowerPoint has automatically selected the Title Slide layout, which is exactly what you want. The boxes marked out on the screen are called placeholders. These show where you will place your text and graphics.

## Minimising and restoring the ribbon                Syllabus 6.1.2.4

You will learn about what individual ribbon buttons do as they become relevant whilst you are creating your presentation. The PowerPoint ribbon is pretty much the same as the ribbons you have experienced in other Microsoft applications.

Sometimes you might want to increase the working area where you type. You can minimise (hide) the ribbon so only the ribbon tabs are displayed. If the ribbon is minimised, you need to know how to get it back!

○ Right-click anywhere in the line containing the ribbon tabs, on the Office button, on the Quick Access Toolbar, or on a ribbon group name.

○ Click Minimize the Ribbon on the shortcut menu that is displayed.

○ To restore the ribbon, right-click in one of the same places as before to un-tick Minimize the Ribbon on the shortcut menu.

**Tip:**

Use **Ctrl-F1** (i.e. press at the same time the **Control** key and the **F1** key on the keyboard) or double-click a ribbon tab to toggle between minimising and maximising the ribbon. At any time when the ribbon is minimised, simply click a ribbon tab to show the ribbon temporarily when you need it.

## Changing defaults and preferences

By default (i.e. unless you tell it otherwise) PowerPoint saves your presentations in a folder called My Documents on the C: drive. You can change this default as well as many other preferences.

▶ Click the Office button, and then click PowerPoint Options on the window that appears.

You will now be able to change the user name and the default directory for opening and saving files.

▶ Click the Save option.

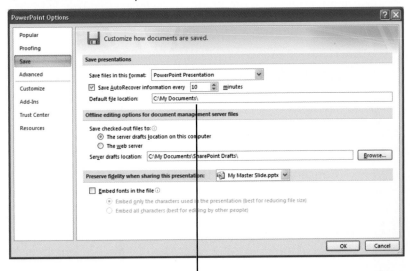

Here you can change the default folder for opening and saving files.

You can also change various other default settings such as how frequently your document is automatically saved.

Clicking Popular on the menu will open a window in which you can change the name of the author of presentations you create.

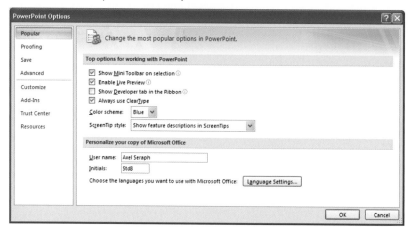

## Getting help

Syllabus 6.1.2.2

If at any time you're unsure of how to do something in PowerPoint, you can search the Microsoft Office PowerPoint Help system. You use this in exactly the same way as for other Microsoft Office 2007 applications. (The Word help system is described on page 170.)

## Adding text to the title slide

Syllabus 6.3.1.2/6.5.2.2

▶ Click in the placeholder box marked Click to add title and type the title Conserving Tigers in the Wild.

▶ Now add a subtitle. Click the subtitle placeholder and type Framework and Strategy for Action 2009.

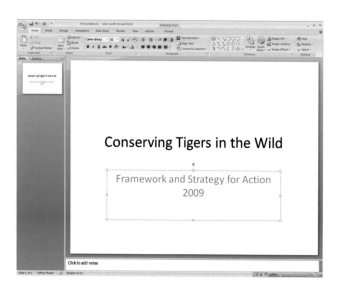

**Tip:**
When you add titles to slides, make sure that each one is different and meaningful. This will help you navigate through a long presentation and make the slides individually recognisable in the Outline view.

## Formatting and moving the text

You can click and drag the placeholder text boxes to move them around the screen. You can also format the text in each text box just as you would in Microsoft Word. Most of the commands you will need for this are in the Font and Paragraph groups on the Home ribbon.

To format or edit text you need to select the placeholder box by clicking its border. When the border has changed to a solid line you know you can start formatting or editing the text.

◉ Select the subtitle text box so that the border changes to a solid line.

◉ Change the font to Times New Roman by clicking the down-arrow on the right-hand side of the Font box in the Font group on the Home ribbon and choosing it from the list that appears.

Font     Font Size

| Times New Roma | ▾ | 32 | ▾ |

 ◉ Make the text italic by clicking on the Italic button in the Font group on the Home ribbon.

**Tip:**
To change the case of selected text, click the **Change Case** button in the **Font** group on the **Home** ribbon, and choose from the options provided. **Aa▾**

◉ The text is already centre-aligned horizontally, but not vertically.

 ◉ To vertically align the text, make sure the placeholder is selected then click the Align Text button in the Paragraph group on the Home ribbon, and choose Middle from the list of options that is displayed.

**Tip:**
To align text horizontally, use the text alignment buttons in the **Paragraph** group on the **Home** ribbon.

Align Left   Align Right

Center   Justify

**Tip:**
You can apply other formatting to text by using the **Font** group buttons.

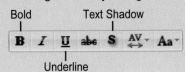

Bold     Text Shadow

Underline

## Resizing and moving placeholder boxes      Syllabus 6.5.1.4

The subtitle would look better if the text appeared on one line rather than two, but without making the text smaller. You can do this by altering the size of the placeholder box using the handles.

*Framework and Strategy for Action 2009*

Some of the handles around the placeholder box

▶ Move the cursor over the left-hand handle so that it becomes an arrow as in the screenshot above.

▶ Click and drag the handle to make the box wider. Repeat this until the text fits on one line. Don't worry that it is now a bit too far left.

▶ Now move the box back to the centre by moving the cursor over its border somewhere where there is no handle, so the cursor becomes a cross.

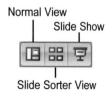

*Fra*

▶ Click and drag the box until it looks central. Click outside the box to deselect it.

**Tip:**

To delete a placeholder box, click its border to select it and then press the **Delete** key. To delete part of the contents of a text box, highlight the text to be removed and then press the **Delete** key.

## Changing the presentation view      Syllabus 6.2.1.1/3

You can change between various views of a presentation by clicking on the icons to the right of the Status bar at the bottom of the PowerPoint screen.

Normal View

Slide Show

Slide Sorter View

**Tip:**

Alternatively, you can change the presentation views by clicking the appropriate button in the **Presentation Views** group on the **View** ribbon.

## Normal view

This is the most useful view and the view you have been using so far. It lets you view the structure of your presentation down the left of the screen, the current slide you are working on and the Notes pane for the current slide.

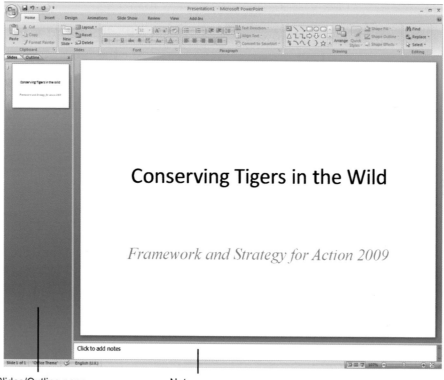

Slides/Outline pane         Notes pane

ⓘ    The Slides/Outline pane has two different tabs. The Slides tab shows small pictures of all the slides so you can quickly see their order and content, and the Outline tab lists only the text on each slide. Click the tabs at the top of the Slides/Outline pane to switch between the views.

Slides tab                     Outline tab

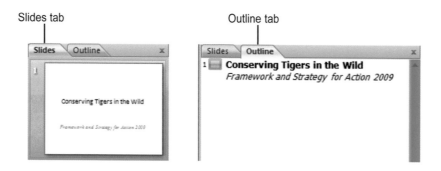

## Slide sorter view

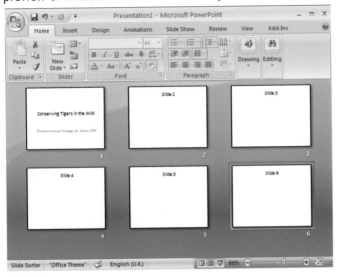

This view helps you to organise your slides when you have more than one slide. Here's a preview of what it will look like when you have more slides:

## Slide show

This is the view you use to give your presentation.

○ Click the Slide Show view icon to view your presentation so far.

○ Exit the presentation by pressing the Esc key.

## The Zoom tool

Syllabus 6.1.2.3

You can change the size of the slide in Normal View by using PowerPoint's Zoom function.

○ Click the View ribbon tab, and then click the Zoom button in the Zoom group on the View ribbon. The Zoom dialogue box is displayed.

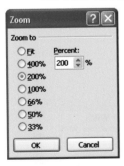

○ Select a higher percentage to make the slide bigger or a smaller percentage to make the slide smaller and view more of it on the screen. For example, to make the slide appear much bigger, either type/select 200 in the Percent: box or select the 200% radio button.

○ This is much bigger than you want it for now! Most of the time you will probably just want the slide to fit into the window. To do this, select Fit from the list.

### Tip:

Use the **Zoom tool** to the right of the **Status bar** to zoom in or out of a worksheet – click the **Zoom level** percentage to open the **Zoom** dialogue box, or draw the slider/click the **+/−** buttons to change the magnification.

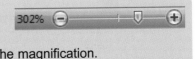

## The Undo and Redo commands

Syllabus 6.3.1.6

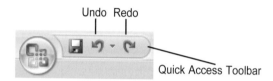

Undo  Redo

Quick Access Toolbar

### Undo

At any time, if you do something that you didn't mean to, or don't like, just click the Undo button. This will undo your most recent action; you can click it more than once to undo recent actions in sequence, starting from the most recent.

Tip:

Click the down arrow next to the **Undo** button to display a list of recent actions. Select the action you want to undo.

### Redo

If you undo something you didn't mean to, just click the Redo button! If you haven't recently used the Undo button, the Redo button won't be active.

Tip:

If you want to repeat an action, for example adding a bullet point or inserting a slide, you can use the **Repeat** button on the **Quick Access Toolbar**. If the action is not repeatable, the **Repeat** button won't appear.

## Saving and closing your presentation

Syllabus 6.1.1.1/3

- ◐ Click the Office button, and then click Save on the menu that appears.
- ◐ Navigate to where you want to save the presentation. Type Tigers as the File name.
- ◐ PowerPoint automatically saves the file as a Presentation file type (i.e. with the file extension pptx). This is what you want for now, but you can select different file types to save the presentation as web pages, for older versions of PowerPoint or as a graphical image (see page 442).
- ◐ Click the Save button.

- ◐ To close your presentation, click the Office button again and then click Close on the menu that appears.

- ◐ Close PowerPoint by clicking the Office button again and then clicking the Exit PowerPoint button.

Tip:

You can save a presentation by clicking the **Save** button on the **Quick Access Toolbar**. If this is the first time you've saved a file you will need to navigate to where you want to save the file and name it in the **Save As** dialogue box.

Note:

You can click **Save As** on the **Office button** menu to save your file with a new name or as a different file type. The original file will stay the same as when you last saved it. Use **Save As** as a way of making a copy of the file.

## Exercise

You are employed in the Human Resources department of a fictitious company that produces and sells maps of different European countries. You are asked to create a PowerPoint presentation that can be used for the induction of new staff. This should provide information about the company and its markets. You will develop this presentation in later exercises.

1.    Load PowerPoint and enter a main heading Mapsters UK Ltd on a title slide. Make this heading Arial, bold size 54.

2.    Enter a subtitle Information for new company employees. Change the font to Forte, bold, size 32.

3.    Adjust the size of the subtitle placeholder box so that it fits on one line.

4.    Centre the subtitle vertically in the placeholder box.

5.    Create a new folder called Presentations.

6.    Save the company presentation as Mapsters.pptx in your new folder.

# Mapsters UK Ltd

*Information for new company employees*

## Ask yourself

❷ Can I run and close Microsoft PowerPoint?

❷ Do I know how to hide and restore PowerPoint ribbons?

❷ Do I know how to get help with Microsoft PowerPoint?

❷ Can I open a new, blank presentation slide?

❷ Do I understand good practice regarding slide titles?

❷ Do I know what the different PowerPoint views are for and how to switch between them?

❷ Can I select a title slide and add text to it?

❷ Can I format, move and delete text in a placeholder box?

❷ Can I resize and move placeholder boxes?

In this chapter you should have created and saved the following files:
Mapsters.pptx
Tigers.pptx

In this chapter you have been introduced to the following buttons and features:

Character Formatting
Font box
in the Font group on the Home ribbon

Align Text
Paragraph formatting
in the Paragraph group on the Home ribbon

Zoom
in the Zoom group on the View ribbon

# CHAPTER

# 38 Editing a Show

In this chapter you will find out:

- ❶ how to open an existing presentation
- ❶ how to start new slides, and add text
- ❶ more about formatting slides
- ❶ how to use PowerPoint's spell-checker
- ❶ how to reorder slides, and reorder text within a slide/between slides
- ❶ about bullet and numbered lists.

## Ribbon groups used in this chapter

In this chapter you will use

this button in the Slides
group on the Home ribbon:

New Slide

this button in the Proofing
group on the Review ribbon:

Spelling

these buttons and features in the Font
group on the Home ribbon:

Font Size    Increase/Decrease
Font Size

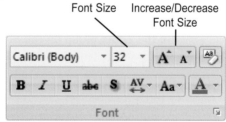

and this button in the Paragraph
group on the Home ribbon:

Increase  Decrease  Line Spacing
List Level

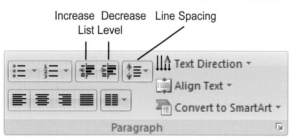

## Opening an existing presentation

- Load PowerPoint.

- Click the Office button, and then click Open on the menu that appears. The Open dialogue box will be displayed.

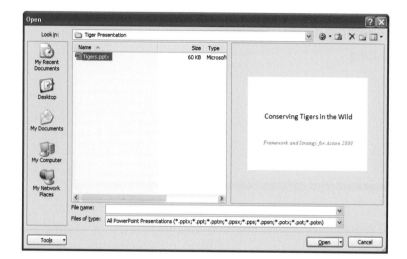

- Navigate to where you saved the Tigers presentation in the last chapter.

- When you have found it, click to select it then click the Open button.

- Make sure you are in Normal View by clicking the Normal View button at the bottom left of the screen. Your presentation title slide will be displayed.

### Tip:

When you click the Office button, you might see the **Tigers.ppt** presentation listed in the **Recent Documents** pane on the right-hand side of the menu that is displayed. Click the file name to open the presentation.

## Starting a new slide

Now you can begin a second slide for the presentation.

- Click the New Slide button in the Slides group on the Home ribbon to place a new slide immediately after the title slide.

By default, PowerPoint has chosen the Title and Content slide which is automatically laid out for a title (in the top placeholder), and a bullet list and content (in the bottom placeholder). This is the layout you want for your second slide, but it is possible to change it if you need to (see page 406).

- Enter the text as shown in the screenshot at the top of the next page, remembering to press Enter each time you start a new point.

---

## Contents

- The challenge – Key threats
- Current population estimates
- The response – Planned action
- Funding

---

**Tip:**

It is good practice to keep the text on a slide to a minimum, using a bullet or numbered list. Your audience is more likely to remember the points you make if you keep them simple and to the point!

## Changing text size                                    Syllabus 6.3.2.1

You can increase or decrease the size of text by using the Font Size buttons in the Font group on the Home ribbon.

   ◉   Select all of the bulleted text on the current slide.

 ◉   Click the Increase Font Size button a few times to increase the size of the text.

**Tip:**

If you make the text too big, you can make it smaller either by clicking the **Undo** button 🔄 or the **Decrease Font Size** button **A˅** .

**Tip:**

You can set the font size precisely using the **Font Size** 32 ▾ box in the **Font** group on the **Home** ribbon.

## Changing line spacing                                 Syllabus 6.3.3.2

The text could do with being more spread out.

   ◉   With the bulleted text highlighted, click the Line Spacing button in the Paragraph group on the Home ribbon.

○ Click **1.5** on the menu that is displayed.

Your screen should now look something like this:

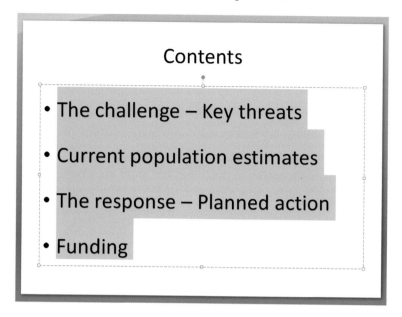

## Checking your spelling

Syllabus 6.6.2.1

By default, PowerPoint checks spelling as you type. Any words that PowerPoint does not recognise will be underlined in red. You can use the spell-checker to review your presentation so errors don't make it look unprofessional.

For the purpose of demonstrating the spell-checker, change the word threats so it is misspelled as thraets.

○ Check your spelling either by clicking the Spelling button in the Proofing group on the Review ribbon.

PowerPoint will try to suggest corrections to all the words it has underlined. These may be words that it thinks are spelt incorrectly or repeated words.

○ Click the correct spelling in the Suggestions: box and then click Change. (If the correct spelling does not appear you can type it into the Change to: box.)

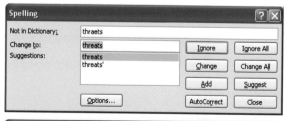

ⓘ If the spell-checker finds a repeated word, the Spelling dialogue box will look slightly different. Click Delete to delete the repeated word.

    **ⓘ**    If the spell-checker finds a word that is actually correct (e.g. a name) then click Ignore.

    **◑**    Click Close to exit the spell-checker at any time. It will tell you when it has checked all the words.

## Adding more slides

You are going to add some more slides to your presentation.

    **◑**    Make sure the Slides tab is selected in the Slides/Outline pane, then click the first slide.

    **◑**    Click the New Slide button in the Slides group on the Home ribbon to add a slide. PowerPoint adds a new slide after the one that is selected.

    **◑**    Click the New Slide button twice more. Don't worry about the Slide Layout just now – you will edit it later.

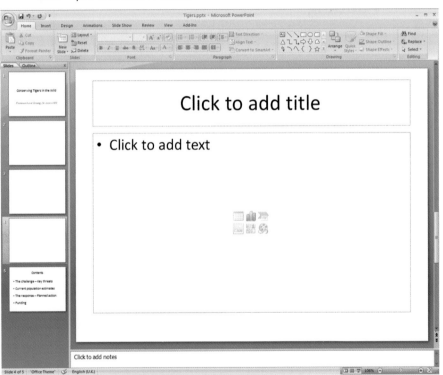

## Adding titles

Syllabus 6.3.1.2

    **◑**    Click the Outline tab in the Slides/Outline pane, then click the icon for the second slide so that Slide 2 appears in the main window.

    **◑**    Enter the text The Challenge – Key Threats either on the slide where it says to add the title, or if you just start typing while the Slide 2 icon is selected you can type it straight into the Outline pane.

▶ Enter the other titles in the same way so that your Outline pane looks like this.

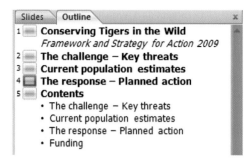

Tip:

Press the **Return** key after entering a title in the **Outline** pane. PowerPoint will automatically insert a new slide. You can easily delete a slide by clicking it in the **Outline** pane and pressing the **Delete** key.

## Changing the order of slides                                   Syllabus 6.3.3.1

At the moment, the contents slide is now at the end of the presentation. You need to move it to be immediately after Slide 1. You are going to move the slide in the Slide Sorter view.

▶ Display the Slide Sorter view by clicking its button as described on page 386.

▶ Click Slide 5 and hold down the mouse button. Drag the slide so that a vertical line appears after Slide 1 as shown below. Drop the slide here.

Tip:

Alternatively, you can drag a slide in the **Outline** pane.

Your slides are now in the right order!

Now add some more text to Slide 3.

- ▶ In the Slide Sorter view, double-click Slide 3. It will be displayed in Normal view.

- ▶ Type the text Poaching driven by illegal wildlife trade as the first bullet item. Press Enter.

You need the next bullet item to be indented a little.

- ▶ Click the Increase List Level button in the Paragraph group on the Home ribbon.

- ▶ Type the text Ban on international trade of tiger parts. Press Enter. You will notice that the text will be a bit smaller than on the first bullet point.

The next bullet point will automatically follow the format of the previous one, which is what you want.

- ▶ Type the text Human pressure on habitats as the second subpoint.

- ▶ Type the rest of the text so that it looks like the screenshot below. You will need to click the Decrease List Level button in the Paragraph group on the Home ribbon to restore the bullets to the left of the slide.

## The challenge – Key threats

- Poaching driven by illegal wildlife trade
  - Ban on international trade of tiger parts
  - Human pressure on habitats
- Habitat loss and fragmentation
- Inadequate international cooperation
- Funding constraints

## Customising bullets

Syllabus 6.3.3.3

You can change the style and colour of bullets to increase the visual impact.

- ▶ Select the text of the two indented bullets.

- ▶ Right-click the highlighted text, move the mouse pointer over Bullets on the menu that is displayed. A selection of commonly used bullets appears.

- ▶ Select a new shape for your bullets.

**Tip:**

> To change a bulleted list to a numbered list, highlight the bullet point text and right click. Move the mouse pointer over **Numbering** button on the menu that is displayed. A selection of commonly used number styles appears. Select the style you want.

## Moving text lines around

The bullet point Human pressure on habitats should actually be under the bullet point Habitat loss and fragmentation. You need to move it down to its new place.

- Click the mouse pointer to the left of the words Human pressure on habitats in the Outline pane where it changes to a four-headed arrow pointer.

- Hold down the mouse button and drag downwards. A line will appear across the text. Keep dragging until the line is underneath Habitat loss and fragmentation and then release the mouse button.

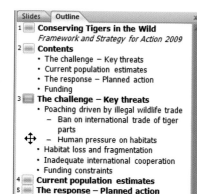

The text will have been moved down the slide.

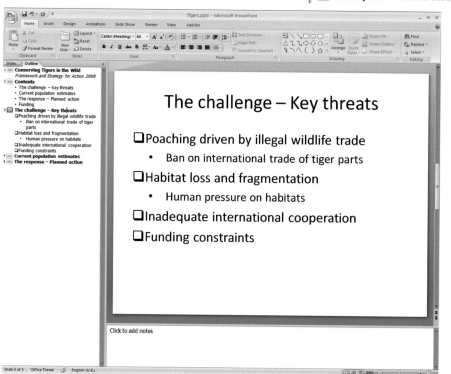

**Tip:**

> You can move text lines in a similar way directly on the slide itself.

**ℹ** You can move text from one slide to another in exactly the same way. Try it. Just click the Undo button on the Quick Access Toolbar when you have finished to restore the slide to look like the one on the previous page.

## Checking your presentation

View your progress so far.

**▶** Look at it first in Slide Sorter view.

When you click the Slide Show button the presentation starts at the selected slide (the one with the highlighted border).

**▶** Click the first slide to select it and then click the Slide Show button.

**▶** Click the Forward button or press the Space bar to move to the next slide.

Clicking the Back button or press the Backspace key to go back one slide. Remember you can exit your presentation at any time by pressing the Esc key.

**▶** Save your presentation and then close the presentation.

## Exercise

At the end of Chapter 37 you began a presentation for the induction of new employees at Mapsters UK Ltd. You will now add more slides to the presentation, edit slides and practise running the slide show.

1. Open the file Mapsters.pptx.

2. Start a new slide that has a simple title and text layout. Insert the heading Company history.

3. Change the size of the text in the bullet points to 22 and enter the following:

   Company (formally known as European Maps UK Ltd) founded in 1920 by George G Girling

   Early work concentrated on industrial and topographic wall maps for the educational market

   In 1961 production moved to tourist maps

   Mapsters series for tourists now comprises 10 maps

   Latest developments – Graphical Information Systems (GIS)

4. Increase the line spacing between the bullet points so that the text box is filled. Run the spell-checker and make any necessary corrections.

5. Add four new slides and give them the titles:

   Company organisation
   Sales by product
   Target markets
   Contents

6.     Add the following bullet points to the last slide:

Company history
Company organisation
Sales by product
Target markets

7.     Move the last slide (Contents) to become the second slide.

8.     Change the order of slides 5 and 6.

9.     Change the order of the text on slide 2 by swapping lines 3 and 4.

10.    Run the slide show, then save and close your presentation.

## Ask yourself

❷    Can I open an existing presentation?

❷    Can I add new slides and add text to them?

❷    Can I use the spell checker to find and correct spelling errors?

❷    Can I reorder slides in a presentation?

❷    Can I reorder text in a slide?

❷    Can I move text between slides?

❷    Do I understand that it is good practice to use lists on a presentation slide?

❷    Can I promote/demote list items and change list formatting?

In this chapter you should have created and saved the following files:
Mapsters.pptx          Tigers.pptx

In this chapter you have been introduced to the following buttons and features:

New Slide
in the Slides group on the Home ribbon

Decrease Font Size       Font Size            Increase Font Size
in the Font group on the Home ribbon

Decrease List Level      Increase List Level       Line Spacing
in the Paragraph group on the Home ribbon

Spelling
in the Proofing group on the Review ribbon

# CHAPTER

# 39 Applying Designs

## In this chapter you will find out:

- about master slides and how to apply them
- about design templates and how to apply them
- how to add text, page numbers and the date to headers and footers
- how to change a layout applied to a slide
- how to insert and edit organisational charts.

## Ribbon groups used in this chapter

In this chapter you will use this button in the Presentation Views group on the View ribbon:

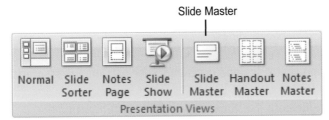

these buttons in the Edit Theme group on the Slide Master ribbon:

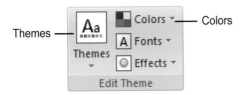

this button in the Slides group on the Home ribbon:

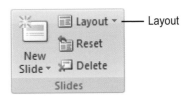

and this button in the Text group on the Insert ribbon:

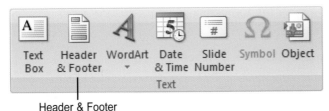

In this chapter you'll brighten up the slides to increase the impact of the presentation. You'll also insert some pictures to add more interest.

## Designing the Master Slide

▶   Open the Tigers presentation.

The Master Slide is a slide that sets the appearance of every other slide in your presentation. For example, if you choose a particular background colour and font for the Master Slide, this background colour and font will appear on all your slides. It's rather like the header and footer in Word – whatever you type in as the header and footer in Word appears on every page, and the same is true in PowerPoint with the Master Slide.

▶   Click the Slide Master button in the Presentation Views group on the View ribbon.

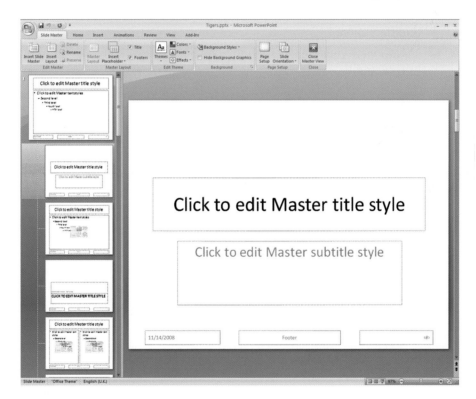

First put a coloured background on the slide. There are two ways to add a background design – you can either select a colour and a fill effect, or you can choose from a range of pre-designed backgrounds called Design Templates.

## Design templates                                                          Syllabus 6.2.2.2

▶   Click the Themes button in the Edit Theme group on the Slide Master ribbon.

A gallery of designs is provided. Pass your mouse over the designs to see the effect of each.

> Choose a design that you like, then click to select it.

> It's very easy to try a different template if you change your mind – just click a different one!

> Now view your presentation in Slide Sorter view. It should look a bit more colourful now!

## Changing the slide background colour                Syllabus 6.2.2.3

You can change the background colour of a slide. If the slide already has a design template selected for it, then you can change the colour of the template. If there is no template then you can just change the colour of the plain background. In fact, if you look in the list of design templates you will see that even the plain white background is a design template – just a very simple one!

> Display the Slide Master again.

> Click the Colors button in the Themes group on the Design ribbon to display a menu of colour schemes.

> Click the scheme you wish to apply to the slides. Click Undo if you don't like the new colour scheme.

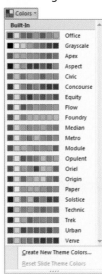

### Tip:

You can apply colour schemes to individual slides. Click the slide you want in Normal view. Then select the colour scheme you wish by clicking the Colors button in the Themes group on the Design ribbon. Right-click a theme in the gallery and select Apply to All Slides or Apply to Selected Slides.

## Adding slide numbers                                    Syllabus 6.2.3.3

You can add page numbers to just one slide, some slides or all the slides. You can also choose to have them only on the Notes pages and not on the actual slides. You can add page numbers whilst you are in Normal View or in the Slide Master.

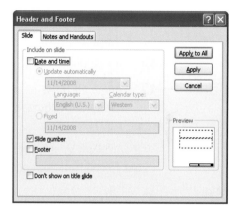

- Open the master slide.

- Click the Header & Footer button in the Text group on the Insert ribbon to display the Header and Footer dialogue box.

- Click to tick the Slide number tick box.

- You have the option to apply these settings only to the slide that is selected, or to all of them. You want page numbers on every page, so click Apply to All.

## Adding text to the footer                               Syllabus 6.2.3.2

You can add text to the footer in just the same way as in Word and Excel. You can choose whether the footer text appears on just the selected slide, or on all slides in your presentation. You are going to add the text World Tiger Conservation Fund 2009 to the footer.

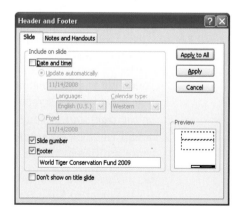

- To add a footer, you use the same window as for the page numbers, so open the Header and Footer window once again.

- You want the footer to appear on the slides, rather than the notes and handouts, so make sure the Slide tab is selected at the top of the window.

- Click in the Footer tick box to activate the footer. You can now type the text World Tiger Conservation Fund 2009 into the text box.

- You want the text to appear on all slides, not just the one selected, so click Apply to All.

## Adding a date to slides

Once again, you will use the Header and Footer window to insert a date on the slides.

- Open the Header and Footer window and make sure the Slide tab is selected.

- Click the tick box next to Date and time, then set the radio button so that the date updates automatically.

- Make sure that the language is set to English (U.K.).

- Click the Apply to All button.

- View all these changes by clicking the Slide Show button.

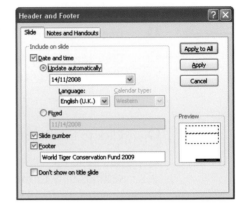

**Tip:**

If you want to show the date, but don't want it to be updated automatically, click the **Fixed** radio button.

- Return to Normal view and save your work.

## Changing the layout of a slide

You can change the layout of a slide at any time, even if you have already entered text. The fourth slide Current population estimates will contain a table and a graph.

- Go to Slide 4 by clicking on it in the Outline pane.

- Click the Layout button in the Slides group on the Home ribbon to display a gallery of slide layouts.

- Click the Two Content layout.

Your slide will look similar to that shown in the screenshot on the right, but of course the design will look different if you chose a different theme.

- Apply the Two Content layout to Slide 5.

You will add some content to the slides in the next chapter, so leave the slides as they are for the moment.

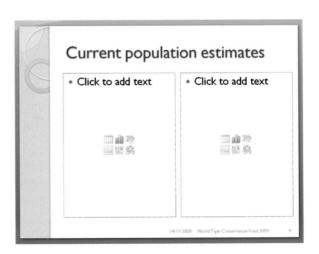

## Creating an organisation chart

Drawing an organisation chart is very straightforward if you use features provided by PowerPoint. You will create a chart showing the structure of the World Tiger Conservation Fund.

- ▶ Create a new slide, slide 6, after the current last slide in the presentation by clicking the New Slide button. Give it the Title and Content layout.

- ▶ View the slide in Normal view.

- ▶ Type the slide title The Organisation Structure and centre the text.

- ▶ Click the Insert SmartArt Graphic icon on the content placeholder to display the Choose a SmartArt Graphic dialogue box.

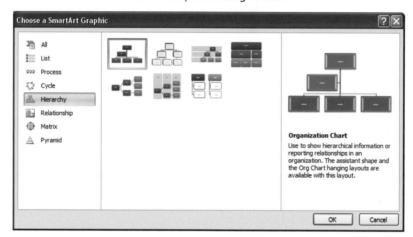

- ▶ Click Hierarchy in the panel on the left-hand side of the dialogue box, and then choose the Organization Chart option in the middle pane. Click the OK button.

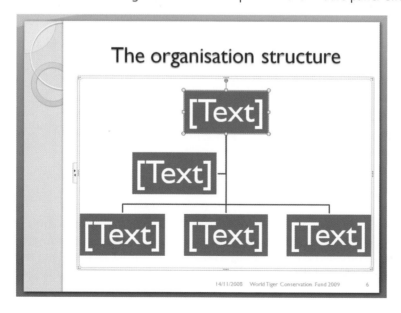

The Chief Executive Officer is Mike Stevenson and he has four Divisional Managers, Mary Wong, Omar Iqbal, Martha Kane and John Hainsworth.

▶ Click in the top box to add some text. Type Mike Stevenson (CEO).

▶ Use the same technique for the other three boxes, adding the names and divisions of the first three managers as shown in the screenshot below.

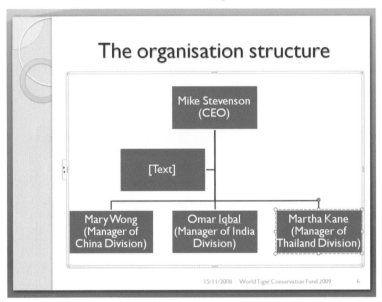

### Inserting managers, co-workers and subordinates          Syllabus 6.4.2.2–3

You need to add the fourth manager as a co-worker to the other managers.

**Tip:**

> All boxes, except the top one for the CEO, will be either co-workers, subordinates or both.

▶ Click the empty box beneath the top-level box that contains Mike Stevenson (CEO) to select it.

▶ Press the Delete key to remove the box.

▶ Right-click the Martha Kane box to display a shortcut menu.

▶ Select Add Shape and then choose Add Shape After to insert a new box to the right of the selected one.

▶ Type the name John Hainsworth (Manager of Siberia Division).

**Note:**

> The steps just described have added John Hainsworth as a **co-worker** to the other three managers. The managers are, of course, also **subordinates** to the CEO, so alternatively you could have right-clicked the CEO box and selected **Add Shape** then **Add Shape Below** to place the fourth box in the same place.

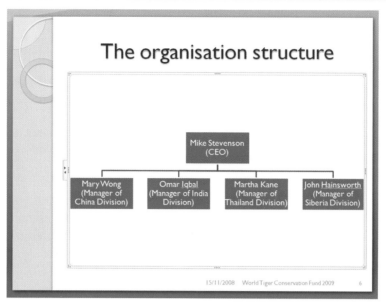

John has two subordinates, fieldworkers George Bradley and Jo Kemple.

- ◉ Right-click the John Hainsworth box and select Add Shape, then Add Shape Below.
- ◉ Type the new person's details in the box: George Bradley (Fieldworker).
- ◉ Repeat for Jo Kemple.

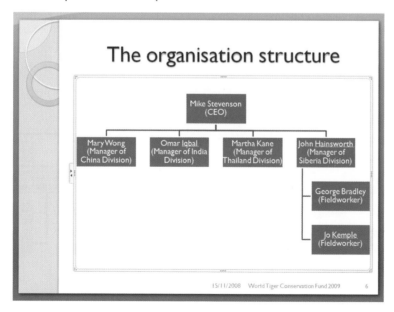

### Deleting managers, co-workers and subordinates     Syllabus 6.4.2.2–3

You remember that there have been some changes. The Thailand Division has been closed down, and Jo Kemple has left. John Hainsworth has retired and George has been promoted to his position.

- ◉ Select the Martha Kane box and press the Delete key.

⯈ Do the same for Jo Kemple.

⯈ Click on John Hainsworth and press the Delete key. George will automatically be promoted. Update the box to show his new role!

⯈ Save your work and close PowerPoint.

**Tip:**

You can delete any box except the top manager by clicking to select it and pressing the Delete key.

## Exercise

In this exercise you will apply a design template to the Mapsters presentation you have been working on in the previous practice exercises. You will add footer information to slides and insert an organisation chart.

1. Open the file Mapsters.pptx.

2. Apply the Flow design template to the whole presentation. (If this isn't present on your copy of PowerPoint, choose another.)

3. Change the colour scheme Module (or something else if it isn't present on your copy of PowerPoint).

4. In the footer of all slides (except the title slide) insert the date and page numbers.

5. Change the position of the page numbers so that they are centred.

6. Create the following organisation chart on slide 4.

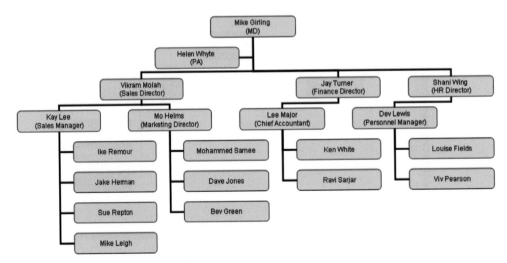

7. Save and close the presentation. You will continue working on this presentation at the end of the next chapter.

## Ask yourself

❷    Do I know what a master slide is and can I apply one to a presentation?

❷    Do I know how to use design templates?

❷    Can I alter slide colour schemes?

❷    Can I add header and footer information to a presentation?

❷    Can I apply formatting and slide information to individual slides and to all the slides in a presentation?

❷    Can I change the layout of a slide?

❷    Do I know how to insert and edit organisational charts?

In this chapter you should have created and saved the following files:

Mapsters.pptx            Tigers.pptx

In this chapter you have been introduced to the following buttons and features:

Slide Master
in the Presentation Views group on the View ribbon

Colors
Themes
in the Edit Theme group on the Slide Master ribbon

Layout
in the Slides group on the Home ribbon

Header & Footer
in the Text group on the Insert ribbon

# CHAPTER 40

# Adding Objects and Tables

In this chapter you will find out:

- about adding objects such as clip art and charts to a slide
- how to change the size of an object
- how to copy and move an object within a presentation and between presentations
- how to insert an object into a master slide
- how to add a table to a slide
- how to insert and delete table columns and rows
- how to add a chart to a slide
- how to add and edit chart data
- how to format chart features.

In this chapter you will use these buttons in the Clipboard group on the Home ribbon:

these buttons in the Illustrations group on the Insert ribbon:

and this button in the Labels group on the Chart Tools Layout ribbon:

## Adding objects

▶ If it is not already on your screen, open the presentation Tigers.pptx.

▶ Click Slide 5 in the Outline pane to display it.

You already prepared this slide for a title and two contents on page 406.

▶ Click where indicated to add text and type Action at:. Press Enter.

 ▶ Add subpoints as shown, pressing the Tab key or clicking the Increase List Level button to indent the lines.

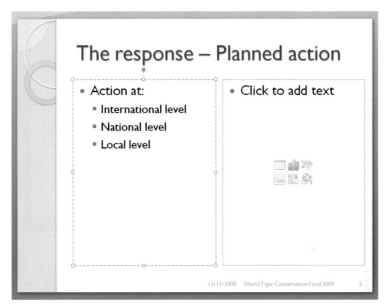

 ▶ Click the Increase Font Size button to make the text slightly larger.

▶ Highlight the text and use the Line Spacing button options to increase the line spacing so that the text fills the whole box.

**Tip:**

You can click the text anywhere in the text placeholder box, and then press **Ctrl+A** to select all the text, rather than highlighting it with the mouse.

## Inserting a clip art image Syllabus 6.5.1.1

Clip art is a collection of pictures and drawings drawn by professional artists for other people to use. It is often free and copyright-free, but it is essential that you check before using an image for publication (see Chapter 6). Microsoft Office comes with a collection of clip art (which extends online). You can use it in all Microsoft Office applications including PowerPoint. Alternatively, you might have a CD with some clip art images that you can use.

 ▶ Click the clip art icon in the bottom right placeholder to display the Clip Art task pane.

- ▶ Search for a picture of a tiger by typing tiger into the Search for: box and clicking the Go button.
- ▶ Click a picture to select it. The picture will now appear on the slide.
- ▶ Close the task pane by clicking the close cross at the top right of the pane.

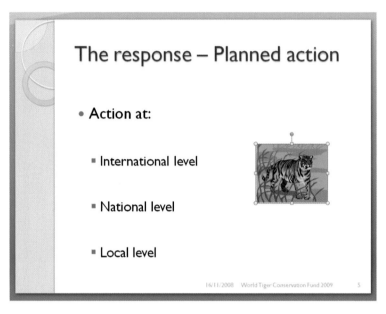

**Tip:**

Don't worry if you have a different selection of clip art images – it doesn't matter which image you use.

## Selecting a graphic object                          Syllabus 6.5.1.2

The little circles surrounding the graphic (picture) are called handles. When the handles are visible, the graphic is selected.

**Tip:**

The **Picture Tools Format** ribbon appears when the graphic is selected.

- ▶ Click away from the graphic and the handles will disappear.
- ▶ Click anywhere inside the graphic and the handles will be visible again.

## Changing the size of an object                      Syllabus 6.5.1.4

You can make the graphic bigger or smaller without changing the width-to-height ratio (its aspect ratio) by dragging any of the corner handles.

- ▶ Make sure the graphic is selected so that the handles are visible.
- ▶ Move the pointer over the top left handle until it is shaped like a diagonal two-headed arrow.

◎     Click and hold down the left mouse button. The pointer changes to a cross-hair.

◎     Drag outwards. When the picture is about twice as wide, release the button.

Tip:

You can use this technique to resize any object inserted from another file.

Tip:

If you change your mind and wish to delete the picture after you have inserted it, simply click to select it and press the **Delete** key.

Your slide will now look similar to this:

◎     Save your work so far.

## Copy or move an object within a presentation     Syllabus 6.3.1.4/6.5.1.3

You would like to use a similar image on the Title slide. You can copy this image without having to insert it from the clip art library.

◎     Make sure Slide 5 is selected.

◎     Click the image of the tiger to select it.

◎     Click Copy in the Clipboard group on the Home ribbon.

ⓘ     You could have selected Cut instead of Copy. This would have copied the image but then deleted the original. Use the Cut button when you want to move images, text and slides from one place to another.

▶ Go to Slide 1 and click Paste in the Clipboard group on the Home ribbon. The image should appear on the slide in a random position.

▶ Move the image by clicking and dragging it. Resize it so it fits below the subtitle.

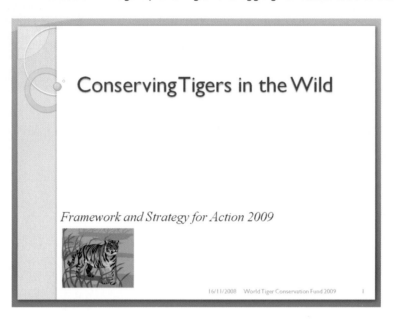

## Copy or move an object between presentations    Syllabus 6.1.1.5/6.3.1.4

You can also copy or move text or objects between open presentations in a similar way.

Suppose you want to use the same tiger picture in another presentation.

▶ Create a new blank presentation as explained on page 381.

▶ Go back to the Tigers presentation by

● clicking the respective taskbar button on the desktop

● clicking the Switch Windows button in the Windows group on the View ribbon, and then selecting the presentation filename on the list, or

● pressing Ctrl+F6 to cycle through the open presentations.

▶ Click to select the image. Click Copy in the Clipboard group on the Home ribbon.

ⓘ Remember you could have selected Cut instead of Copy. This would have copied the image but then deleted it from the original presentation.

▶ Now go back to the new presentation and click Paste in the Clipboard group on the Home ribbon. The image will appear on the slide.

▶ Move and size the image appropriately.

▶ Save the new presentation as More tiger information and close it.

## Inserting an object into the Master Slide          Syllabus 6.2.3.1

You will now insert a tiger graphic into the Master Slide for the non-title slides. This can be done by opening the file containing the graphic then simply copying and pasting the image onto the slide. You can also import it directly, which is what you'll do here.

▶ Either find a tiger picture you like on a website or use the tiger pictures you downloaded earlier.

▶ Make sure the Slide Master is in view.

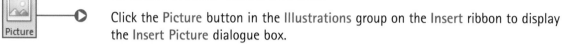

▶ Click the Picture button in the Illustrations group on the Insert ribbon to display the Insert Picture dialogue box.

**Tip:**

To delete an inserted image, click to select it and press the **Delete** key.

▶ Locate the tiger pictures that you've downloaded. Click to select one then click the Insert button.

▶ Now resize the graphic to be quite small, and position it in the top-right corner.

The image will now appear in the corner of all your slides.

▶ Run the slide show and check that the image doesn't obscure any text. Resize it on the master slide if necessary.

ⓘ If you want to delete this image, make sure you're in the Slide Master, select the image by clicking it, then press the Delete key.

You could instead insert any object into the master slide, for example:

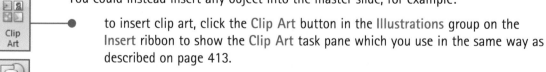

● to insert clip art, click the Clip Art button in the Illustrations group on the Insert ribbon to show the Clip Art task pane which you use in the same way as described on page 413.

● to insert a drawn object (such as a shape or a line), click the Shapes button in the Illustrations group on the Insert ribbon. This is covered in more detail in Chapter 41.

▶ Select the Normal view to exit the slide master.

## Adding a table                                    Syllabus 6.3.4.1

You are now going to add a table to slide 4.

⊙   Display slide 4.

⊙   Click the Insert Table icon in the left-hand placeholder to display the Insert Table dialogue box.

⊙   Set the number of columns to 3, and the number of rows to 3, then click OK.

A table grid will be displayed in the left-hand placeholder.

⊙   Fill in the grid as shown below.

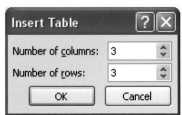

| Insert Table | | ? ☒ |
| --- | --- | --- |
| Number of columns: | 3 | ↕ |
| Number of rows: | 3 | ↕ |
| OK | | Cancel |

| Estimate | Siberian | Sumatran |
| --- | --- | --- |
| Minimum | 360 | 400 |
| Maximum | 406 | 500 |

Do not worry if the layout does not look very neat. You will adjust the rows and columns, and format the text later.

**Tip:**

Tables are not only used to display rows and columns of figures. They are often used by website designers to position images and text neatly on a page.

## Inserting table rows and columns                  Syllabus 6.3.4.3

You decide that you want to include some data about a third tiger population. You need to add a new column to the left of the Siberian column.

⊙   Right-click in any cell in the Siberian column to display a shortcut menu.

⊙   Click Insert, and then click Insert Columns to the Left. A blank column is inserted to the left of the selected column.

⊙   Now add the new data shown.

| Estimate | Amoy |
| --- | --- |
| Minimum | 20 |
| Maximum | 30 |

**Tips:**

You can delete a column or row by first selecting it and then selecting **Delete Columns** or **Delete Rows**, respectively, on the shortcut menu.

Insert a new row by clicking **Insert Rows Above** or **Insert Rows Below** on the shortcut menu.

## Formatting a table                    Syllabus 6.3.4.2/6.3.4.4

⊙   Your table is in desperate need of tidying up! Select all the cells in the table.

**Tip:**

Place the text insertion cursor in the table, column or row you wish to select and click the **Select** button in the **Table** group on the **Layout** ribbon. Then select **Select Table, Select Column** or **Select Row** from the menu options as required.

 ▶ Choose a font and then change the font size using the buttons in the Font group on the Home ribbon, so the text fits neatly in the table cells. Change the text colour if you want to.

▶ As you move your mouse pointer over the borders between rows, or over the borders between columns, the pointer will change to a double-headed arrow. Drag the borders to change the row heights or column widths so your slide looks similar to this.

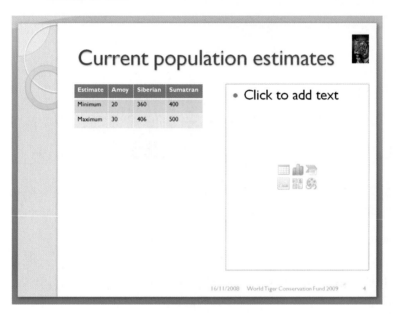

▶ Save your presentation so far.

## Adding a column chart                          Syllabus 6.4.1.1

You will now add a chart to Slide 4. It will show the current population estimates of different species of tigers that you have included in the table.

▶ Select Slide 4, if it is not already, by clicking it in the Outline pane. It already has a Content placeholder on its right-hand side.

 ▶ Click the Insert Chart icon in the placeholder to display the Insert Chart dialogue box.

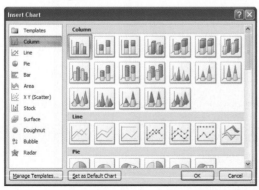

- ◖ Select the Column chart type in the left-hand list, then select the Clustered Column format in the gallery on the right-hand side of the dialogue box.

- ◖ Click the OK button. PowerPoint will display a sample datasheet in Excel format and the bar graph for the sample data.

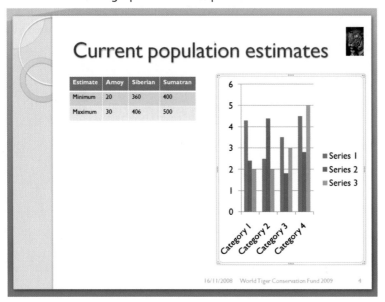

To make the chart you need to replace the sample data in the datasheet with the tiger population data shown on the slide. Delete any sample data that remains after entering the tiger population data.

| | A | B | C |
|---|---|---|---|
| 1 | | Min. estimate | Max. estimate |
| 2 | Amoy | 20 | 30 |
| 3 | Siberian | 360 | 406 |
| 4 | Sumatran | 400 | 500 |

As you type, the chart is updated with the new text and figures. When you have finished it will look similar to the next screenshot.

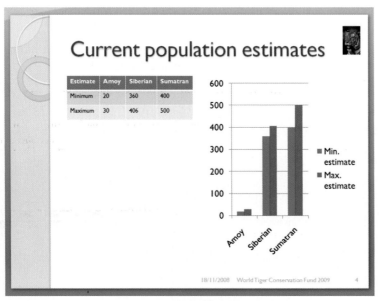

○ Close the Excel datasheet.

○ Click somewhere on the slide outside the chart area to deselect it.

Do not worry if some of the labels appear to be missing or look different at this stage. You will apply formatting so that the chart looks correct on the slide.

## Sizing a chart                                    Syllabus 6.4.1.2/6.5.1.4

ⓘ To adjust the chart size, click it and drag a corner handle inwards to make it smaller and outwards to make it larger.

ⓘ To delete a chart, click to select it and press the Delete key, just as you would to delete any object.

## Editing a chart

Suppose you have made a mistake in one of the figures or headings in the chart.

○ Select the chart so a frame appears around it.

○ Click the Edit Data button in the Data group on the Chart Tools Design ribbon to open the Excel datasheet.

○ Edit the data as you require in the datasheet.

You can apply formatting to all the different parts of a chart. You can see what the chart parts are called by pausing the mouse pointer over a feature to display a screen tip.

○ Identify the some chart features such as the Legend, Category Axis and Value Axis.

○ Right-click the Category Axis and select Format Axis... from the shortcut menu to display the Format Axis dialogue box, where you can change the formatting.

## Adding a chart and axis title                         Syllabus 6.4.1.4

○ Click the Chart Title button in the Labels group on the Chart Tools Layout ribbon to display a menu of options.

○ Select where you want the chart title to be placed.

○ Type the title you want in the Chart Title placeholder that appears.

**Tip:**

> You can also add titles to the axes by clicking the **Axis Titles** button on the **Labels** group on the **Chart Tools Layout** ribbon.

○ You don't need a chart title for this example (the slide title is enough), and the axes are self-explanatory, so click the Undo button on the Quick Access Toolbar to remove the title.

## Changing the background colour                        Syllabus 6.4.1.6

- Select the chart.

- Right-click in the Chart Area and select Format Chart Area... from the shortcut menu to display the Format Chart Area dialogue box.

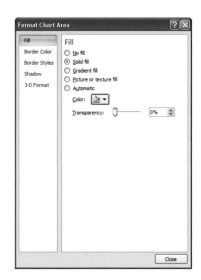

- Click Fill in the list on the left-hand side of the dialogue box.

- Click the Solid fill radio button. The background will change to the last used colour.

- Click the Color: button and choose a colour from the palette that appears.

**Tip:**

The **Chart Area** is the area around the chart. To be sure you're in the right place, just pause the mouse pointer over that area and a screen tip will appear telling you where you are.

## Changing the column colour                        Syllabus 6.4.1.7

- With the chart still selected, right-click one of the columns, then select Format Data Series... from the shortcut menu. The Format Data Series window appears.

- Click Fill in the list on the left-hand side of the dialogue box, which will now look similar to the Format Chart Area dialogue box above.

- Click the Solid fill radio button. The colour will change to that last used.

- Click the Color: button and choose a colour from the palette that appears.

- ⓘ This will have changed the colour of only one of the data series. To change the other colour of the other series, repeat the steps above, having first right-clicked a column that you want to change.

**Tip:**

You can use all these formatting techniques on different types of graph and chart.

## Adding a pie chart                Syllabus 6.2.2.5–6/6.4.1.1–3/6.4.1.5/6.4.1.7

You decide that you would like to display the population data as a pie chart. For the moment you would like to keep the table and column chart until you have seen whether the pie chart is what you want for your presentation.

- Select Slide 4 on the Slides pane, then right click it to show a shortcut menu.

- Click Copy.

- Right click the slide again in the Slides pane and click Paste. A copy of Slide 4 appears after it, and has become Slide 5.

- Click the chart on Slide 5 to select it.

- Click the chart to select it.

- Click the Insert ribbon tab, and click Chart in the Illustrations group to display the Change Chart Type dialogue box. This is similar to the Insert Chart dialogue box you met on page 419.

- Select the Pie chart type in the left-hand list, then select the Pie format in the gallery on the right-hand side of the dialogue box.

Tip:

You can change the chart type by right clicking a chart and selecting **Change Chart Type** from the options on the shortcut menu that is displayed, and then choosing from the **Change Chart Type** dialogue box gallery.

- Click OK to display the pie chart on the slide.

Tip:

You can use exactly the same methods as described to insert and format other types of chart.

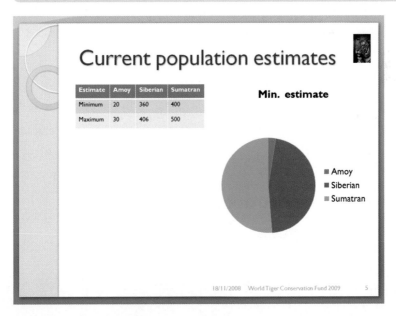

Only the minimum estimate figures have been used and this is fine for the purpose of the slide.

- Click the Chart title placeholder and edit the title so it reads Minimum estimate.

- Right-click in one of the sectors and select Add Data Label from the shortcut menu.

▶ Right-click the sector again and select Format Data Labels... on the shortcut menu. The Format Data Labels dialogue box is displayed.

▶ Make sure that Label Options is selected in the list on the left-hand side of the dialogue box.

▶ Select the Percentage and Outside End options.

▶ Click Close.

▶ Some chart features might be obscured (such as the legend), so you might need to move them.

**Tip:**

On a line graph or bar chart, you would tick **Value** to display the number that is in the datasheet.

Finally, you are going to change the colours of the sectors.

▶ With the chart selected, click the Series area of the pie chart circle, then click the largest sector so only it is selected.

▶ Right-click the selected sector and click Format Data Point... from the shortcut menu to display the Format Data Point dialogue box, which is similar to the Format Chart Area dialogue box you used on page 422.

▶ Click Fill in the list on the left-hand side of the dialogue box.

▶ Click the Solid fill radio button.

▶ Click the Color: button and choose a colour form the palette that is displayed.

▶ Try formatting different features of the chart. See if you can end up with something like this:

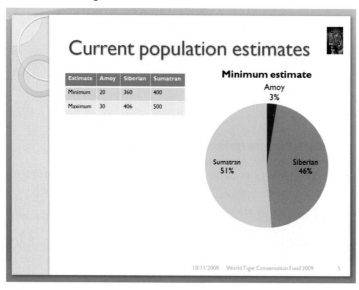

When you are happy with how your chart looks, you can remove the original slide containing the table and column chart from your presentation.

◉    Right-click Slide 4 in the Slides pane.

◉    Select Delete Slide from the shortcut menu that appears.

Your new pie chart slide now becomes Slide 4.

◉    Save and close your presentation.

## Exercise

Now you will add a graphic to the Mapsters presentation you have worked on in previous practice exercises. You will also add a chart showing the company sales by product (i.e. maps of European countries).

1. Open the file Mapsters.pptx.

2. Find a clip-art image of a globe that would be suitable as a company logo for Mapsters Ltd.

3. Insert it into every slide except the title slide, in the top right-hand corner.

4. Size the image to fit.

5. Insert a pie chart into the Sales by product slide based on this table.

6. Give the chart a title and display the data labels as percentages. Run the slide show. Save and close the presentation.

|  | 2008 (£k) |
|---|---|
| Austria | 60.9 |
| Belgium | 89.4 |
| Eire | 86.7 |
| France | 170.4 |
| Germany | 120.4 |
| Italy | 130.9 |
| Portugal | 86.3 |
| Spain | 140.3 |
| Switzerland | 98.9 |
| UK | 80.6 |

## Ask yourself

❷      Do I know what objects are and how to add them to a slide?

❷      Can I change the size of an object?

❷      Can I copy or move an object within a presentation?

❷      Can I copy or move an object between presentations?

❷      Can I insert an object into a master slide?

❷      Can I insert a table into a slide and format it?

❷      Can I insert and delete table rows and columns?

❷      Can I add a chart to a slide?

❷      Can I add and edit chart data?

❷      Can I format and edit chart features?

In this chapter you should have created and saved the following files:
Mapsters.pptx
More tiger information.pptx
Tigers.pptx

In this chapter you have been introduced to the following buttons and features:

Copy
Paste
in the Clipboard group on the Home ribbon

Chart
Picture
in the Illustrations group on the Insert ribbon

Chart Title
in the Labels group on the Chart Tools Layout ribbon

# Special Effects

In this chapter you will find out:

- ❗ how to add a slide transition effect
- ❗ how to add special effects to text
- ❗ how to format text and objects
- ❗ about lines, arrows and shapes, and how to format them
- ❗ how to rotate and flip objects
- ❗ how to select a group of objects
- ❗ how to bring objects to the front, and send them to the back, of a slide.

In this chapter you will use these buttons and features in the Transition to This Slide group on the Animations ribbon:

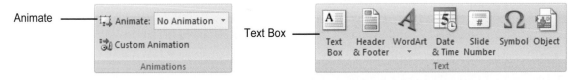

Slide Transition
gallery

Slide Transition
effects

this button in the Animations group on the Animations ribbon:

this button in the Text group on the Insert ribbon:

Animate

Text Box

this button in the Arrange group on the Picture Tools Format ribbon:

and these buttons in the Drawing group on the Home ribbon:

Rotate

Arrange

Shape formatting

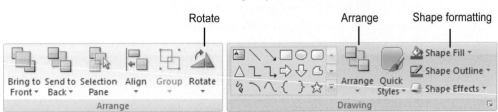

In this chapter you will add sounds and animation to your presentation. You can also add transition effects for when each screen opens.

▶ Open the presentation Tigers.pptx.

## Adding slide transitions

Transitions change the way a slide opens. For example, you can make the next slide open like a blind or a curtain.

▶ Display the Slide Sorter view.

▶ Click Slide 1 to select it.

▶ Click the Animations ribbon tab and select Split Vertical Out from the gallery in the Transitions to This Slide group. The transition is previewed in the Slide Sorter view.

Click to scroll through the gallery

Click to display the whole gallery

This will make the first screen open like a curtain, as if it were opening in a theatre.

You could also add a sound to this transition by choosing one from the Transition Sound list box in the Transitions to This Slide group on the Animations ribbon. However, be very careful about adding a special effect such as sound – unless the sound is particularly appropriate and the effect is not used too often, it can detract from the purpose of the presentation.

You can also change the speed at which the transition occurs. Try the different options.

If you want the same transition between all the slides, click the Apply to All button.

**Tip:**
Select **No Transition** from the slide transitions gallery to remove a transition effect.

## Adding special effects to text

PowerPoint also allows you to add animation effects to objects such as clip-art images, charts and bulleted lists. Again, use the effects sparingly. You can add animations to different slide elements using the Normal view.

▶ Show the Normal view and show Slide 1.

▶ Select the title placeholder containing the text Conserving Tigers in the Wild.

▶ Click the down-arrow on the Animate list box in the Animations group on the Animations ribbon and select Fly In from the list that appears.

○ Try out the effect in Slide Show view.

Tip:

Select **No Animation** from the list box to remove an animation effect.

## Formatting text and images                           Syllabus 6.5.2.2

Now you will create a simple logo for the World Tiger Conservation Fund.

○ Click the Text Box button in the Text group on the Insert ribbon.

○ Click and hold the mouse button and drag the mouse to draw a text box at the top-left of the slide.

○ Type the letters WTCF in Arial, bold, size 24.

## Adding a shadow to text                               Syllabus 6.3.2.2

○ Select the letters WTCF.

 ○ Click the Text Shadow button in the Font group on the Home ribbon.

**WTCF**

## Adding lines to a slide                        Syllabus 6.5.1.1/6.5.2.1

Now add a horizontal line above the letters.

Shapes you can use are displayed in the Drawing group on the Home ribbon. You can also display the gallery of shapes by clicking the Shapes button in the Illustrations group on the Insert ribbon.

Line

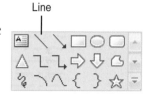

○ Click the Line shape. The mouse pointer changes to a crosshair.

○ Whilst holding down the Shift key, click and hold the mouse button to drag out a horizontal line above the letters. Release the mouse button when you are happy with the line.

**WTCF**

Tip:

Select the **Scribble** shape from gallery to draw freehand lines.

ⓘ The Shift key restricts the number of angles the line can take which makes it easier to draw a horizontal line. Try drawing it without!

ⓘ If you want to move the line slightly higher or lower, move the mouse pointer over the line until it becomes a cross with arrowheads, then click and drag.

## Formatting a line

### Changing line colour

▶     Click the line to select it.

 ▶     Click the Shape Outline button in the Drawing group on the Home ribbon to display a menu

▶     Click to select a different colour, such as a dark blue, from the palette.

### Changing line width

 ▶     Click the Shape Outline button again, click Weight and then select 6 pt.

### Changing line style

 ▶     Click the Shape Outline button again, click Dashes and then select the Round Dot style.

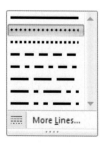

▶     Save your work.

That's all you need for the simple logo, but here are some of the other drawing tools that you can practise using.

**Tip:**

Adding shapes to a slide on page 432 describes how to add other types of shapes to slides. Practise drawing and formatting some of these. Perhaps you can design a better logo for the WTCF?

## Adding an arrow Syllabus 6.5.1.1/6.5.2.1/6.5.2.4

- ◉ Add a new slide, Slide 7, at the end of your presentation and apply the Blank design template.
-  ◉ Select the Arrow shape in the shapes gallery and drag a vertical line downwards on the slide. An arrowhead will appear when you release the mouse button.
- ◉ Format the arrow by right-clicking it and selecting Format Shape... from the shortcut menu. The Format Shape dialogue box is displayed.
- ◉ Click Line Style in the list in the left-hand side of the dialogue box.
- ◉ Change the style of the arrowhead by selecting from the options available when you click the buttons in the Arrow settings section.
-  ◉ Click the Up Arrow shape and drag out a wide arrow on the slide.

## Rotating or flipping an object Syllabus 6.5.1.5

You'll now practise rotating/flipping the block arrow you've just drawn.

- ◉ Select the object.
- ◉ Click the Rotate button in the Arrange group on the Picture Tools Format ribbon.
- ◉ Choose an option from the displayed menu. Leave the arrow pointing upwards.

## Adding text to a shape Syllabus 6.5.2.2

You can add text to shapes such as block arrows, rectangles, squares, ovals and circles.

- ◉ Right-click the block arrow to show a shortcut menu.
- ◉ Select Edit Text and type This way up. PowerPoint aligns the text centrally in the shape.

## Selecting and grouping drawn objects Syllabus 6.5.2.6

- ◉ You can select more than one object by clicking the first object, holding down the Shift key, then clicking other objects. Select the two arrows you've just drawn.
- ❶ Grouping objects is useful if you want all the separate objects to be treated as one object. This means you only need to click once to select them all, and if you move one of the objects, all the others will be moved too.
- ◉ With both the objects selected, right-click any one of the objects to display a shortcut menu.
- ◉ Click Group and then select Group from the list of options.

Try selecting the grouped objects and moving them around – they will move together.

◗ Ungroup the arrows by right-clicking the group and selecting Group, and then Ungroup.

◗ Delete the thin line arrow.

## Sending objects to the front or back          Syllabus 6.5.2.1/7

When you've got two objects overlapping, PowerPoint will automatically place the most recent object on top. If this isn't what you want, you need to change the order of the objects, and either send one of the objects to the back or bring one to the front.

◗ Use the techniques you've been practising to draw a circle over the block arrow. It will appear over it.

> **Tip:**
> Select the **Oval** shape ⬭ and hold down the **Shift** key as you drag out the shape to form a circle.

◗ You'd like the arrow to be on top, so you will send the circle to the back.

◗ Right-click the circle and select Send to Back from the shortcut menu, then choose the Send to Back option. The circle will be moved behind the arrow.

You could have selected the arrow first and brought it in front of the circle by clicking the Bring to Front option on the shortcut menu displayed when you right click it.

> **Tip:**
> Selecting **Send Backward** or **Bring Forward** will move an object one level if there are multiple objects.

◗ You don't need Slide 7 for your presentation, so delete it, and save the file.

## Adding shapes to a slide          Syllabus 6.5.1.1/6.5.2.1

As well as lines, you can add a range of shapes such as boxes and circles to a slide. You can modify these shapes in exactly the same way as lines. You'll run through this briefly by adding a rectangle at the top of Slide 1.

◗ Select Slide 1.

◗ Click the Rectangle button in the Shapes gallery.

◗ Click and drag the mouse pointer to draw a large rectangle like this:

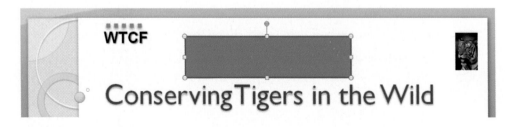

Tip:
To draw a square, hold down the **Shift** key as you drag out the shape.

## Formatting shapes                                    Syllabus 6.5.2.3/6.5.2.5

### Fill colour

 Make sure the rectangle is selected and click the Shape Fill button in the Drawing group on the Home ribbon.

● Select a light blue colour from the palette.

ⓘ If you don't want any fill colour in the shape, choose No Fill instead of a colour.

### Border colour

 With the rectangle still selected, click the Shape Outline button and make the border the same light blue as the fill.

### Shadow

 With the rectangle still selected, click the Shape Effects button in the Drawing group on the Home ribbon and choose one of the shadow options.

● Now tidy up the title slide by deleting the shape you have just added – select it then press the Delete key.

## Moving or copying a line or shape

To move or copy a drawn object, right-click the object and select Cut or Copy on the shortcut menu. Right-click on the destination slide (either within the presentation or in a different, open presentation) and select Paste on the shortcut menu.

## Deleting a line or shape

To delete a drawn object on either a normal slide or the master slide, click the object and press the Delete key.

## Aligning a line or shape on a slide                   Syllabus 6.5.1.6

 To align a drawn object on a slide, click the object and then click the Arrange button in the Drawing group on the Home ribbon.

● Select Align on the shortcut menu and then make sure Align to Slide is ticked.

● Click the Arrange button again and Align, and now select how you want the shape to be aligned (e.g. left, right, centre etc.).

## Adding and modifying a text box                    Syllabus 6.3.2.3

Now add a text box to Slide 4.

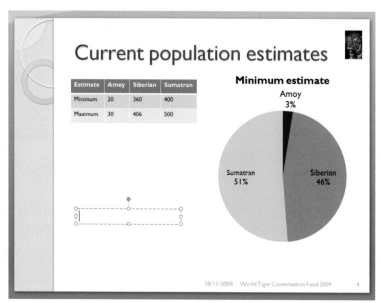

- Select Slide 4 and click the Text Box button in the Text group on the Insert ribbon.

- Click and hold the mouse button to drag out a text box anywhere below the chart.

- Type the text Source: WWF Species Status Report.

### Repositioning and resizing

- Size the text, and click and drag the handles until the text box is positioned as shown below:

### Changing the text colour

- With the text box still selected, click the down-arrow on the Font Color button in the Font group on the Home ribbon.

- Select a dark blue colour.

- Save your work.

- Check the presentation by running Slide Show. Make changes if you think any are necessary.

- Close your presentation and PowerPoint.

## Exercise

There is just one slide left to complete on the Mapsters presentation that you have been working on at the end of each presentation chapter. This exercise asks you to complete that slide and add slide transitions and special effects.

1.  Open the file Mapsters.pptx.

2.  Produce the following diagram on the Target Markets slide using shapes and formatting you have learnt:

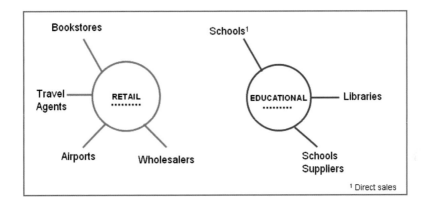

3.  Add a Blinds Horizontal transition between all slides. Choose to advance slides on a mouse click.

4.  Insert a special effect that makes the bullet points on the slides fly in from the left at a medium speed.

5.  Add a slight shadow to the headings on all pages.

6.  Run the slide show and make any necessary adjustments. Save and close your work.

## Ask yourself

&#10067;    Do I know what slide transition effects are, and can I add them to a presentation?

&#10067;    Can I add special effects to slide text?

&#10067;    Can I apply formatting to text and objects?

&#10067;    Can I format lines, arrows and shapes?

&#10067;    Can I rotate and flip objects on a slide?

&#10067;    Do I know what grouping objects means, and can I use it?

&#10067;    Can I bring objects to the front of a slide, and send them to the back?

In this chapter you should have created and saved the following files:
Mapsters.pptx
Tigers.pptx

In this chapter you have been introduced to the following buttons and features:

Slide Transition effects
Slide Transition gallery
in the Transitions to This Slide group on the Animations ribbon

Animate
in the Animations group on the Animations ribbon

Text Box
in the Text group on the Insert ribbon

Rotate
in the Arrange group on the Picture Tools Format ribbon

Arrange
Shape Effects
Shape Fill
Shape Outline
in the Drawing group on the Home ribbon

# Show Time!

CHAPTER

42

**In this chapter you will find out:**

- about running a slide show
- how to navigate slides during a presentation
- how to hide a slide so it isn't shown during a presentation
- about slide notes, and how to add and display them
- how to print slides, notes and handouts
- how copy slides between open presentations
- about different file formats.

In this chapter you will use this button in the Page Setup group on the Design ribbon:

Page Setup ———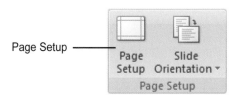

and this button in the Preview group on the Print Preview ribbon:

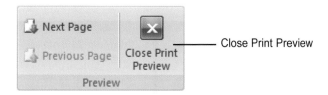 ——— Close Print Preview

In this chapter you'll find out how PowerPoint can help you during your presentation. Many of these features work best when you are giving the presentation on a big screen and controlling it from your computer.

○ Open the document called Tigers.pptx if it is not already open.

## Starting a show on any slide                    Syllabus 6.6.2.4

To start a show on a particular slide, all you need to do is make sure that slide is selected before clicking the Slide Show button.

## Navigating your way around a presentation      Syllabus 6.6.2.5

○ Once in Slide Show mode, right-click a slide to display a shortcut menu.

ⓘ To find your way around a presentation you can click the Next and Previous options. This will take you to either the next or previous slide in the presentation.

| Next |
| Previous |
| Last Viewed |
| Go to Slide ▶ |
| Custom Show ▶ |
| Screen ▶ |
| Pointer Options ▶ |
| Help |
| Pause |
| End Show |

### Tip:

You probably will not want to display this shortcut menu every time you want to change a slide. Instead, you can click the controls that appear at the bottom left of the slide. An alternative way to go to the next slide, which does not even require using the mouse, is to press the Space bar. To go back a slide press the Backspace key.

○ If you want to move to a particular slide, click Go to Slide. This will bring up another submenu, where you select the slide by its title. Go to the Contents slide.

## Hiding slides                                   Syllabus 6.6.1.5

Suppose that you don't want to show Slide 4 in your presentation.

○ In Normal view, right-click Slide 4 in the Slides pane.

○ Select Hide Slide from the shortcut menu.

Hidden slide indicator

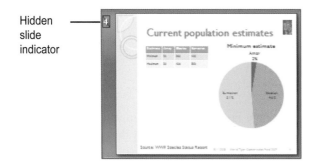

This slide will now not appear when you run your presentation. You can see in the Slides pane or Slide Sorter if a slide is hidden because the slide number is crossed out.

▶  Unhide the slide by following exactly the same procedure.

## Using Notes Syllabus 6.6.1.3

To assist you in your presentation you can make additional notes about each slide to prompt you. The notes are not visible in Slide Show view. You usually print them as your speaking notes when giving the presentation.

▶  Select Slide 4 once again.

The pane below the slide is for adding notes. To make it easier to write notes, make this pane bigger by clicking and dragging the border above the pane.

— Click and drag here

— Notes pane

▶  Now you can type some notes. Type Adapted from WWF Species Status Report 'Wanted Alive! Tigers in the Wild!', or make up your own note.

▶  Save your work.

## Slide setup Syllabus 6.6.1.4/6.6.2.2

Occasionally you might need to display your presentation in a specific format.

▶  Click the Page Setup button in the Page Setup group on the Design ribbon to display the Page Setup dialogue box.

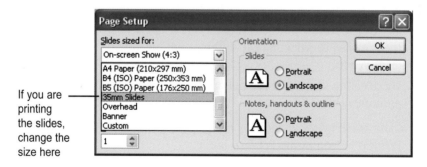

If you are printing the slides, change the size here

ⓘ  To change the orientation of the slides, just select either the Portrait or Landscape option in the Slides section.

ⓘ  You can choose an appropriate output format using the Slides sized for: list. The options you may be asked about for ECDL are On-screen show, Overhead and 35mm Slides.

▶  Click OK when you are happy with the settings.

## Printing

● To print anything, click Print on the Office button menu to display the Print dialogue box.

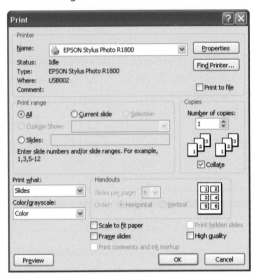

The Print dialogue box is similar to those in other Microsoft Office applications.

### Printing slides

● To print only slides, make sure Slides is selected in the Print what: section.

● You can change which slides are printed using the Print range section.

● Set the number of copies in the Copies section.

● Preview the slide printouts by clicking the Preview button.

ⓘ You can also preview and print Handouts, Notes Pages and Outline View from either the Print window or from the Preview, by selecting the different options under Print What:.

● Try selecting some of these options to see the different print previews.

● Close the Preview window by clicking the Close Print Preview button in the Preview group.

### Printing handouts

This is very similar to printing slides.

● Open the Print dialogue box.

● This time select Handouts from the Print what: list.

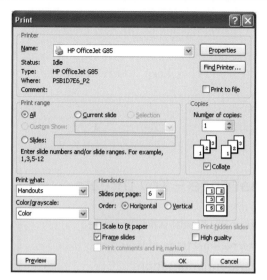

● Notice that the Handouts section can now be used. You can choose how many slides to print on a page, and also change the order from Horizontal to Vertical. Try choosing different numbers of slides per page.

● Again, click the Preview button to see what it will look like. You can also change the number of slides on a page in the preview by using the Print what: list.

### Printing Notes Pages

● To print the notes, just make sure Notes Pages is selected in the Print what: list in either the Print dialogue box or in the Print Preview.

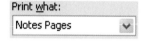

## Copying slides

Syllabus 6.1.1.5/6.2.2.5

● You can copy slides between presentations. To try this out open a new presentation (see page 381) – do this whilst keeping the Tigers.pptx presentation open.

You will add two slides to this presentation by copying and pasting slides from the Tigers.pptx presentation.

● Go back to the Tigers presentation (see page 416 to remind yourself how to switch between open presentations).

● In Slide Sorter view, select both Slide 2 and Slide 3 by clicking them whilst holding down the Ctrl key.

● Right-click the selected slides and click Copy on the shortcut menu.

ℹ Remember you could have selected Cut instead of Copy. This would have copied the slides but then deleted them from the original presentation.

● Return to the new presentation and right-click Slide 1.

● Select Paste from the shortcut menu.

The two slides will be copied to the new presentation. The background has not been copied because the slides take on the formatting of the new presentation.

If you want to keep the original formatting, click the Paste Options button, which appears under the slides you pasted, and click Keep Source Formatting.

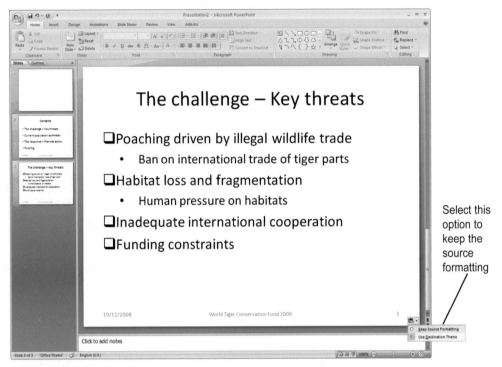

Select this option to keep the source formatting

Tip:

If the Paste Options button does not appear, click PowerPoint Options on the Office button menu. Select Show Paste Options buttons in the Advanced section of the window.

▶ Save the file as Tigers2.pptx.

## Saving in different file formats                    Syllabus 6.1.1.4

You have a choice of many file formats other than the normal .pptx format. You will now save the Tigers2 file as a template.

▶ Click the Office button, move the mouse pointer over Save As on the menu and click the Other Formats option to open the Save As dialogue box.

▶ Navigate to the Tiger Presentation folder.

▶ Type the filename Tigers2 in the File name: box.

▶ Click the down arrow to the right of the Save as type: list box to see a large selection of different file types.

▶ Select PowerPoint Template (*.potx).

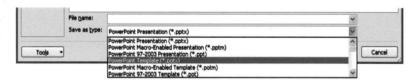

▶ Click the Save button to save the Tigers2 presentation.

Among the other format options are the following:

ⓘ Select Web Page to save the presentation for a website.

ⓘ You can also choose to save the presentation for use in a different version of PowerPoint.

ⓘ If you want to save a presentation in Rich Text Format, select Outline/RTF, but you will lose the graphical content.

ⓘ You can choose to save a single slide or all slides in a presentation as a graphic.

Sometimes it is a good idea to save different versions of a presentation as you develop it. This way you can easily retrieve the slides you liked if you took them out of a later version.

Identifying different versions of a file is as simple as saving it with its name plus a version number (e.g. Version 1 or v4 etc.).

## That's it!

You've now finished the Tigers presentation – yours should look similar to this.

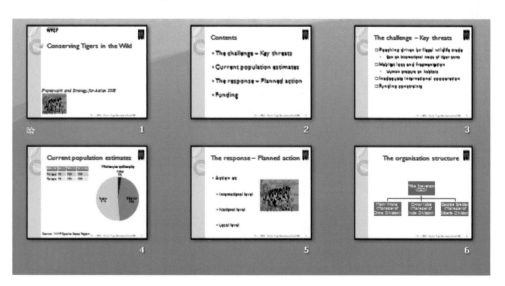

▶ Save and close your presentation, then close PowerPoint.

## Exercise

In this exercise you will practise printing the Mapsters Ltd presentation.

1. Open the file Mapsters.pptx.

2. Check the slides in Print Preview and make any necessary adjustments.

3. Return to Normal view and add some notes in the Notes pane of each slide.

4. Print the slides on one page of A4 paper in portrait orientation.

5. Now print the slides on separate pages together with the notes.

6. Run the slide show.

7. Save and close your work.

## Ask yourself

❓   Do I know how to run a slide show from the beginning or from a particular slide?

❓   Can I move forward to the next slide, or back to the previous slide during a slide show?

❓   Can I go to a particular slide during a slide show?

❓   Can I add notes to a slide?

❓   Do I know about different printing options, and can I print slides, notes and handouts?

❓   Can I copy slides between open presentations?

❓   Can I save a presentation in file formats appropriate to different purposes?

In this chapter you should have created and saved the following files:
Mapsters.pptx
Tigers.pptx
Tigers2.pptx

In this chapter you have been introduced to the following buttons and features:

Page Setup
in the Page Setup group on the Design ribbon

Close Print Preview
in the Preview group on the Print Preview ribbon

# Module 7
## Information and Communication

The module is divided into two sections. Chapters 43–47 on *Information* will help you to understand some of the concepts and terms associated with using the Internet, and to appreciate the security considerations. You will be able to:

- accomplish common web search tasks using a web browser
- use search engine tools
- bookmark websites
- print web pages
- navigate around and complete web-based forms.

In chapters 48–50 on *Communication*, you will learn some of the concepts of electronic mail (e-mail), and gain an appreciation of some of the security considerations associated with using e-mail. You will be able to:

- use e-mail software to send and receive messages
- attach files to e-mail messages
- organise and manage message folders within e-mail software.

This training, which has been approved by the ECDL Foundation, includes exercise items intended to assist Candidates in their training for an ECDL Certification Programme. These exercises are not ECDL Foundation certification tests. For information about authorised ECDL Test Centres in different national territories, please refer to the ECDL Foundation website at www.ecdl.org

# Module **7**

# Contents

# Browsing

In this chapter you will find out:

- about the Internet and the World Wide Web, and what the differences are
- about web browsers and browsing
- how to run and close Microsoft Internet Explorer
- about the web addresses and how to enter them in a browser to view web pages
- how to navigate pages within and between websites
- how to refresh and stop a web page
- how to get help.

## The Internet                                                    Syllabus 7.1.1.1–2

The Internet consists of a huge number of computers, all over the world, connected together. It is an International network of networks. Once connected, you can use the Internet to send e-mails, browse the Web and transfer files.

The World Wide Web and e-mail are probably the best-known facilities that use the Internet. The Web consists of hundreds of millions of web pages stored on computers the world over, which you can access from your computer. Most large companies and organisations have a website, and so do more and more individuals.

## Web browser software                                    Syllabus 7.1.1.3/7.1.1.5

To view web pages, you need a software application called a browser. A browser converts the web page program code into images, text, links and layout that can be displayed on the computer screen. The Microsoft Internet Explorer 7 browser is used in this book. Other PC web browsers are Mozilla Firefox, Google Chrome and Opera.

A browser can show a web page located anywhere (locally on your own computer, or remotely on a network or Internet computer). However, unless the computer is connected to an Internet Service Provider or ISP, you will not be able to show pages accessed online via the Internet. When you connect your computer to the Internet, you connect to an ISP's computer that stores and transmits data to other ISPs and thus to other users. Your connection will either be permanent or dial-up.

# Module 7 Information and Communication

## Getting started

Syllabus 7.2.1.1

- ◉ *Either* double-click the Internet Explorer icon (if it is on your desktop)
- ◉ *Or* click Start, All Programs, then Internet Explorer.
- ◉ If a dialogue box appears, enter your username and password to connect.

A web page will now appear on the screen. On a new installation, this is probably a page that was set as a default by your ISP or computer manufacturer. You will find out how to change this in Chapter 45.

## Entering an address

Syllabus 7.2.1.2–3

You can go to a different page by entering another address.

- ◉ Click in the Address bar at the top of the screen. The text will be highlighted.

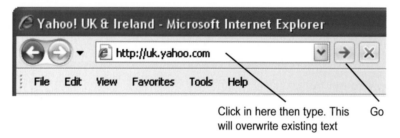

Click in here then type. This will overwrite existing text     Go

- ◉ Type in www.payne-gallway.co.uk and click the Go button or press Enter.

This should bring up the Payne-Gallway website at the opening or home page. It will look similar to the picture below, but it may not be identical since people and companies often change their web page content to keep it up to date. (The address in the address bar might also change – this is because you have been redirected to another address.)

### Tip:

Right-click a link on a web page to display a shortcut menu.
Click Open in New Tab to show the website on a tab.
Click Open in New Window to show the website in a new window.
(Syllabus 7.2.1.3).

❶ Web pages may be longer than the screen. To see the whole page, either click in the scroll bar or press the Page Down key. Ctrl+End takes you to the bottom of the page, Ctrl+Home back to the top.

Tip:
> If you are looking for something on the page, choose Find on this Page... from the Edit menu and enter the word or phrase you are looking for.

## Navigating the Web                                                Syllabus 7.2.3.1

Most web pages have links called hypertext links or hyperlinks. These enable you to jump to another page within the website, or to another place on the same web page (for example, to the top if it's long), or even to other websites. When you move the mouse pointer around the screen, its shape changes to a hand when it is over a link. Links are usually blue, underlined text, but they may also be pictures.

When you click a link, the browser jumps to the new location.

▶ Click the link word Vocational on the Payne-Gallway home page to open a page showing some IT-related products from the publisher.

Tip:
> The page may look quite different when you come to look at it.

▶ Click some more links for practice.

Tip:
> Click an unused tab across the top of the page display area, and type a new URL in the Address bar. You can use the tabs across the top of the page display area to switch between open web pages (Syllabus 7.2.1.3).

## Moving to pages already visited

To go back to the previous page:

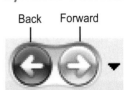

Back    Forward

▶ Click the Back button at top of the screen.

▶ Click Back repeatedly until you are back at the home page.

Notice that the links you have already clicked have changed colour to tell you that you've already followed them.

▶ Now click the Forward button to take you forward through the pages you have already looked at. The buttons appear faded if you cannot use them.

ⓘ The down-arrow to the right of the arrows allows you to jump straight to a page by clicking its name from the displayed list.

> **Tip:**
> You can use the **Alt** key with left or right arrow for **Back** and **Forward**, respectively.

## The web page address

Every web page has a unique address known as the Uniform Resource Locator (URL). The exact location (the computer) on which the web page is located is represented specified by the URL. It has distinct parts separated by dots, each part having a special significance. A typical address is:

http://www.bbc.co.uk

http:// means Hypertext Transfer Protocol. This is the set of rules used by the Internet for sending and receiving data between computers. Some addresses may have https:// for a secure (protected) page with sensitive information. ftp:// (File Transfer Protocol) is another protocol which is used for transferring files.

There's no need to type in http:// as the browser adds it automatically.

www means World Wide Web and is in most, but not all, web page addresses.

bbc.co.uk is the domain name, showing the organisation owning the site and it has several parts.

co is the type of site, in this case a UK commercial organisation. International company domain names generally end in .com.

Some other codes are .gov for government, .org for non-profit organisations, .ac for educational sites (.edu in the USA), and .sch for schools.

If the site is neither .com nor US-based there is usually a country code – .uk for the UK, .fr for France, .de for Germany, .es for Spain, .it for Italy, .ch for Switzerland, .ie for the Republic of Ireland, and so on.

Pages accessed from the home page URL, but forming part of the same site, are written after a / symbol (e.g. www.bbc.co.uk/music displays the BBC Music web page on the BBC website). There may also be the name of a file at the end of an address, such as

/index.htm. Web pages are written in a language called HTML (Hypertext Markup Language) and each page is a file usually ending in .htm.

Here are some sample web addresses – you can probably guess who they belong to.

| | | |
|---|---|---|
| www.disney.com | www.cam.ac.uk | www.bmw.de |
| www.nationalgallery.org.uk | www.harvard.edu | www.louvre.fr |
| www.worldwildlife.org | www.nasa.gov | www.lastampa.it |

## Entering an address from the address bar                    Syllabus 7.2.3.4

 The address box in the address bar has a down-arrow at the right-hand end. If you click this, a list opens with the URLs of recently visited web pages.

○ Click one and notice the browser jumps to that page.

Alternatively, start typing an address in the address bar. If you have recently visited the website, Internet Explorer will match what you type so you don't have to type the complete URL.

> Tip:
>
> If this doesn't happen, look up **AutoComplete** in Help.

○ Start typing the URL www.bbc.co.uk

As soon as you get to www.b Internet Explorer lists all the addresses matching what you have typed.

○ Once you see the address you want, select it on the list.

> Tip:
>
> You can bookmark your favourite websites so you can quickly go to them without having to type in the URL each time. See page 463 to find out how to do this.

> Tip:
>
>  Go quickly to the start page that is set on your computer by clicking the **Home** button. See page 468 for how to change the start page (**Syllabus 7.2.3.3**).

## Refreshing a web page                                 Syllabus 7.2.1.5

The browser stores the pages you browse in a file known as a cache on your hard disk. If you ask for the same page again, it is the stored page that is opened. If you are not sure whether you are looking at the latest version of the page (it will be obvious on a page that is dynamically refreshed like a news page), or you get a message that a web page cannot be displayed, click the Refresh button. This then reloads the page from the Internet, not from the cache.

## Stopping a page downloading                           Syllabus 7.2.1.4

If a page is taking too long to open (this might happens if a page has a lot of pictures or if there is a problem finding the website), click the Stop button.

## Missing page

You may find that your browser cannot find a page although you clicked a link to it, and it displays something like this.

---

**The page cannot be found**

The page you are looking for might have been removed, had its name changed, or is temporarily unavailable.

---

Please try the following:

- If you typed the page address in the Address bar, make sure that it is spelled correctly.
- Open the www.payne-gallway.co.uk home page, and then look for links to the information you want.
- Click the Back button to try another link.

HTTP 404 - File not found
Internet Information Services

---

This might occur because a website has been removed or is temporarily unavailable. The URL may be incorrect (perhaps because you have typed it incorrectly or a link you clicked is directed at a web page that has been removed or has had its address changed). It could also be due to a problem with the site server or because of heavy demand for that site.

## Ending a browsing session                             Syllabus 7.2.1.1

Close Internet Explorer by clicking the Close icon at the top right of your screen, or by selecting File, Exit from the main menu.

> Tip:
> If you have a dial-up connection to your service provider, you might need to disconnect so that you do not continue paying for using the phone line.

## Getting help

If at any time you're unsure of how to do something in Internet Explorer, you can search the Internet Explorer Help system.

◉ Click the Help on the main menu, then Contents and Index.

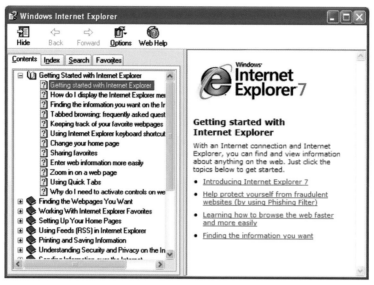

**Tip:**

You could press the F1 key to access Help instead.

The topics are marked by Book icons: clicking a topic lists the items below.

◉ Click an item to see the associated help information on the right.

You can also search the help index by entering a keyword.

◉ Click the Index tab and type in a keyword representing the topic you want help on.

◉ Topics relating to the keyword are displayed; click one to show the help information. Alternatively you can enter your keyword on the Search tab. If all else fails there is also Microsoft online help from the Web Help button.

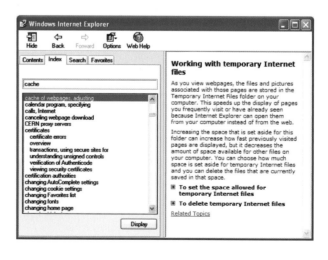

◉ Close the Help window when you have seen enough.

# Module 7 Information and Communication

## Exercises

1. Open Internet Explorer and make sure you are connected to the Internet.

2. Enter the URL www.bbc.co.uk/music

3. Find on this page all instances of the word jazz.

4. Bookmark this page.

5. Go to the site www.multimap.com and bookmark it.

6. Enter your postcode to display a small-scale map of your home area.

7. Click the Print button to print out the map.

8. Disconnect from the Internet if you have a dial-up connection.

9. Close Internet Explorer.

## Ask yourself

❓ Do I know the difference between the Internet and the World Wide Web?

❓ Can I start and close a web browser?

❓ Do I know what a web address comprises and can I enter an address into a browser to display a web page?

❓ Can I navigate within and between web pages?

❓ Can I refresh a web page and stop one from loading into a browser?

❓ Can I use the browser's help feature?

# Search Engines

**In this chapter you will find out:**

- about search engines, encyclopaedia and dictionaries
- about searching using keywords or phrases
- how to refine a search using advanced search features
- about copying text and graphics from a web page to another application
- how to save a graphic as a file
- how to save and print a web page
- about temporary Internet files and how to manage them.

## Using a search engine      Syllabus 7.1.1.6/7.3.2.1

It's easy to spend hours browsing the Web, jumping randomly from page to page, but, although it can be fun to see what this turns up, you usually want to find information on a specific topic. You can use a search engine to do this. There are many different search engines – Google, Yahoo! and AltaVista are examples of well-known ones.

A search engine is software which enables you to find information on almost any conceivable topic.

This book uses Google as an example search engine, but the techniques described are similar for other search engines.

- Start Internet Explorer.

- Type the address www.google.co.uk into the Address bar and click the Go button to display the Google website home page.

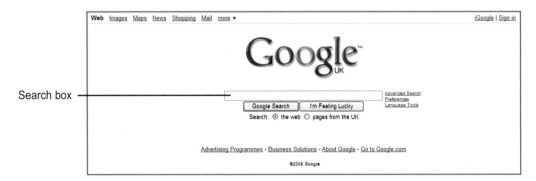

Search box

455

## Searching by keyword

Google allows you to type a word or phrase, and then comes back with a list of related web pages. Suppose you wanted to find the Prime Minister's official website.

▶ Type 10 Downing Street into the search box and click the Google Search button.

Google comes back with a list of links to websites that match your search words.

▶ The first link is the 10 Downing Street home page. Click the link to view the Number 10 website.

◉    Go back to the Google home page.

This time you'll search for items on bell ringing.

◉    Type ringing in the search box, and click Google Search.

This finds a huge number of references. Among them are links to pages about bird
ringing. You need to refine the search to filter the results to show mainly websites on
bell ringing.

## Including and excluding pages       Syllabus 7.3.2.3

You can tell Google to exclude topics you don't want by adding a keyword with a minus
in front. Similarly, if you are particularly interested in a topic, such as bells, you can add
keywords with a plus in front.

◉    Try adding –bird +bell and click Google Search.

This is better, but you might be interested only in bell ringing in London or Oxford.

◉    Add +London OR Oxford to the search string.

Here the OR must be in capitals. This will narrow the results further but in some cases
you might need to filter the search results further to find what you want.

**Tip:**

> If you want to specify bell ringing in both London and Oxford, you would put
> **London AND Oxford·**
> If you want to keep words together, then type the phrase in quotes, such as
> **"single Oxford"** (which will find bell ringing methods called 'Single Oxford', rather
> than web pages with the word 'Oxford' on them, and occurrences of web pages
> with the word 'single' on them, but not necessarily together).

## Copying text from a web page                              Syllabus 7.4.1.3

Suppose you want to copy some of the text and graphics from a website into a Word
document.

- ▶ Open a blank document in Word.
- ▶ Go back to Internet Explorer by selecting it from the taskbar at the bottom of
  the screen.
- ▶ Open the 10 Downing Street home page once again.
- ▶ Drag to select a few lines of text.
- ▶ From the Edit menu, choose Copy.
- ▶ Go back to Word and choose Paste.

**Tip:**

> There are two ways to copy a web address, depending on where they are.
> • To copy the URL in the **Address bar**, right-click it and select **Copy** from the
> shortcut menu.
> • To copy a link from a web page, right-click it and select **Copy Shortcut** from the
> shortcut menu.

**Note:**

> You may only copy for your own personal use. Copyright material may not be
> reproduced without permission.

## Copying and saving graphics from a web page               Syllabus 7.4.1.3

It is better to copy the graphics separately from the text.

- ▶ In Internet Explorer, right-click the picture you want to
  copy to display a shortcut menu.
- ▶ Select Copy.
- ▶ Return to Word and select Paste.

The method described places the picture on the clipboard. Sometimes you might want to keep a copy of a picture as a file. To save a web page picture as a file, right-click it, and select Save Picture As... from the shortcut menu, then browse to the folder you want to put it in.

The shortcut menu also lets you select options for printing and e-mailing a selected picture.

## Saving a web page                                          Syllabus 7.4.1.1

You can save a web page to look at later.

◉　In the browser, choose File, Save As....

◉　Select a folder and type Downing Street as the file name.

◉　Select Webpage, complete as the file type and click the Save button.

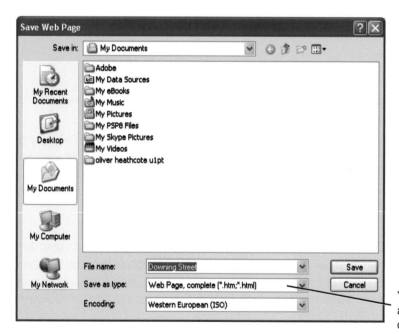

You can save a web page in different formats

This saves the page to your hard disk as a .htm file. You can open it later with the browser by clicking File, Open... and navigating to where you saved it. You can also save it as text-only if you don't want any graphics.

**Tip:**
You can save a web page as text-only if you don't want any graphics by selecting the Text File file type.

## Printing a web page

 You can print an entire web page simply by clicking the Print button, or by selecting File, Print... from the main menu. However, there are some print options to change the page margins and orientation.

▶ Choose File, Page Setup....

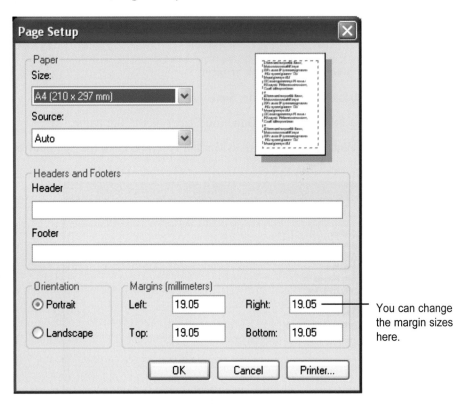

You can change the margin sizes here.

This dialogue box lets you select the paper size and whether you want the page printed vertically (portrait) or horizontally (landscape), as well as the top, bottom, left and right margin sizes. The printed page might have details such as the page title, date and time at the top and bottom but you can change these and add text of your own using the Header and Footer boxes.

▶ Select File, Print Preview and preview the printed page(s). From the toolbar at the top you can zoom in or out, browse the pages or print.

**Tip:**
Rest the mouse pointer over a button to display a screen tip telling you what the button does – several of them are the same as the options on the **Page Setup** dialogue box.

● Click the Print Document button on the preview window toolbar, or close Print Preview and choose File, Print... from the main menu. Both methods display the Print dialogue box.

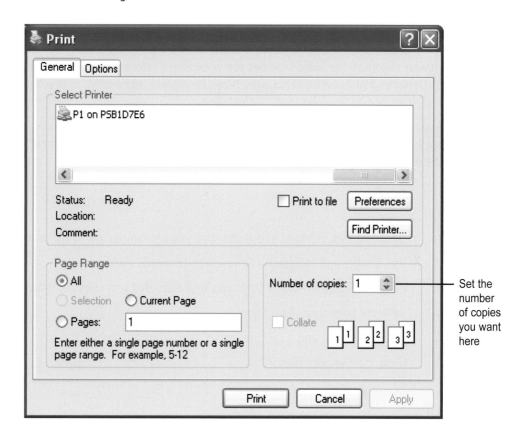

Set the number of copies you want here

You can use the options in the Print dialogue box to print the whole web page (which may extend to several printed pages), only particular pages, or just a part that you have selected (which avoids wasting ink and paper on almost empty pages). Similarly for web pages built with frames you can print individual frames from the Options tab.

## Temporary Internet files                                         Syllabus 7.2.2.5

Internet Explorer keeps data on the web pages you visit in a cache. They are temporary Internet files that the browser can access more quickly than downloading the page afresh. However, they use up disk space rapidly, especially if you use the Internet a lot, and you will need to delete them from time to time.

● Click Internet Options on the Tools menu.

● Click Delete in the Browsing history area of the General tab.

● Click the Delete files... button in the Temporary Internet Files area of the Delete Browsing History window that appears.

## Encyclopaedia and dictionaries                    Syllabus 7.3.2.4

The Web is a great place for finding information, but its very nature means that anybody can create a web page. You should trust only information on well-known websites. This doesn't mean that the information on other sites is wrong, only that you should use your common sense before believing everything you read!

Having said that, the Web provides some excellent reference sources, such as dictionaries and encyclopaedia, which can be general or specific to a subject. Use your search engine to find one that interests you.

A good dictionary is dictionary.com (dictionary.reference.com), and examples of encyclopaedia include Wikipedia (www.wikipedia.com) and Encarta (encarta.msn.com). Use them like a search engine by searching for keywords.

## Exercises

1.  Open Internet Explorer and make sure you are connected to the Internet.

2.  Use Google and Wikipedia to research Leonardo da Vinci.

3.  Print a selected area of a page you find that contains relevant information.

4.  Save the page as a .htm file.

5.  Copy some text and a picture into a new Word document and save it.

6.  Close Internet Explorer.

## Ask yourself

❷  Do I know the difference between a search engine, a browser, web-based encyclopaedia and web-based dictionaries?

❷  Can I use keywords and phrases in a search engine to find information on the Web, and refine a search using advanced search features?

❷  Can I copy text and graphics from a web page to another application?

❷  Can I save a web page graphic as a file?

❷  Do I understand the copyright restrictions that apply to the use of web page content?

❷  Can I save a web page, and do I understand the difference between some of the basic file formats a web page can be saved in?

❷  Do I understand the different print options available, and can I preview and print a web page?

# Bookmarks and Settings

**In this chapter you will find out:**

- about bookmarks, and how to bookmark a web page
- how to create a bookmark folder and move a bookmarked web page into it
- about viewing and managing a history list of previously visited web pages
- about the browser start page and how to change it.

## Bookmarking web pages                                    Syllabus 7.2.4.1–2

As you use the Web more you will often find you need to go back to pages you have visited previously. Bookmarking is a way of keeping your most frequently used sites in a list, for easy recall. In Internet Explorer this list is called the Favorites list.

In Internet Explorer, open the Favorites Center by clicking the Favorites Center icon on the button. The Favorites Center opens. If it is not already showing, click the View Favorites button to show the Favorites list.

Favorites Center button

View Favorites button

Favorites Center

You may find that the list already contains some suggested websites, perhaps put there by your ISP or by Microsoft, but the list becomes really useful when you start to add your own favourite sites, and you can click them to display them.

> Use a search engine to find a useful website that contains information on something that interests you, for example a hobby, a sport, a TV programme etc.

Notice that the website address appears in the browser's Address bar when the page opens. It may be long and not easy to remember. This is the address that you want to bookmark so you can easily find the website again without having to search for it or type it each time.

> Click the Add to Favorites button and choose Add to Favorites... from the shortcut menu that appears. The Add a Favorite dialogue box is displayed.

You will usually find that the Name field has been filled in for you. You can replace it with a name of your choice by typing in its place.

By default the entries are be created in the Favorites folder, but you might find it easier to organise related websites in folders. You will learn how to create a Favorites folder in the next section.

> Click the Add button.

> Open the Favorites Center once again and display the Favorites list.

The website you just added will be displayed. The entries in the list appear in the order that they were added. You might want to change the order, perhaps by moving the most useful ones to the top.

> Click the Add to Favorites button once again, and this time click Organize Favorites... from the shortcut menu. The Organize Favorites window is displayed.

> Tip:
>
> To revisit a website that you have placed in the **Favorites Center**, simply navigate to where you placed it, then click on its name.

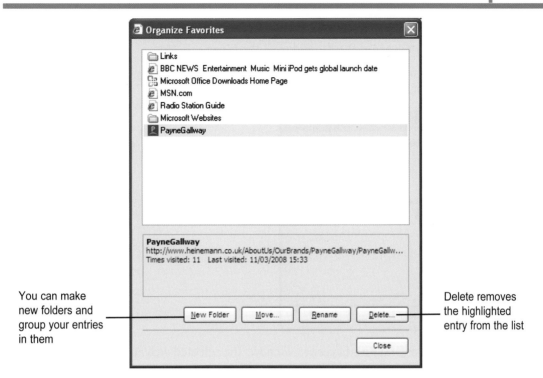

You can make new folders and group your entries in them

Delete removes the highlighted entry from the list

Sometimes you might want to delete items from the Favorites list or reorganise it so that the most used sites are near the top of the list.

Tip:

To change the order of items in the list, just drag them up or down. To remove an unwanted entry, select it and click the Delete button.

## Creating a bookmark folder                                            Syllabus 7.2.4.3

As the list builds up, it is advisable to group the entries in specific folders that contain related websites.

- Click the New Folder button and type the name for your folder, for example, Reference.

- Click Close to close the window and you will now see the new folder in the Favorites list.

Tip:

To delete a bookmark folder, right-click the folder name in the Favorites list and select Delete on the shortcut menu that appears.

## Adding web pages to a bookmark folder                                  Syllabus 7.2.4.4

You can now move entries to the folder or add them to it directly when you create a bookmark by using the Create in: box on the Add a Favorite dialogue box (see the screenshot on the previous page).

○ To move an existing bookmark, open the Organize Favorites window again.

○ Select an entry in the list and click the Move... button.

○ Navigate to the folder you want using the Browse For Folder window, and click the OK button.

○ Close the Organize Favorites window. The selected website is moved into the new folder.

## The History list                                    Syllabus 7.2.2.2/7.2.3.4

Internet Explorer keeps track of all the pages you have visited and when. This is kept in the History list.

○ Display the Favorites Center, and click the View History button.

Favorites Center button

View Feeds button

View History button

List of websites visited at different times

The History shows the websites that you (or someone else) recently visited. The pages visited are grouped by day and/or by period. Clicking a calendar icon expands or contracts it, and selecting a link displays the page.

○ Click the icon for Today to expand it (if it is not already expanded) and see the sites you have visited today.

Tip:

As well as viewing the History list by date, you can also order it by Site or by Most Visited. Click the down-arrow to the right of the View History button to display the available options.

Tip:

To delete an entry form the browsing history list, right-click the website name and select Delete on the shortcut menu that appears. You can delete a whole group by right-clicking a calendar icon and deleting it in the same way.

## Setting and deleting the browser history

Syllabus 7.2.2.2

How far back your History list goes depends on how your browser is set up. The browser in this example is set to keep web pages for 20 days. To change the time that pages are kept in history:

○ Select Tools, Internet Options to display the Internet Options window.

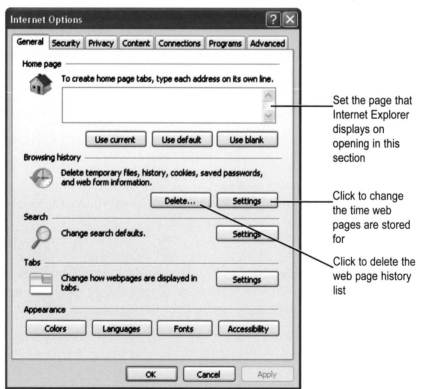

Set the page that Internet Explorer displays on opening in this section

Click to change the time web pages are stored for

Click to delete the web page history list

○ On the General tab, click the Browsing history Settings button to open the Temporary Internet Files and History Settings dialogue box.

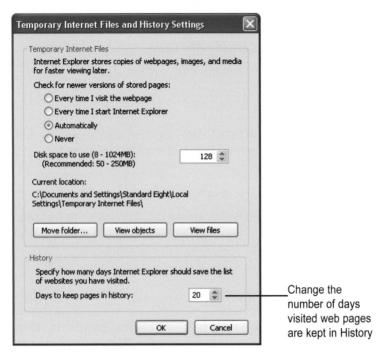

Change the number of days visited web pages are kept in History

○ Set the number of days you want to keep web pages for in the Days to keep pages in history: box.

○ Click the OK button.

Tip:

You can delete all the web pages from the History list by clicking the Delete... button in the Browsing history section on the General tab of the Internet Options window. Then click the Delete history... button on the Delete Browsing History window.

## RSS feeds                                                                  Syllabus 7.1.1.7

RSS variously means Rich or RDF Site Summary, but is often referred to as 'Really Simple Syndication'. An RSS feed displays updated content (perhaps for a news or a financial website) without the user having to visit or refresh the source page.

## Changing the start page                                                    Syllabus 7.2.2.1

It is sensible to set Internet Explorer to open showing a website that you often visit or that particularly interests you, for example a news site or a search engine. You can easily change the start page using the Internet Options General tab shown on page 467.

○ Go to the page you would like to be the start page, for example the BBC home page.

○ Select Tools, Internet Options.

○ Click the Use current button.

Tip:

You can set several 'start' pages in Internet Explorer 7. Simply add them to the Home page section of the Internet Options window. The different pages will open on different tabs displayed across the top of the browser viewing area.

## Displaying and hiding built-in toolbars                     Syllabus 7.2.2.6

Internet Explorer has several toolbars to help you find your way around. However, if you display them all at the same time, there won't be much area left to display a web page. In any case, you might use some of the toolbars infrequently.

As with other applications, you can display and hide the toolbars.

▶   Select View, Toolbars from the main menu.

▶   Click the toolbar name in the displayed submenu to display or hide the toolbar. (A tick next to the toolbar name means the toolbar will be visible.)

## Exercises

1.   Open Internet Explorer and show the Favorites list.

2.   Click Organize Favorites.

3.   Create a new bookmark folder called Shopping.

4.   Go to www.amazon.co.uk and add it to the new folder.

5.   Go to www.192.com, www.royalmail.com and www.yell.com and add them to the Links bar.

6.   Close Internet Explorer.

## Ask yourself

❓   Do I know what a bookmarked web page is, and can I bookmark a favourite web page?

❓   Can I create a bookmark folder and move a bookmarked web page into it?

❓   Can I organise and delete a list of favourite web pages?

❓   Do I know how to view a history of visited web pages, and can I manage how long web pages entries are listed?

❓   Can I set a start page that opens first when the browser is opened?

# CHAPTER

# 46 Downloading Files

**In this chapter you will find out:**

- ❗ about downloading via the Internet
- ❗ how to download graphic, sound and video files
- ❗ how to download document files
- ❗ how to download executable files
- ❗ about the risk from viruses downloaded with files, and how to protect against them.

## What is downloading?

Syllabus 7.4.1.2

Downloading is the process of transferring a file from a remote computer to your own over a network (see page 24). When you download a file from a website, the network is the Internet. You can download any type of file: pictures, video clips, sounds and programs.

The process of opening a web page on your computer involves downloading. The software code that your browser interprets to display the page has to be downloaded via the Internet from the computer that hosts the page.

You'll need to keep downloaded files well organised in folders where they can easily be found again when you need them. If you don't know how to make a new folder, refer to Module 2.

The time taken to download a file depends mainly on two things: the speed of your connection to the Internet (a broadband connection will download a file more quickly than a dial-up connection), and the size of the file being downloaded.

## Downloading graphics, sounds and video

Syllabus 7.4.1.2

Images on websites have been downloaded to your computer along with the website code. You have already found out, on page 458, how to save these images to your hard drive (or elsewhere). However, many search engines now have a search facility specifically for finding images. For example, if you click Images on the Google home page, and then type a criteria in the search box, only images matching the criteria will be found.

Click here to
search for
images

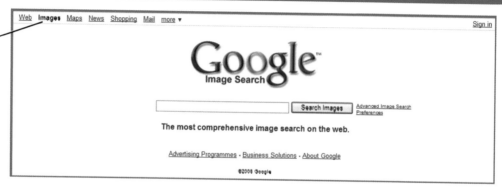

Search engines can find hundreds of images, but many of them are not free to copy. Chapter 6 explains in detail about copyright.

Alternatively, you can visit websites dedicated to images. These are called picture libraries. Example of picture library websites are www.corbis.com and www.freeimages. co.uk. If you don't want to pay for an image, make sure your choice is royalty-free. Also check the conditions of use to make sure you won't be infringing the copyright.

Image files can be very large unless they are compressed. Some graphic file formats, such as .jpg, compress the image file, making it smaller in size for storage and quicker to download, but without noticeable loss of quality

You can also find and download sound files. For some files, Windows may prompt you to download special software. Like graphic files, some sound files might be subject to copyright restrictions.

You can copy the file by right-clicking a sound icon and choosing Save Target As..., which will prompt you to choose a folder to put the file in.

Windows Media Player will play all types of sound files, including MP3 compressed files. (See Podcasts below.)

Some links simply play a sound file without downloading it – a process known as streaming. Many sites offer this, such as radio channel websites that allow you to stream digital recordings of programmes and news reports etc.

Video can be downloaded for watching later, or it can be streamed. You may be prompted to download special software such as RealPlayer or Quicktime. Files tend to be large.

## Podcasts

Syllabus 7.1.1.8

Podcasts are audio and video files that can be transferred to portable media players (such as Apple's iPod), mobile phones or PCs. Some radio stations offer podcasts of programmes for people who missed the original broadcast, and bands are increasingly offering their music as podcasts downloadable from their websites.

Podcasts can be set to download or alert the user automatically so, for example, episodes in a series of related broadcasts won't be missed.

## Malware Syllabus 7.1.2.4–5

There is a risk that a file you download could be infected with malware – malicious software that can have various effects ranging from mischief to damaging your computer. Malware can take many forms, such as:

- 🛈 Virus – code that uses other programs, such as macros and e-mail attachments, to 'spread' through a computer and between computers. At best, infected computers are prone to unreliability, but important data can also be lost.

- 🛈 Worm – similar to a virus except that it doesn't rely on other programs to propagate itself.

- 🛈 Trojan horse – code that ostensibly performs a benign task but at the same time is doing something harmful to your computer and/or data.

- 🛈 Spyware – software that records how a computer is being used and sends the information to a third party. It may log key strokes, thereby recording passwords and personal details that could be used in identity theft.

Make sure you have virus checker software installed to catch the viruses and malware as they arrive. (See pages 39 and 72 for more on viruses.)

## Downloading document files Syllabus 7.4.1.2

Some search engines allow you to search for specific types of file. Click the Advanced Search link in Google and try entering tiger as the keyword and .doc as the file type. This lists Word document files only. Click a link and specify the folder to put it in.

Tip:

> Files such as Word documents can contain macros (small programs written to perform specific tasks in the document). Macros are very useful, but they can be placed in a document with malicious intent that could affect the performance of your PC. Before downloading and opening a document, make sure that you are doing so from a reputable website, and that you have up-to-date anti-virus software installed and running.

Sometimes documents you download have names ending in .pdf (Portable Document Format). These files cannot harbour viruses, but you need a program such as Adobe Reader to view them. If this is not already on your machine you can download it free from www.adobe.com

## Downloading software Syllabus 7.4.1.2

There's a lot of software available on the Internet. You can search for and download freeware, shareware and open-source software (discussed on page 37). You can also download drivers, and purchase and download brand new software and upgrades.

▶ Click the link on the web page to download the file you want.

You will be prompted with a security warning – heed it!

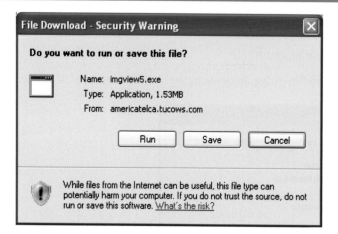

○ If you are happy that you can trust the source, then click the Save button to download the software onto your computer. This will display a Save As dialogue box that is similar to those you have used when saving application files.

○ Navigate to where you want to save the file (usually the My Downloads folder), then click the Save button.

A window showing the download progress is displayed.

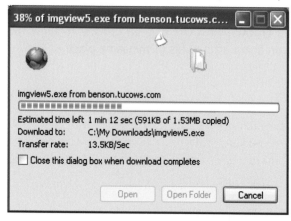

○ Once the file has downloaded, click the Open Folder button to show the downloaded file in your folder.

You can now install the program.

○ Double-click the file in the folder and the install window will appear.

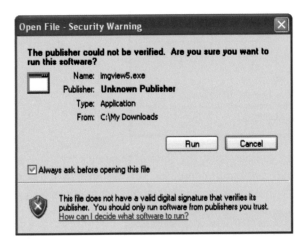

○ Without changing any settings, click Run and follow the install instructions for the particular piece of software you have downloaded. Once installed, you can run it from the Start, Programs menu or by double-clicking the icon on the desktop.

When you download a program file, it will have a name ending in .exe (meaning it is an executable file). The program may install itself and start running automatically. Sometimes a program file is compressed to make downloading faster. (See page 69 for how to extract a compressed file.)

## Pop-ups                                                 Syllabus 7.2.2.3

Sometimes a download can be temporarily interrupted because the browser's pop-up blocker is turned on. Pop-ups are windows that appear while you are browsing. They usually contain advertisements and can be a frustrating intrusion, so the blocker is often turned on to stop them.

○ Select Tools, Pop-up Blocker, Turn Off Pop-up Blocker to allow the download to continue. Turn it on again afterwards in the same place.

## Exercises

1.  Open Internet Explorer.

2.  Use AltaVista to download a royalty-free sound file.

3.  Use Google to download a few royalty-free image files.

4.  Download a freeware image viewer (e.g. from www.tucows.com) and use it to display the image files.

## Ask yourself

❓  Do I know what downloading is?

❓  Can I download a graphic, sound or video file?

❓  Can I download a document file?

❓  Can I download an executable file?

❓  Do I understand the risk of potential virus infection posed by downloading certain types of file, and what precautions to take?

# CHAPTER 47

# Online Forms and Security

In this chapter you will find out:

- ❗ about payment methods for, and security of, online shopping
- ❗ about web-based forms and how to use their features
- ❗ how to recognise a secure website
- ❗ about cookies and how to manage them
- ❗ about some safety precautions you can take to protect yourself online.

## Shopping online

Consumer websites are great places for shopping. In general, you pay by credit card, but some sites operate a system where money is transferred directly into and out of your bank account (for example PayPal).

Many well-known high street retailers now have a web presence that allows you to buy goods via the Internet. Others, such as Amazon and eBay, do not have 'real' shops and sell over the Internet alone.

Online shopping on a secure site (see below) is no less safe than high street shopping, and has the advantages that prices can be cheaper, you can view products from sources all over the world, and there are fewer crowds!

## Completing a web-based form                                  Syllabus 7.3.1.1

When you have chosen what you want to buy, you will need to fill in a web-based form giving delivery and payment details. This stage of the transaction needs to be secure to ensure that your identity and payment details are not visible to others who might use them maliciously and defraud you.

Forms are frequently used on web pages. They allow you to type in information about yourself, and to easily answer questions that the company needs answers to in order to deal with your purchase or enquiry correctly. A web-based form is usually linked to a database, and works in a similar way to a database form (see Chapter 33).

A web-based form can also display information that might change depending on the information you type in. This is called an interactive form because it updates itself as you enter or change values.

Here are some screenshots that show some of the web-based forms you will have to fill in to renew a UK passport. They are annotated to show some of the different form features you might find on an web-based form.

**ⓘ** Radio buttons – these allow you to make a single selection from several options provided. The selected option has a dot. Only one option can be selected at a time.

**ⓘ** Tick boxes also allow you to choose from a list of options, but, unlike radio buttons, you can select more than one option at the same time. The boxes are usually square. Click the square to select/deselect it. A selected option is shown by a tick symbol.

**ⓘ** List boxes – these allow you to make a selection from a pre-defined list. Click the down-arrow to the right of the box to display the drop-down list of options.

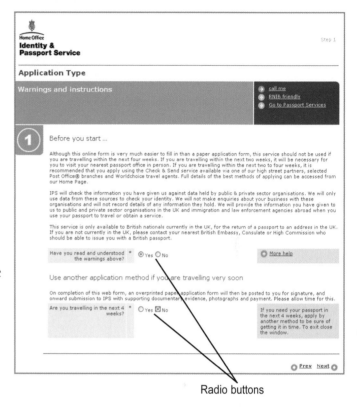

Radio buttons

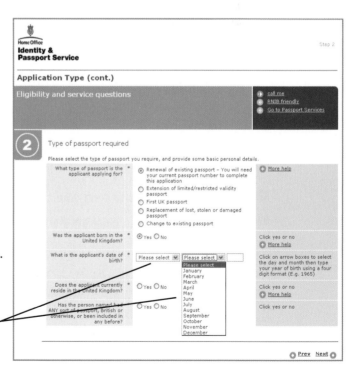

List boxes, and a drop-down list

ℹ️ Text boxes – These allow you to type in information. They are often used on forms for name and address information, but you may find larger text boxes that allow you type in more detailed text (for example, a customer care form might let you give more information about a complaint you have).

Text boxes

## Submitting and resetting a web-based form — Syllabus 7.3.1.2

When you have filled in the form, you need to check it carefully before electronically sending it to the company. In the passport example above, you will need to check each page before you click the Next button to move on (although you can also move back through the pages).

All forms will have a Submit button (sometimes called Send or similar). They might also have a Reset button. (These buttons will appear on the last page of a multi-page form.)

ℹ️ Submit – click this to send your completed form to the company.

ℹ️ Reset – click this to clear all the fields on the form.

## Security on the Web — Syllabus 7.1.2.1–3

When using a website you are sometimes open to fraud: a site may not be who it says it is in order to obtain credit card information.

There are several things you can do to protect yourself and make sure you are using a reputable company.

ⓘ A secure page is granted a Digital Certificate (by a Certificate Authority) confirming that the site is secure and genuine. Information is exchanged via encrypted messages encoded using keys so that only authorised people can read it. The site sends its public key which the recipient uses together with its private key to encode the message. Look for the https:// prefix on the website address, and for the padlock symbol.

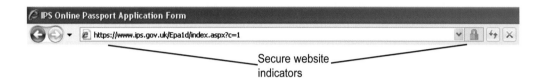

Secure website indicators

## Cookies Syllabus 7.2.2.4

These are small files that companies put on your computer to record your settings and preferences. The website software also uses the cookie data to see what pages you visited. This helps the website customise the view for your next visit, perhaps steering you to other products you might like. Cookies are usually harmless, only sending back information that you provide. Allowing a website to create a cookie does not give that or any other site access to the rest of your computer, and only the site that created the cookie can read it. This is fine provided that sites do not share the cookie information with others who might, for example, direct specific advertisements at children. Internet Explorer accepts cookies by default but you have some control over them.

▶ Select Tools, Internet Options. On the Privacy pane you have six settings ranging from Block All Cookies to Accept All Cookies.

You even have the option of blocking/allowing cookies from named sites (click the Sites button and complete the Per Site Privacy Actions dialogue box).

Tip:
You can delete all the cookies by clicking the Delete... button in the Browsing history section on the General tab of the Internet Options window (see page 467). Then click the Delete cookies... button on the Delete Browsing History window.

## Firewall Syllabus 7.1.2.6

When you are online continuously, it is advisable to install a firewall to stop anyone hacking into your computer and copying information or making changes (see page 40).

## Online safety Syllabus 7.1.2.7–9

There are some basic precautions you should take to minimise the risks of fraud, identity theft or unwarranted intrusion into your private life (such as bullying, harassment or predation by malevolent individuals or companies).

ⓘ Always use a user name and password to log onto the Internet.

ⓘ Never divulge your password to anyone or save the password for automatic use whenever you log on.

ⓘ Always check the security features of a website before you give address and/or credit card details.

ⓘ Always adhere to the safety rules listed on page 33.

In addition to the above precautions, when children can use a computer to browse the Web, you should use the parental control features provided in Internet Explorer.

▶ Select Tools, Internet Options, and click the Content tab.

▶ Click the Enable... button in the Content Advisor section of the window.

▶ Explore the features under the Ratings, Approved Sites and General tabs, to control access to websites and to set passwords.

ⓘ Use the Ratings tab to set the level to which the user is allowed to view websites with content on, for example, drugs, sex, gambling etc.

ⓘ Use the Approved Sites tab to specify specific websites that are always viewable or that are never viewable regardless of the generic setting applied on the Ratings tab.

ⓘ Use the General tab to set a password that will prevent unauthorised changes to the settings set on the Ratings and Approved Sites tabs. Here, you can also supervise use of restricted sites by typing a password to allow access.

Note:

Windows Vista, but not Windows XP or earlier, has a feature that allows a time duration to be set that limits the time a PC can be used. Games software often has a facility to set restrictions on the type of game that can be played. Parents can use these features to help supervise and control their children's computer usage.

## Exercises

1.  Use Google to find a railway timetable such as www.nationalrail.co.uk

2.  Use an interactive form to find some sample fares for one adult and one child travelling from Oxford to Shrewsbury one way. Note the effect on the cost and journey time of time of day, fastest/cheapest, number of changes, railcard.

3.  Copy the times of a fastest and a cheapest journey into a Word document and save it.

4.  Print out selected details.

## Ask yourself

❓ Do I know how to use web-based forms?

❓ Can I recognise a secure website?

❓ Do I know what cookies are, and how to control them?

❓ Do I understand some of the risks posed by online activities, and how to minimise them?

# 48 Preparing an E-mail

**In this chapter you will find out:**

- ❶ about types of electronic communication
- ❶ about e-mail and e-mail addresses
- ❶ about Microsoft Outlook Express and how to use it to send and receive e-mails
- ❶ about the outbox and the address book
- ❶ how to get help
- ❶ how to format text in an e-mail
- ❶ how to spell-check text in an e-mail
- ❶ how to attach files to e-mails
- ❶ how to indicate the priority of an e-mail.

## Electronic communication                    Syllabus 7.5.1.1/3–6

The following chapters are primarily concerned with e-mail (electronic mail) but there are other forms of electronic communication such as:

- **Short message service (SMS)** – An SMS message is better known as a text message and is usually associated with mobile phones.

- **Voice over Internet Protocol (VoIP)** – VoIP is a voice telephony system that uses the Internet to let users speak to each other. Calls to others with an Internet phone service account, such as with Skype, are free or charged at local rates.

- **Instant messaging (IM)** – IM is a low-cost communication method where a message typed at one computer appears 'immediately' on the recipient's screen if both parties have broadband access. An IM user can see whether a particular recipient is online and so start 'talking' immediately. IM also has the ability to transfer files.

Websites and electronic communication have spawned online or virtual communities in which members can participate in social networking, forums and games. These groups of people 'interact' using the Internet to communicate with one another without meeting. Social networking websites (such as Facebook and Friends Reunited), Internet forums and chat rooms bring together people with a common interest and provide means for them to discuss, ask questions and learn from their peers.

Collaborative websites can be built that take input from any user who wishes (or is permitted) to participate. Probably the most well-known collaborative website is Wikipedia, which is an encyclopaedia entirely constructed of pages of information posted on it from users worldwide. Other users can add to topics already on the site or they can comment on the accuracy of an entry.

Games are no longer limited to one computer, and players can compete with each other online around the world in role-playing scenarios using the Internet.

## E-mail                                                             Syllabus 7.5.3.1

E-mails can be sent over the Internet to anybody who has an e-mail address. It arrives almost instantaneously and at low cost anywhere in the world. The recipient picks it up when they are ready.

This makes e-mail a tremendous boon to life both at home and the office, but it should be used with care, especially in business. Messages should be short, to the point and courteous and sent only to those who need them. Beware discussing confidential or sensitive information, because e-mail is neither private nor secure. E-mails can easily be forwarded or intercepted, to come to light later in embarrassing circumstances.

To use e-mail, you need both an e-mail address and a program to handle it. Both are available free.

Note:

> There are two types of e-mail connection – permanent, which is always online, and **dial-up**. Dial-up is always slow but tariffs may reduce the cost. Permanent connections are usually broadband and so are much faster (and cost more).

## E-mail addresses                                                   Syllabus 7.5.1.2

An e-mail address is similar to a website address. The format is always:

$$username@domain\_name$$

Here, username is you and domain_name is either the Internet Service Provider (ISP) who gives access to the Internet, or a website address. For example, Sam Brown's personal address might look similar to any of these:

sam.brown@virgin.net

sam-brown@aol.com

sam@brownfamily.demon.co.uk

Alternatively, if you have your own registered website name, your e-mail address can be a part of the site name – oliver@payne-gallway.co.uk for example. This has the advantage that if you switch ISPs your e-mail address remains the same.

An e-mail address has no spaces and is usually all in small letters. It **must** be entered correctly or the e-mail will bounce – that is, come back undelivered. Every e-mail address is unique.

## Using Outlook Express Syllabus 7.6.1.1/7.6.3.5

The program often used to handle e-mail is Microsoft Outlook Express, which comes with Microsoft Windows. It is what is used in this book. Outlook Express can be used to handle e-mail from most ISPs.

Note:

> Another type of e-mail – web-based e-mail – does not require a special program because you access your e-mail from a website using the browser. This means you have to be online for longer while you deal with mail but the advantage is you can check your mail from any computer anywhere that's on the Internet, which is particularly useful when travelling. A popular web-based e-mail is Microsoft's Hotmail: you open a free account at www.hotmail.com

Click the Outlook Express icon on your desktop or in the Start menu, otherwise select Start, All Programs, Outlook Express.

If there are other people using your computer, you may need to identify yourself by selecting File, Switch Identity and choosing your name from a list of users.

The Outlook Express window lets you:

- ❶ compose messages
- ❶ send and receive e-mails
- ❶ reply to e-mails
- ❶ forward e-mails
- ❶ print e-mails
- ❶ keep contact names in an Address book
- ❶ file old e-mails in folders.

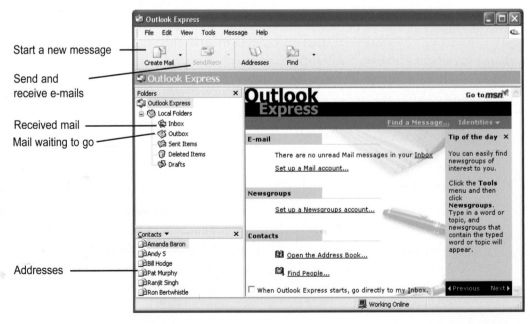

The general window layout can be altered in View, Layout... allowing you to display or hide the built-in toolbars.

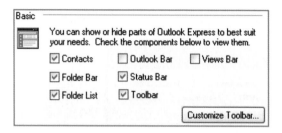

## Composing an e-mail

To start a new e-mail to someone, you need to know their e-mail address.

Create Mail

◉ Click the Create Mail button on the toolbar.

The New Message window opens.

◉ Type the e-mail address in the To: box.

◉ Leave the Cc: box blank. This is used if you want to send a copy of the e-mail to someone else.

◉ Type something in the Subject: box to say what the message is about. It is good practice always to type something as the subject. Not only does it tell the recipient what the message is about, but it will help them and you organise and find e-mails in the future.

◉ Type your message in the main window (the message box).

Click here to send your e-mail ———

Enter the recipient's e-mail address —

What the message is about. Always fill this in —

Message box ———

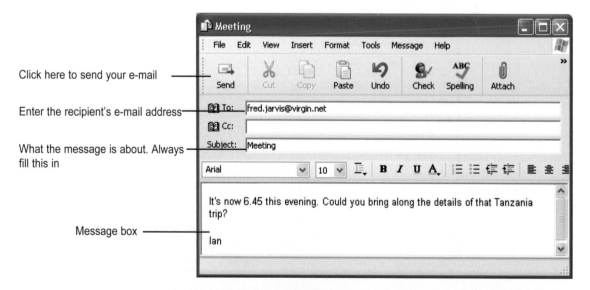

There are two sending options – sending an e-mail immediately or putting it in the Outbox to send later. You can write messages to several people and store them in the Outbox. When you are ready, you can send them all at once, which is useful if you have a dial-up connection because you don't have to keep dialing your ISP.

Holding e-mails in the Outbox also gives you time to edit or delete it if you change your mind.

▶ On the Outlook Express main menu, select Tools, Options... and on the Send tab untick Send messages immediately.

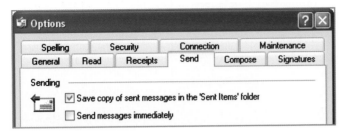

▶ Display the message window again, and click the Send button on its toolbar.

▶ If prompted to Connect, click Cancel.

## The Outbox

The New Message window closes and your e-mail is now in the Outbox. It has not actually been sent yet.

To edit a message in the Outbox:

▶ Click Outbox in the Folders pane to select it. The e-mails waiting to be sent are displayed.

▶ In the Message list pane, double-click the message header of the message you want to edit.

Folders pane

Drag the bars to adjust the pane sizes

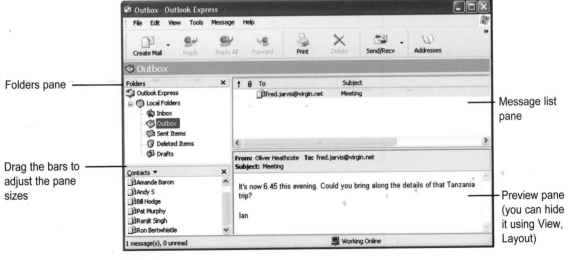

Message list pane

Preview pane (you can hide it using View, Layout)

▶ An Edit window appears and you can edit the message.

▶ Click Send to put it back in the Outbox.

▶ If prompted to Connect, click Cancel.

## Getting help

If you get stuck, try using the Outlook Express Help system – choose Help, Contents and Index or just press the F1 key.

You use the help system in a similar way to help pages for other applications.

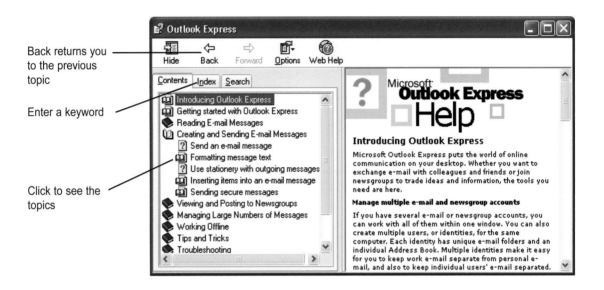

Back returns you to the previous topic

Enter a keyword

Click to see the topics

## The Address Book

The Address Book is used to save the addresses of people you regularly send e-mails to, so that you don't have to type in their address each time.

○ Click the Addresses button in the main window to display the Address Book window.

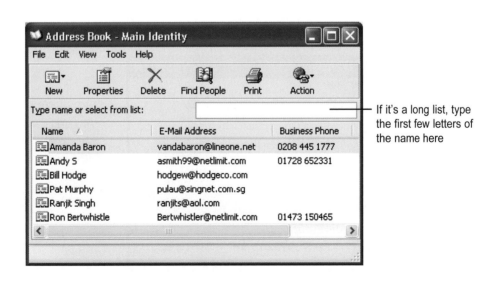

If it's a long list, type the first few letters of the name here

## Entering a new address

The Address Book window lists any contacts who have been already entered.

▶ Click the New button on the Address Book toolbar and choose New Contact... from the drop-down menu. This opens a blank Properties window where you can type in the details of the new contact.

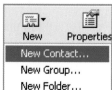

Type their name

Choose how you want it shown in the Contacts list

Type their e-mail address

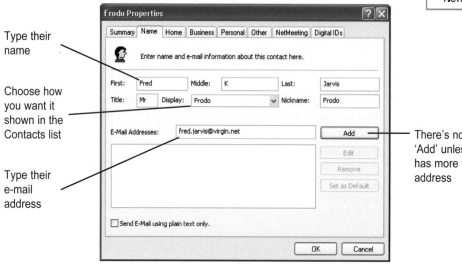

There's no need to click 'Add' unless the person has more than one e-mail address

▶ On the Name tab, enter the First: and Last: names and Title:, with Middle: and Nickname: as well if you like.

▶ Click the arrow on the right of the Display: box and choose how you want the name displayed.

▶ Type the contact's e-mail address in the E-mail Addresses: box.

▶ Click the OK button to enter the address.

The name is now listed in the Address Book window.

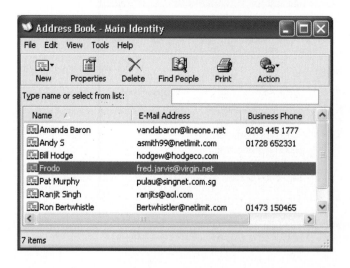

Tip:

You can remove an entry with the Delete button.

If you need to change it, for example to add the home address:

Properties

- Select the name in the list and click the Properties button.

- On the Home tab, enter the details and click OK.

The Properties window lets you keep all sorts of details and is very useful

- Now enter two more addresses and close the address book.

**Tip:**

> You can configure Outlook Express to automatically add addresses by selecting **Tools**, **Options...**, **Send** tab, and ticking **Automatically put people I reply to in my Address Book**.

**Tip:**

> You can also set up a group of recipients (New button, New Group...) and select the contacts to go into it for a group mailing. With New Folder... you can start a new list.

## Adding to the Address Book from an e-mail                 Syllabus 7.7.2.2

When you receive an e-mail from somebody not in your Address Book, you can quickly add the sender's address to the list.

- Right-click the message in the Message List pane.

- Select Add Sender to Address Book on the shortcut menu that is displayed.

| |
|---|
| **Open** |
| Print |
| Reply to Sender |
| Reply to All |
| Forward |
| Forward As Attachment |
| Mark as Read |
| Mark as Unread |
| Move to Folder... |
| Copy to Folder... |
| Delete |
| Add Sender to Address Book |
| Properties |

## Group e-mails                                              Syllabus 7.7.2.3

If you send regular e-mails to a large group – say a newsletter – you can make a Group in the Address book. Now you just choose the group name as one recipient.

- Open the Address Book.

- Click the New button and select New Group.... The Properties window appears (see the screenshot overleaf).

- Type a name for the new group in the Group Name: text box.

- Click the Select Members button.

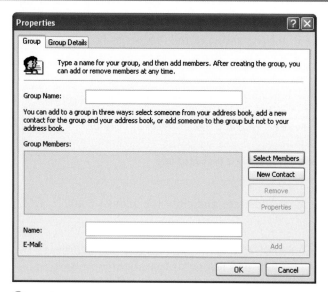

○ Select each person you want in the group from the list of contacts, clicking the Select -> button to add them to the group.

○ Click OK when you have finished adding contacts.

○ The Properties window now shows the contacts in the Group Members: section. Check the list is correct. You can delete a group member by selecting it on the list and clicking the Remove button, or you can add a new contact by clicking the New Contact button.

○ Click OK.

Tip:

When you want to send an e-mail to a group, simply type the group name or select it from the Address Book. If you do not want group members to see each others' addresses, send the message as Bcc (see page 491).

## Using the Address Book                                Syllabus 7.7.2.1

You can now enter addresses straight from the Address Book when you send an e-mail.

○ In the Outlook Express main window, click Create Mail.

○ In the New Message window, click the icon to the left of To:.

The Select Recipients window opens (see the screenshot at the top of the next page).

## Selecting recipients                           Syllabus 7.5.3.4/7.6.1.3

In the Select Recipients window:

○ Select an entry in the Name list and click To: -> to transfer it to the Message Recipients: list.

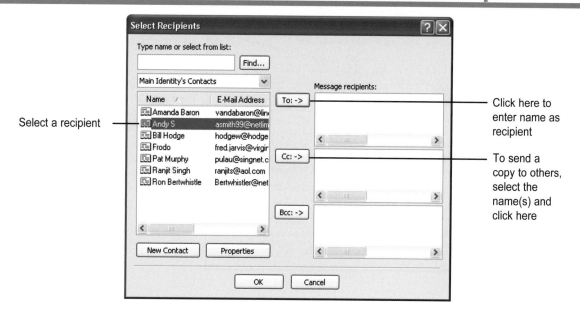

Select a recipient

Click here to enter name as recipient

To send a copy to others, select the name(s) and click here

In the same way you can send a copy of your e-mail to someone else just to keep them posted.

○ Select another entry in the Name list and click Cc: -> to copy it over.

Note:

Cc stands for Carbon copy (the name refers back to the days when carbon paper was used with typewriters to make a copy of a document as it was typed). When the recipients reads an e-mail, they can all see who else it was sent to. To send someone a copy without the other recipients knowing, enter their name in the Bcc: -> box. (This stands for Blind carbon copy.)

○ Click OK to return to the New Message window.

The recipients you have chosen will appear in the recipient text boxes.

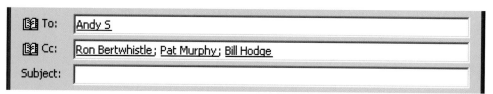

○ Type in a subject line and a message.

## Formatting a message

You can use the buttons on the Formatting toolbar to make text bold, underlined etc. Notice the formatting options appear faded until you click in the message area.

○ Type two or three lines, then try moving, deleting, copying and pasting words.

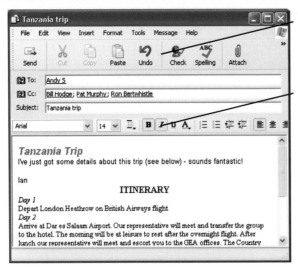

The **Standard** buttons include cut, copy, paste and undo

The **Formatting** toolbar has the usual word-processing features (font, style, colour, bullets, indents)

**Tip:**

You can move selected text within a message by clicking and dragging, just as in Word. Text can also be copied between any messages you have open, using the **Cut**, **Copy** and **Paste** buttons or the **Edit** menu.

**Tip:**

Although you can format your message using Outlook Express, not all recipients will see the formatting if their e-mails are text-only or they use some other e-mail programs. It is better to send e-mail messages as text-only.

## Spell-checking                                    Syllabus 7.6.1.5/7.6.1.8

○    Now try opening a Word document, select and copy some paragraphs and paste them into your e-mail message. If you need a Word document download the resource file for Module 7 from the Payne Gallway website (see page 93).

The spell-checking tool finds and corrects both spelling mistakes and repeated words. For example, if you had the text:

You will be leabing in the the evening.

○    Click the Spelling button to find the first mistake 'leabing'.

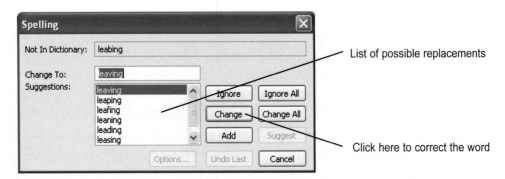

List of possible replacements

Click here to correct the word

> ○ Choose the correct word from the Suggestions: list (or type the word you want into the Change to: box).

> ○ Click Change to replace the misspelt word with the first option and look for the next mistake.

> ○ Click Delete to remove the repeated word 'the'.

## Indicating e-mail priority

Syllabus 7.6.1.9

If the e-mail is urgent you can indicate this by clicking the Priority button arrow and selecting High Priority (or Message, Set Priority, High). The e-mail won't get there any sooner but it will stand out.

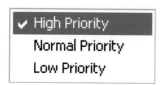

## Good practice

Syllabus 7.5.3.2

It is important that the Subject field should be accurate and the message spell-checked and not too long. This is called Network etiquette or netiquette. When the message is ready click Send to move it to the Outbox.

## Attaching a file

Syllabus 7.5.3.3/7.6.1.6

As well as text you can also attach one or more files to an e-mail. Each could be a word-processed document, spreadsheet, graphics file etc. However, it is not good practice to attach a document that contains your message. Always put your message in the e-mail itself, and keep attachments for files that you want to send in support of your message.

> ○ Create a new message and enter the address, subject and some text.

To attach a file in the New Message window:

> ○ Click the Attach button on the toolbar.

> ○ In the Insert Attachment window, navigate to the file, select it and click Attach.

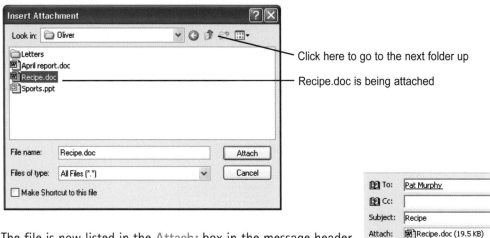

Click here to go to the next folder up

Recipe.doc is being attached

The file is now listed in the Attach: box in the message header.

Tip:

If you change your mind, select the file in the **Attach** box and press **Delete**.

Tip:

If the total size of the file you are sending is more than half a megabyte (500 kB) then you should compress or **zip** it (see page 69) – you might have broadband, but has the recipient? Also, your or your recipient's ISP may restrict the size of file you can send or receive. Some organisations' e-mail systems reject **.exe** files.

Your e-mail is now complete and ready to send. When you send the e-mail, any attached files go too.

## Exercises

1.  Look up Addressing e-mail messages in the Help system.

2.  Open the Address Book and add three new addresses. (If you are in a class they could be other class members.)

3.  Create a new mail message with one of the addresses in the To: box and the others in Cc: and Bcc:.

4.  Enter Attached file as the subject and Here's the file as the text.

5.  Attach a Word .doc file to the e-mail (preferably no bigger than 200 kB).

6.  Give the e-mail a high Priority.

7.  Click Send to put the e-mail in the Outbox. (Do not connect.)

## Ask yourself

❓ Can I name different means of electronic communication?

❓ Do I know the format of an e-mail address?

❓ Do I know how to use an e-mail application to send and receive e-mails?

❓ Can I use the address book feature in an e-mail application?

❓ Can I prepare text for sending by formatting and spell-checking it?

❓ Can I attach a file to an e-mail?

❓ Do I know how to indicate the priority of an e-mail?

# CHAPTER 49

# Sending and Receiving E-mails

In this chapter you will find out:

- ❗ more about the Outbox and how to send an e-mail
- ❗ how to look again at sent e-mails and to read received e-mails
- ❗ how to open and save an attachment to an e-mail
- ❗ more about the risks posed by viruses
- ❗ how to reply to a received e-mail
- ❗ how to forward a received e-mail to new recipients
- ❗ how to personalise an e-mail with a 'signature'
- ❗ about good e-mail practice and precautions you can take to minimise the risk from fraudulent activities.

## Sending e-mails from the Outbox                     Syllabus 7.6.1.9

Clicking the Send button on the New Message window places the e-mail in the Outbox. Earlier you configured Outlook Express so that e-mails were not sent immediately they were placed there (which could happen with an 'always on' broadband connection, or if a dial-up connection was already made to your ISP).

When you are happy that you do not want to make any changes to the e-mail(s) in the Outbox, you are ready to send them to the recipient(s).

○ Click the Send/Recv button on the toolbar.

This sends the e-mails from the Outbox and puts any incoming e-mails in the Inbox.

In reality, an outgoing e-mail is routed via the Internet to the recipient's mailbox (which is often dedicated space on an ISP's server). Conversely, clicking Send/Recv tells Outlook Express to look in your mailbox (at your ISP) to see if there are any e-mails for you. If there are e-mails, they are downloaded to the Inbox on your computer.

If you have a dial-up connection and are offline, you will be prompted to go online. In this case click Yes. Enter your password and then click the Connect button.

> **Tip:**
>
> If you have a dial-up connection, click the **Tools, Options..., Connection** tab, and make sure that the **Hang up after sending and receiving** tick box is clear. This will ensure you do not leave your phone line connected!

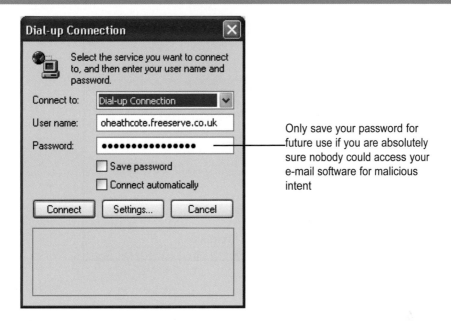

Only save your password for future use if you are absolutely sure nobody could access your e-mail software for malicious intent

A window may appear telling you what is happening.

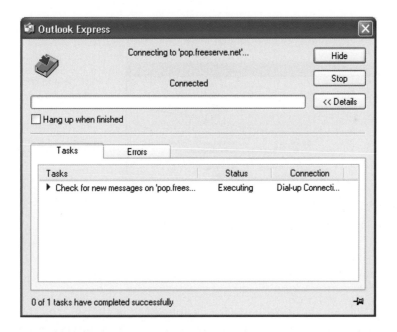

## Viewing sent e-mails

Sometimes it is useful to be able to look again at an e-mail you sent previously to remind yourself what you said. All the e-mails you send are saved automatically and kept until you delete them.

Click Sent Items in the main window to see what you sent (see the screenshot overleaf).

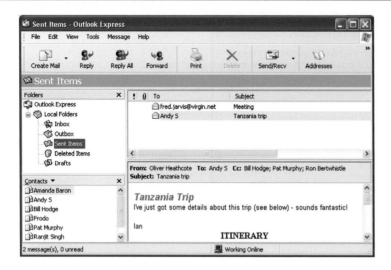

## Receiving e-mails

Syllabus 7.6.1.1

> Click Inbox to show any e-mails received.

Note:

You are likely to receive unsolicited e-mails – known as spam. These are usually advertising but they are sometimes sent just to annoy or even with malicious intent.

The number shows how many new (unread) e-mails you have

Click here to change the sort order. To change the columns shown, right-click here and choose Columns...

Unread

Read

Preview pane

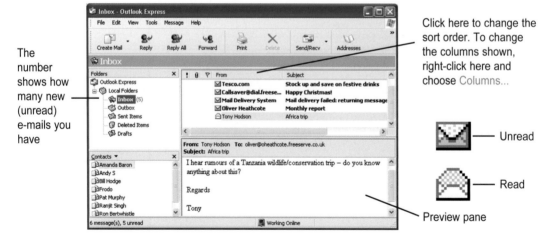

Received e-mails are shown with icons indicating Read or Unread. You can sort the e-mails by sender, date and so on either by View, Sort By, or by clicking the column header. If you select the message title, the content is shown in the Preview pane, but it is easier to view it in a separate window.

Tip:

Right-click a column header and select Columns... to specify which columns are displayed (Syllabus 7.6.3.1).

○ Double-click the message name in the Message List pane.

Click here to close the e-mail

Next and Previous buttons show the other Inbox e-mails

The Message View window lets you:

ⓘ read and print out the message

ⓘ type a reply

ⓘ forward it to someone else

ⓘ print a message by clicking the Print button.

Tip:
You can have more than one e-mail open at once. Switch between them using Alt+Tab.

Tip:
If you right-click the sender's name in this window, or on the e-mail in the message list, you can add the sender to the Address Book.

## Receiving an attachment                                    Syllabus 7.6.1.6

If you receive a file with an attachment, the message header has a paper-clip icon beside it (see the screenshot overleaf).

Note:
The size of attachment that you can receive may be restricted by your ISP or your available computer memory.

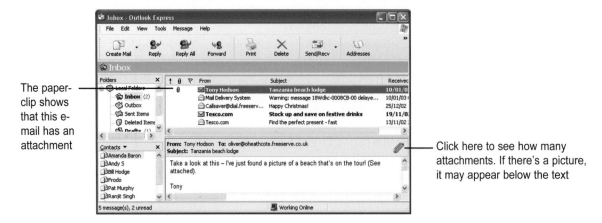

The paper-clip shows that this e-mail has an attachment

Click here to see how many attachments. If there's a picture, it may appear below the text

## Saving an attachment                                Syllabus 7.6.2.3

You might want to save an attached file to your hard disk if you want to keep it permanently. Otherwise, when you delete the e-mail you'll delete the attachment too.

▷   Click File, Save Attachments....

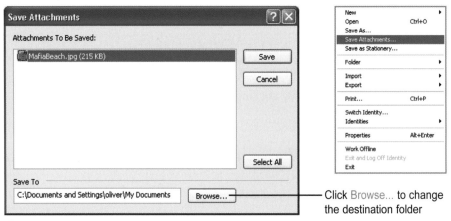

Click Browse... to change the destination folder

▷   Use the Browse... button to navigate to a folder where you want to save the attachment.

### Tip:
You can open an attachment without saving it by opening the e-mail and double-clicking the file name in the **Attach:** box. However, first make sure you can trust the sender and the file in case it carries a virus.

## Virus alert!                                         Syllabus 7.5.2.3

Make sure you have an up-to-date virus checker installed. While most file types are safe, it is wise not to open files with .exe, .scr, .pif or .vbs extensions unless you are expecting them.

## Opening an unrecognised e-mail Syllabus 7.5.2.1/3

There is a risk of infecting a computer with a virus just by opening an e-mail – there's no danger from plain text but if the e-mail is in the form of a web page there may be buttons that have unseen effects. You can delete a suspicious-looking e-mail without opening it by hiding the Preview pane first (View, Layout...) then right-clicking the e-mail and choosing Delete.

If you don't trust a file attachment, save it first then scan it with the virus-checker before opening it.

## Replying to an e-mail Syllabus 7.6.2.1/7.6.3.2

 ◯ Click the Reply button on the toolbar.

The reply window is all set up for you to type a reply to the sender only.

The To: box is already filled in ──────────

So is the subject line ──────────

Type your message here ──────────

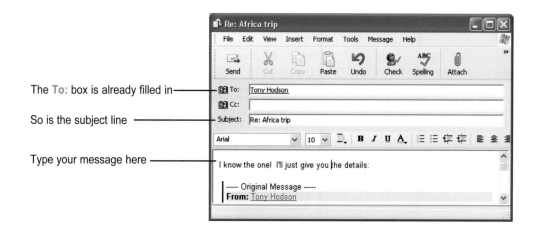

Clicking Reply All sends a reply to anyone else that the e-mail was sent to.

◯ Type your message and click Send.

The reply should normally be kept brief. The original message is often included in the reply as a reminder. If you don't want this (perhaps if the original message was very long), choose Tools, Options... on the Main Outlook Express window and, on the Send tab, untick Include message in reply.

The e-mail will be put in the Outbox so you can send it in the usual way.

**Tip:**

Choose **Tools, Options...** on the main Outlook Express window and, on the **Send** tab, tick **Include message in reply** to send the original message text as part of your reply.

## Forwarding an e-mail
Syllabus 7.6.2.2

An e-mail message sent to you might be of interest to someone else too. Try forwarding an e-mail.

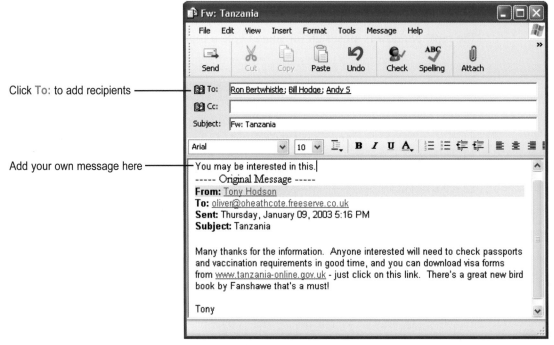

◉   Double-click the message name in the Inbox to show the Message View window.

◉   Click the Forward button.

The forwarding window is set up for you with the original subject line. The cursor is in the message area with the forwarding message below.

◉   Click To: to add the recipient's name.

◉   Add your own message if you like and click Send.

Click To: to add recipients

Add your own message here

## Signatures

You may like to add a standard ending to some messages without having to type it all in every time. To do this, go to Tools, Options..., Signature and enter the text – or even a scanned image of your signature! If you don't select to insert the signature on all your e-mails, you can insert it on individual e-mails by clicking Insert on the New Message window, then Signature.

## Digital signatures
Syllabus 7.5.2.4

As e-mail becomes increasingly used to send confidential information, it is important to be sure that e-mailed documents are not intercepted and can be read only by the intended recipient(s). To send a secure e-mail you must obtain a digital ID from a certification authority (see Outlook Express Help). Then, from the New Message window, choose Tools, Digitally Sign and a digital ID that matches your e-mail address will be added. To encrypt the e-mail as well choose Tools, Encrypt. You can read a digitally signed e-mail like a normal e-mail, but there is a security warning if it has been tampered with. You can read an encrypted e-mail from a contact once you have sent them a digitally signed e-mail.

A digital ID consists of a public key, private key and a digital signature. Digitally signing an e-mail adds your digital signature and a public key, together comprising a certificate. To read an encrypted e-mail requires your private key.

## Some other e-mail dangers Syllabus 7.5.2.1–2

ⓘ Some e-mails may employ sneaky ways to trick you into opening an attachment – such as 'Install this upgrade immediately'. Always delete unsolicited e-mails and attachments without opening them.

ⓘ E-mails may be forgeries and not from the address given.

ⓘ E-mails may try to steal your identity. With a message informing you that your account is about to expire and you have 12 hours to reactivate it, they lure you to a bogus website posing as an online bank or building society. They then instruct you to enter your log-in details. This is called phishing. Remember that no serious financial institution would ever request this by e-mail. If you do want to check details on a site, open a new browser window (File, New) and type in the address manually rather than clicking a link in a suspicious e-mail. In any case, you should never be asked to enter sensitive information on a web page where the address is not https://, ... and certainly never divulge your password.

## Exercises

1. Open Outlook Express.

2. Get someone to send you an e-mail with an attachment.

3. Click Send/Recv to collect e-mail for your address.

4. View the message in the Preview pane.

5. Double-click the header to view the message in a new window.

6. Send a reply to the e-mail.

7. Forward the e-mail to another address.

## Ask yourself

❓ Do I know how to send and receive e-mail?

❓ Do I know how to open and save an attachment to an e-mail?

❓ Can I reply to and forward e-mails?

❓ Can I personalise an e-mail by adding a signature?

❓ Do I understand the risks posed by e-mails, and how to minimise them?

# Managing E-mails

In this chapter you will find out:

- how to sort e-mails
- how to search for e-mails
- how to delete e-mails
- how to use folders to organise e-mails
- how to save an e-mail as a draft
- how to print an e-mail.

Sent and received e-mails very quickly start to build up in the Inbox and Sent Items so that you have to scroll a long way to find an e-mail. You need to sort the e-mails, delete those you don't need and file those you do.

Your computer memory and hard disk space (or your ISP in the case of web-based mail) may restrict the number of e-mails you can store.

## Sorting e-mails                                 Syllabus 7.6.3.3–4/7.7.1.2

You can sort e-mails in a folder by sender, subject or date, by clicking the column header (clicking again reverses the order).

Priority, Attachment and Flag ——

In the left-hand columns, the Priority shows if a priority level was set by the sender.

Attachments (shown by a paper clip) were discussed in the last chapter. Clicking in the Flag column shows a Flag icon to draw your attention. (Click again to remove it.) You can sort on these three columns as well.

The Read/Unread markers can be changed from the Edit menu.

## Searching for e-mails

Syllabus 7.7.1.1

With large numbers of e-mails it is useful to search for matching sender, recipient, subject, content and/or date details.

◉ Click the Find button, enter search parameters and click Find Now.

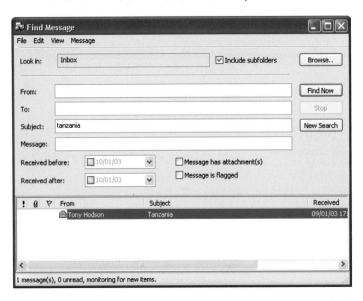

## Deleting e-mails

Syllabus 7.7.1.5/7.7.1.7

To delete e-mails:

◉ Select the e-mails you don't want and click the Delete button.

This moves them to the Deleted Items folder so they are not actually lost immediately. When this folder starts to fill up, choose Edit, Empty 'Deleted Items' folder. Alternatively, to delete them automatically, choose Tools, Options..., Maintenance tab, and check Empty messages from the 'Deleted Items' folder on exit.

## Organising e-mails

Syllabus 7.7.1.3–4/7.7.1.6

As with files, it's a good idea to group together related e-mails in easily recognisable folders. To file e-mails:

◉ Select the e-mail in the main window.

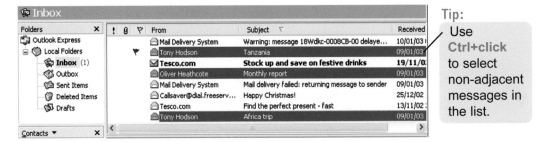

Tip:
Use Ctrl+click to select non-adjacent messages in the list.

○ Choose Move to Folder... from the Edit menu.

Tip:
You can also drag a e-mails between folders (but not into the Outbox).
You can recover a deleted e-mail from Deleted Items by dragging and dropping in another folder.

The Move window shows all the Local Folders set up in your copy of Outlook Express. You will probably need to make a new folder for your own use.

○ Click the New Folder button and type a name for the folder, such as Personal.

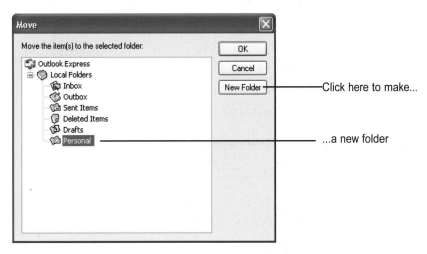
Click here to make...
...a new folder

○ Click OK, then OK again to move the e-mail from its current folder to the new folder.

Tip:
You can delete a folder from the Folders list by right-clicking its name and selecting Delete from the shortcut menu that appears.

## Saving a draft                                      Syllabus 7.6.1.7

If you get interrupted in the middle of writing a long e-mail and aren't sure when you can continue, or maybe you need to get some information before finishing the e-mail, then you can save it in the Drafts folder until you are ready to finish and send it.

○ In the New Message window, click File, Save. You will be shown a confirmation message.

○ Click OK.

○ When you want to finish the message, double-click it, make any necessary changes, and send it in the usual way.

## Printing a message                                  Syllabus 7.6.2.4

You can print a message from most windows by clicking the Print button or File, Print.... The Print dialogue box is similar to others you have met in other applications. In it you can set the pages to print and the number of copies.

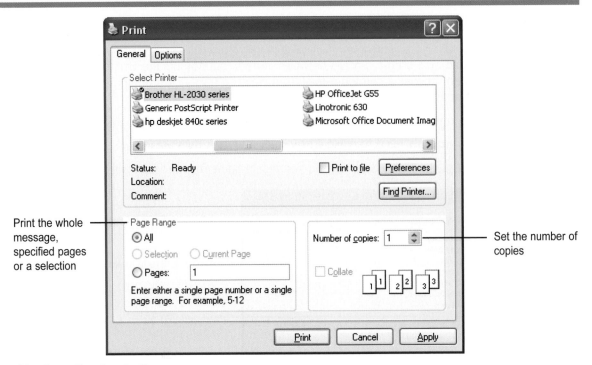

Print the whole message, specified pages or a selection

Set the number of copies

## Closing Outlook Express

○  Select File, Close.

## Exercises

1.  Open Outlook Express. For this exercise, you need at least six e-mails in the Inbox.

2.  Delete an e-mail and view it in the Deleted Items folder.

3.  Empty the Deleted Items folder.

4.  Sort the e-mails by sender, then content, then date received.

5.  Mark an e-mail as unread.

6.  Create a new folder and name it Special.

7.  Select three e-mails together and move them into the new folder.

8.  Mark one e-mail with a flag.

## Ask yourself

❓ Can I sort a list of e-mails by different criteria, such as read/unread, date, sender/recipient?

❓ Can I search a list of e-mails for different criteria, such as sender, recipient, subject and date?

❓ Can I delete unwanted e-mails?

❓ Can I create e-mail folders and use them to organise e-mails?

❓ Can I create a draft e-mail and send it when it is finished?

❓ Can I print a copy of an e-mail?

# Module 8

## BCS IT User Syllabus

The module is divided into two sections.

Chapters 51–55 on the BCS Module 1 on *IT Security for Users* will help you to understand some of the concepts and terms associated with the legal use of IT, and to appreciate the security considerations.

Sadly, the growth in the use of IT, both at home and in business, has led to new crimes that exploit it. These illegal activities are commonly known as cyber crimes, and they take many forms: from the annoying program that might cause a message to be displayed on a screen on a certain date to the deliberate attempt to obtain money illegally from private online bank accounts.

Individuals and corporate businesses are both vulnerable to security breaches, and it is vital that everything possible is done to minimise the risk of data falling into the wrong hands.

In chapters 56 and 57 on the BCS Module 2 on *IT User Fundamentals*, you will learn about some of the concepts of maintenance and solving IT problems.

Chapter 58 details how the BCS revised IT User Syllabus maps to ECDL syllabus 5.0.

# Module **8**

# Contents

# System Performance Security

In this chapter you will find out:

- ❶ about spam and malicious programs, and how to protect a computer against them
- ❶ about hackers and hoaxes.

## Unwanted messages

You are likely to receive unsolicited e-mails – known as spam. These are usually advertising (admail) but they are sometimes sent just to annoy or even with malicious intent.

Most ISPs provide an efficient first line of defence to spam, but obviously they cannot always tell what messages are genuine and what messages are unwanted. If spam is a significant problem, particularly if a lot is coming from the same source, you might like to set up a message rule to filter it. A rule is an instruction for your e-mail software to look out for a certain type of message and to deal with it automatically. Typically, the rule will pick up messages from a named sender and delete them immediately.

Spam can be minimised by installing anti-spam software, but it is difficult to block all spam reliably while still letting genuine e-mail messages through to your computer. One technique used by anti-spam software is to detect keywords (such as those that might be offensive), however spammers (those who send spam) try to find ways around the filters by deliberately misspelling these words. Another technique blocks e-mails sent from known addresses, but again the spammers often regularly change their addresses to circumvent this filter.

> **Note:**
>
> Never open an e-mail message from a sender unknown to you or that you were not expecting – delete it immediately. If you do open a message such as this, never open any attachments it might have, and do not click any hyperlinks within the message text – both could breach your computer's security defences and leave it vulnerable to malicious programs.

> **Note:**
>
> A lot of malicious spammers take the 'blunderbuss' approach in deciding to whom their messages are sent. This means that the addresses are generated automatically and thousands of e-mails are sent in the hope that a few addresses are genuine and the message will be delivered. Never reply in any form to a spam message, unless you are certain it is legitimate, because if you do the spammers will know that one of their many tries has reached a real recipient – your e-mail address will then become an even more vulnerable target.

## Malicious programs

There is a risk that a file you download, including an e-mail, could be infected with malware – malicious software that can have various effects ranging from mischief to seriously damaging your computer. Malware can take many forms, such as:

- Virus – code that uses other programs, such as macros and e-mail attachments, to 'spread' through a computer and between computers. At best, infected computers are prone to unreliability, but important data can also be lost.

- Worm – similar to a virus except that it doesn't rely on other programs to propagate itself. They can do damage to networks simply because they can take up processing power and use bandwidth as they copy and spread.

- Trojan horse – code that ostensibly performs a benign task but at the same time is doing something harmful to your computer and/or data.

- Spyware – software that records how a computer is being used and sends the information to a third party. It may log key strokes, thereby recording passwords and personal details that could be used in identity theft (see page 519).

- Adware – software that automatically displays advertisements on a computer's screen.

- Rogue dialer – this malware targets computers that use a dial-up connection to access their ISPs for e-mail and web access by changing the usual contact phone numbers to premium rate numbers, sometimes leaving the computer connected even though the user has closed the session. The user will be unaware that the rogue dialer has done this until they receive an unusually high phone bill.

Once files on your computer are infected with a virus, it can spread to other computers on your network or belonging to your e-mail contacts.

Precautions to avoid your PC being infected with a virus include the following:

- You should not share or lend floppy disks or flash drives that could introduce viruses into your system without first checking the files on them for viruses.

- You should take care when downloading files from the Internet. The proliferation of viruses over recent years is partly due to e-mail communication. Never open an e-mail message or an e-mail attachment from someone that you don't recognise – it could introduce a virus to your system.

Note:
Some e-mails may employ sneaky ways to trick you into opening an attachment – such as 'Install this upgrade immediately'. Always delete unsolicited e-mails and attachments without opening them.

Note:
You should check files on removable storage media for viruses. They could infect your system.

**Tip:**

Do not set Outlook Express to display automatically the content of a received message in the Preview pane. The process of rendering the text contained in an HTML-formatted e-mail to display it can unleash a virus or send an alert to the dubious source letting it know that your e-mail address is valid. If you are unsure of the origin of an e-mail, right-click the unopened message header in the Inbox and select Properties. Click the Message Source button on the Details tab to display the message content. Scroll down to the message. If the text is in HTML then close the Properties windows and delete the e-mail from the Inbox without opening it.

Hundreds of new viruses are unleashed each month so you should install anti-virus and anti-spyware software which should be capable of not only detecting the malware, but also of removing it from the infected file (this is called disinfecting the file). Ensure that the anti-virus software includes an automatic online update service so that your computer is protected against the latest malware.

## Infiltration

The UK Computer Misuse Act (1990) legislates against the unauthorised use of both hardware and software: a process known as hacking. Those who illegally access others' computer systems are called hackers, and they might hack either directly at a workstation or over a network (including the Internet).

Hacking could be as simple as using somebody else's illegally gained password to access a computer, but circumventing the many security features in today's computer systems is not always so easy. There are many reasons why a hacker might want illegal access to a computer system. They include:

- To obtain data. This might be an individual's passwords, bank account details or other personal information. In a business system, this might be commercial secrets that will give a competitor a market advantage, or to obtain names and e-mail addresses of customers from a database.

- To discredit a company or other body. This might be to 'hijack' or deface a website for political or propaganda reasons.

- To prove a point. A hacker might wish to expose a flaw in a high-profile computer system.

- For fun. Some hackers gain unauthorised access simply to prove to themselves that they can do it.

Although a hacker might have simply found out a password by watching the legal user type it in, it is more usual for the hacker to operate remotely using the Internet. Malware, such as that described in the preceding section, is used to record keystrokes and to exploit loopholes in browser software. Hackers often use sophisticated software and techniques to circumvent security systems.

A hardware or software firewall detects and provides limited defence from unauthorised access from the Internet to a computer or network. Microsoft Windows XP and Vista include firewall software. It is important that this is configured correctly and is switched on.

Most manufacturers react quickly to shortcomings that are revealed in their software's security. They do this by releasing program updates, called patches, that prevent any future exploitation of the loophole.

Note:

Once a potential security flaw has been revealed in, for example, browser software, it is important to install the manufacturer's patch as soon as it is released. You should set software to download updates automatically as they become available so your computer is protected to the latest security level at all times.

## Hoaxes and scams

Among all the malware and security threats that hinder the safe use of computer systems are messages that are simply an annoying waste of time. Some constitute spam, others are e-mails from well-meaning friends and colleagues passing on warnings of viruses, that on investigation turn out to be bogus.

Many hoaxes and scams are very obvious, for instance, an e-mail:

- ⓘ   might ask you to deposit funds in an off-shore bank account to help an individual gain residency in your country, with the promise of repayment at a later date

- ⓘ   might purport to be from a bank and ask you to visit a website to change your password or give your account details – a practice known as phishing (see page 519)

- ⓘ   might take the form of 'electronic' chain letter with a threat to the recipient if they do not pass on the message to a given number of new addresses

- ⓘ   might advise you to delete a file from your disk because it says it is a virus, whereas in reality it is crucial to the correct working of the operating system or other software.

You should never act on any of these or similar messages, other than to delete them.

Others messages are less obvious and are designed to raise false alarm. For example, you might receive notification of a virus – usually a message telling you to look out for and not to open any e-mail with a particular subject. You can check the existence of the virus on your anti-virus software manufacturer's website. If it turns out to be a hoax, it is good practice not to pass on the message to others, so not to propagate unnecessary alarm, and to tell the person who sent you the warning that it is a deception, putting their mind at rest.

Tip:

Always check misunderstanding and prevent unnecessary scares by checking the validity of a message. Most hoaxes and scams are well known and can be researched on reputable websites.

# Information Security

In this chapter you will find out:

- ❗ about controlling access to data
- ❗ about identity theft.

## Identity and authentication

The security of data, both on an individual's computer and on a company's networked servers, is vitally important. Access to that data must be controlled to prevent its deletion or it falling into an unauthorised person's hands. The UK Data Protection Act (1998) legislates on the storage of personal data requiring, among other things, that it is safe from unpermitted access.

Most networks require a user to identify themselves by typing a user ID which is then authenticated by typing a password before they can gain access to the computer system. Together, these allow the user to log on to their network account. The user ID assigned to you is open to view. The password is secret and does not appear on the screen when you type it in – the letters may be replaced by asterisks as you type. You can change your password whenever you like.

The network administrator can use network management software to assign which servers and drives an individual can access with their account, and set what rights (e.g. read, write, delete, copy) are allowed.

If you are authorised to access particularly sensitive data that only certain people are allowed to view, you may need to enter a personal identification number (PIN) or second password.

Note:

Identification and authentication methods such as swipe cards or biometric readers (e.g. fingerprint readers) are used on some computers that could give access to data that needs a high level of security.

Tip:

When leaving a computer unattended, even for a short while, use a password protected screensaver to prevent prying eyes seeing what is on your screen or an unauthorised person using your open network account to access servers or disk drives.

Always log off a network when you have finished working on it (and switch off the computer if you are leaving work) unless there is some special reason why you should leave it running and logged on (e.g. monitoring or processing data overnight), in which case you should use an alternative means of preventing access, such as a keyboard lock.

You should change your password/PIN regularly in case somebody has found it out. How often you should change it might form part of a company's network management policy, and, indeed, the network operating system might be configured to tell you automatically to do so after defined periods.

If, for any reason, you feel that your password/PIN has been found out, you should change it immediately.

Tip:
Change your password/PIN at least every month. Change it more often if your company security policy requires you to or if the data you access is particularly sensitive. Your IT help desk staff will be able to tell you how to do this for your company's network, or you can search the Windows Help and Support Center on a stand-alone PC.

## Confidentiality

As explained, access rights are used to protect confidential, commercial and vital data, but they also safeguard the privacy of individuals.

If you are entrusted with authorised access to these types of data, there are some basic rules you should follow when using a password or PIN so that others do not have the opportunity to find it out or use it successfully.

- Never write down the password/PIN. Commit it to memory.
- Never tell your password/PIN to another person.
- Do not use an obvious word or name as a password. A combination of at least six letters and numbers is best.
- Change your password/PIN regularly.

You should always save confidential data to secure drives on network servers and not to a local drive on a desktop PC, laptop or other portable storage media (see Portable devices on page 521). The data is then less vulnerable to hacking, and automatic backups ensure recovery if the data is accidentally deleted.

Note:
It is better to remember a password/PIN than to use the AutoComplete password feature available in some browsers where the user ID is linked to its stored password (and a hacker only needs to find out the ID to gain illegal access).

## Identity theft

The use of user IDs and passwords is a strong defence that protects data falling into the wrong hands, so, not surprisingly, the cyber criminal now spends a great deal of time trying to find them out so that they can pose as the bona fide user and enjoy all the access rights of that person. If successful, the criminal has committed identity theft.

To minimise being a victim of identity theft, you should be extremely careful of how you give out or dispose of any personal data that could be gathered and used by a thief. The rules about password usage and confidentiality obviously apply, but you should also be careful with all other personal information, both on paper and online, such as credit card numbers and statements, your address, bank account details etc. In fact, it is best to shred or burn personal details that could be illegally gathered over time to build up a portfolio of information that might be used to defraud or discredit you.

A phishing e-mail may try to steal your identity. For example, a message might tell you that your online bank account access details are about to expire and that you have to reactivate it. The fraudsters then lure you to a bogus website posing as an online bank or building society, and ask you to enter your log-in details. Remember that a serious financial institution will never request these details by e-mail.

Tip: -

Check with your bank whether or not they are interested in seeing phishing e-mails you might receive. Some welcome them because they analyse them in an effort to keep ahead of the criminal's next move and perhaps even track them down.

Note:

Never inappropriately disclose your personal data or that of others to which you are entrusted.

# CHAPTER 53

# Technology Security

In this chapter you will find out:

- about network security and Bluetooth connectivity
- about security risks associated with portable devices.

## Networks

A network within a company's premises or in a home office is protected by security measures, such as a firewall or proxy server, from the public and less secure Internet. Private, leased network connections are available to those who wish to pay for security, but the rest of us transmit and receive data over the world's public telephone communication channels, be they copper wires, fibre optic cables or microwave links etc. These are inevitably less secure than private networks, thereby making the data they carry more vulnerable to being intercepted and used for illegal purposes.

When banking or shopping online, or when sending confidential or valuable data to a website via a public network, you need to be sure that your data is safe while in transit. Encryption ensures this. If a site uses encryption, data is encoded before sending and can only be decoded by a computer that has the necessary key. Sites that use encryption have digital certificates to guarantee that they are who they say they are.

Secure sites can be recognised by the letters https at the start of the address instead of the usual http.

Tip:
View a website's digital certificate if you want to check that it is safe to send data securely.

Note:
Any Wi-Fi-enabled computer within range of a Wi-Fi router can covertly access the Internet and files on other computers in the Wi-Fi network unless suitable access controls are in place.

When you configure a router or set up an account on a website, such as an online banking site, you will often be given a default password to let you use it in the first instance. You should change this as soon as you have used it for the first time, and thereafter change it regularly as described on page 518.

Note:
Keeping default passwords and security settings leaves your computer vulnerable to unauthorised access.

You should also change your browser's default Internet security settings to those that suit your network usage. You will need to consult the user guides for firewall and router configuration settings.

## Connectivity

A wireless communication protocol that overcomes some of the limitations of traditional wireless networks, and allows data to be exchanged between IT devices within range of one another, is called Bluetooth. Bluetooth-enabled devices include PCs, laptops, mobile phones, cameras and printers. An advantage of using Bluetooth connectivity is that, unlike a Wi-Fi network, the network devices do not have to be configured individually to communicate with each other. However, security is compromised because of the simpler set-up procedures. Unless some precautions are put in place, a Bluetooth-enabled device is potentially accessible to any other Bluetooth-enabled device within communication range.

Here are some security considerations when using Bluetooth connectivity. (You might need to read the relevant user guide to find out exactly how to configure your device.)

- Turn off Bluetooth or hide your device when you are not using it to transmit or receive files. ('Hide' means set your device to its non-discoverable or non-connectable mode.)

- Check the sender is known to you before accepting a file.

- Set up a password protected connection (sometimes called pairable mode).

- Turn on encryption if your device allows it.

## Portable devices

Portable devices (such as laptops/notebooks/tablets, PDAs, mobile phones, disks and flash drives etc.) by their very nature are targets for a thief, but they are also easily lost by the owner – USB flash drives and floppy disks can be easily left on tables, on seats or in pockets. Replacement equipment can be bought and, if the data has been backed up, the owner can continue work after some expense and time. However, confidential business files and personal details can fall into criminal hands, with potentially disastrous consequences, if the portable devices are not properly protected. This protection can include:

- Visible security marks to make hardware less attractive to steal.

- Security cables and locks to make it harder to remove devices.

- Portable storage media kept under lock and key when not in use. In transit, they must be protected and monitored at all times. Old media must be securely disposed of.

- Password-protected access to disk drives, folders and files to help to keep data safe.

- A system of signing in and out portable devices to help instil the security and vigilance requirements among staff.

# CHAPTER 54

# Guidelines and Procedures

In this chapter you will find out:

> ❗ about laws and company policies on security and privacy.

## Security and privacy policies

Many of the security and privacy considerations discussed in this module are relevant to UK Acts of Parliament such as:

- ℹ️ The Copyright, Designs and Patents Act (1988)
- ℹ️ The Computer Misuse Act (1990)
- ℹ️ The Data Protection Act (1998)
- ℹ️ The Electronic Communications Act (2000)
- ℹ️ The Freedom of Information Act (2000)
- ℹ️ The Regulation of Investigatory Powers Act (2000)

In the UK, all individuals and companies are subject to the legislations of these Acts, so businesses usually provide staff with guidelines and procedures they can follow to ensure that nobody is breaking the laws. These policies are usually written so they help compliance within the context of the company's type of work.

Many companies will provide these guidelines, perhaps as part of a staff handbook, and give training to new staff as part of their introduction.

### Note:

In many companies which have special security or confidentiality needs, the guidelines might be displayed where they can be read as a reminder.

The handbook will usually tell staff where they can get further guidance if they want it. If a company has an IT help desk, its staff should be able to advise on IT security issues in the first instance. The HR/personnel department should be able to help with privacy policy.

### Tip:

Find out from your supervisor who you should approach for advice on security or privacy issues or if you are unclear of the procedure you should follow.

Follow the guidelines as published, making sure that you understand each policy item it requires you to follow.

Note:

A company's policies could contain many rules on many topics, for example password use, Internet use, storage of data on local drives, downloading etc. You might even be required to conduct risk assessments when new procedures are introduced, or periodically to check that the existing procedures are working adequately.

Note:

You must always follow a company's security and privacy guidelines. Failure to do so could lead to disciplinary action or dismissal. Remember that the procedures are often there to comply with legislation, so you could also be breaking a law.

The security guidelines will also tell you who you must notify if you think or know that the company's IT security has been threatened or breached.

Note:

A security breach does not necessarily mean that it has been committed by an outsider to the company. It could be a colleague you saw acting negligently or you might have left your laptop in a taxi!

# 55 Data Security

In this chapter you will find out:

- about the importance of backups.

## Security

Not all thefts and loss of data occur because the equipment is portable (see page 521). Desktop computers might be stolen in some burglaries, or data copied from disk drives to floppy disks or flash drives. To minimise these risks you should do all or some of the following, depending on how sensitive the data is:

- Lock the equipment to the desk using a cable lock.
- Keep the equipment in a secure room.
- Use locks on floppy disk drives.
- Do not have floppy disk drives or USB ports.
- Use locks on keyboards.
- Do not permit sensitive data to be stored on the computer's local drives.
- Password-protect folders on disk drives.

## Backups and safe storage

Computer data and application source files can be very valuable and can be all too easily lost, for example because of fire/flood, theft, file corruption, disk crash, virus infection or accidental deletion etc. Copying files for backup purposes ensures that you have a recent copy of your data in case disaster strikes. For home users it may be enough to make a backup once a week, or after any significant work has been done or new files loaded. In businesses, backups are typically made on a daily basis, or more frequently, depending on the nature and importance of the data. Large companies will usually have special software and hardware to manage the backups ensuring that copies are made regularly.

Backups are a vital lifeline to individuals and companies so they need to be kept safe from theft, fire and flood. The most convenient form of backup storage for home users is likely to be a USB flash drive, CD, DVD or external hard drive. For larger amounts of information, perhaps on a company network, a tape drive is normally used. This is a unit that copies the contents of the hard drive onto a magnetic cassette tape or DAT (Digital Audio Tape). The backup media must be clearly labelled.

If a problem occurs with the hard drive the data can all be copied back from the tape. One limitation of this procedure is that it can take some time to find a particular piece of data stored sequentially on the tape.

As broadband Internet access becomes more widely available, remote backup services are becoming more popular. This means backing up via the Internet to a remote location. This can protect against some disaster scenarios, such as a whole building being destroyed, taking PCs and backup tapes with it. One limitation can be the speed of the Internet connection which is usually a lot slower than the speed of local data storage devices, so backing up large amounts of data can be a problem. There are also potential security risks for company-sensitive information stored effectively by a third party.

Note:

In a corporate network environment staff are encouraged to use disk space allocated to them on a server. These servers are automatically backed up each night so data can be easily recovered if the user loses the original.

Tip:

An individual in the home environment will not necessarily have access to a secure area to store their data and application software. Nevertheless, it is important that essential data is backed up and the source files of software are kept, in case of catastrophe or the need to transfer everything to a new computer.

Keep the regular backup somewhere safe where you can change it periodically (e.g. online storage), but you could consider putting long-term backups and source disks (with other set-up information such as licence numbers etc.) in a locked box and asking a friend or a family member to look after it.

In this chapter you will find out:

- about the importance of maintenance of both hardware and software

- about printer maintenance.

As with anything, things can go wrong with your computer system when you use it: the hardware can break and software might cease to function as expected. The probability of some of these things happening can be lessened by carrying out preventative maintenance to keep your system in good order, but inevitably moving parts (such as fan motors) or parts that are subject to repeated handling will need to be replaced when they break or wear out.

## Hardware

Modern computer hardware is extremely reliable so long as it is used as the manufacturer intended. Quality control techniques have increased hardware life to the point where it rarely fails before the technology becomes obsolete. However, failures can still occur, sometimes bringing disastrous consequences (such as data loss or even fire) to individuals or companies.

Some examples of hardware that can fail are:

- bearings in disk drives

- motors in fans and disk drives

- backup batteries

- fuses and power supply components (e.g. capacitors)

- electronic components (including PCBs, keyboard switches, LED indicators, infrared transceivers etc.)

- displays (especially VDU tubes)

- laptop screen hinges and cables

- CD-ROM tray mechanisms

- power cables, and other cables and connectors

- moving parts in printers and scanners.

Many of these examples are not easy to repair without the correct tools and specialist technical knowledge, so in some cases replacing the part is the best option.

Tip:

Unless you are a competent technician you should recognise your limitations: it is safer to know where you can find the help you need rather than risk damaging the hardware or injuring yourself.

Most hardware comes with an owner's manual or disk that details the component parts of the equipment, with part numbers, maintenance instructions, and support contacts (such as telephone numbers and websites). The manufacturer's guidelines on what can be repaired or replaced and how the maintenance should be carried out must always be followed to ensure that the work is performed correctly and safely.

Note:

Although most of the electronics in computer equipment is powered by low voltage supplies, mains voltage is also present (usually in the power supply). Always disconnect the mains supply cable before opening the equipment casing, and never work on components with the case open and the power turned on. Do not allow water to get into the case.

Note:

The semiconductor components within computers (e.g. memory chips and processors) are easily damaged by electrostatic voltages. Simply touching these components without taking suitable precautions (i.e. ensuring both you and the equipment are at the same ground potential) will irreparably break them.

Repairs and replacements such as described above are non-routine maintenance tasks because they are needed infrequently and at irregular intervals (if at all). However, routine maintenance can be easily and safely performed to ensure the hardware continues to work correctly and so the user can use it efficiently.

Some examples of routine maintenance of any ICT hardware are:

- Clean all ventilation grilles. Excessive build-up of dust will prevent air flow through the equipment casing. This will cause electronic components to overheat and eventually fail. Also clean or replace air filters if this can be done safely.

- Clean keyboards. Dust and dirt falling between the keys will eventually jam the key switches making the keyboard unreliable.

- Clean screens and plates. Grease (from fingers) and dust will build up on the glass of LCD and CRT screens making them difficult to use. Unless the glass plates of flat-bed scanners are kept clean, the marks will also be scanned and appear on the reproduced image.

- Clean cases. Regular cleaning, if only dusting, of exposed surfaces keeps the equipment looking new and protects your investment. Infrared signals between hardware devices might be degraded by dirt on transmitters and receivers, so it is important to keep these clean.

ℹ Check connectors and cables. Most connectors have integral clips or screws to hold them in place. However, because another user of the equipment might have been less than diligent, it is good practice to check routinely that connectors are correctly and firmly seated. Cables should be routinely tidied, making sure that cable runs (both in desks and floors etc.) are used if available. This will ensure that the workspace is less hazardous and that the equipment is more reliable and more efficient to use.

ℹ Clean the ball and rollers on corded mice.

Cleaning can usually be done using a soft damp cloth or brush. Marks on screens and cases should be removed using a suitable solvent spray or impregnated wipe. Always follow the hardware manufacturer's guidelines about what solvents can be used.

Note:

Cleaning materials such as solvents can be dangerous. They are often toxic and flammable. Protect yourself and the environment by always following the cleaning product's instructions on safe use and disposal.

Note:

Soap and cleaners containing alcohol will damage the anti-glare and anti-static coating on screens.

Tip:

Always read the manufacturer's guidelines on what can and should be routinely maintained, and how often.

## Printers

Printers are hardware and are subject to similar routine and non-routine maintenance requirements as described above. However, because they use up materials (consumables) in the printing process, such as ink and paper, routine maintenance also includes the replacement of the materials.

The methods of replacing consumables depend on the type of printer (e.g. impact, inkjet, laser), the printer model and the manufacturer. Therefore it necessary to read the manufacturer's guidelines to ensure that the correct procedure is followed and the correct replacement parts are installed.

Routine maintenance on printers includes:

### Replenishing the print medium

Refill the paper tray or feed hopper with the recommended paper (i.e. correct weight and finish) or transparency film for the type and model of printer. Some printers will only take one size of paper, but if different sizes can be used, then make sure that the feed guides are correctly positioned so the paper enters the printer without misalignment.

Impact printers often use continuous feed (fan-fold) paper with holes in tear-off strips down the side edges. This type of paper needs to be fed into the printer so the holes are aligned with the sprockets that pull the paper through the printer.

### Replacing ink

**Laser printers:** Toner is contained in a cartridge that can be easily replaced when empty. The user guide for the printer will give the part number of the recommended replacement cartridge and installation instructions. Often cheaper alternatives are available, or toner cartridge refills are offered, but unless the source is highly recommended there is a risk of printer damage and sub-standard printing (e.g. poor colour reproduction). Using the incorrect parts and ink is likely to invalidate the manufacturer's warranty.

New toner cartridges are carefully packaged to prevent toner leakage while in store or transit. It will be necessary to follow the instructions that come with the cartridge to prepare it before putting it in the printer. This usually involves removing plastic protection strips, and shaking it to evenly spread out toner that has settled while in store.

Empty toner cartridges should be sent back to the manufacturer for refilling and resale. Most manufacturers provide this as a pre-paid service to encourage recycling.

**Inkjet printers:** Depending on the make and model of the printer, inkjet cartridges are single colour or multi-colour. The cartridges are usually held in a cradle that moves at right angles to the direction of paper feed through the printer. When not being used, the cradle is 'docked' to one side of the printer and can often be unreachable. For this reason, the cradle needs to be moved into an accessible place before the cartridge can be changed. The printer's user guide will describe how to move the cradle, remove the empty cartridge and replace it.

The ink cartridge is simply a container for the ink which is fed to the print head on the cradle. Some new cartridges have a seal to prevent ink leaks. The seal is broken when the cartridge is installed in the printer. The delicate electronics on some makes of cartridge are protected by a plastic strip that has to be removed before the cartridge is installed.

Like toner cartridges, and for the same reasons, only approved cartridges and ink should be used. Most makes of inkjet cartridge can be recycled.

**Impact printers:** The ink in the ribbon that is struck by the character keys will eventually run out or the ribbon fabric itself will wear too thin causing the printed characters to appear faded. The ink-soaked ribbon is usually contained in a plastic cassette for easy replacement in a printer.

**Plotters:** A plotter's coloured pens will need replacing according to the manufacturer's guidelines.

### Improving print quality

Running out of ink will obviously degrade the print quality: the printed characters will first appear faded and then disappear altogether. However, with toner, this can happen unevenly across the width of a page.

Tip:

> The life of the toner cartridge can be extended by gently rocking it a few times to redistribute the toner more evenly along its length. Do not vigorously rock the toner cartridge because this might cause toner to leak out.

Poor (uneven) print quality from inkjet printers usually means that the print heads need cleaning. This can happen if the printer is unused for long periods. Read the user guide to find out how to clean the heads for a particular printer.

After a new ink cartridge has been installed, the printer automatically aligns the print heads to ensure the best quality printout. However, the heads might need realigning between cartridge changes: vertical lines become misaligned and horizontal banding appears. The printer's user guide will explain how to align print heads to improve the print quality.

Tip:

> Use the printer's test page facility to view the print quality to help you decide whether or not the print heads need cleaning or aligning.

Plotters that are used for highly accurate drawing usually need calibrating by a specialist.

## Clearing paper jams

During the printing process, sheets of paper are fed through the printer by a series of rollers. The printing process in laser printers is more complicated than in inkjet printers, and so the sheets of paper are more likely to become jammed in the mechanism, especially if the incorrect quality paper is used or the inside of the printer has not been kept clean. It is therefore important to follow the manufacturer's guidelines regarding approved media, and to keep clean the accessible areas inside the printer.

Laser printers have panels that can be opened to view the location of the paper jam and to allow the jammed paper to be cleared. The component parts of some large laser printers can also be taken out to help clear the blockage.

The paper's route through most inkjet printers is more or less entirely visible, and the mechanism is simpler, making jams less likely, and easier to clear if they do occur.

Note:

> Some jams in laser printers can occur before the fuser unit. This means that the toner will not have been fused to the paper and is easily transferred to whatever the paper comes into contact with: skin, clothing, desktops etc. Carefully dispose of the unwanted paper and use cold water if it is necessary to clean any toner smudges.

## Software

Software doesn't fail unless the program code becomes corrupted. However, over time, applications can show signs of slowing down when they access data or fetch new parts of their code from the hard disk.

### Defragmenting a disk

Program and data files are rarely stored contiguously on the computer's hard disk. This means that the files are broken up and stored in different locations on the disk with the disk operating system managing where they are placed. This situation is made worse as files are deleted and the disk operating system stores parts of new files in the locations that become unused. This break-up of files causes the disk to become fragmented. The time to retrieve files from a severely fragmented disk slows down because the disk operating system needs to access many more storage locations.

Non-routine maintenance of software should include defragmenting the hard disk from time to time to ensure that the stored files are located more contiguously and unused locations are not scattered.

Tip:

Make sure that there are no programs (including the screen saver) running on the computer because any interruptions caused by these programs will slow down the defragmentation process.

○ Click All Programs on the Start menu and select Accessories, System Tools, Disk Defragmenter.

○ The Disk Defragmenter window is displayed. Select the disk you want to defragment.

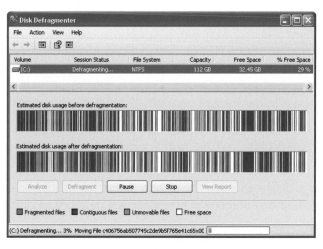

Tip:

Click the Analyze button to view whether or not the disk will benefit from being defragmented before starting the process.

○ Click the Defragment button to start defragmenting the selected disk.

Maps of the estimated disk usage before and after defragmentation are displayed in the Disk Defragmenter window.

### Deleting unwanted files

Over time, a computer's hard disk will become cluttered with unwanted files. These might be old program files, old data files or temporary files that have not been deleted automatically by the operating system. These all fill the hard disk and cause the system to run more slowly.

Uninstall unwanted programs using the method described in Installing/uninstalling a software application on page 80 in Module 2.

Tip:
> Make sure you have the original source media for the application file before you uninstall it from the hard disk. You can then reload the software at any time if you find that you need it again.

All data held on the computer's hard disk should be reviewed regularly to check its relevancy, and deleted if it is no longer required (see page 67 – Deleting files and folders). In any case, the Data Protection Act (see Chapter 6 on page 34) requires that personal data should be kept no longer than is necessary. Data that is required, but infrequently, should be backed-up to archive storage from where it can be retrieved if needed.

When an application is run, temporary files are created on the hard disk as part of the normal operation of the program. When the application is closed correctly, these files are automatically deleted from the hard disk. If, for any reason, an application or the computer crashes (i.e. an incorrect shut-down procedure happens), then the temporary files will remain on the hard disk, using valuable disk space that will eventually slow down the operation of the system.

Tip:
> You can find and delete temporary files by searching for files with a tmp extension on your hard disk. For example, type *.tmp in the search facility (see page 70) to find all the temporary files on the hard disk. Other temporary files have a tilde (~) symbol as the first character.

Microsoft Windows also provides a clean-up utility to help you choose which files can safely be deleted.

▶  Click All Programs on the Start menu and select Accessories, System Tools, Disk Cleanup.

▶  A dialogue box is displayed while the system assesses what can be deleted from the computer's hard disk and how much space will be saved by doing so.

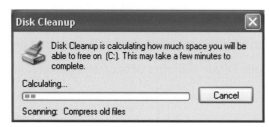

○ When the system has assessed the hard disk, the Disk Cleanup for dialogue box is displayed. Click the Disk Cleanup tab if it is not already selected.

Tip:

A description of the different types of temporary files is displayed in the Description section of the Disk Cleanup for dialogue box when you click the file type in the Files to delete: section.

○ Click the boxes to the left of the file types listed in the Files to delete: section of the dialogue box to select which files you want to delete.

Tip:

Temporary Internet Files are discussed more fully in Module 7 on page 461.

○ Click OK to delete (or compress) the selected files.

Note:

The Files to delete: section of the Disk Cleanup for dialogue box also lets you compress files without deleting them. This will give you with more usable disk space.

The More Options tab on the Disk Cleanup for dialogue box gives three further clean-up options. A brief description of the options is given in each section. Click the Clean up... button to select the option.

ⓘ Windows components – These are optional features of Windows that may have been included in the original installation of Windows and that you may never use.

ⓘ Installed programs – This opens the Add or Remove Programs dialogue box that is explained on page 80.

ⓘ System Restore – System Restore points are discussed below. Selecting this option deletes all but the most recent restore point, thereby freeing up disk space.

Tip:

Run the Disk Defragmenter after cleaning up the hard disk to optimise the use of disk space released by deleting files.

## System restore

Microsoft Windows has a facility that allows you to return your system to a configuration that worked at an earlier point in time. This is useful if, for example, the system ceases to work correctly after you have installed new software.

- Click Control Panel on the Start menu and then select Performance and Maintenance.
- Click System Restore in the See Also panel in the left-hand panel of the Performance and Maintenance window.

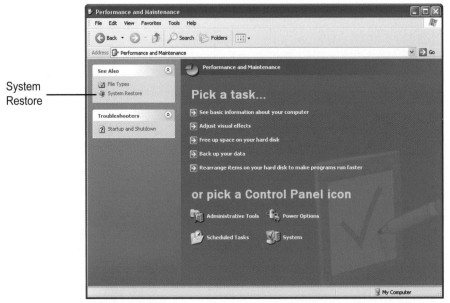

- Click Restore my system to an earlier time on the Welcome to System Restore window and click the Next button.

Tip:

You can set how much disk space is allocated to system restore files by clicking Start, Control Panel, Performance and Maintenance, System, and selecting the System Restore tab. Move the Disk space usage slider to change the disk space used, or click the Turn off System Restore box to turn off the facility.

Note:

Windows automatically sets restore points but you can set your own restore point for the current configuration as well. Click Create a restore point to set your own restore point, then click the Next button. Type a descriptive name and click the Create button.

> Select a restore date and restore point using the calendar and descriptions shown on the Select a Restore Point window.

> Click the Next button and confirm that the restore point is the one you wish to use.

> Read the on-screen notes and then click the Next button to begin the restoration.

Note:

You will be given the opportunity to undo a restoration.

## Memory resident programs

The number of programs resident in the computer's memory at any particular time will affect the performance of the computer. The more programs that are running, the less memory is available to an application you are using. Some memory resident programs are necessary to the well-being of your computer (e.g. anti-virus software) and should not be closed down. However, other utilities might have been loaded automatically when the system was booted up or you might have left open an application you used earlier for a specific purpose and forgot to close it after you had finished with it. You should close down any programs you are not using, especially if your computer has limited memory and/or you experience your applications slowing down.

## Software updates

Most software goes through rigorous checks before being released for sale. The manufacturer will specify what the minimum system requirements are to guarantee that the product will work. However, it is impossible to test program code on every type of computer and with every type of program that it might be run alongside.

Sometimes a genuine 'bug' might be present and updates that patch the error will need to be installed. Many software providers provide free updates to registered users of the application. These updates are downloaded to the computer automatically or on demand. Sometimes the computer will need to be rebooted for the patch or update to take effect.

Microsoft regularly release updates that correct discovered flaws in the Windows operating system and in Internet Explorer that could affect the security of a system.

> Click Control Panel on the Start menu and select Security Center.

> Make sure that the Automatic Updates option is set to On in the Security Center.

## Drivers

Sometimes a piece of hardware (e.g. a printer) that worked on one system might not work on another. This might be because the driver for that hardware (i.e. the software that allows communication between the hardware and the computer) is out of date or incompatible. Drivers can be downloaded from the manufacturer's website.

Other reasons why an updated driver might be needed include:

- the original driver has been corrupted/deleted
- an updated driver might include new features not previously available.

## Upgrading

At some time in the life of a piece of software, the manufacturer will decide to release a new version. There are several reasons for this, including:

- The number of patches released on the previous version now justify a new version of the software that incorporates them all.
- Technology has advanced and techniques have changed.
- The market demands new features.
- A new version keeps the manufacturer's name in the public's eye.

The advantages of upgrading include having the latest version of the software, thereby ensuring that any previous problems have been eradicated. Compatibility with the latest hardware is ensured, meaning that you do not have to download drivers for any new hardware you might have.

However, the new features in the upgraded software might introduce new bugs that will only be corrected as and when the manufacturer finds out about them and a patch is made available.

# Problems

> ❶ about problems that might arise and how to resolve them.

In an ideal world every time you use your computer it should work perfectly. Unfortunately, things can and do go wrong. The types of problem might be hardware or software related, or a combination of the two; therefore it is important to have a good understanding of how your computer system works and how it is configured. It is also important to know the limit of your understanding and where to get help with a problem.

Typical hardware and software problems that might occur include:

- ❶ an inability to print
- ❶ loss of Internet access
- ❶ program locking up and not responding
- ❶ an inability to save
- ❶ incorrect or unexpected operation caused by a virus
- ❶ slow operation
- ❶ intermittent operation
- ❶ error messages.

The list cannot be exhaustive, and each problem might be caused by any number of reasons, both hardware and software related. As an example, if faced with an inability to print, you will need to investigate the following in no particular order:

- ❶ Is the printer turned on?
- ❶ Is the printer connected?
- ❶ How is the printer connected – stand-alone or network?
- ❶ If stand-alone, is the cable connected at the printer? Is it connected at the computer?
- ❶ If networked, is it a wireless or cable network?
- ❶ If cable networked, is the network cable connected at the printer. Is it connected to the router? Is the computer communicating with the network correctly? Has the computer lost other network connectivity? If so, has the network card failed?

- If wireless networked, has the signal path been blocked? Has the wireless router failed? Is your computer communicating with the network correctly?

- Is there paper in the printer? Is there a paper jam?

- Has the printer hardware failed?

- Is the printer driver corrupted?

- Is your print job stuck in a long print queue?

- Are you using the software correctly?

- Is the printer there? Has it been changed to a different model? (In a corporate environment, it has been known for a printer to be moved or changed without all the users being informed!)

These are only some of the reasons that a print problem might occur, but it shows the questions needed to resolve the issue and why an understanding of the system helps.

Most manufacturers provide help and support in the form of manuals and on-screen help pages on disk and/or web-based (for example, the Help and Support Center in Microsoft Windows – see page 87). Often the problem is identified by asking you to answer a series of 'troubleshooting' questions that eventually tell you how to correct the difficulty.

You might not be able to solve some of the problems you encounter. This might be because the problem is related to hardware that needs a technician to repair or replace it, or because it is related to software that you cannot change. In these cases, you will need expert help. Most manufacturers offer some type of support. This might be free, free for a limited period, or charged for. It might be necessary to pay to speak to an expert immediately, or, alternatively, free e-mail support might be given by an expert, providing you are prepared to wait until your query reaches the top of a queue.

In a corporate environment, the IT department will run a help desk that you can contact for on-site help. The technicians on the help desk will be experts in the systems used by the company.

When you report a fault, you are likely to be asked for specific details about the software and computer system you have. Make sure you take details of any error messages that appear and be prepared to give the exact details of what you were doing when the problem occurred.

Tip:
Professional IT technicians in help desk teams record what they did to resolve problems (often with specialist software). This way they can quickly provide help to problems they have previously encountered. Even in the home, it is good practice to keep a list of problems and their resolutions. By doing this, you can learn from experience and possibly avoid spending time and money searching for the answer again.

Tip:
See also Module 2, chapter 10, pages 86–88 for more about getting help with problems.

# BCS to ECDL Syllabus 5.0 map

## BCS Module 1 Revised IT User Syllabus

The BCS Module 1 on IT Security for Users is covered in Module 8, pages 513–525.

## BCS Module 2 Revised IT User Syllabus

The BCS Module 2 on IT User Fundamentals maps to the ECDL syllabus 5.0 reference numbers as shown in the following table. Note that some of the BCS Module 2 specification items appear as Module 1 items in the ECDL syllabus 5.0.

| BCS Revised IT User Syllabus | | | ECDL Syllabus 5.0 |
|---|---|---|---|
| Category | Skill set | Reference | Reference and page |
| 2.1 Operating system | 2.1.1 First steps | 2.1.1.1 | 2.1.1.1 page 45 |
| | | 2.1.1.2 | 2.1.1.2 page 51 |
| | | 2.1.1.3 | 2.1.1.3 page 84 |
| | | 2.1.1.4 | 2.1.1.4 page 50 |
| | | 2.1.1.5 | 2.1.1.5 page 86 |
| | 2.1.2 Setup | 2.1.2.1 | 2.1.2.1 page 76 |
| | | 2.1.2.2 | 2.1.2.2 pages 77–78, 83–84 |
| | | 2.1.2.3 | 2.1.2.3 page 79 |
| | | 2.1.2.4 | 2.1.2.4 page 80 |
| | | 2.1.2.5 | 2.1.2.5 page 81 |
| | 2.1.3 Working with icons | 2.1.3.1 | 2.1.3.1 page 46 |
| | | 2.1.3.2 | 2.1.3.2 pages 47–48 |
| | | 2.1.3.3 | 2.1.3.3 pages 75–76 |
| | | 2.1.3.4 | 2.1.3.4 page 75 |

| BCS Revised IT User Syllabus | | | ECDL Syllabus 5.0 |
|---|---|---|---|
| Category | Skill set | Reference | Reference and page |
|  | 2.1.4 Using Windows | 2.1.4.1 | 2.1.4.1 pages 48–49 |
|  |  | 2.1.4.2 | 2.1.4.2 pages 48–49 |
|  |  | 2.1.4.3 | 2.1.4.3 page 46 |
| 2.2 File management | 2.2.1 Main concepts | 2.2.1.1 | 2.2.1.1 pages 60–62 |
|  |  | 2.2.1.2 | 2.2.1.2 pages 85–86 |
|  |  | 2.2.1.3 | Page 8 & 2.2.1.3 page 61 |
|  |  | 2.2.1.4 | 1.5.2.1 page 40, 2.2.1.4 page 67, and pages 524–525 |
|  |  | 2.2.1.5 | 1.5.2.1 page 40, 2.2.1.5 page 67, and pages 524–525 |
|  | 2.2.2 Files and folders | 2.2.2.1 | 2.2.2.1 pages 61–62 |
|  |  | 2.2.2.2 | 2.2.2.2 pages 63–64 |
|  |  | 2.2.2.3 | 2.2.2.3 pages 63–64 |
|  |  | 2.2.2.4 | 2.2.2.4 pages 62–63 |
|  | 2.2.3 Working with files | 2.2.3.1 | 2.2.3.1 page 54 |
|  |  | 2.2.3.2 | 2.2.3.2 pages 52–53 |
|  |  | 2.2.3.3 | 2.2.3.3 page 65 |
|  |  | 2.2.3.4 | 2.2.3.4 page 65 |
|  |  | 2.2.3.5 | 2.2.3.5 pages 61–62, 64 |
|  |  | 2.2.3.6 | 2.2.3.6 page 64 |
|  | 2.2.4 Copy, move | 2.2.4.1 | 2.2.4.1–3 pages 65–66 |
|  |  | 2.2.4.2 | 2.2.4.1–3 pages 65–66 |
|  |  | 2.2.4.3 | 2.2.4.1–3 pages 65–66 |
|  | 2.2.5 Delete, restore | 2.2.5.1 | 2.2.5.1 page 67 |
|  |  | 2.2.5.2 | 2.2.5.2 page 67 |
|  |  | 2.2.5.3 | 2.2.5.3 page 68 |
|  | 2.2.6 Searching | 2.2.6.1 | 2.2.6.1 pages 70–71 |
|  |  | 2.2.6.2 | 2.2.6.2 pages 70–71 |
|  |  | 2.2.6.3 | 2.2.6.3 pages 70–71 |
|  |  | 2.2.6.4 | 2.2.6.4 pages 70–71 |
|  |  | 2.2.6.5 | 2.2.6.5 page 72 |

| BCS Revised IT User Syllabus | | | ECDL Syllabus 5.0 |
|---|---|---|---|
| Category | Skill set | Reference | Reference and page |
| | 2.2.7 File compression | 2.2.7.1 | 2.3.1.1 page 69 |
| | | 2.2.7.2 | 2.3.1.2 page 69 |
| | | 2.2.7.3 | 2.3.1.3 page 69 |
| 2.3 Maintain systems | 2.3.1 Maintenance | 2.3.1.1 | Pages 526–536 |
| | | 2.3.1.2 | Pages 526–536 |
| | | 2.3.1.3 | Pages 526–536 |
| | | 2.3.1.4 | Pages 526–536 |
| | | 2.3.1.5 | Pages 526–536 |
| | | 2.3.1.6 | Pages 526–536 |
| | 2.3.2 Problems | 2.3.2.1 | Pages 537–538 |
| | | 2.3.2.2 | Pages 537–538 |
| | | 2.3.2.3 | Pages 537–538 |
| | | 2.3.2.4 | Pages 537–538 |
| 2.4 Print management | 2.4.1 Printer options | 2.4.1.1 | 2.4.1.1 page 81 |
| | | 2.4.1.2 | 2.4.1.2 page 82 |
| | 2.4.2 Print | 2.4.2.1 | 2.4.2.1 page 57 |
| | | 2.4.2.2 | 2.4.2.2 pages 57–58 |
| | | 2.4.2.3 | 2.4.2.3 page 58 |
| | 2.4.3 Printer maintenance | 2.4.3.1 | Pages 528–530 |
| | | 2.4.3.2 | Pages 528–530 |
| | | 2.4.3.3 | Pages 528–530 |
| | | 2.4.3.4 | Pages 89 and 536 |
| 2.5 Health and safety | 2.5.1 Health | 2.5.1.1 | 1.4.4.1 pages 30–31 |
| | | 2.5.1.2 | 1.4.4.2 pages 30–31 |
| | | 2.5.1.3 | 1.4.4.3 pages 30–31 |
| | | 2.5.1.4 | 1.4.4.4 page 31 |
| | 2.5.2 Safety | 2.5.2.1 | 1.4.4.2–4 pages 30–31, 1.4.5.1–2 page 32 |
| | | 2.5.2.2 | Pages 31, 34 and 522–523 |
| | | 2.5.2.3 | Page 528 |

| BCS Revised IT User Syllabus | | | ECDL Syllabus 5.0 |
|---|---|---|---|
| Category | Skill set | Reference | Reference and page |
| 2.6 Security | 2.6.1 Identity/Authentication | 2.6.1.1 | 1.5.1.1 page 38 and 517–518 |
| | | 2.6.1.2 | 1.5.1.2 page 38 and 517–518 |
| | | 2.6.1.3 | Page 41 |
| | 2.6.2 Data security | 2.6.2.1 | 1.5.2.1 page 40, 2.2.1.4 page 67 and pages 524–525 |
| | | 2.6.2.2 | 1.5.2.2 page 40, and page 515 |
| | | 2.6.2.3 | 1.5.1.1–3 pages 38–39, pages 517–518 and page 521 |
| | 2.6.3 Viruses | 2.6.3.1 | Page 39, 2.3.2.1 pages 72–73, and page 514 |
| | | 2.6.3.2 | Page 39, 2.3.2.2 pages 72–73, and page 514 |
| | | 2.6.3.3 | Page 39, 2.3.2.3 pages 72–73, and page 514 |
| | | 2.6.3.4 | Page 513 |
| 2.7 Law | 2.7.1. Copyright | 2.7.1.1 | 1.6.1.1 page 36 |
| | | 2.7.1.2 | 1.6.1.2 page 36 |
| | | 2.7.1.3 | 1.6.1.3 page 36 |
| | | 2.7.1.4 | 1.6.1.4 page 37 |
| | 2.7.2 Data protection | 2.7.2.1 | 1.6.2.1 page 34–36 |
| | | 2.7.2.2 | 1.6.2.2 page 34–36 |
| | | 2.7.2.3 | 1.6.2.3 page 34–36 |

# Index

# Index

# Index

# Index

# Index

# Index

# Index